A Products Liability Anthology

AF719318

ANDERSON'S
Law School Publications

ADMINISTRATIVE LAW ANTHOLOGY
by Thomas O. Sargentich

ADMINISTRATIVE LAW: CASES AND MATERIALS
by Daniel J. Gifford

ADMIRALTY LAW ANTHOLOGY
by Robert M. Jarvis

APPELLATE ADVOCACY: PRINCIPLES AND PRACTICE (Second Edition)
Cases and Materials
by Ursula Bentele and Eve Cary

A CAPITAL PUNISHMENT ANTHOLOGY
by Victor L. Streib

CASES AND PROBLEMS IN CRIMINAL LAW (Second Edition)
by Myron Moskovitz

THE CITATION WORKBOOK
by Maria L. Ciampi, Rivka Widerman and Vicki Lutz

COMMERCIAL TRANSACTIONS: PROBLEMS AND MATERIALS
Vol. 1: Secured Transactions Under the UCC
Vol. 2: Sales Under the UCC and the CISG
Vol. 3: Negotiable Instruments Under the UCC and the CIBN
by Louis F. Del Duca, Egon Guttman and Alphonse M. Squillante

A CONSTITUTIONAL LAW ANTHOLOGY
by Michael J. Glennon

CONSTITUTIONAL TORTS
by Sheldon H. Nahmod, Michael L. Wells, and Thomas A. Eaton

CONTRACTS
Contemporary Cases, Comments, and Problems
by Michael L. Closen, Richard M. Perlmutter and Jeffrey D. Wittenberg

A CONTRACTS ANTHOLOGY
by Peter Linzer

CORPORATE AND WHITE COLLAR CRIME: AN ANTHOLOGY
by Leonard Orland

A CRIMINAL LAW ANTHOLOGY
by Arnold H. Loewy

CRIMINAL LAW: CASES AND MATERIALS
by Arnold H. Loewy

CRIMINAL PROCEDURE: TRIAL AND SENTENCING
by Arthur B. LaFrance and Arnold H. Loewy

ECONOMIC REGULATION
Cases and Materials
by Richard J. Pierce, Jr.

ELEMENTS OF LAW
by Eva H. Hanks, Michael E. Herz and Steven S. Nemerson

ENDING IT: DISPUTE RESOLUTION IN AMERICA
Descriptions, Examples, Cases and Questions
by Susan M. Leeson and Bryan M. Johnston

ENVIRONMENTAL LAW (Second Edition)
Vol. 1: Environmental Decisionmaking: NEPA and the Endangered Species Act
Vol. 2: Water Pollution; Vol. 3: Air Pollution; Vol. 4: Hazardous Wastes
by Jackson B. Battle, Mark Squillace, Maxine I. Lipeles and Robert L. Fischman

ENVIRONMENTAL PROTECTION AND JUSTICE
Readings and Commentary on Environmental Law and Practice
by Kenneth A. Manaster

Continued

FEDERAL INCOME TAXATION OF PARTNERSHIPS AND OTHER PASS-THRU ENTITIES
by Howard E. Abrams

FEDERAL RULES OF EVIDENCE (Second Edition)
Rules, Legislative History, Commentary and Authority
by Glen Weissenberger

FIRST AMENDMENT ANTHOLOGY
by Donald E. Lively, Dorothy E. Roberts and Russell L. Weaver

INTERNATIONAL HUMAN RIGHTS: LAW, POLICY AND PROCESS
Problems and Materials
by Frank Newman and David Weissbrodt

INTERNATIONAL LAW ANTHOLOGY
by Anthony D'Amato

INTERNATIONAL LAW COURSEBOOK
by Anthony D'Amato

INTRODUCTION TO THE STUDY OF LAW: CASES AND MATERIALS
by John Makdisi

JUDICIAL EXTERNSHIPS: THE CLINIC INSIDE THE COURTHOUSE
by Rebecca A. Cochran

JUSTICE AND THE LEGAL SYSTEM
A Coursebook
by Anthony D'Amato and Arthur J. Jacobson

THE LAW OF DISABILITY DISCRIMINATION
by Ruth Colker

THE LAW OF MODERN PAYMENT SYSTEMS AND NOTES
by Fred H. Miller and Alvin C. Harrell

LAWYERS AND FUNDAMENTAL MORAL RESPONSIBILITY
by Daniel R. Coquillette

PATIENTS, PSYCHIATRISTS AND LAWYERS
Law and the Mental Health System
by Raymond L. Spring, Roy B. Lacoursiere, M.D., and Glen Weissenberger

PROBLEMS AND SIMULATIONS IN EVIDENCE
by Thomas F. Guernsey

A PRODUCTS LIABILITY ANTHOLOGY
by Anita Bernstein

PROFESSIONAL RESPONSIBILITY ANTHOLOGY
by Thomas B. Metzloff

A PROPERTY ANTHOLOGY
by Richard H. Chused

THE REGULATION OF BANKING
Cases and Materials on Depository Institutions and Their Regulators
by Michael P. Malloy

A SECTION 1983 CIVIL RIGHTS ANTHOLOGY
by Sheldon H. Nahmod

SPORTS LAW: CASES AND MATERIALS (Second Edition)
by Raymond L. Yasser, James R. McCurdy and C. Peter Goplerud

A TORTS ANTHOLOGY
by Lawrence C. Levine, Julie A. Davies and Edward J. Kionka

TRIAL PRACTICE
Text by Lawrence A. Dubin and Thomas F. Guernsey
Problems and Case Files with *Video* Presentation
by Edward R. Stein and Lawrence A. Dubin

A Products Liability Anthology

Edited with Comments by

Anita Bernstein

Chicago-Kent College of Law
Illinois Institute of Technology

LAW LIBRARY
JUL 31 2000
GOLDEN GATE UNIVERSITY

Anderson Publishing Co.

A PRODUCTS LIABILITY ANTHOLOGY

© 1995 by Anderson Publishing Co.

All rights reserved. No part of this book may be used or reproduced by any means without written permission from the publisher and author.

Library of Congress Cataloging-in Publication Data

A products liability anthology / edited with comments by Anita Bernstein.

p. cm.

ISBN 0-87084-704-X

1. Products liability--United States. I. Bernstein, Anita.

KF1296.A75P765 1995

346.7303'8--dc20

[347.30638]

94-45933

CIP

For Sylvia Zucker Bernstein

LAW LIBRARY
JUL 3 1 2000
GOLDEN GATE UNIVERSITY

Contents

Preface

When I was a first-year law student, in 1982, the Yale torts casebook (Shulman, James & Gray) covered, or rather buried, products liability in a chapter called "Suppliers of Goods and Remote Contractors." The next thirteen years have been eventful: *Restatement (Third) of Torts: Products Liability*, treatises and casebooks, hundreds of articles, a tort reform movement, references to the subject by three U.S. presidents, legislation in Europe and Japan and elsewhere around the world, Supreme Court decisions, Dan Quayle's crusade, Dateline's fake explosion, toxic shock syndrome, Agent Orange, asbestos "plans," silicone implants. Once I even saw my specialty mocked in *Mad Magazine.*

Products liability has burgeoned, to be sure; and yet, as scholars keep reminding us, the subject is just as old as it is new. When Edward Levi needed an area of law to show how judges build common-law principles through incremental logic for his *Introduction to Legal Reasoning*, he chose products liability. The phrase sounds new, but its heritage is venerable. And as this collection (the only products liability anthology that I know of) shows, products liability not only has antecedents stretching back into biblical and Roman times, but is also a subject of great breadth.

Consider the contributors. More than half the pieces in this collection are written by credentialed experts in products liability, including James Henderson and Aaron Twerski, compilers of the new *Restatement*. This expertise is supplemented—enriched, I think—by the work of others who became products liability contributors *ad hoc*: lawyer-epidemiologists, a judge making a sermon from the bench, two students, a business school professor, law professors who specialize elsewhere, a law firm speaking in behalf of more than a hundred organizations and the great contracts scholar Grant Gilmore, who muses elegantly on many of the themes that permeate this collection.

Although I believe that each piece in the anthology represents an important addition to the literature, this book isn't Products Liability's Greatest Hits. Such a compilation would be indigestible and could not cohere. Instead, it consists of discrete pieces fitted together, mosaic fashion. In each part of the book, articles play off each other, sometimes differing with an adjacent piece and sometimes choosing to emphasize other facets of a similar argument. I think of each part as a panel-style dialogue. Of course, within the larger products liability dialogue, more voices are speaking and more topics warrant discussion than these 41 pieces can indicate.

Now, as I wrap up my work, I am hoping that this book will be useful to a diverse audience. Because it is aimed primarily at the law school classroom, I have kept law teachers in mind throughout its preparation, and I will gladly make available a supplement of notes, questions for students, references to related materials, and thoughts about pedagogy to instructors who request it. I encourage other readers to contact me with their suggestions and criticisms. Should this anthology be useful to you outside of a classroom, I would be gratified to hear why and how.

Lisa Wortman, my indefagitable research assistant, made the production of the book possible. I am grateful also to the copyright holders of the works reprinted here, for their cooperation with the republication process. I received financial support from the Marshall D. Ewell Fund at Chicago-Kent.

Writing this Preface gives me a chance to thank several colleagues and mentors who know the pleasures of products liability and have shared them with me over the years: Leslie Bender, Guido Calabresi, Jacob Corré, Richard Epstein, Paul Fanning, Patrick Glenn, Michael

Green, Steven Heyman, Ewoud Hondius, Geraint Howells, Christian Joërges, Frances Kao, Jon Kroeper, Stuart Madden, Giandomenico Majone, Jonathan Mintz, David Owen, David Partlett, Jerry Phillips, Roger Podesta, William Powers, George Priest, Robert Rabin, Margaret Jane Radin, Marco Ricolfi, Diana Runcie, Gary Schwartz, Marshall Shapo, Jane Stapleton, Carel Stolker, Stephen Sugarman, Hans-Claudius Taschner, Nicolas Terry, Ellen Vos, Otto van Wassenaer von Catwijck, Jack Weinstein, Malcolm Wheeler, and Richard Wright.

Anita Bernstein
Chicago-Kent College of Law
565 Adams Street
Chicago, Illinois 60661
(312) 906-5039
E-mail: abernste@kentlaw.edu

Permissions to republish works in this Anthology are gratefully acknowledged.

Richard L. Abel, The Real Tort Crisis—Too *Few* Claims, 48 Ohio St. L.J. 443 (1987). Reprinted with the permission of the author and the Ohio State Law Journal.

John B. Attanasio, The Principle of Aggregate Autonomy and the Calabresian Approach to Products Liability, 74 Va. L. Rev. 677 (1988). Reprinted with the permission of the Virginia Law Review and Fred B. Rothman, Inc.

Leslie Bender, Feminist (Re)Torts: Thoughts on the Liability Crisis, Mass Torts, Power, and Responsibilities. 1990 Duke L.J. 848 (1990). Reprinted with the permission of the author.

Sheila L. Birnbaum, Unmasking the Test for Design Defect: From Negligence [to Warranty] to Strict Liability to Negligence, 33 Vand. L. Rev. 593 (1980). Reprinted with the permission of the Vanderbilt Law Review.

Guido Calabresi and Jon T. Hirschoff, Toward a Test for Strict Liability in Torts, 81 Yale L.J. 1055 (1972). Reprinted with the permission of the authors and Yale Law Journal Company.

Richard A. Epstein, Modern Products Liability Law (1980). Reprinted with the permission of the author and Greenwood Publishing Group, Inc.

Richard A. Epstein, The Risks of Risk/Utility, 48 Ohio St. L.J. 469 (1987). Reprinted with the permission of the author and the Ohio State Law Journal.

Grant Gilmore, Products Liability: A Commentary, 38 U. Chi. L. Rev. 103 (1970). Reprinted with the permission of the University of Chicago Law Review.

H. Patrick Glenn, Judicial Authority and the Liability of the Manufacturer, or *Jusqu'ou Peut-on Aller Trop Loin?*, 38 Am. J. Comp. L. 555 (1990). Reprinted with the permission of the American Journal of Comparative Law.

James A. Henderson, Jr., Judicial Review of Manufacturers' Conscious Design Choices: The Limits of Adjudication, 73 Colum. L. Rev. 1531 (1973). Reprinted with the permission of the Columbia Law Review.

James A. Henderson, Jr. & Theodore Eisenberg, The Quiet Revolution in Products Liability: An Empirical Study of Legal Change, 37 UCLA L. Rev. 479 (1990). Reprinted with the permission of the UCLA Law Review and Fred B. Rothman, Inc.

James A. Henderson, Jr. & Aaron D. Twerski, Doctrinal Collapse In Products Liability: The Empty Shell of Failure To Warn, 65 N.Y.U. L. Rev. 265 (1990). Reprinted with the permission of the New York University Law Review.

Peter W. Huber, Safety and the Second Best: The Hazards of Public Risk Management in the Courts, 85 Colum. L. Rev. 277 (1985). Reprinted with the permission of the Columbia Law Review.

Peter W. Huber and Robert E. Litan, Overview, in The Liability Maze: The Impact of Liability Law on Safety and Innovation (1991). Reprinted with the permission of the authors and The Brookings Institution.

J.A. Jolowicz, Product Liability in the EEC, in Comparative and Private International Law: Essays in Honor of John Henry Merryman on His Seventieth Birthday (David S. Clark ed., 1990). Reprinted with the permission of Duncker & Humbolt Publishers.

Frances P. Kao, Pornography as Product. Printed with the permission of the author.

Howard Latin, "Good" Warnings, Bad Products, and Cognitive Limitations, 41 UCLA L. Rev. 1193 (1994). Reprinted with the permission of the UCLA Law Review.

Revised Annotated Reprimand by Chief Judge Miles W. Lord, 9 Hamline L. Rev. 7 (1986). Reprinted with the permission of the Hamline Law Review.

Robert M. McKenna, The Impact of Product Liability Law on the Development of a Vaccine Against the AIDS Virus, 55 U. Chi. L. Rev. 943 (1988). Reprinted with the permission of the University of Chicago Law Review.

Michael B. Metzger, Corporate Criminal Liability for Defective Products: Policies, Problems, and Prospects, 73 Geo. L.J. 1 (1984). Reprinted with the permission of the Georgetown Law Journal and Georgetown University.

David G. Owen, The Moral Foundations of Products Liability Law: Toward First Principles, 68 Notre Dame L. Rev. 427 (1993). Reprinted with the permission of the author and the Notre Dame Law Review.

David G. Owen, Problems In Assessing Punitive Damages Against Manufacturers of Defective Products, 49 U. Chi. L. Rev. 1 (1982). Reprinted with the permission of the author and the University of Chicago Law Review.

William C. Powers, Jr., The Persistence of Fault in Products Liability, 61 Tex. L. Rev. 777 (1983). Reprinted with the permission of the Texas Law Review Association.

George L. Priest, Products Liability Law and the Accident Rate, in Liability: Perspectives and Policy (Robert E. Litan & Clifford L. Winston eds., 1988). Reprinted with the permission of The Brookings Institution.

George L. Priest, The Current Insurance Crisis and Modern Tort Law, 96 Yale L.J. 1521 (1987). Reprinted with the permission of the author and the Yale Law Journal Company.

George L. Priest, A Theory of the Consumer Product Warranty, 90 Yale L.J. 1297 (1981). Reprinted with the permission of the author and the Yale Law Journal Company.

William L. Prosser, The Assault Upon The Citadel (Strict Liability to the Consumer), 69 Yale L.J. 1099 (1960). Reprinted with the permission of the Estate of William L. Prosser and the Yale Law Journal.

William L. Prosser, The Implied Warranty of Merchantable Quality, 27 Minn. L. Rev. 117 (1943). Reprinted with the permission of the Minnesota Law Review.

Michael Rustad, In Defense of Punitive Damages in Products Liability: Testing Tort Anecdotes With Empirical Data, 78 Iowa L. Rev. 1 (1992). Reprinted with the permission of the Iowa Law Review.

Victor E. Schwartz and Liberty Mahshigian, National Childhood Vaccine Injury Act of 1986: An Ad Hoc Remedy or a Window For the Future? 48 Ohio St. L.J. 387 (1987). Reprinted with the permission of the authors and the Ohio State Law Journal.

Gary T. Schwartz, Product Liability and Medical Malpractice in Comparative Context, in The Liability Maze: The Impact of Liability Law on Safety and Innovation (Peter W. Huber & Robert E. Litan eds., 1991). Reprinted with the permission of the author and The Brookings Institution.

Alan Schwartz, The Case Against Strict Liability, 60 Fordham L. Rev. 819 (1992). Reprinted with the permission of the Fordham Law Review.

Marshall S. Shapo, A Representational Theory of Consumer Protection: Doctrine, Function and Legal Liability for Product Disappointment, 60 Va. L. Rev. 1109 (1974). Reprinted with the permission of the Virginia Law Review and Fred B. Rothman, Inc.

Sidley & Austin, The Need for Legislative Reform of the Tort System: A Report on the Liability Crisis From Affected Organizations, 10 Hamline L. Rev. 2 (1987). Reprinted with the permission of the Hamline Law Review.

Joan E. Steinman, Women, Medical Care, and Mass Tort Litigation, 68 Chi.-Kent L. Rev. 409 (1992). Reprinted with the permission of the author and the Chicago-Kent Law Review.

Stephen P. Teret & Michael S. Jacobs, Prevention and Torts: The Role of Litigation in Injury Control, 17 Law, Med. & Health Care 17 (1985). Reprinted with the permission of the authors and the American Society of Law, Medicine and Ethics.

W. Kip Viscusi, Toward a Diminished Role for Tort Liability: Social Insurance, Government Regulation, and Contemporary Risks to Health and Safety, 6 Yale J. Reg. 65 (1989). Reprinted with the permission of the Yale Journal on Regulation.

John W. Wade, On The Nature of Strict Tort Liability for Products, 44 Miss. L.J. 825 (1973). Reprinted with the permission of the Mississippi Law Journal.

Ernest J. Weinrib, The Insurance Justification and Private Law, 14 J. Legal Stud. 681 (1985). Reprinted with the permission of the Journal of Legal Studies.

Malcolm Wheeler, The Need for Narrow Tort Reform: Abolishing Strict Product Liability, in Product Liability Reform: Debating the Issues (Kenneth L. Chilton ed., 1990). Reprinted with the permission of the author and the Center for the Study of American Business.

NOTE ON EDITING

All materials in this Anthology have been edited. Footnotes, asterisks, brackets and ellipses are used sparingly, so as not to jar the reader more than necessary. Deletions are indicated with asterisks only where they interrupt the flow of the work. Most editorial additions appear in brackets, but occasionally a word or two, or a punctuation mark, has been added without indication. Most of the subheadings appeared in the original writings, but a few new ones have been created to improve readability.

Readers are urged to bear in mind that it was the full-length originals that called out to be republished in an anthology. The original works should certainly be retrieved by anyone who wishes to quote from them. All are readily available in law libraries, except for the Kao essay (p. 194) published here for the first time, and the Bernstein essay (p. 177).

Part I
The Defective Product

This part of the anthology addresses the question of how to determine whether a product is defective. Writers have been most interested in two facets of this question: defective design and problems involving the failure to warn. Even if a maker knows the best possible way to design a product or warn about an unavoidable defect, this best possible way—perfection—cannot usually be achieved. A reasonableness inquiry creeps into the analysis.

Some writers resist this tendency; others embrace it. Sheila Birnbaum urges courts to be forthright about the need to resolve design-defect questions with reference to negligence principles. Her exhortation has been heeded; this article, part of a relatively early symposium on products liability, is widely cited in judicial opinions. In another famous article, John Wade sets out several criteria, often called the Wade factors or the Wade risk-utility test, that combine negligence principles with other concepts to determine whether a design is defective. These criteria have been challenged, but seldom so fundamentally as in the next piece in the section: Richard Epstein attacks negligence-like tests in general and the risk-utility approach in particular. Finally, James Henderson suggests that even if the proper test were devised, courts might not be competent to determine the defectiveness of product designs.

A. What Makes a Design Defective?

Sheila L. Birnbaum, *Unmasking the Test for Design Defect: From Negligence [to Warranty] to Strict Liability to Negligence*, 33 VAND. L. REV. 593 (1980)*

Courts have struggled to rework the basic standards for imposing liability in design defect cases. A consistent, uniform, and just approach to defining the term "defect" has not yet been achieved. Courts have tenaciously repeated the original rationales underlying a theory of strict products liability without inquiring into the continued viability of these notions. Manufacturers, for example, are thought to be in the best position to distribute the costs of product-related injures by purchasing insurance or increasing prices of their products. They are also deemed to be in the best position to control the risk of injuries through safety-conscious design, testing, and inspection programs. Thus, a theory of strict liability, which assures compensation to those injured by defective products, is said to provide the needed economic incentive for manufacturers to design safer products.

*Used by permission.

One must question, however, whether strict liability in design cases is any more efficacious than a negligence standard in providing an incentive to manufacturers to design safer products. Manufacturers can forcefully argue that greater incentive might be supplied by a tort, or fault, approach. At least in negligence, when issues of reasonableness and due care are central to the inquiry, the conscientious manufacturer can take heart that the effort and expense he devotes to product safety will make a difference. He can rely on a court of law distinguishing between the safety-conscious and vigilant manufacturer on the one hand, and the lax and careless one on the other. The negligence approach would also add some much-needed stability and predictability to the tort litigation system, which would doubtless have a calming effect on insurers.

The primary goal underlying any standard of liability for product-related injuries resulting from defective design should be not compensation, but the reduction of the incidence of injuries. As a matter of rational social policy, it is of foremost importance to build into the rule of law an approach aimed at deterring conduct that exposes consumers and users to unreasonable risks of harm. Presumably, if courts and juries were to take cognizance of a manufacturer's efforts at designing a safe product, underwriters would feel confident in formulating insurance rates based on considered judgments of the real risks involved vis-à-vis the specific safety-oriented conduct of the individual manufacturer. In addition, the conscientious manufacturer and the consumer would no longer have to pick up the tab for the careless or negligent manufacturer. Broadly spreading the risk of product-related injuries, without more, meets only a secondary goal of compensating injured plaintiffs. Only by fusing the rule of law governing design cases to a notion of faulty conduct will the rationale of providing manufacturers with a true incentive to design safer products have any meaning.

One must note that strict liability does seem to work efficiently and fairly in cases of manufacturing defects, doubtless because the test for defectiveness is built-in and readily ascertainable by reference to the manufacturer's own production standards as well as those customarily observed in the industry. Serious analytic difficulties arise, however, when strict liability is applied in conscious design defect cases, in which the very determination of the existence of a defect is the central issue to be resolved.

The traditional consumer expectations test is, by and large, hopelessly inadequate as a vehicle for discerning a standard for defectiveness in design cases. When the defect is patent, the test often leaves the loss on the injured consumer, who may be assumed in law to have accepted the risk of injury. When the defect is latent and the product complicated in design, we cannot say with any certainty that consumers know what to expect because they usually do not know how safely the product could or should have been made. If this proposition is true, then presumably jurors, who are themselves ordinary consumers, do not know what the plaintiff or the hypothetical objective consumer expected in the way of safety. How, then, can jurors charged under a consumer expectations test make a determination of whether to impose liability? In all probability, they guess.

Many jurisdictions have, in fact, turned away from the consumer expectations approach and apply instead some form of a risk-utility balancing test for determining defectiveness in design cases. Nevertheless, in an attempt to define the test in terms that are uniquely suitable and exclusively applicable to products liability cases, courts have taken what is essentially a negligence calculus and turned it into something else by relying on two fundamentally suspect assumptions. First, following Deans Wade and Keeton, the courts impute scienter of the danger to the manufacturer on the ground that it is unfair to burden the injured plaintiff with the difficult task of proving that the manufacturer was negligent. Second, since the risk-utility analysis is, through the magical imputation of scienter, no longer deemed a negligence test, the balancing of factors must necessarily yield a conclusion that focuses on the nature or condition of the product rather than on the conduct of the manufacturer.

The argument that plaintiff would be tremendously disadvantaged by having to prove negligence on the part of the manufacturer was originally posited in connection with early manufacturing defect cases. Indeed, it is probably true that a plaintiff would find it enormously difficult and sometimes even impossible to prove the negligent conduct that led to the soda bottle with the hairline fracture that ultimately exploded and caused plaintiff's injuries. At some particular moment in time on an otherwise uneventful day, a worker on the assembly line might have been distracted and careless or some slight malfunction in the plant equipment may have damaged a few bottles that somehow managed to slip through the quality-control check points undetected. To be sure, manufacturing defects are an inevitable by-product of mass production, which may or may not even be attributable to negligence. Because of the random and unpredictable nature of the occurrence of a manufacturing flaw, however, a plaintiff cannot be expected to be able to pinpoint the negligence, if any, that was involved. Manufacturing defects are almost always by definition accidents; and so in these cases the goal of deterrence is not as prominent as the need for compensating the victims of these assemblyline errors.

The design defect case, on the other hand, presents a very different configuration of elements. A design defect is neither random, nor unpredictable, nor inevitable. It is the result of deliberate and documentable decisions on the part of the manufacturer. Here the plaintiff does not struggle to find some fleeting indicia of negligent conduct; instead, he seeks to impugn an entire product line by condemning a manufacturer's judgment, as manifested by his conscious choice of available options. Vastly expanded and liberalized discovery rules enable the plaintiff to prove that the manufacturer's deliberate design decision was an ill-considered one. Plaintiffs have ready access to technical data and expert witnesses, making the assumption that it is unduly difficult or impossible to prove the manufacturer's negligence in design cases fallacious. Furthermore, as almost every vigorously litigated design defect case shows, plaintiffs do in fact come forward with detailed technical evidence tending to prove that the manufacturer was either aware of the nature and gravity of the risk posed by the challenged product or that he could have designed the product more safely. Imputed scienter is thus essentially an unnecessary fiction that does not theoretically or even pragmatically serve the questionable foundation upon which it is based. The goal it does serve, however, is that it may eliminate defenses based upon state of the art and scientific or technological unknowability. This, of course, raises the spectre of absolute liability, which no court has as yet openly sanctioned.

The second questionable assumption courts have relied on in applying strict liability in design defect cases is that since the risk-utility balancing test will not require proof of negligence, the conclusion derived cannot be cast in terms of negligence. Thus, as the California Supreme Court has insisted, the trier of fact must focus on the product, not on the manufacturer's conduct. This is nothing more than semantic artifice. The ineluctable conclusion is that the competing factors to be weighed under a risk-utility balancing test invite the trier of fact to consider the alternatives and risks faced by the manufacturer and to determine whether in light of these he exercised reasonable care in making the design choices he did. Instructing a jury that weighing factors concerning conduct and judgment must yield a conclusion that does not describe conduct is confusing at best.

It is doubtful that any court in this country would impose upon a manufacturer the duty of designing an absolutely safe product. In fairness, all that one can ask is that the manufacturer exercise due care in designing products that do not involve unreasonable danger to consumers and users. Dean Prosser described this as a negligence standard; the risk-utility balancing test is but a detailed version of Judge Learned Hand's negligence calculus. Calling a theory of liability based on a duty of due care and a standard of reasonable conduct anything other than negligence is pure sophistry. Of course, this would be harmless if the trier of fact had the jurisprudential acumen of the legal scholar—but courts are sending lay jurors off to deliberate with nearly incomprehensible instructions, leaving them to formulate random and unpredictable judgments.

Liability for conscious design defects is tortious liability, and the time has come for courts to stop creating obfuscatory tests that can only confuse jurors and deny litigants a consistently fair and just result. Imposing a negligence standard for design defect liability is in many cases only to define in a coherent fashion what litigants are in fact arguing and what jurors are in essence analyzing. When this is not the case, it should in all fairness be the case. The confused and inconsistent body of product liability case law that has emerged in the last fifteen years seriously undermines the integrity of the tort system. As a constructive response, it is time for courts to adopt, unequivocally and forthrightly, a pure negligence/risk-utility test in design defect cases.

John W. Wade, *On The Nature of Strict Tort Liability for Products*, 44 Miss. L.J. 825 (1973)*

Whatever the rationale, strict liability for products has become a significant portion of tort law. This type of strict liability differs in several respects from the strict liability of the type arising from the case of *Rylands v. Fletcher* (or that involving the keeping of dangerous animals). The latter type—whether the test is the penning up of a dangerous force seeking to get loose and cause mischief, or the making of a non-natural use of the land, or the conducting of an ultrahazardous activity, or the conducting of an abnormally dangerous activity—involves the deliberate engaging in an activity which is known to create serious dangers which cannot be eliminated by the exercise of ordinary care. The activity is one which is inappropriate to the place in which it is being carried on, but which has so much utility that the courts have not wanted to call it negligence. They have simply decided that it should pay its own way and compensate for the injuries which it imposes. Its similarities to, and differences from, strict liability for products have not yet been clearly worked out by the courts or fully analyzed by the commentators.

Strict liability for products is clearly not that of an insurer. If it were, a plaintiff would need only to prove that the product was a factual cause in producing his injury. Thus, the manufacturer of a match would be liable for anything burned by a fire started by a match produced by him, an automobile manufacturer would be liable for all damages produced by the car, a gun maker would be liable to anyone shot by the gun, anyone cut by a knife could sue the maker, and a purchaser of food with high calories would have an action for his overweight condition and for an ensuing heart attack. The liability would be like that created by a particularly stringent dramshop law.

There must be suitable ways of limiting the liability—both as to its initial existence and as to its scope and extent. The courts have had no difficulty in finding ways to do this. Scope and extent

*Used by permission.

of liability have usually been controlled by the concepts of proximate cause or risk (including abnormal use) and of plaintiff's fault (including contributory negligence, assumption of risk, and misuse). Original existence of liability is usually controlled by analyzing the nature of the product. It is this last approach which has proved most fruitful in solving the issues. And it is here that much of the dispute—and litigation—has arisen.

The initial approach to the problem was in the language of the warranty cases. It was said that there was an implied warranty that the goods were of merchantable quality, or were suitable for the purpose for which they were sold. In the case of foodstuffs it was said that they must be wholesome. The reasonable expectations of the buyer were utilized as guidelines in making the determination. But while the analogy was helpful in the strict liability cases it was not fully suitable. The implied warranty arose in a commercial setting. It involved primarily people who were contracting with each other. The suit was for commercial damages, for loss of bargain, because the product did not perform as expected. Tort damages for injury incurred were given only incidentally, as consequential damages. The test was not fully attuned to the tort recovery. In many situations, particularly involving design matters, the consumer would not know what to expect, because he would have no idea how safe the product could be made.

* * *

Determining Whether a Product is Defective

Quite obviously, a product must be harmful or unsafe because of something wrong with it. The "something wrong" may have come about quite unintentionally because of a miscarriage in the manufacturing process, so that the product was not what it was intended to be; it may, on the other hand, have come about, even though the product was exactly as it was intended to be, because of a poor design or the failure to attach a warning or suitable instructions. The California court [in Cronin v. J.B.E. Olson Corp., 501 P.2d 1153 (Cal. 1972)] would read all of this into the single word "defective." The *Restatement (Second) of Torts* uses two expressions—"defective" and "unreasonably dangerous"—which may seem redundant. They might have been joined together with an "or" rather than an "and." But they were not; and this has created some problems of its own.

If it is either tautological or requiring too much to insist that the product be both defective and unreasonably dangerous, the question then arises as to which term is the more appropriate. There are difficulties with either one alone, as analysis will show.

The term "defective" raises many difficulties. Its natural application would be limited to the situation in which something went wrong in the manufacturing process, so that the article was defective in the sense that the manufacturer had not intended it to be in that condition. To apply it also to the case in which a warning is not attached to the chattel or the design turns out to be a bad one or the product is likely to be injurious in its normal condition, is to use the term in a Pickwickian sense, with a special, esoteric meaning of its own. It is not without reason that some people, in writing about it, speak of the requirement of being "legally defective," including the quotation marks. To have to define the term to the jury, with a meaning completely different from the one they would normally give to it, is to create the chance that they will be misled. To use it without defining it to the jury is almost to ensure that they will be misled.

In addition, a product may be defective and still not be likely to cause injury. An automobile, for example, may have something wrong with the ignition so that it will not start properly, or the clock or the radio may not work correctly. If so, it is obviously defective, but it is not harmfully defective. Perhaps the adverb "harmfully" needs to be added to the adjective. Without it, the test sounds more like one used in a commercial setting than in a tort setting. It suggests the idea of an action on a sales contract for rescission or for damages for loss of bargain. Finally, the term "defective" gives an illusion of certainty by suggesting a word with a purported specific meaning rather than a term connoting a standard involving the weighing of factors.

On the other hand, the term "unreasonably dangerous" raises difficulties of its own. It may suggest an idea like ultrahazardous, or abnormally dangerous, and thus give rise to the impression that the plaintiff must prove that the product was unusually or extremely dangerous. The California court suggests that it carries connotations of negligence, and thus nullifies the effect of setting up strict liability for products instead of requiring the plaintiff to prove negligence. It does, however, indicate more clearly that we are dealing with a standard involving consideration of a number of factors.

There are other terms that might be used. For example, unsafe, or harmful, or injurious—or, in the case of foodstuffs, unwholesome. Like the original *Restatement* term "dangerous," these terms are subject to the objection that they might create liability on the part of the manufacturer of an ordinary knife on the ground that it cuts and therefore might injure somebody. The adverb "unreasonably" was added to the word "dangerous." If it connotates too strongly the idea of negligence, perhaps another adverb like "undue" could be used. In an earlier article, I had suggested the expression "not reasonably safe." Today, I think I would offer the expression "not duly safe."

All of these terms seem to be much better than the word "defective." They are tort words, indicating the idea of causing tortious damage to someone, rather than the idea of a contract action for failure to receive what had been contracted for. They include the tort concept of creating a danger for a bystander, as well as one for the consumer who had purchased the chattel and therefore had at least an indirect contractual relationship.

Whatever word or phrase is used, a further explanation or indication of meaning is needed. In the absence of authorities on strict liability, early commentators resorted to cases based on warranty liability-whether express or implied. They thus used contract language. How good did the product have to be? What were the expectations of the parties? Are these actual expectations or reasonable ones? What might the manufacturer expect the consumer to expect? This is all warranty language. It essentially is a contract approach. It sounds as if the action is based on the ground that the buyer did not receive what he contracted for, so that he is entitled either to return it and get his money back or to keep it and sue for the difference between the value in its actual condition and the value it would have had if it had complied with his reasonable expectations. True, if the product caused injury, recovery might be had to compensate for it. But these are consequential damages, coming almost as an afterthought. Their availability may depend on the rules of *Hadley v. Baxendale,* rather than those of proximate cause in tort. Under the warranty approach, there is no available basis for liability other than that for purchasers who might have had "expectations" from the manufacturer or supplier.

All of this might have been justified in the days when strict tort liability was in its formative stage. Now that strict liability has become the dominant theory, with a definite indication that the liability may apply for any user whether he is a purchaser or not, and even for bystanders who would be endangered and were injured by the product, it is time to abandon the warranty way of thinking and its terminology just as we have abandoned other "impedimenta" of the warranty approach, such as required notice of defect within a reasonable time, and disclaimers.

The time has now come to be forthright in using a tort way of thinking and tort terminology. There are several ways of doing it, and it is not difficult. The simplest and easiest way, it would seem, is to assume that the defendant knew of the dangerous condition of the product and ask whether he was then negligent in putting it on the market or supplying it to someone else. In other words, the scienter is supplied as a matter of law, and there is no need for the plaintiff to prove its existence as a matter of fact. Once given this notice of the dangerous condition of the chattel, the question then becomes whether the defendant was negligent to people who might be harmed by that condition if they came into contact with it or were in the vicinity of it. Another way of saying this is to ask whether the magnitude of the risk created by the dangerous condition of the product was outweighed by the social utility attained by putting it out in this fashion.

* * *

A Proposed Test

If there is agreement that the determination of whether a product is unreasonably dangerous, or is not duly safe, involves the necessary application of a standard, it will, like the determination of negligence or of strict liability for an abnormally dangerous activity, require the consideration and weighing of a number of factors. I offer here a revised list of factors which seem to me to be of significance in applying the standard:

(1) The usefulness and desirability of the product—its utility to the user and to the public as a whole.

(2) The safety aspects of the product—the likelihood that it will cause injury, and the probable seriousness of the injury.

(3) The availability of a substitute product which would meet the same need and not be as unsafe.

(4) The manufacturer's ability to eliminate the unsafe character of the product without impairing its usefulness or making it too expensive to maintain its utility.

(5) The user's ability to avoid danger by the exercise of care in the use of the product.

(6) The user's anticipated awareness of the dangers inherent in the product and their avoidability, because of general public knowledge of the obvious condition of the product, or of the existence of suitable warnings or instructions.

(7) The feasibility, on the part of the manufacturer, of spreading the loss by setting the price of the product or carrying liability insurance.

When the issue of lack of due safety is submitted to the jury, what should be said in the instructions? The instruction will obviously use the term or terms sanctioned in the state for expressing the test—e.g., unreasonably dangerous, not duly safe, defective (in the manufacture or design). But these terms are usually not enough to give the jury an adequate impression as to the test which they are applying. Something more is needed. Prior to *Cronin,* the California-approved instructions defined unreasonably dangerous as being "dangerous to an extent beyond that which should be contemplated by the ordinary consumer who purchases it, with the ordinary knowledge common to the community as to its characteristics." Under *Cronin,* with the elimination of the requirement that the product be unreasonably dangerous, this definition will apparently go out, but something at least similar will have to be substituted; the term "defective" without any explanation, will provide practically no guidance to the jury and may be quite misleading.

The California instruction is not unsatisfactory, but it has at least two drawbacks. First, it gives something of an impression that the product must be specially or unusually dangerous. This, it would seem, is the real reason why the court in *Cronin* discarded it. Second, like all definitions in terms of consumer expectations it carries a flavor of commercial loss rather than tort injury and seems to confine the scope of liability to those who "consume" the product. There is also a hint of reliance on an undertaking by the defendant-an element which does not need to be present.

The following may be offered as a substitute: "A product is not duly safe if it is so likely to be harmful to persons or property that a reasonably prudent manufacturer or supplier, who had actual knowledge of its harmful character, would not place it on the market. It is not necessary to find that this defendant had knowledge of the harmful character of the product in order to determine that it was not duly safe." This language gives the tort flavor. It uses the familiar concept of a reasonable prudent man; which juries have always been able to handle; but it differentiates clearly between negligence and strict liability. It applies equally to manufacturing errors and bad designs. It is clearly objective in nature, giving no hint of depending on the subjective expectations of either party.

Should the jury be told about the list of seven factors which were set forth above? The answer should normally be no. The problem here is similar to that in negligence. The *Restatement of Torts* has analyzed negligence, described it as a balancing of the magnitude of the risk against the utility of the risk, and listed the factors which go into determining the weight of both of these elements. This analysis is most helpful and can be used with profit by trial and appellate judges, and by students and commentators. But it is not ordinarily given to the jury.

Richard A. Epstein, *The Risks of Risk/Utility*, 48 OHIO ST. L.J. 469 (1987)*

The legal revolution of the past twenty-five years has dramatically changed tort law, but not for the better. The inexorable expansion of liability has taken place on two fronts. The scope of the defendant's basic liability has increased, while the available defenses have been whittled away. This one-two combination has worked dramatic effects that could not be gleaned from looking at each change in isolation. While the changes have been massive, the justifications offered for them have been inadequate.

In a short paper it is quite foolish to attempt to assay the entire landscape of tort doctrine, from causation, to proof, to foreseeability, to privity, to assumption of risk. Nonetheless, it is important to stress that this vast array of doctrinal changes have not occurred at random. Quite the contrary they all reflect a uniform, if misguided, vision of the role of tort law in particular and of legal rules in general. My hope is to isolate one central methodological weakness of modern tort law and to show, however briefly, the influence it exerts on a large number of doctrinal areas. That weakness is the incurable judicial fondness for replacing fixed rules of tort liability with open-ended balancing tests. The now common risk/utility test, as developed by Professor Wade, is the foremost illustration of the new approach and the unfortunate social consequences that it produces.

Rule, Don't Balance

My basic thesis is that rules should be preferred to balancing tests, both for basic liability and for defenses. To be sure, this opposition between rules and balancing is not ironclad. Every system

*Used by permission.

has to have a little "give" in the joints to take care of the complex or unanticipated cases that do not fall neatly into the available paradigms. Bright line rules are not etched with laser sharpness. Yet the overriding distinction between rules and balancing tests remains structurally important notwithstanding the occasional blurriness at the edges. The critical inquiry is whether each case that comes before judge or jury must receive the same level of anxious consideration that is properly reserved for the most difficult ones. The advantage of well-crafted rules is that they can account for the routine case in a predictable and sensible fashion, while reserving the give in the system for the few atypical cases that remain. Traditional rules of thumb are serviceable over the broad run of cases. These should be preserved against the wholesale or frontal attacks that have been made against them.

The function of the rules is to demarcate the zones of decision for individual choice. When we speak of courts and nations, jurisdictional rules work best when they are clear and well focused. This is why principles of territoriality, the political analogue to property, persist into modern times, even though political decisions have manifest economic spillover effects beyond territorial borders. An equally pressing need exists for clear rules to specify initial entitlements, and to define their violation. Indeed as societies become more complex, the gains from simple rules become ever greater. Families and small groups can adopt complex rules to govern behavior because, given their commonality of interest, they can monitor each other's behavior to assure compliance, and make the necessary informal adjustments to novel or troublesome situations. But for large social groups, the desirable rules must be easily communicated across the large numbers of individuals who are bound by them. Rules of thumb or simple rules, make the law workable.

The question then becomes, do we have any easy surrogates which tell us when rules are simple and when they are complex. Here the litmus test of a *complex* rule is any which makes use of the idea of "reasonableness" and the implicit cost-benefit, or risk/utility calculus that it contains. In some sense it might be thought that to criticize any legal system for its reliance upon a reasonableness test is to misstate a source of legitimate modern concern. After all, how can a test which has been with us for so long, as a central part of the law of negligence, be the source of any fresh doubts about the soundness of the tort system? The answer is that while the reasonableness standard itself is old, its application has traditionally been hemmed in by the application of a variety of hard-edged rules that did not depend upon the case-by-case use of any risk/utility formula as such.

[Epstein next provides some examples of bright-line rules: the prohibition of force, custom in the law of medical malpractice, and the rule that land occupiers are liable for harms caused by latent defects or "traps" in the land. As a final example he mentions the products liability "patent danger" rule.]

The risks of the risk/utility formula have been most pronounced in the law of products liability. Here the relationship between the basis of liability—negligence or strict—and the definition of product defect—latent defect or risk/utility analysis—is of exceptional importance. The choice between negligence and strict liability is relatively unimportant if liability is confined to latent defects only. The expansion of liability to patent defects has enormous consequences, even if liability is confined to negligence theories. The reason the early law of products liability produced no serious disruption of commercial insurance markets was that the wall between latent and patent defects was not breached, even as strict liability had become the order of the day.

To put the point in perspective, if one had to summarize the traditional law before, say, 1968, in a couple of propositions, these are the two I would choose: First, ordinarily no liability for products with patent defects, and second, liability for latent defects only if the product caused damage in ordinary use. The application of these two tests was designed to make sure that liability existed only when (1) there was differential knowledge or access to knowledge between the parties, and (2) no misconduct of the plaintiff (who typically is using the product at the time of injury and well able to prevent the loss) helped bring about the loss in question.

This system of liability may give the wrong answer in some cases. Still as a rule of thumb it gives a clear, cheap, and correct answer in most cases. The distribution of cases along the latent/patent axis is such that there are few cases when the line between latent and patent is in doubt. By working to insure the easy transmission of information, this account strengthens market institutions by helping consumers make informed choices. Private contracts work fitfully at best before individual consumers have purchased or used a wide variety of goods, and the prohibition against latent defect spares producers from having to devise ways of providing independent guarantees that the product sold meets its promised quality standards. What seller of foodstuffs is able to provide warranties to all the people who eat its products? The utter want of any concern about "contracting out" of products liability rules is pretty strong evidence of how close the common law rules once adhered to the social optimum.

The risk/utility formulas are a very different kettle of fish, as a bare listing of the Wade factors shows:

> (1) The usefulness and desirability of the product—its utility to the user and to the public as a whole.
>
> (2) The safety aspects of the product—the likelihood that it will cause injury, and the probable seriousness of the injury.
>
> (3) The availability of a substitute product which would meet the same need and not be as unsafe.
>
> (4) The manufacturer's ability to eliminate the unsafe character of the product without impairing its usefulness or making it too expensive to maintain its utility.
>
> (5) The user's ability to avoid danger by the exercise of care in the use of the product.
>
> (6) The user's anticipated awareness of the dangers inherent in the product and their avoidability, because of general public knowledge of the obvious condition of the product, or of the existence of suitable warnings or instructions.
>
> (7) The feasibility, on the part of the manufacturer, of spreading the loss by setting the price of the product or carrying liability insurance.

While Professor Wade wrote as if his factor analysis offered a convenient rationalization of existing tort law, he was an unwitting firebrand. Risk/utility represents nothing less than a totally revolutionary way of looking at products liability. The latent defect tests reinforce market disciplines. The risk/utility test is a massive, if unintended, assault on markets and private ordering, for defendants are now required to justify independently every decision that they and their customers have made with respect to a product's use. No longer is it sufficient to say that the defendant informed the plaintiff of the hazards involved. Instead it becomes necessary to go behind the consent of consumers by finding expert testimony to reconstruct their past decisions from the ground up. And for what end?

Surely it is not to control administrative costs. The traditional rules have massive administrative efficiencies that are frittered away under Wade's risk/utility test. Substantive certainty is sacrificed as well. Risk/utility opens up every machine tool and every generic product to case-by-case attack within the judicial system: after all, the mere fact that the risk was assumed can no longer be treated as decisive on the reasonableness of the risk in question, even if relevant in some attenuated sense.

For all the intrusiveness of his test, Wade never explains why *ex post* collective judgments are superior to the *ex ante* judgments people make on their own. Yet surely the obviousness of the danger (which surely conveys something of its seriousness as well) is protection against both ordinary mistake and manufacturer misrepresentation or deceit, both of which harken back to the traditional concern with latent defects. And when the defect is patent, the ability to sell the product in the first instance is surely diminished, so that there is a powerful market check against systematic product abuse, one which the risk/utility test wholly ignores.

To see both the magnitude and the weakness of this entire risk/utility approach, it is instructive to ask the questions: Where does the application of the risk/utility test end, and why? If it can be used to decide whether certain features of a machine tool should be replaced, why cannot it be used to answer the question of whether entire classes of products, from handguns to convertible automobiles to alcohol should be marketed at all? There is nothing in the disorganized array of relevant factors that prevents a single headstrong jury from making fundamental decisions about what may be marketed and what may not be sold at all. Indeed, whenever the defendant has obtained a directed verdict or summary judgment, the judicial decision sooner or later returns to the ''open and obvious'' test whose supposed inadequacy ushered in the risk/utility test in the first instance. In truth, it is no principled way to identify one domain where open and obvious dominates and another where risk/utility prevails. While we have been largely spared risk/utility in generic product cases, the risk/utility test continues to work its mischief by undermining countless standardized product warnings and designs.

There is, moreover, nothing about the parade of utilitarian factors that justifies the risk/utility test on any utilitarian grounds. Quite the opposite, its cost and unreliability suggest that it should be banished from the legal system. The older view, which said, let us control force and fraud, does have application to products liability. It explains why the latent/patent distinction, while widely rejected today, has far more intellectual staying power than the voguish, complex, multifactored test that has replaced it. The latent/patent distinction can yield the clean yes/no answer necessary on the issue of liability. In contrast, the Wade factors are utterly untranslatable into yes/no inquiry. We are asked, for example, to take a wide range of variables with continuous distributions, but without preassigned weights, and to meld them into a single yes/no judgment on the question of product defect.

A cursory inspection of the text shows how difficult that task is to execute. Who can decide what the total levels of social utility are, as set out in factor #1? Nor is there any single ''substitute product'' against which the challenged product can be compared, as factor #3 might suggest. There are in reality a large number of different products (all of which can be configured in different ways) which may be the baseline on comparative analysis. These alternative products may not ''eliminate'' the risk, as suggested in factor #4. They may reduce it by an uncertain amount. Alternatively they may increase the probability of injury but reduce the anticipated severity of the injuries that do occur. Nor must a substitute product meet the ''same'' need. It could only meet some portion of the need and perhaps at some greater, or different, cost. And the ability to respond to changes in liability rules may be met only in part by changes in price or insurance coverage, as noted in factor #7.

With variables so numerous, the ingenuity of lawyers should never be doubted when the stakes in litigation are very high and discovery underregulated. The test is couched in an offhand way that makes difficult matters of degree look as though they involved simple distinctions in kind. It is a utilitarian nightmare. What starts out as a faithful application of the utilitarian calculus ends up as an unprincipled battle of the experts. Everything is admissible; nothing is quantifiable; nothing is dispositive. The degree of freedom left to the trier of fact after trial is as great as it was before. All too often, anything from a plaintiff's verdict for punitive damages to a defendant's verdict of no liability is consistent with the evidence. And it is all quite unnecessary; "awareness" in factor #6 points to the key element of knowledge, and usually gives more useful information than everything else taken together.

Nonetheless, once courts are committed to risk/utility, it quickly becomes clear that they have no formal test of liability equal to the task of sorting out the cases they must decide. Courts have quite naturally been most reluctant to grant any defendant (or plaintiff) a summary judgment, which is likely to be reversed on appeal in any event. Instead, judges are encouraged to hide behind the verdict, which decides without reasoning. The rise of the jury in modern law is no accident. It is an inevitable consequence of the present level of doctrinal poverty. Error costs and administrative costs continue to rise, and only the lawyers and experts, whose skills are necessary to navigate the morass, are able to turn a profit. For in these times the best legal and professional talent is strictly necessary to handle any complex case.

So we return to our original theme. One can find the odd difficult case under the older common law rules. But as a general rule, it is quite easy to decide who has hit whom, who has complied with the rules of the road, who has complied with statute or custom, or who has sold a product with a latent defect dangerous in ordinary use. These are rules with bite in routine cases. It is not equally possible to decide whether a product is too dangerous or too safe. The legal system today spends an enormous amount of energy and effort to make these impossible substantive judgments. In so doing it insures that no product nor any medical treatment is ever safe from judicial challenge. The spate of balancing tests that are so common today is a recipe for continued institutional dislocation. And that, alas, is the road down which modern courts and legislatures have taken us, today more than ever before.

James A. Henderson, Jr., *Judicial Review of Manufacturers' Conscious Design Choices: The Limits of Adjudication,* 73 Colum. L. Rev. 1531 (1973)*

The Concept of Polycentricity

In several articles, Lon Fuller developed the hypothesis that certain judgmental problems, to which he applies the adjective "polycentric," are inherently unsuited to being solved by adjudication. An understanding of his thesis necessarily begins with an understanding of the nature of the adjudicative process. Fuller defined adjudication as a social process of decision which assures to the affected party a particular form of participation—that of presenting proofs and arguments for a decision in his favor. Fuller was quick to recognize that adjudication is not the only social process of decision in which those affected are guaranteed some form of participation. Elections provide for participation through voting, and contracts provide for participation through negotiation. Rather,

*Used by permission.

it is the kind of participation available in court—the implications growing from Professor Fuller's phrase "presenting proofs and arguments"—that sets adjudication apart as a social process of decision.

The primary implication in the concept is the requirement that the presentations be addressed to an impartial tribunal that is bound to determine the relevant facts and to apply established rules to reach reasoned results. Fuller's definition of adjudication, in other words, implicitly includes the requirement that the proofs and arguments be based upon rules sufficiently specific in their content to enable the parties to argue rationally that a proper application of the rules dictates a certain result which the impartial tribunal is obligated to reach. It follows from this emphasis upon the unique form of participation afforded to litigants in adjudication that only those problems that lend themselves to adversary proofs and arguments of the sort described above are amenable to solution by means of adjudication.

The characteristic of most legal problems that renders them adjudicable is the unique manner in which the various issues presented in a case are logically related to each other. In presenting the proofs and arguments in a legal problem, the parties are able to take up and consider each issue separately, in an orderly sequence, although the issues are not necessarily unrelated to each other. A party's argument on the second issue may relate to and depend upon his argument on the first; and, similarly, his argument on the third issue may be related to his argument on the second. But in addressing himself to each successive point in turn, a litigant may momentarily exclude the others and assume, for the sake of his argument, that the court will render a favorable decision on the preceding points upon which he relies. Thus, where one person sues another seeking to recover for breach of contract, a number of interrelated issues may be presented, including issues of offer, lapse, acceptance, breach and measure of recovery. Regardless of the number of issues to be decided, the substantive law of contracts will have arranged and interrelated them in a way that allows the parties to address themselves in argument to each in turn, to the momentary exclusion of the others. The litigants will be able to isolate analytically any given issue in the case (e.g., whether a communication from one party to the other constitutes an offer) and to talk of a favorable decision in relation to that issue without simultaneously considering all of the others.

The manner in which established rules of decision render meaningful participation feasible may most clearly be understood by considering what would happen if for some reason the rules did not or could not perform the function of isolating issues for decision. What if, in other words, all of the issues in cases typically brought to courts for decision were related to one another in such a way that it was impossible for a litigant to address himself to any one issue apart from a consideration of all the others? Under those circumstances, a litigant's initial argument relating to any single issue would change in substance depending upon how the court might react to every other issue. Thus, a case containing a number of interdependent issues for decision might present innumerable analytical permutations to which the parties would logically be required to address themselves.

Meaningful participation in the decision through formal proofs and argument, in the manner described earlier, would be impossible. The parties would never be able to work their way logically through an unbroken chain of reasoning, nor would they be able to assert with any confidence that under applicable law the court was bound to accept any one of the myriad of possible approaches to the exclusion of all the others. At the end of the trial, when the last word from the parties had been uttered, the court would be left to arrive at a solution of the problem on its own, largely unaided and uninfluenced by either the arguments or the law. The parties would have been denied meaningful participation by the nature of the problem presented; and whatever the court might decide, its decision would not deserve to be called principled.

It is to this type of problem that Professor Fuller applies the adjective "polycentric." As both the term itself and the preceding discussion indicate, polycentric problems are many-centered problems, in which each point for decision is related to all the others as are the strands of a spider web. If one strand is pulled, a complex pattern of readjustments will occur throughout the entire web. If another strand is pulled, the relationships among all the strands will again be readjusted. A lawyer seeking to base his argument upon established principle and required to address himself in discourse to each of a dozen strands, or issues, would find his task frustratingly impossible. As he moved from the first point of his argument to the second and then to the third, he would find his arguments regarding the earlier points shifting beneath him. Unlike most of the traditional types of cases in which litigants are able, in effect, to freeze the rest of the web as they concentrate upon each separate strand, the web here retains its natural flexibility, adjusting itself in seemingly infinite variations as each new point, or strand, in the argument is reached.

Even though polycentric problems are not suited to adjudication, it does not follow that they are incapable of rational resolution. Adjudication is, of course, only one of several social processes of decision, and there are other such processes—contract negotiation and the exercise of managerial authority—that are ideally suited to solving polycentric problems. The guarantee of a player's right to be quarterback, for example, can best be accomplished by contract negotiation. Allowed to sit down informally and "talk things out," the players and the coach can arrive at a mutually acceptable agreement on the assignment. On a somewhat broader scale, it is to this process of negotiation that the law of contracts prospectively delegates a major portion of responsibility for the achievement of legally binding solutions to the polycentric problem of resource allocation.

The exercise of managerial authority is also well suited to providing rational solutions to polycentric problems. Managerial authority is exercised when one person has the authority to impose his own judgment upon the circumstances which he confronts. It should be observed that the manager in this situation acts very differently from a court. He is not bound to apply any law in reaching a decision and, in fact, is free to make judgments through the exercise of his unfettered discretion. The exercise by coaches of managerial authority, of course, is the primary process by which football team lineups are designed.

Finally, before applying the foregoing analysis of the limits of adjudication to the governing products liability, two important points must be made. First, the thesis that courts are "unable" to solve polycentric problems is an overstatement. Strictly speaking, the hypothesis advanced above is that courts are ill-suited to solving polycentric problems, not that they are absolutely incapable of doing so. The more polycentric the problem, the less equipped are the courts to deal with it. Professor Fuller uses the example of a sledge hammer, which is very well suited to driving stakes and which will serve in a pinch for cracking nuts, but which may be thought of as hopeless for opening cans. Nonetheless, if the need is great enough, as where any solution is preferable to no solution at all, the sledge hammer can be used to open cans, just as courts can be employed to provide some kinds of responses to even the most polycentric problems. The point is that in both instances the results would be exceedingly messy.

Second, having recognized that courts can, if the situation demands, provide some kinds of responses to polycentric problems, one should also recognize the very real threat to the integrity of the adjudicative process inhering in any broad-scale judicial commitment to doing so. The source and nature of this threat are not difficult to understand. The very essence of the rule of law lies in the formally guaranteed opportunity afforded to parties to participate meaningfully in the social processes of decision. Whenever persons affected by such decisions are denied their right to participate—as when, for example, public elections are rigged—the threat to the integrity of those social processes of decision is substantial. And so, if courts were ever to begin routinely to provide responses to highly polycentric problems, the judicial process would be effectively subverted. Because of the absence of sufficiently specific rules upon which to argue or decide such cases, the litigants would be denied the traditionally guaranteed opportunity to participate meaningfully in the decisionmaking process. Of course, they would still take part in the proceedings, but only in the limited sense of making speeches—not as litigants offering proofs and arguments for a decision according to law. Their posture before the court would become very much like that of a supplicant before a manager, appealing to the latter's discretion. And the courts, confronted systematically with polycentric problems in connection with which the litigants' proofs and arguments are essentially useless, would inevitable be forced to resort to bases for decision bearing little, if any, relation to the presentation of the legal issues. Were such a denial of the litigants' rights to meaningful participation to become commonplace, the adjudicative process would become nothing more than an elaborate masquerade.

Polycentricity and the Establishment of Product Safety Standards

There can be little doubt that the problems confronting the products engineer with respect to the establishment of specific standards for the design and manufacture of his product are not less polycentric than those facing the football coach as he undertakes to assign positions for his players. Because absolute safety is not attainable and—in any event—is not the sole desirable objective of the product's design, the engineer must place relative values upon a multitude of factors. The decisions he must make regarding these factors are as interrelated and interdependent as the strands of an intricate web. Intelligent answers to the question of "How much product safety is enough?"—the question that will concern us throughout—can be provided only by a process that considers such factors as market price, functional utility, and aesthetics, as well as safety, and achieves the proper balance among them. Ultimately, the question reduces to "What portion of society's limited resources are to be allocated to safety, thereby leaving less to be devoted to other social objectives?"

Accepting that the products engineer faces extremely polycentric problems in designing his products and their methods of manufacture, it is clear that a court would face the same degree of polycentricity were it to attempt to establish independent product safety standards with which to review the engineer's decision in a products liability case. Unless the court were in some way able to avoid establishing independent standards, it would be required to take into account the same factors that the products engineer did originally. To be sure, the court might weigh these factors differently—legal standards in this context are properly thought of as minimum standards—but the requirement that these numerous, interrelated factors be weighed at all would cause the judicial establishment of product safety standards to retain all of this task's inherent polycentricity.

It follows that the process of adjudication administered by the courts is not institutionally suited to establishing product safety standards. Were courts to attempt independently to adjudicate the relative reasonableness of various product designs and methods of manufacture, they would encounter the same difficulties that were predicted above in connection with any attempt by a court to assign various players to their positions on a football team. Every alternative advanced by either party would have to be evaluated in light of many factors, of which safety is but one. This does not mean the courts are powerless. They may, for example, adopt and apply specific standards established elsewhere by decisional processes more suited to that task, or they may develop alternative approaches which eliminate altogether the necessity of passing judgment upon the reasonableness of the various product designs and manufacturing techniques brought before them for review. The task which courts are not suited to undertake, however, is that of establishing product safety standards by themselves.

Of course, it is true that in applying the general concepts of negligence in non-products cases courts have been establishing safety standards of one sort or another for more than a century, and have to some extent been exposed to the difficulties inherent in the solution of polycentric problems. Certainly the negligence standard of reasonable care is very general, providing relatively few specific guidelines for decision. I submit, however, that the courts were lured from the secure, essentially unicentric world of early nineteenth-century strict liability into the potentially polycentric world of negligence-based liability by the strong pull of substantive policy, and that they have been flirting with disaster ever since. The difficulties were submerged from the start by two institutions: the reasonable man test and the jury. The flesh-and-blood moralistic qualities of the reasonable man were ideally suited to helping both lawyers and courts address themselves to solutions to the polycentric problems which the relatively non-technical cases of the time presented. And the jury, which has been delegated much of the responsibility for actually deciding the ultimate issues raised under the general reasonableness standard, is ideally suited to burying in a collective laymen's verdict whatever analytical difficulties may be encountered at the law-application stage.

These two devices served the courts in combating even the relatively low levels of polycentricity presented by the early cases. Nonetheless, the administration of the negligence concept over the last one hundred years is ultimately consistent with my hypothesis, for it must be conceded that it has been accomplished only with notable signs of strain and difficulty. The confusion generated by the doctrine of *res ipsa loquitur* is but one example.

That the limits of adjudication have influenced the courts' approach to negligence cases may be further substantiated by reviewing what has happened in a non-products field in which advancing technology early threatened the courts with difficult polycentric problems—medical malpractice actions. From the beginning, the courts have delegated the establishment of specific standards in malpractice cases to the collective managerial authority of the medical profession. This approach to malpractice cases is arguably at least partially attributable to the necessity of avoiding highly polycentric problems. Judges with any natural instinct for survival would no more think of trying to establish an independent standard with which to permit the jury to evaluate a defendant doctor's performance of an appendectomy than they would think of trying to establish independent standards for assigning players to a football team or—assessing an engineer's consumer product.

* * *

Judicial Determination of Design Standards

Assuming the validity of the hypothesis that adjudication is unsuited to answering the question of "How much design safety is enough?," it follows that a broad-scale judicial commitment to the independent review of conscious design choices would bring with it a very real threat to the integrity of the judicial process. Confronted with the hopeless difficulties of trying to redesign products via adjudication, and presumably unable to resist the social pressures generally favoring injured plaintiffs, courts would inevitably resort to some form of judicial coin-flipping, *i.e.*, they would begin to determine defendants' liability on some arbitrary basis rather than on the purported basis of the reasonableness of the product designs brought before them. Efforts to establish meaningful design standards would be abandoned in favor of allowing juries to determine defendants' liability upon no more substantial grounds than their own untutored "good judgment," or whim.

The shift in the basis of manufacturers' liability would be disguised, consciously or otherwise, by heavy reliance upon the unsupported opinions of experts relating to the ultimate issue of the reasonableness of defendants' conscious design choices. The absence of any viable product safety standards with which to decide these cases, however, would be obvious even to the casual observer. In effect, the adjudicative process would largely become a sham. Although such tactics might render these cases manageable in the short run, they would do so at the cost of a serious erosion of confidence in the courts by those litigants who would correctly come to realize that they have been denied effective access to the adjudicative process by such subterfuge.

* * *

Conclusion

To those consumer advocates who look upon their efforts to achieve greater product safety as a struggle approximating all-out war, the preceding analysis is apt to ring of treason. Having argued that courts are not suited to participate directly in the establishment of product safety standards, I may appear to be calling for the removal from the battlefield of an effective weapon in the consumer protection arsenal. But I have called for no such thing. Assuming the battlefield of particular interest here is the one upon which product safety standards are established, I am calling not for the removal of the courts from that field but for a recognition that the courts have never really occupied it in the first place. Moreover, to attempt to assign them now to the task of reviewing manufacturers' conscious design choices would, in effect, be to send them on a suicide mission. The superficial attractiveness of courts attempting such an effort detracts not at all from the realities of the limits of adjudication as I have described them.

If I should be wrong in my prediction that legislative responses in the area of product design and judicial attention on marketing will reduce pressures sufficiently to allow courts generally to resist independent attempts to adjudicate the reasonableness of defendant manufacturers' conscious design choices and if, instead, the coming years should find most courts making such attempts, then we will have entered a regrettable phase in the development of products liability. The courts will have been badgered into trying to deliver more than the process of adjudication is capable of delivering, and the end result will be the subversion of that process and its displacement by a thinly disguised lottery. If this occurs, it will be incumbent upon the legislature to replace the common law system of manufacturers' liability for conscious design choices with some more orderly, fair and rational system for compensating the victims of product-related injuries.

B. Failure to Warn

"Warnings aren't free," chorus James Henderson and Aaron Twerski in their numerous writings on this topic. More than any other scholars, they have educated readers about the thorny doctrinal problems raised by the premise that product sellers should warn users about defects that cannot reasonably be eliminated in manufacture. In the article excerpted below, Henderson and Twerski write in support of beleagured manufacturers who cannot, no matter how diligently they try, communicate warnings effective enough to prevent significant harm.

While Henderson and Twerski express concern that the current state of doctrine—or rather, doctrinal collapse—obliges defendants to pay more than they should for their failure to warn, Howard Latin reaches an opposite conclusion, although he agrees with Henderson and Twerski that warnings cannot prevent serious harm in the aggregate. Latin approaches product warnings from a social-science perspective. Warnings, he writes, continually fail. And the costs of this failure ought to fall more, rather than less, on defendant manufacturers.

James A. Henderson, Jr. & Aaron D. Twerski, *Doctrinal Collapse in Products Liability: The Empty Shell Of Failure To Warn*, 65 N.Y.U.L. Rev. 265 (1990)*

Commercial distributors of products owe users and consumers a duty to warn of product-related risks that are not obvious. Failure to warn when a reasonable person would have warned exposes defendants to tort liability, as do other forms of unreasonably risky conduct in a negligence regime. In contrast to other areas of tort, however, the precast negligence standards are inadequate for the tasks to which they have been assigned. The doctrine purporting to govern these cases has collapsed upon itself. To reestablish coherence, significant changes are necessary; fine-tuning will not suffice.

To understand the nature of the difficulties with failure-to-warn doctrine, we contrast it with defective-design litigation. With allegedly defective designs, defendants often can show that an alternative design suggested by the plaintiff would have made things worse, and therefore courts hearing design cases must conduct elaborate cost-benefit analyses to test these claims. By contrast, in failure-to-warn cases the common assumption is that warnings can often be improved upon but can never be made worse; that is, the issue at stake is always whether the defendant ought to have supplied consumers with more, and by definition better, information about product risks. Whether the defendant should have supplied more information seems, therefore, an intuitively manageable, eminently adjudicable question.

We believe, however, that the shared wisdom regarding the negligence standard in failure-to-warn cases overlooks two flaws. Concepts such as risk foreseeability, risk-utility balancing, and proximate causation are so devoid of content in the failure-to-warn context that they cannot hope to test the bona fides of the plaintiff's claim. We conclude that even a well-tended failure-to-warn garden probably cannot support growth. The real problem, it turns out, is not with the weeds. It is steeped in the soil of negligence itself.

The "Strict Liability v. Negligence" Debate

Modern American products liability started off on the wrong doctrinal foot twenty-five years ago and has never regained its stride. To understand the nature of the problem, one must examine it in historical context. The American Law Institute gave birth to this analytic confusion with the highly influential section 402A of the *Restatement (Second) of Torts*, which states that strict liability applies equally well to cases involving manufacturing defects, design defects, and failures to warn. Strict liability can be applied coherently in manufacturing defect cases because a product's defectiveness can be determined without resort to negligence-oriented cost-benefit balancing. But

*Used by permission.

in both defective-design and failure-to-warn cases, cost-benefit balancing is inevitably required to determine product defectiveness. Because cost-benefit balancing is also at the heart of negligence, it is no easy matter in design and warning cases to discover a difference between strict liability and negligence.

Having adopted strict liability across the board, courts found themselves trapped by their own rhetoric. Strict liability, as everyone knows, is a doctrine more favorable to plaintiffs than is negligence. Thus, courts which found that in the midst of "strict liability" cases they were knee-deep in traditional negligence balancing, undertook a prolonged search for the strict liability "edge." After years of frustration, many courts have finally abandoned the search and declared that, for all intents and purposes, strict liability, as applied to generically dangerous product cases, was simply negligence by another name. However, many courts continue to insist that strict liability provides some practical benefit to claimants that negligence doctrine does not. In doing so they have been forced either to articulate outrageous positions that both deeply offend traditional notions of moral responsibility and prevent tort law from achieving its objectives, or to create verbal distinctions that have little practical consequence other than to confuse litigants and commentators.

Liability for Failing to Warn About Unknowable Risks

Courts might distinguish between product-oriented strict liability theory and conduct-oriented negligence theory by dispensing with the reasonable foreseeability standard which lies at the heart of negligence theory. A plaintiff could then recover for damages caused by a defective product even though the risk that the plaintiff claims should have been warned against was unforeseeable at the time the product was distributed. Given this distinction, a negligence standard, with its focus on the conduct of the manufacturer, would impose liability for failure to warn only when the defendant knew, or should have known, of the relevant information. In contrast, a reasonable manufacturer could be found liable under a strict liability standard even if he had no access to the information that later became available.

However tempting it may be for courts to hold distributors "strictly" liable for unknowable risks, doing so prevents the achievement of either of two contrasting objectives underlying tort law, as identified by the majority of commentators. One view regards tort law as essentially enhancing non-instrumental norms of fairness which mediate between conflicting individual preferences. The other view interprets tort law as essentially furthering instrumental, allocative efficiency objectives, which help competitive markets put resources to their highest uses without attempting to mediate between individual preferences.

If we assume, under the fairness view, that a basic postulate of legal duty is that the conduct the law seeks to induce is capable of being performed and, as a corollary, that the law eschews imposing duties to perform impossible tasks, then imposing liability for failure to warn of unknowable risks is grossly unfair. On the other hand, imposing liability for failing to warn of scientifically unknowable risks also strikes hard against the efficiency objective. As a number of commentators have noted, manufacturers cannot, by hypothesis, insure against risks that even reasonably careful persons do not know exist. As a consequence, when strict liability is imposed retroactively for risks about which the defendants could not have known at distribution, defendants can only charge the losses against earnings or capital, or go out of business. Either way, inefficiencies result. Later entrants to the market enjoy a decided advantage over earlier entrants who are saddled with obligations that they could not insure against or avoid by exercising reasonable care. A rule that penalizes longevity and contradicts fundamental rules of risk spreading by asking the impossible of manufacturers is counterproductive and likely headed for oblivion. Negligence, not strict liability, should, and eventually will, govern the time dimension issues in products liability litigation.

Although strict liability here serves neither fairness nor efficiency, a small cadre of courts have nevertheless followed the lead of the New Jersey Supreme Court and have imposed liability for defendants' failure to warn of risks which were scientifically unknowable when the product was marketed. The New Jersey court did restrict its earlier holding to asbestos cases; thus, under current New Jersey law, for all other warnings cases predicated on strict liability, the defendant now bears "the burden of proving that the information was not reasonably available or obtainable and that it therefore lacked actual or constructive knowledge of the defect." It is questionable whether this partial retreat is meaningful. Given that defendants are unlikely to carry the burden of proving a negative, the modified New Jersey rule may be the functional equivalent of true strict liability. Whatever the label, the point is the same. Liability for unknowable risks is a weed that should not be allowed to take root in the failure-to-warn garden.

The Causation Presumption

Many courts have held that when the defendant fails to provide an adequate warning, it is presumed that such a warning would have been read and heeded by the user had it been given. This presumption serves to get the plaintiff over the hurdle of establishing causation in all but the weakest of cases. The rationale most often given for the presumption is that it is a mirror image of a presumption that defendants enjoy under comment *j* to section 402A of the *Restatement (Second) of Torts*. That comment provides:

> Where warning is given, the seller may reasonably assume that it will be read and heeded; and a product bearing such a warning, which is safe for use if it is followed, is not in defective condition, nor is it unreasonably dangerous.

It is argued that if a seller is entitled to a presumption that a warning will be read and heeded, a plaintiff should be entitled to the converse causation presumption when no warning, or an inadequate warning, is given. We will consider later the substantive merits of granting the plaintiff this causation presumption. Our more limited objective here is to show that the logic of the courts that rely formally on comment *j* is seriously flawed. Plaintiffs may deserve a presumption regarding causation, but such a presumption cannot be derived logically from comment *j*.

A closer analysis of the causation presumption is required to see why it does not derive logically from comment *j*. If a risk is not obvious to a substantial number of users and consumers, and a proper warning will suffice to bring that risk to the attention of most such users and consumers, then the defendant owes a duty to provide such a warning. Once such a warning is provided, the product is no longer in a defective condition, as it is not unreasonably dangerous to consumers. And when the product is reasonably safe and nondefective, the question of causation in the particular case involving the particular plaintiff is never reached. Thus, when comment *j* says that "the seller may reasonably assume," it is not referring to a presumption that any individual plaintiff actually did read and heed the warning; to the contrary, it is certain from the outset that at least some consumers will not have done so. Rather, comment *j* says that if the warning is adequate and is likely to reach many, even if not all, consumers, then, for purposes of determining whether the defendant has discharged his underlying duty to warn, it reasonably may be assumed that consumers will act on the warning. Once the conclusion is reached that the defendant has satisfied this duty, the plaintiff's claim fails at the threshold and the question of individualized causation never arises.

To insist that any particular plaintiff should enjoy a presumption of individualized causation when adequate warnings are not given because the defendant enjoys such a presumption when warnings are given is to rely on false logic. Comment *j* never addresses the causation issue, as such, nor does it create any presumption of individualized causation benefiting defendants. All it says is that, if the defendant provides an adequate warning, he fulfills his duty of care, and that, in determining the adequacy of the warning, courts will examine its likely effects on reasonable consumers generally, not the actual effects on particular consumers. Thus, to rely on comment *j* to derive a presumption of actual, individual causation for plaintiffs in failure-to-warn cases is to commit serious error.

Causation should, in appropriate cases, be the acid test of negligence law. In theory, it should force a plaintiff to move from establishing the defendant's violation of an abstract standard of care to proving the concrete effects of that violation on this plaintiff. By forcing an answer to the question, "What difference would it have made in this case?" causation doctrine provides some quality assurance that the standard of care has been established correctly. It is altogether too easy to theorize about standards of care applied to society at large. But if it is likely that the particular plaintiff's injury would have occurred in any event, then perhaps the gap between what is and what should have been is not as significant as was first thought—if it would not have mattered to this particular victim, then perhaps the effects of the defendant's behavior on society at large have been exaggerated.

Once again, it is useful to compare failure-to-warn with design-defect cases. In product cases alleging defective design, causation doctrine operates reasonably well. A plaintiff typically sets forth a hypothetical alternative design and seeks to prove that, had the safer alternative been in place, the injury would have been avoided or reduced. Many design cases provide a rich factual background which helps to define the causation question. For example, motor vehicle design cases are generally supported by hard data such as auto speed, skid marks, trajectories, and the like. Similarly, in industrial machinery cases, where allegations of inadequate safety devices are often made, the injury-causing event is typically not clouded in mystery: a user whose hand is caught and injured can usually identify the physical characteristics of the machine, how her hand was trapped, where she was standing, the work environment surrounding the machine, and so on. In short, the causation issue in most design cases is rendered manageable by hardware and hard facts.

In the typical failure-to-warn case, the very opposite is true. To establish causation a plaintiff should, in theory, be required to prove not only that she would have read, understood, and remembered the warning, but also that she would have altered her conduct to avoid the injury. How is the plaintiff to carry these burdens? No hard facts or scientific data frame the question. A plaintiff typically can offer little more than self-serving testimony and anecdotal evidence to establish her proximate causation case. Being purely speculative, the plaintiff's arguments at once state both the minimum and maximum case. The good causation case and the bad are remarkably alike. If courts were to "get tough" with plaintiffs on the causation issue, almost no one would survive a defendant's motion for summary disposition. And yet anything less than getting tough sends most causation issues to the jury. Faced with choosing between these extremes, courts understandably defer to juries' discretion. The plaintiff's causation case is made excessively easy because any other reaction would make the case unacceptably difficult.

If the plaintiff's prima facie causation case is too easy to establish, the tools available to defendants to rebut it are almost nonexistent. Unlike design cases, in which defense experts are free to demonstrate that the hypothetical design would have fared no better, the defendant responding to the causation issue in a warning case has little to say and rarely finds it in his interest to say it. In many cases, the only factually plausible, causation-related line of defense is the assertion that the plaintiff was either too lazy to have read or too dull-witted to have understood a more pointed warning. Thus, only a personal attack on the plaintiff's shortcomings can blunt the unverifiable anecdotal offensive. Yet the cost to the defendant in potential jury displeasure at such an attack is hard to overestimate.

If the plaintiff can establish causation by mere say-so, however, and if the defendant is powerless to rebut, causation plays little role in establishing the actual validity of most failure-to-warn claims. Unfortunately, the need to rely on anecdotal evidence is not likely to disappear any time soon. The tribunal must construct a conceptual bridge between the absence of the desired information and the injury which plaintiff suffered, in order to establish the necessary causal link. For this bridge-building process to have any meaning, the factfinder must be able to hypothesize as to how the plaintiff would have used the missing information had the defendant supplied it. Such projection requires a model of how consumers absorb this information and under what circumstances they alter their behavior in response.

Constructing a credible causation model is no easy task. In fact, a huge body of literature dealing with decision theory and cognitive learning suggests that predicting how additional information would have affected any given individual may be well nigh impossible. A number of factors make such predictions difficult. First, considerable empirical evidence indicates that many people do not process information in a logical and predictable manner. Second, not only the type of information presented, but also the manner in which it is presented can have a substantial effect on the decision. Thus, unless we know the manner in which the withheld information would have been transmitted, we often cannot credibly predict its effect. Third, the prior beliefs and information of a given individual significantly affect the impact on her decisions of any additional information. Unless we uncover the pre-existing base on which the additional information would have stood, we cannot determine the effect it might have had.

A concrete example will clarify the nature of these difficulties. Regarding the effects upon behavior of the manner in which information is presented, experimenters have discovered, not surprisingly, that the order in which information is presented has a significant impact on its perception by the individual who must ultimately utilize the data to reach a decision. Unlike suggested design changes, suggested alternative or additional warnings cannot be comprehended by the user all in one piece. The consumer must read warnings sequentially and digest them piecemeal. As one moves from more important warnings to those of lesser urgency, the number of warnings that must be supplied increases exponentially at each descending level. The plaintiff typically asks for only one warning—the one precisely relating to the risk that materialized in his injury. But the defendant has the right to insist that other, equally important warnings also not be obscured as a result.

Thus, when faced with the causation question at any level of risk, one must ask not only how many warnings should have been given, but how they should have been sequenced with regard to each other. If warnings of similar magnitude could be comprehended by the user simultaneously, their relative positioning might be unimportant. However, given that users cannot assimilate warnings simultaneously, warnings must be arranged in a sequence. Sequencing inevitably denotes relative importance and will have an impact on the weight a consumer attaches to the risk.

It follows that resolution of the causation question in failure-to-warn cases frequently depends on variables that cannot be resolved coherently in the courtroom. For the analysis in a multiple-warnings case to make sense, one must determine the sequence in which the hypothetical warnings should have appeared, and how the user or consumer would have reacted to alternative sequencing. The former question may not be determinable, and the latter question is surely not litigable. We can only conclude that the causation issue lacks substantive content in much of failure-to-warn litigation. Too often, causation is a mirage—whatever the factfinder wishes it to be.

Given the difficulties of litigating the causation issue in these failure-to-warn cases, the question arises whether it should be abandoned altogether in warnings claims. This question may well be moot, because the courts have already effectively abandoned it: the willingness of judges to pass most causation questions to the jury is evidence that they attach little practical importance to the issue. In addition, the adoption by many courts of the causation presumption has almost entirely negated the issue in those jurisdictions.

Theory aside, it is clear that, for the reasons set forth above, causation plays no such role in warnings cases. Courts have practically mooted the issue because they lack any realistic way of adjudicating it. Thus, causation joins preliminary risk-utility screening and risk-utility balancing as an empty doctrinal shell in failure-to-warn cases. This situation is deeply disturbing. A plaintiff's prima facie case should not be capable of being constructed from pure rhetoric. The analogy to a car with a gas pedal and no brakes is not inappropriate, for there are no longer any effective checks on a failure-to-warn claim. The drive toward liability is now almost unhindered.

Finally, we note that the gulf between design litigation and failure-to-warn litigation is very great. In the design case not only does risk-utility have true substantive content, but the causation issue is usually determinable because it is developed through the kind of hard facts that can be the subject of legitimate expert testimony. As a result, courts handling design cases treat the causation issue seriously. They tend not to favor the plaintiff with presumptions to help him overcome the proof hurdle. By contrast, in most failure-to-warn cases, the liability standard is without content and the causation analysis completely ad hoc. The collapse of negligence doctrine as a guide to decisionmaking in warnings cases could not be more complete.

Confusing Risk-Reduction and Informed-Choice Warnings

Courts generally recognize that product warnings serve two distinct but related functions. First, warnings may reduce the risk of product-related injury by allowing consumers to behave more carefully than if they remained ignorant of risks associated with product use. By behaving more carefully, consumers help to achieve the efficiency objective of tort law. Second, warnings may provide consumers with the information necessary to choose whether or not they wish to encounter certain kinds of risks on a "take it or leave it" basis. While assuring more informed consumer choices increases efficiency, it also reflects fairness concerns more clearly than do risk-reduction efforts. Risk-reduction warnings cases are common to almost all product categories and form the central focus of this Article. Informed-choice warning litigation is generally limited to prescription drugs and cosmetics, although occasionally other products are implicated. As with all legal distinctions, the lines between these two types of warnings often blur. Even in a classic case of the product user being able to use the product more safely thanks to clear warnings, the user may also decide to decrease his level of usage in order to reduce the residual risks of injury. And even when the warning says "one out of one million people who take this drug become blind as a result," the consumer who chooses to go ahead and take it can be on the lookout for early symptoms that might reduce the severity of his injury if he turns out (inescapably, once he decides to consume) to be one of the unlucky few.

The difference between risk-reduction and informed-choice warnings is closely analogous to the distinction between a medical malpractice case premised on negligent conduct and one based on the theory of informed consent. The negligence case tests the reasonableness of the doctor's conduct. It looks to risk reduction. The informed-consent claim, while acknowledging that the standard of conduct was adequate (and therefore that risk reduction is not involved), questions the privilege of the doctor to act at all without providing the patient with adequate information to decide whether he wishes to encounter the risk. Scholarship dealing with medical malpractice reflects an understanding that, with regard to standard of care and causation, the negligence standard used in typical risk-reduction cases may not be appropriate for informed-choice issues. For example, considerable controversy exists regarding whether the standard of adequate disclosure required of the physician to the patient should be that provided by a reasonable doctor (the negligence standard) or that expected by a reasonable patient (the informed-choice standard). Similarly, opinions differ strongly regarding the burden the plaintiff should bear in establishing decision-causation: need the plaintiff prove that he would have made a contrary decision had he been provided with additional information?

Compared with their medical malpractice counterparts, products failure-to-warn cases reflect little judicial sensitivity regarding the distinction between risk-reduction and informed-choice warnings. Courts most often treat all failure-to-warn cases as of one cloth. However, it is possible that if they fully appreciated the distinction they might, for example, be less willing to apply the causation presumption in risk-reduction cases. In informed-consent cases, where the function of a particular warning would have been to empower the plaintiff by allowing him to decide whether he wished to expose himself to the risk at all, second-guessing the decision the plaintiff would have made had he received the warning defeats the objective sought to be achieved: to transfer the decision from the defendant to the plaintiff. In these cases, therefore, the presumption for the plaintiff is justified. By contrast, when the role of the warning is the more traditional one of risk reduction, the plaintiff's burden arguably should be higher. In the context of pure risk-reduction cases, the defendant's failure to warn constitutes less of a personal insult to the plaintiff and more of a wasteful generator of social costs. To make a valid case, the plaintiff arguably should be required to show that such waste has, indeed, been caused by defendant's failure to warn—that, having received a proper warning, the plaintiff would have behaved differently and avoided injury.

* * *

Recommendations

In order to reconstruct an effective failure-to-warn doctrine, the failure-to-warn garden must first be weeded by eliminating the fundamental doctrinal errors which prevent this area of products liability law from reaching its objectives. However, elimination of these doctrinal errors alone is not enough. The doctrine must be wholly reconstructed; the very soil of the garden must be reconstituted. Even an error-free failure-to-warn doctrine is fraught with problems. Indeed, they are sufficiently disturbing to suggest that failure to warn should be abandoned and replaced with a more manageable and effective means of reviewing the adequacy of manufacturers' efforts to convey risk information.

Such a drastic solution, however, presents a dilemma. We believe no responsible system of products liability law can properly function without a cause of action which imposes responsibilities on manufacturers to warn consumers about hidden, product-related risks. Yet, once one starts down the slippery slope of finding liability for failure to warn, few brakes exist to prevent sending most, if not all, cases to the jury on instructions which refer to nonverifiable events and generate inconsistent verdicts. This inevitable slide to inconsistency seems to flow necessarily from the fact that manufacturers are being asked unreasonably to rescue consumers from their natural state of imperfect knowledge and understanding. Common law judges have moved with caution in creating exceptions to the general rule of no duty to rescue others from peril. Perhaps what has happened in failure-to-warn cases is that courts, uncharacteristically, have gone too far in imposing an open-ended duty to rescue. As a result, courts have predictably encountered severe problems of claims management.

Refusing to Impose Liability for Failure to Include Insignificant Increments of Information

Earlier we described the relative ease with which plaintiffs can press upon courts their need for tiny increments of additional information that might have helped them to avoid injury. We also noted the difficulties encountered in fairly establishing causation for such small informational increments. In addition, we argued that as product warnings address each new level of risk, the lists of warnings become increasingly longer and consumer focus more attenuated and difficult. We see no solution to these problems unless judges begin adopting a hardheaded attitude toward such claims. Courts simply should refuse to hold defendants liable for their failure to include one more tiny piece of information. Several types of claims, especially those involving obvious dangers, low risk foreseeability, and minor verbal shadings, must be approached with a firm anti-liability presumption.

Deferring to Institutions Capable of Evaluating Warnings in the Aggregate

Courts could pay more serious attention to conclusions reached by those who possess the institutional capability of evaluating warnings in the aggregate. However, for reasons that we find difficult to understand, courts have not deferred to the determinations of product safety agencies such as the Food and Drug Administration or Consumer Product Safety Commission. The analysis usually begins and ends with the statement that agency standards are minimum, not maximum, standards and that courts are therefore free to disregard them.

We submit that this approach is misguided. The problem of determining the proper wording of a warning may not necessarily require expertise to be solved. But perceiving and judging the wide spectrum of possible warnings does require significant expertise. Furthermore, it is the kind of expertise that is not easily transferrable to the judicial theater. The knowledge sought is not the knowledge of an isolated fact or judgment, but rather the totality of possible warnings for the product or product type. Accordingly, a dose of judicial humility is called for. Courts recognizing the limits of their institutional capabilities should refuse to second-guess the judgments of agencies who possess not only expertise but also a capacity for knowledge and memory which the courts cannot match. If the regulation aims at reducing the particular risk that materialized in the plaintiff's injury, the fact that a warning conforms to a regulation promulgated by a federal agency should practically foreclose liability for failure to warn. In those instances, courts should require plaintiffs to show by clear and convincing evidence that the agency's regulation was insufficient.

In one class of failure-to-warn cases, the courts appear to have followed something like the agency-deference approach suggested here. The federal courts of appeal, in the recent spate of cigarette-cancer cases, have effectively eliminated all failure-to-warn actions arising subsequent to 1966, when the Federal Cigarette Labelling and Advertising Act became effective. Admittedly, the cases have been decided under the guise of federal preemption of states' rights to regulate warnings. However, as commentators have noted, the federal preemption argument does not follow easily from controlling precedent. The more logical explanation is that the courts are convinced that the litigation cycle that would follow from a contrary holding would be unmanageable. The specter of trial courts making findings of inadequacy based on the failure of defendants to have added small increments of warnings to those legislatively mandated is one that the appellate courts do not welcome. The prospect of such increments effectively being mandated on a state-by-state basis is equally unappealing to courts. We believe that the holdings in these cases are rather the product of common sense or common law preemption than that of federal preemption.

In addition to legislative deference, courts should accord some weight to industry standards regarding product warnings. Defendants have put forward industry custom as a defense in failure-to-warn litigation less frequently than compliance with governmental standards. Courts have good reason, of course, to be more suspect of the custom defense simply because it may be in the interest of industry to conform to a sub-optimal standard of care. Nonetheless, widespread industry custom with regard to product warnings deserves serious attention by the courts. Once again, an entire industry has the ability to assess the warning issue in a manner that a court faced with seriatim litigation cannot hope to accomplish. We do not suggest that a black letter rule of judicial deference to industry-wide standards be adopted. We do argue that courts should give substantial weight to evidence that an entire industry, or a substantial portion thereof, has chosen to handle product warnings in a certain way.

Increased Utilization of Experts

With respect to design, it is almost inconceivable that a case involving any significant complexity would be tried without both sides relying heavily on experts. The expert testimony could be expected more often than not to be rigorous, reflecting confidence in its conclusions. In contrast, courts have made clear that experts are not required in connection with the issue of whether the defendant supplied adequate warnings of product-related risks, even when the case involves complex technology. This reasoning generates a dangerous asymmetry, because plaintiffs often choose to rely on experts in warnings cases. And although it is often the case that the expert testimony relates to whether the defendant reasonably should have known of the risks not warned of, or to the technical background describing the risk and its non-obvious qualities (in which cases warnings experts tend to show the same rigor as they display in design cases), in a large percentage of failure-to-warn cases the main function of plaintiffs' experts is to offer speculative and conclusory opinions that the warnings supplied by defendants were inadequate. While some courts object to this use of experts in warnings litigation, a greater number approve.

These patterns must change. Whenever expert testimony would help jurors to assess the validity of a failure-to-warn claim, judges should require both sides to support their arguments regarding obviousness, sufficiency, and causation with testimony from qualified experts who give more than conclusory opinions that warnings are or are not adequate, or that better warnings would or would not have made a difference. We are urging, in effect, that courts pressure litigants to develop more adequate behavioral models with which to sort out valid and invalid warnings claims. At the same time, courts should eschew reliance on the uninformed discourse that currently dominates warnings litigation. Juries are competent to judge some issues on their own, and should be left to do so. On balance, we would like to see more, rather than less, expert testimony in these cases. But, in any case, courts must insist that it be rigorous.

At a time when the role of experts in products litigation generally has come under heavy attack, it may seem odd to insist that behavioral experts be utilized more frequently. Indeed, our own analysis has suggested that expert testimony can be especially problematic in the failure-to-warn context. However, in an area so devoid of substance and so overblown with mere posturing, judicial insistence that experts speak with greater authority makes considerable sense. As we have observed, the sciences relevant to warnings claims are softer than those that inform decisions regarding allegedly defective designs. However, experts could serve to educate the courts as to the truly difficult policy choices that attend this special genre of products litigation. Courts could insist, on threat of dismissal of actions, that plaintiffs bring forth the relevant expertise. And they could insist, on threat of giving cases to juries on instructions favorable to plaintiffs, that defendants respond in kind. In this area of the law, adding expertise to the evidentiary mix at trial could be a real blessing.

Elimination of Causation Presumptions

We showed above how a presumption of proximate causation cannot be derived logically from comment *j* to section 402A of the *Restatement*. Now we argue that such a presumption makes no good sense on the merits. In failure-to-warn cases, causation analysis is already a flight into fancy. When a presumption favors the plaintiff, the defendant is basically precluded from the opportunity to convince a court to rule as a matter of law that the failure to warn was not the proximate cause of plaintiff's harm. In some instances, giving the plaintiff the benefit of the doubt regarding causation is fair to both sides. For example, when the victim is killed in an accident with respect to which there are no eyewitnesses, and it is clear that a reasonable person in the decedent's position probably would have read and heeded the missing warning, allowing a jury to conclude that the decedent would have heeded an adequate warning is appropriate. However, when all the circumstantial evidence (save the plaintiff's self-serving testimony) points the other way, shifting the burden to the defendant prevents a court from disposing of even a patently weak claim as a matter of law. Because the defendant must prove that her failure to warn was not the cause of injury, the court is almost duty-bound to send virtually every proximate causation issue, no matter how weak the factual basis, to the jury for determination. If we truly seek an active judicial role in controlling the kinds of warnings cases that reach the jury, the causation presumption must be abandoned in favor of a more fact-intensive approach.

Conclusion

In the branch of products liability commentary devoted to generically dangerous products, much attention has been paid in recent years to liability for defective product designs. In contrast, failure-to-warn litigation has largely escaped serious analysis. Almost everyone appears to have assumed that traditional negligence doctrine is adequate to the task of deciding warnings cases. Breaking ranks with the majority of commentators, we argue that negligence doctrine in the context of failure-to-warn litigation is little more than an empty shell. In most cases, the elements of the warnings cause of action require plaintiffs to do little more than mouth empty phrases. From the plaintiff's perspective, there is undoubtedly a certain attractiveness to a tort without a meaningful standard of care or any serious requirement of proving causation. From a broader social perspective, however, such a tort is too lawless to be fair or useful.

To cure this collapse of failure-to-warn doctrine, we urge that judges engage more aggressively in both lawmaking and law-applying. We have considered the possibility of replacing the nonfeasance-oriented failure-to-warn regime with a misfeasance-oriented system of misrepresentation-based liability. Perhaps if the judicial climate today were, as it was a decade ago, firmly committed to expanding products liability wherever possible, we would recommend that such a drastic change be implemented by statute. However, we perceive that judges today may be more receptive to arguments of the sort we are making.

If this perception is accurate, and if we have fairly and persuasively presented the shortcomings in current failure-to-warn doctrine, perhaps courts will respond generally with good sense and moderation. If they do not, legislation along the lines of our analysis may yet be called for. It is imperative that failure-to-warn litigation become subject to the rule of law. Talk is cheap, but courts must recognize that the education of consumers through product warnings is not. For too long these easy cases have made bad law. The time for change has come.

Howard Latin, *"Good" Warnings, Bad Products, and Cognitive Limitations*, 41 UCLA L. Rev. 1193 (1994)*

Why Warnings Often Prove Ineffective

The comment *j* presumption of Section 402A of the *Restatement (Second) of Torts* embodies the behavioral assumption that "reasonable" users can be expected to receive, correctly interpret, and obey every comprehensible warning accompanying every product they use or encounter. Yet, people are exposed each day to innumerable risks created by appliances that may malfunction or be mishandled; by potentially toxic pollutants, food additives, and other chemical substances; by cosmetics, drugs, and cleansing agents that may be improperly applied and are inherently dangerous for some sensitive individuals; by machine tools, presses, and other industrial or occupational equipment; and by hazardous transportation and recreation devices. Indeed, almost all products present substantial risks if improperly manufactured, designed, or used. People would have to read, understand, remember, and follow innumerable product warnings to protect themselves from all product-related risks they may confront. Moreover, risk assessment is only one realm of decisionmaking, and people must devote some of their limited time and attention to many other types of choices.

Failure to Read Product Warnings

In the aftermath of a serious injury, a court may assume that the user's failure to read product warnings stemmed from unusually careless or deliberately risky behavior. In reality, there are numerous reasons why consumers may not notice or read warnings, and most of these circumstances are neither easily avoidable nor clearly "unreasonable."

Functional Illiteracy. A 1986 Census Bureau study found that about 13 percent of American adults are illiterate in English. A higher proportion of the populace is functionally illiterate or has great difficulty in deciphering instructions that entail any significant degree of complexity. Product users who only read with difficulty may often ignore warnings to reduce time demands and cognitive strain. For example, one discussion of product warnings noted that an aluminum extension ladder may be accompanied by as many as 44 distinct warnings and directions. A representative of the American Ladder Institute conceded: "[Y]ou need Evelyn Wood just to read the labels." Why should the law presume that users will read all product warnings when manufacturers recognize just the opposite is often true?

Predictably Inattentive or Incompetent User Groups. Some products are intended for children, unskilled laborers, and other users who are frequently inattentive, unable or unwilling to devote the

*Used by permission.

time and effort needed to read detailed warnings. For example, courts have dismissed several design-defect actions against BB-gun manufacturers because child users failed to read or follow directions accompanying the weapons. The warnings implored users never to point the guns at any human being, and injuries would seldom occur if this instruction were always followed. Yet BB-gun manufacturers can readily foresee that their products will be used carelessly by children on many occasions. Current legal doctrines allow these manufacturers to rely on demonstrably ineffective warnings rather than requiring them to develop the safest feasible product designs or marketing practices.

Misplaced or Unavailable Directions. A recurring problem with warnings and instructions is that consumers often need more information to use a product safely than can be put on the product itself. Manufacturers may provide instruction manuals, tags, or package inserts that can be detached and misplaced while the product is still in use. In other cases, buyers may keep the instructions in places that are not readily accessible to product users. Motor vehicles, for example, are often resold without the operator manuals, and employees frequently must operate machinery without the instruction manuals provided when the equipment was first installed. People will seldom stop using expensive equipment simply because the directions or warnings have been misplaced.

Reliance on Explanations by Intermediaries. Consumers often ignore written warnings because they rely instead on explanations provided by human intermediaries who ostensibly possess relevant expertise: patients normally follow their doctors' advice irrespective of the directions printed on drug packages, employees usually depend on training provided by supervisors, and buyers often rely on the advice of salespersons. Product warnings communicated in this manner may be incomplete, ambiguous, or obsolete, and may underemphasize safety concerns to increase sales or productivity. Under the comment *j* presumption and learned intermediary rule, however, manufacturers are insulated from liability if intermediaries provide inadequate warnings even when the manufacturers can readily foresee that the warnings will often be garbled or ignored by the intermediaries.

Reliance on General Knowledge and Experience. People may ignore written instructions in the belief that they already understand how the product can be used safely. It is doubtful that most consumers will read detailed warnings and directions accompanying hammers, aspirin, bicycles, light bulbs, detergents, and many other products that are in widespread use. Instead, people may assume they are already familiar with safe practices based on general knowledge and prior experience with common products. Yet considerable evidence indicates that people often overestimate the extent of their knowledge and fail to assess accurately many common hazards.

Reliance on presumed knowledge may also induce overconfidence and resulting failures to read product warnings in fields that require expertise. In *Mays v. Ciba-Geigy Corp.*,[1] a commercial pipe installer relied on a demonstration he had seen years before and on his decade of experience, rather than reading the extensive instructions accompanying a new product. In *Richards v. Upjohn Co.*,[2] a doctor failed to remain current by reading the latest package inserts and pharmacological manuals, and therefore continued to prescribe a drug for a purpose that had once been approved but was later found unsafe. Manufacturers can predict that experts will often rely on their expertise instead of double-checking directions provided with products similar to ones they have used in the past.

Information Overload. There is a debate in the social sciences literature about whether extended descriptions of product attributes will induce information overload. Some experiments have found that "too much" information may lead to confusion or paralysis in consumer choices. Other

---

[1]661 P.2d 348 (Kan. 1983).

[2]625 P.2d 1192 (N.M. Ct. App.), *cert. denied*, 615 P.2d 992 (N.M. 1980).

experiments indicate that most people adopt heuristics or "rules of thumb" enabling them to disregard much of the available information; as one example: "It is well known in marketing that many consumers have a general tendency to buy either the cheapest brand or the most expensive brand. This tendency represents a shopping strategy that greatly reduces decisionmaking costs at the supermarket." Considerable research suggests that consumers in real settings stop assimilating information long before the point of decisionmaking paralysis.

In other words, detailed product descriptions and warnings can prove counterproductive because (a) consumers only choose to read or evaluate part of the information provided and (b) "too much" information makes it more difficult for people to select the most important features for consideration. Under this view, "too much" information can be just as much of an impediment to effective user comprehension of product hazards as "too little" knowledge would be.

Competing Demands on Time and Attention. Warnings have required increasing amounts of consumer time and attention as products proliferate and manufacturers attempt to avoid liability by providing more extensive statements of risks and safe practices. Many products are accompanied by labels with several paragraphs of directions in fine print, and many others require users to read instructional booklets. Yet, social science studies have stressed the significant time-intervals and effort required for people to read, interpret, and memorize information. Once it is recognized that decisionmaking capacities are limited and that people have many competing demands made on their time and attention, the failure of consumers to read some product warnings becomes foreseeable and inevitable.

In contrast to the comment *j* presumption that users will read whatever information manufacturers choose to impart, product liability caselaw amply demonstrates that people often do not read warnings when they need (or simply want) to focus attention on some other pressing (or merely interesting) concern. Users who examine the front of a product may not notice warnings printed on its back or bottom. People may only read directions that pertain to their intended operations and may consequently miss warnings presented in other passages or places. Consumers may assume that any significant danger would be prominently featured and therefore not read instructions presented in fine print. Having once read the warnings associated with a product, people may thereafter rely on imperfect memory rather than inspection of the warnings attached to similar products. Many consumers imitate the behavior of other people and simply assume that they will somehow "hear" of significant risks and safe usage practices. In many cases, consumers ignore warnings and uncritically rely on manufacturers to market safe products. These kinds of realistic attention-conserving strategies are not demonstrably "unreasonable" in light of limited time, attention span, expertise, and cognitive capacity.

Whether or not ideal consumers "should" examine all warnings and directions, the caselaw provides empirical support for the conclusion that product users frequently do not read them. People cannot know in advance which warnings will be personally relevant, and yet they cannot devote careful scrutiny to all disclosures. Moreover, in many contexts people do not *choose* to ignore warnings; product users cannot find them, cannot read them, or do not notice that they exist.

Failure to Understand "Good" Warnings

Understanding of a warning may fall anywhere on a continuum between complete knowledge and total incomprehension. Before a product warning can be accepted as "good," a court must decide whether reasonable consumers would adequately grasp the meaning and implications of the warning. The *ex post* nature of this judgment may induce juries and judges to overestimate a typical user's degree of comprehension. Social science research has found that "people consistently exaggerate what could have been anticipated in foresight . . . [and] believe that others should have been able to anticipate events much better than was actually the case." People also tend to attribute harmful effects disproportionately to human mistakes rather than environmental or situational circumstances. In the aftermath of an accident, "hindsight bias" and "attribution error" increase the likelihood that courts will find the warning was comprehensible and the product user was unreasonable in failing to follow it.

Imperfect Tradeoffs Among Detail, Clarity, and Impact. Many risks are complex and cannot be explained in simple terms; that is ordinarily true, for example, of drug warnings that describe a range of contraindications and possible health hazards. Attempts to give comprehensive descriptions of all risks and relevant circumstances would often decrease the clarity or impact of warnings about especially significant hazards and protective measures. Moreover, psychological studies show that many people are not adept at grasping crucial points in complex narratives. Other research findings indicate that the effectiveness of a warning is very dependent on the particular format selected, but exhaustive disclosure is incompatible with clear and vivid message formats.

Selectivity in the volume and type of information provided often improves the comprehensibility of warnings. On the other hand, omission of information reduces the ability of product users to understand some material risks and precautionary measures. If relevant information is not provided, users inevitably face the prospect of "surprises." No tradeoff among clarity, comprehensiveness, and impact can prove optimum for all warning contexts and all product users.

Textual Ambiguity. Statements of any significant complexity may contain ambiguity and this form of uncertainty frequently arises in product warnings. In addition to tradeoffs between detail and clarity, producers must make trade-offs between their conflicting desires to promote sales while disclosing material risks. A message declaring that the product is desirable, efficacious, and safe for use, but also hazardous and subject to misuse, may confuse potential buyers. Many risks are inherently complex and require evaluative expertise outside the bounds of common knowledge. Warnings often employ qualitative descriptive terms, such as "hypersensitive" or "allergic reaction," that are vague and may not be intelligible to some users. A manufacturer's attempt to explain complex subjects concisely in layman's terms must often create ambiguity.

Space constraints and limitations on the user's attention span would prevent producers from defining every term in every instruction. In [one experiment testing the interpretation of warnings, a hammer] was accompanied by this warning: "Caution! A hammer can be used to chip if struck against another hammer face or other hardened surface resulting not only in damage to the hammer but possibly in bodily injury." This warning on its face applies equally well to striking nails, the *raison d'etre* of hammers, and provides no criteria enabling users to discriminate between proper and improper hardened surfaces. This ambiguity may not appear significant to a court after an injury results, but the warning's failure to distinguish between approved and improper hard surfaces may deprive it of any meaningful content before the accident.

People try to resolve ambiguity through information search, estimation, interpretation, and guesswork, but they will undertake such measures only if they recognize that ambiguity exists. Yet, many people appear reluctant to acknowledge that ambiguity and uncertainty are present. Consumers may not recognize ambiguity in warnings before an accident occurs and courts may underestimate the ambiguity after subsequent events have clarified product risks and appropriate preventive measures.

Uncertainty about the Consequences of Misuse. Product instructions often provide little or no explanation of the potential harm from a user's failure to follow them. The directions at issue in *Cooley v. Carter-Wallace, Inc.*,[3] for example, listed body areas where "Nair" should not be applied, including the "vaginal/genital" areas, but failed to reveal what harm might otherwise

[3] 478 N.Y.S. 2d 375 (App. Div. 1984).

occur. The plaintiff applied the depilatory to his scrotum following his doctor's recommendation to use Nair or a similar product before undergoing a vasectomy. The court in *Cooley* found that the warning was inadequate partly because the product appeared "innocuous" and "a prospective user could fairly assume that any possible adverse effect of the product would be mild, whereas the product was actually capable of producing serious and permanent injury." The opinion also suggested that a warning cannot be legally adequate, however precise the instructions for use, unless "qualitatively sufficient to impart the particular risk of harm."

Many other judicial decisions adopted the contrary treatment, precluding actions by consumers who failed to follow "good" directions even in the absence of any description of attendant risks. Indeed, the dissenting opinion in *Cooley* contended that the "warning at issue clearly and unambiguously stated that the product was not to be used in the genital areas" and "plaintiffs simply chose to ignore it." The dissent concluded that Cooley's failure to use the product as "intended and directed" should preclude recovery: "To hold otherwise would impose an unreasonable burden on manufacturers by requiring them to enumerate every anticipated injury which could result from misuse of their product."

It is difficult to see how consumers can make "rational" risk calculations if they are not aware of the stakes. Yet, informing product users of every potential risk associated with intended uses and foreseeable misuses can be expensive, might deter worthwhile product uses, and would exacerbate problems of space and time constraints, ambiguity, and dilution of impact. In practice, many products provide instructions alone, or only an incomplete listing of potential hazards, and users consequently may not understand the risks created by any deviation from the specified directions.

Inadequate Evaluative Expertise. People may not grasp the meaning of product warnings because they lack the necessary education and evaluative skills. Consumer behavior studies have found that people often do not use all information provided or they fail to use it in a competent manner. Other studies have shown that people with higher education levels tend to consider more information and derive more meaning from it. Yet, many products are used by people who cannot be expected to possess proficient cognitive and evaluative skills.

Individual Variations in Capabilities, Motivations, and Beliefs. Effective communication of warnings and instructions is not a simple serial process in which manufacturers transmit information to product users who passively absorb it. Comprehension of product risks involves complicated interactions of diverse psychological and environmental factors. People's ability to understand information is influenced by educational backgrounds, personality traits, and motivation levels, by socioeconomic status and group affiliations, and by idiosyncratic personal experiences and prejudices. Consumers have varied information processing capabilities and attitudes; they may organize facts in different ways; they may use different strategies for confronting different types of risks. In short, decisionmaking capacities and proclivities vary greatly among different people and in different settings.

When new information becomes available, people often continue to believe what they want or expect to believe—one study concluded that "the contest between expectations and evidence is apt to be an unequal one." Another study found that people avoid new information that contradicts established beliefs. As one psychologist emphasized, "[o]nce people's minds are made up, it is difficult to change them." Because prior beliefs about product safety vary widely, the responses of people to new information in product warnings will correspondingly diverge.

Competing Demands on Time and Attention. Cognitive and attentional capacities are inherently limited, which means that understandings of product warnings may partly depend on the fortuitous absence of competing demands for time and attention. Thus, cognitive limitations may induce some people not to read warnings and others not to think sufficiently about their import. In this regard, extensive warnings can be counterproductive because they distract consumer attention from consideration of relatively significant factors.

Social science studies have found that a substantial proportion of human behavior becomes habitual, programmed, or impulsive in order to reduce cognitive and attentional demands. In order to achieve an efficient level of safety, consumers must understand product risks and precautionary instructions not only when they purchase the product but every time they use it. To the extent product use becomes habitual or programmed, users cannot be presumed to understand the risks in a meaningful sense because they do not think about those risks at the times of greatest danger.

Cognitive Heuristics and Biases

The consequences of individual variability are compounded by the presence of cognitive heuristics and biases. This fertile area of psychological research indicates that people commonly adopt a variety of simplifying strategies and biases that are inconsistent with "rational" behavior and often lead to erroneous judgments.

The Representativeness Heuristic. Many people are not adept at statistical reasoning and often draw invalid conclusions when confronted by probabilistic data. The representativeness heuristic reflects the tendency of people to make improper probability estimates because they generalize from inadequate samples or superficial analogies. In other words, people may rely on limited data and inapplicable comparisons while ignoring underlying statistical probabilities or "base rates."

Even if consumers do not generalize from their limited experiences, they may treat advertising and promotional claims as representative of a product's virtues without recognizing the doubtful reliability of the manufacturer's assertions. Manufacturers are much more likely to advertise goods as safe than to emphasize their dangers, which suggests that people who take product ads as representative of actual product attributes may underestimate the risks.

The Availability Heuristic. The availability heuristic suggests that people often assess risks on the basis of salience, how vivid and easy to recall the risks are, not on their objective probabilities.

Even for relatively risky products, harm will be an unusual occurrence. Consumers may overvalue the harm when it does happen, but safe usage will be far more typical and hence more available in most product-use contexts. It is true that people may overestimate the risks of airplane travel in the aftermath of a plane crash and may exaggerate the danger posed by activities such as nuclear energy and toxic waste dumping that are often the subjects of unfavorable publicity. Yet, the vast majority of common product risks—adverse reactions to cosmetics and drugs, falls from ladders, injuries from power tools and lawnmowers, electrocution from hair dryers or other common appliances—are seldom publicized nor intrinsically vivid. Most uncommon hazards are even less likely to be available because by definition they rarely produce notable injuries. When a product-related injury occurs and is widely publicized, people may temporarily overestimate the particular hazard; yet, the salience of that product risk will recede as other types of accidents and other issues attract public attention. Vivid risks seldom remain immutably vivid and available because newly publicized hazards gradually supplant old ones.

No balanced discussion of the availability heuristic should omit recognition that availability is limited and usually transitory, nor that safe experiences with virtually all products are far more frequent than injuries. Once these facts are acknowledged, it should be clear that the great majority of product risks cannot be available to product users. Because people seldom think about unavailable risks, the effect is precisely the same as if they were unduly optimistic about those product hazards.

Cognitive Dissonance. Cognitive dissonance leads people to reject or underemphasize information inconsistent with their beliefs and actions. Consumers must evaluate many products with both positive and negative attributes: A Corvette, for example, may be fast and stylish but also dangerous and costly. If people are attracted by attributes such as style or power, dissonance may lead them to undervalue safety considerations. If someone has enjoyed ownership of a particular sports car in the past, he may suppress information that current models are dangerous. If a home buyer finds one neighborhood attractive or has lived there peacefully in the past, she may discount a statistically high crime rate. People seldom make decisions as *tabulae rasae* and any prior beliefs or conflicting impulses may lead to cognitive dissonance affecting their selections of products.

* * *

Failure to Follow "Good" Warnings

Consumers who read and understand "good" product warnings may still not heed them for several reasons that courts may not recognize as "reasonable" behavior in the aftermath of a product-related accident.

Imperfect Memory. To conserve time and effort, people often rely on memory rather than rereading warnings and instructions every time they use products. Yet human memory is inherently limited and imperfect. An experiment on the efficacy of drug warnings found that only sixty-five percent of the student subjects could recall all identified side effects when asked to do so shortly after the information was provided. Thus, as time passes, drug users may forget a specific contraindication, machine operators may forget to check whether a safety device is engaged, users of cosmetics and hair care products may forget how long the application should last. People may forget a vital instruction or misremember and wrongly believe they are following the directions precisely.

In *Conti v. Ford Motor Co.*,[4] for example, the plaintiff was injured when her husband forgot to disengage the clutch before starting his manual transmission car. He undoubtedly knew the proper procedure but neglected to depress the clutch that one time. The court concluded that no warning would have prevented this "momentary inadvertence." Information is unlikely to prevent accidents caused by forgetfulness or inattention, but safer product designs could guard against some forms of predictably imperfect consumer behavior.

Overconfidence. People may not respond properly to many risks designated in warnings because they are unduly optimistic about their ability to avoid these hazards. Social science research has found that unjustified optimism is a common propensity in many, though not all, risk contexts. Overconfidence may sometimes result from ignorance about the full ramifications of the risk. Particularly when the hazard is complex, which is often true in the realm of product safety decisions, overconfidence "seems to arise from assessors' inability to appreciate how difficult or easy a task is." One social scientist concluded that people often fail to realize how little they know and how much they need to know.

The prevalence of attribution error is another potential source of overconfidence. People tend to ascribe accidents and other undesirable results to bad human judgments rather than variable environmental factors. They may disregard some risks if they believe careful behavior will prevent accidents and they consider themselves unusually capable and careful. For example, studies have found that most people think they are better than average drivers, which suggests that they assume they will suffer fewer injuries than the "bad" drivers to whom they attribute causation of most

[4] 743 F.2d 195 (3d Cir. 1984), *cert. denied,* 470 U.S. 1028 (1985).

automobile accidents. This expectation may explain why many people underestimate the probability of a serious automobile accident despite the high incidence and salience of crashes.

Reflexive Actions During Emergencies. People frequently do not follow safety instructions when they must respond rapidly or even instinctively to emergency circumstances. In many cases, machine tool operators have attempted to clear obstructions or correct other problems without first shutting down the equipment as the directions required. In traffic emergencies, drivers often exceed the safe—handling tolerances of their vehicles. No matter how detailed safety instructions may be, people will not always have the time needed to follow them during crises. As one court concluded: "[A] warning is not effective in eliminating injuries due to instinctual reactions, momentary inadvertence, or forgetfulness on the part of a worker. One of the primary purposes of safety devices is to guard against such foreseeable situations."[5]

Disregard of Low-Probability Risks. Social science findings indicate that people often ignore low probability risks even when catastrophic harm is threatened if the risks materialize. This occurs partly because people in everyday life are exposed to so many low-probability hazards that a major investment of time and effort would be required to think about most of these risks in any meaningful way. Research also indicates that people fail to consider low-probability risks because they do not understand how to weigh and balance the significance of these risks in their decisional processes. By definition, people are seldom injured through exposure to low-probability risks and therefore do not obtain much experiential feedback on those risks. Moreover, product warnings seldom cite statistical probabilities for most risks, but instead use qualitative terms such as "small" or "occasional" that are not very informative.

Lack of Manufacturer Credibility. Consumers sometimes fail to follow product warnings because they do not find the disclosures credible. Home-care cosmetics products may direct purchasers to conduct a "patch" test every time and then wait twenty-four hours before applying them. Many hammers are sold with directions to wear goggles during all uses. Q-tips and other cotton swabs warn people never to insert them into the ear canal. Producers of many kinds of machinery tell operators to turn off or stop the equipment before making any adjustments or corrections. Do manufacturers really believe people normally follow these warnings or is their main objective to limit potential liability? Under current tort doctrines, courts examine the adequacy of product warnings through a process of semantic interpretation without any requirement that manufacturers show their warnings and instructions will usually be followed. Yet, social science research demonstrates that source credibility is a significant issue. As warnings proliferate in number and length, consumers may come to believe that some (or many) are included more to protect manufacturers against potential liability than to inform users of significant dangers.

* * *

It is necessary to emphasize again that nothing in this behavioral analysis suggests that product warnings and other legally-mandated disclosures are useless or counterproductive, only that they will often prove ineffective. The critical legal issue is not whether "good" warnings should be provided, but whether they should be treated as legally acceptable substitutes for safer product designs and marketing strategies.

---

[5] Uloth v. City Tank Corp., 384 N.E.2d 1188, 1192 (Mass. 1978) (citation omitted).

Part II
Focus on the Consumer

A rival of the risk-utility test to determine product defectiveness is "consumer expectations," a principle expressed in Section 402A of the *Restatement (Second) of Torts*. In *Barker v. Lull Engineering Co.*, 573 P.2d 443 (Cal. 1978), a products liability landmark, the California Supreme Court held that the two tests enjoy coequal status. Yet they are dissimilar. Risk-utility analysis can be applied to virtually every products liability case, whereas consumer expectations seem inapposite in several situations—for example, where the product was not a consumer product (e.g., asbestos and other toxic substances) or where the injury is suffered by someone who is not the consumer. Consumer expectations, moreover, do not lend themselves to a checklist-style test a la the Wade factors (*see* Part IA, above); instead, they suggest a way of including themes of disappointment and betrayal into doctrinal analysis. The article by Marshall Shapo is a venerable expression of this view.

Taking a different approach to the consumer, Richard Epstein argues that he or she can be a source of harm. Epstein begins by addressing arguments made by Justice Stanley Mosk in *Daly v. General Motors Corp.*, 575 P.2d 1162 (Cal. 1978). He next argues in support of traditional plaintiff's-conduct defenses, mainly contributory negligence and assumption of risk.

Marshall S. Shapo, *A Representational Theory of Consumer Protection: Doctrine, Function and Legal Liability for Product Disappointment*, 60 Va. L. Rev. 1109 (1974)*

How Defect Relates to Product Function and Purpose

Performance Specifications. If consumers could articulate fully their reasons for choosing products, they probably would tend to do so in terms performance specifications. Thus, unsurprisingly, a substantial body of public regulation has arisen to compel certain classes of products to measure up to defined standards. This is so with respect to physical hazards, as in the case of motor vehicle safety requirements, and also regarding products primarily entangled with pocketbook problems, as in the case of food standards It is well established in the general law of negligence that industry standards are not dispositive with respect to liability, and the development of public regulation operates to confirm this rule. A producer may call something he makes a "motorcycle helmet,"

*Used by permission.

and it may look like what people call a motorcycle helmet, but if it is made of materials approximating the durability of cardboard, lawmakers may prevent him from selling it under that name.

Durability. The inquiry of "how good a product has to be" necessarily partakes of the question of how long it may be expected to last. It is difficult to quarrel with the general proposition that producers cannot be expected to make goods that "will not wear out over a period of years." In one case the court agreed with a dogmatic statement by the maker's witness a hammer that chipped after three months was "not a proper hammer." After preliminary decision of whether the period of use falls below the range of normal expectations, the court generally will leave the defect question to the jury, as it did in the case of a hammer that chipped after eleven months. The question is one of product function in a background of expectation. One could visualize a society where hammers lasted for only a few whacks, like grinding wheels, and this naturally would affect both product use and assignment of liability. It is important to ask how products operate in fact, but this issue should always be tied to the question of whether their portrayal by their sellers is accurate on the factor at issue.

Resilience. Discussion of the durability problem leads to related questions concerning how well products must meet expectable strains. For many products trauma is par, and generally the representational background cases involving goods of that kind will provide grounds for a rather broad judicial definition of purpose. It is implicit in a decision allowing a cause of action for the breaking of an auto seat belt that the belt must be strong enough to hold when an accident takes place. Similarly, in *Storey v. Exhaust Specialties Parts, Inc.*, the court approved an offer of proof to show that the standard for the manufacture of aluminum auto wheels is that of the ordinary steel wheel, noting that "[i]n every day experience people constantly compare the specifications or qualities of one kind of material against another for a given use."[1] Defect thus partakes of the concept of indifference curves in economic theory, with consumers trading off among all kinds of product combinations to fulfill particular functional requirements.

Stresses on Consumer Choice. A formulation that focuses on function defined by representational background will also help to rationalize cases of expectable consumer departures from what might be called the contemplative standard. Consumers sometimes eschew information gathering or precautions in times of hurry and stress because the situation makes investigation or caution too costly in practical fact. This presents difficult problems, and it may be only a partial response to argue that consumers tend naturally to underrate risk to themselves. Yet some regulation has catered to that point of view, and if it derives partly from a paternalism of arguable rigor and wisdom as well as from a more solid concern with social welfare externalities, it often represents a sensible recognition of the realities of consumer choice.

* * *

The Right to Rely

If the consumer has a "right to rely" on a product's performance, this should substantially determine the question of whether the law ought to grant relief when the product disappoints expectations.

Trust. Reliance springs from the circumstances of a transaction. In many cases it derives generally from the consumer's dependence on the ability of the seller to produce a certain result. Reliance arises not so much from a single specific facet of the transaction as from a general atmosphere

---

[1] 54 Wis.2d 345, 195 N.W.2d 602 (1972); 255 Ore. 151, 154, 464 P.2d 831, 832 (1970).

which some might call one of trust, and which might be described more dispassionately and technically as an environment charged by the seller's portrayal with the implicit understanding that he will save the buyer certain costs of investigation.

Representational Background and Fact of Sale. The appearance of goods may also help to generate a right to rely, especially in situations in which the consumer reasonably but wrongly assumes that the product will not harm him physically. Sometimes a direct representation will fuse with appearance, as in the case of an "off" switch that turns out to conceal a powerful electric current. Such a fusion may lie just in the background, not a basis for a holding based on language itself but an auxiliary vehicle for producer liability. A classic in this respect is the case of the rubber shower mat that omitted suction cups in its center section, which was imprinted with the words, "This mat is placed here for your convenience and protection to make your stay with us more enjoyable."[2] Strict liability was the chosen theory; the case is noteworthy for the irony that the representation, quite possibly unread, was itself the physical agent that rendered the product unreasonably dangerous.

The right to rely can arise from a general representational context, and this may subsume all else, including the 402A concept of unreasonable danger—perhaps even the starkest concept of defect. This broad reliance concept would reach beyond the objective standard of the "ordinary consumer" to a recognition that modern advertising can play on particular sensitivities about which advertisers must be assumed to know. Thus, the right to rely has a subjective aspect, rooted in particularized needs for gratification and in the special desires—even the quirks—of individuals, as well as in "the compulsive in all of us." From this perspective, one can see that even appeals to caprice deserve a legal response that recognizes the underlying seriousness of the game.

Appearance in Context. One may go further yet, not only beyond words but beyond the marriage of product and language. There may be a right to rely on appearances alone. Consumers will assume that something appearing to be a truck will have a transmission that consistently engages—a trucklike transmission. They infer from the contextual appearance of a motorcycle helmet that it will provide substantial protection against the impact of collision. Subject to complex trade-offs in the doctor-patient relationship, they tend to believe that drugs designed to make them well will not make them sick. And indeed, at the borderland of representations, when they come near products that present an innocent appearance, they take them at face value. The "right to rely" thus becomes an alter ego for the non-representational theories as well as a significant factor in the representational ones, at least in cases of purchase or direct use and metaphorically in some bystander cases. Of course, considerations of equity and loss spreading appear importantly, sometimes dispositively, looming more prominent as the facts move away from conventional bargains. Also evident, if often implicit, is a judicial impulse to achieve efficiency. So, as normative judgment blends with behavior estimate, it is with complex motives that the lawmaker undertakes to bypass the extraordinary explanations that a truly full bargain would require between producer and consumer—over the counter, at the sickbed, or on the job. But it should be emphasized that the root of bargain and of choice, even at their most casual, is in the representation.

* * *

In summary, I believe that lawmakers will find the most responsive legal solution of consumer disappointment problems primarily in a consideration of the general background of product por-

[2] Wagner v. Coronet Hotel, 10 Ariz. App. 296, 458 P.2d 390 (1969).

trayal, an examination of seller motivation, and an analysis of consumer response to product images in the context of opportunities for choice in product encounter. This is so in private litigation, where the judge must rely on hindsight, and for the public regulator, who must make his guesses in advance. For both the same basic considerations prevail, although often with different emphases. In private suits, sometimes courts will cast the crucial question in terms of a duty to warn. In other cases the central problem may appear as one of contributory fault. On some occasions the problem of proof will come to the fore, and at other times the tribunal must focus on the question of the proper remedy. Always insinuating themselves in common law actions will be questions of whether issues are for judge or jury, and to complete the circle, controversy about whether the best problem-solver is court or legislature. These and other matters merit independent examination in light of this analysis, but the answers to the core of questions posed by the representation principle should shed light on almost all issues that arise in injurious encounters between consumer and product.

Toward a "Consumer Tort." Because of the difficulties that terminology has posed for judicial efforts to grasp the essence of the problem, it may be appropriate to epitomize my theory. Phraseology will not solve the problem, but it could serve a useful descriptive function if this study has advanced efforts toward solution. It may be time for a term more comprehensive than "misrepresentation" or "products liability," and more descriptive than "strict liability in tort."

I would thus suggest that courts dealing with individual lawsuits for disappointment with product performance should speak of "an action for consumer injury," or more simply "the consumer tort," to describe both actions based on the common law and those drawn explicitly or by implication from statutes. Either phrase would not only evoke the relatively disadvantaged position of the consumer with respect to expertise and organization, but also would imply his typical position as a receiver of the communication barrages that portray goods.

Statement of the Thesis

The thesis is this:

> *Judgments of liability for consumer product disappointment should center initially and principally on the portrayal of the product which is made, caused to be made or permitted by the seller. This portrayal should be viewed in the context of the impression reasonably received by the consumer from representations or other communications made to him about the product by various means: through advertising by the appearance of the product, and by the other ways in which the product projects an image on the mind of the consumer, including impressions created by widespread social agreement about the product's function. This judgment should take into consideration the result objectively determinable to have been sought by the seller, and the seller's apparent motivation in making or permitting the representation communication.*
>
> *These determinations of liability should consider, generally, the integrated image of the product against the background of the public communications that relate to it; and should refer, specifically, to those communications concerning the characteristics or features of the product principally related to the element of disappointment, and to the question of whether these characteristics or features reasonably might have aroused conflict with respect to the decision to buy or otherwise to encounter the product.*

Although this thesis may serve as a supporting vehicle for analysis within existing doctrinal frameworks, ideally it would provide a completely new approach to the examination of product frustration problems. Considerations relevant to decisionmaking on the basis of this model would include:

1. The nature of the product as a vehicle for creation of persuasive advertising images, and the relationship of this factor to the ability of sellers to generate product representations in mass media;
2. The specificity of representations and other communications related to the product;
3. The intelligence and knowledge of consumers generally and of the disappointed consumer in particular;
4. The use of sales appeals based on specific consumer characteristics;
5. The consumer's actions during his encounter with the product, evaluated in the context of his general knowledge and intelligence and of his actual knowledge about the product or that which reasonably could be ascribed to him;
6. The implications of the proposed decision for public health and safety generally, and especially for social programs that provide coverage for accidental injury and personal disability;
7. The incentives that the proposed decision would provide to make the product safer;
8. The cost to the producer and other sellers of acquiring the relevant information about the crucial product characteristic and the cost of supplying it to persons in the position of the disappointed party;
9. The availability of the relevant information about the crucial product characteristic to persons in the position of the disappointed party and the cost to them of acquiring it;
10. The effects of the proposed decision on the availability of data that bear on consumer choice of goods and services;
11. Generally, the likely effects on prices and quantities of goods sold;
12. The costs and benefits attendant to determination of the legal issues involved, either by private litigation or by collective social judgment;
13. The effects of the proposed decision on wealth distribution, both between sellers and consumers and among sellers.

Richard A. Epstein, Modern Products Liability Law (1980)*

Courts have always treated the plaintiff's conduct as a proper source of inquiry in all manner of torts actions, no matter what the substance of the plaintiff's original cause of action. Not only is contributory negligence regarded as an appropriate defense in the typical highway accident case, but analogous defenses based upon plaintiff's conduct are viable in traditional causes of action based explicitly upon strict liability principles. Provocation is available as a defense in strict liability actions brought against the owner of a wild animal. The default of the plaintiff, however defined, is a defense to actions patterned upon *Rylands v. Fletcher* for the escape of hazardous substances collected and stored on the defendant's premises. Both contexts exhibit the same theme: the plaintiff

*Used by permission.

has engaged in conduct that would expose him to liability if it injured a third person. There is no obvious reason, therefore, why that conduct should be ignored because the plaintiff has helped to injure himself instead. It is true that no person can sue himself; nonetheless, his conduct can be taken into account in actions that might otherwise promise full relief. The plaintiff who shares in the production of his own harm can raise no obvious moral claim against being required to shoulder a part of his own loss. Within this framework, strict liability does not preclude an examination into plaintiff's conduct; to the contrary, it invites it.

The basic equities of the situation are unchanged, moreover, even when applied to products liability actions. Justice Mosk [of the California Supreme Court] has made arguments of *symmetry*, echoing those of comment *n*, that are designed to give some a priori credibility to the argument that as negligence is no part of the prima facie case, it should be no part of the defense. A closer examination of the situation demonstrates, however, that no single conceptual refinement can bear the immense burden of undoing all contributory negligence defenses. Justice Mosk is on sound ground when he notes the administrative advantages of strict liability compared to negligence. He fails to note, however, the small cash value of the doctrinal change, given the extensive use of res ipsa loquitur, and the repeated insistence on a very high standard of care. The tiny change brought about by the movement from negligence to strict liability as the basic cause of action provides no warrant for a massive revolution in the law of affirmative defenses. If anything, one expansion of plaintiff's rights should caution against any further, independent shift in the same direction. Courts that relax one requirement—defendant's negligence—in the plaintiff's case for administrative ease need not dismantle another barrier to recovery—contributory negligence—which has its own independent justifications.

* * *

Incentive Arguments

Justice Mosk has also laid great stress upon the undesirable incentive effects that would be fostered by an acceptance of the contributory negligence defense in liability actions. Although the point must be made with some caution, it seems in broad outline that the incentive arguments do more to support than undermine that defense. The customary justification for contributory negligence is, of course, that it imposes upon the plaintiff those incentives that encourage cost-effective measures that help prevent his own injuries. The usual response to this argument is that a plaintiff, faced with the possibility of death or serious injuries, need not be subjected to legal sanctions in order to compel his cooperation in the loss-control process. Instead, the argument continues, the powerful incentives should be directed toward the defendant, especially in the products liability context. Defendants are typically business firms, often large, that can and do make the appropriate cost calculations. They can "design out" product error and protect the plaintiff against the hazards of systematic neglect. Plaintiffs are isolated individuals who may not even know the applicable rules governing their own conduct. It is idle to expect them to respond to the indirect pressure created by the manipulation of the liability rules. To the extent that contributory negligence either reduces or eliminates the incentives created by the prima facie case, the argument continues, the law cuts back on one of its own essential missions, that of putting the liability upon the parties best able to make and act upon the appropriate cost-benefit analysis.

This argument, it should be stressed, is not wholly without force, yet it is subject to a number of important caveats.

First, there is a danger that the argument could prove too much. Airplane pilots and automobile drivers clearly risk harm to themselves when they inflict harm upon innocent third parties. Yet no one would suggest that we remove all tort sanctions against them because of the dangers they face in their activities. Why then should defenses based upon plaintiff's conduct be removed simply because the plaintiff exposes himself to injury?

Second, there is good reason to believe that many individuals will respond to the additional incentives even if faced with the possibility of personal loss. They will, in all likelihood, respond to such incentives when faced solely with property damage, especially if tort awards are fixed to make them indifferent between the property destroyed and the cash received on account of its destruction. Likewise, individuals may well respond to legal incentives even where life and limb are placed in peril. The reduction of the speed limits to fifty-five miles an hour is in all likelihood responsible for the sharpest drop in accident rates in the past thirty years, and this is an era featuring both the extensive safety regulations under the National Highway Safety Act and the well-nigh universal adoption of the crashworthiness doctrine. If individual drivers were held adequately in check by fear for their own lives, then it would be ironic to assume that the threat of a small fine, coupled with a possible increase in insurance rates, or the suspension of a license would have much influence upon their behavior. Yet the decline in death rates suggests that the marginal contribution of these additional sanctions has indeed had that effect.

What is true of these statutory sanctions may well be true of the private law sanctions as well. Individual parties need not know the refinements of the tort law in order to respond to the milieu that it creates; it is quite sufficient that they know as a crude truth that they will lose all or most of their recovery if they work like fools in the shop or drive like hot-rodders on the highway. The sanctions involved may be contingent in impact and uncertain in extent, but unless all individuals are oblivious to all probabilistic facts, it seems likely that the presence of contributory negligence defenses will have some favorable influence upon their conduct, and through it upon the accident rates. Ignorance is not a fixed fact of nature. If the defense is accepted, the individuals ignorant of it today will surely be informed of it tomorrow, whether it be by a public service announcement about highway safety or from an insistent warning by a union shop steward.

Third, the conduct of private parties (to the extent that it has not been rendered futile by judicial regulation) also points to the importance of the contributory negligence defense in products liability actions brought by product users and consumers. It is commonly accepted (especially by critics of the marketplace) that, in the absence of judicial regulation, most manufacturers would require, and most consumers would accept, rules that barred misbehaving plaintiffs. As with virtually all terms between buyer and seller, there is every reason to believe that the durable distribution of risks between manufacturers and their customers represents the efficient distribution of risks between the two parties. These restrictions upon recovery might be motivated in part by a commendable desire to reduce the administrative costs associated with accidents. They can also be interpreted as a market judgment that the incentives of a contributory negligence defense are worth preserving. The ultimate economic question is, of course, whether the incentives that are removed from the defendant are replaced by equal or more insistent incentives upon the plaintiff. While the result may vary from case to case and product to product, the perceived behavior of the interested parties creates a strong presumption that the incentive properties of affirmative defenses are indeed preferable to those under some alternative regime.

Fourth, the practical aspects of products liability litigation point in the same direction as the theory. The distinctive feature of these products liability actions is that the plaintiff is uniquely in the better position to prevent the harm. He typically has possession and control over the product at the time of its use and has information about the immediate environment in which it operates. The traditional negligence law allows these spatial and temporal priorities to work for the plaintiff when the defendant had "the last clear chance" to prevent harm. Recognition of the contributory negligence defense in products cases could also show the importance of the "proximate" in theories of proximate cause and ultimate tort liability in yet another context. The operator or user of a product certainly had clear and effective means to avoid the harms in question. Incentives directed toward the elimination of foolish conduct should not be dismissed as unnecessary or unworkable, even in a regime that seeks to create strong incentives upon manufacturers.

Fifth, the implied premise of this discussion of contributory negligence is that the rest of products liability law has already set into motion a set of ideal incentives for the control and regulation of the defendant's conduct, such that the recognition of any form of contributory negligence can only "dilute" the incentives placed upon the manufacturer. Yet, all is not well in the basic products liability cause of action, particularly with cases involving challenges to product warnings and design. If the incentives created in these areas are indeed both perverse and undesirable, then a strong set of contributory negligence defenses has a desirable tendency to correct the imperfections that have crept into other portions of the law. The offset will be far from perfect because the contributory negligence defense will apply with equal force to the strongest construction defect case and the weakest design defect case. The guess here is that the contributory negligence defense is of greatest importance where a product is alleged defective because of its inability to prevent injuries resulting from "foreseeable misuse" or "open and obvious" defects. As these cases tend to give rise to the most strained interpretation of the defect question, it seems reasonable to believe that the contributory negligence defense will come into play precisely in those cases in which it is most needed.

The incentive arguments of Justice Mosk, then, are not without their strength, but the arguments that can be marshaled on the other side seem to have greater merit. As is so often the case with incentive arguments, the results are inconclusive without empirical evidence, and the empirical evidence that is required is, only because of the difficulty of the subject matter, never forthcoming.

* * *

Product Misuse

The discussion of contributory negligence helps shape the analysis of the product misuse issue, as both defenses serve to identify those forms of conduct by the plaintiff that bar or reduce recovery. Indeed, the overlap is so great that a principled distinction between the two types of defenses becomes difficult to draw. An Oklahoma case has, for example, held that the misuse defense covers the use of a product to an improper end, but not its "use for a proper purpose but in a careless manner."[1] This test would bar recovery where an automobile is used as a boat, but not where it is driven at excessive speeds under the influence of alcohol. Such a distinction, even if intelligible, is indefensible in principle, given the soundness of the contributory negligence defense in products liability actions. The principles of redress, economic incentives, and even loss spreading all militate against the suggested distinction between improper means and improper ends.

With this said, it is still necessary to avoid two common errors about product misuse, one which impermissibly restricts and the other which impermissibly broadens the defense. On the one hand it is incorrect to treat the manufacturer's precise intentions, express or implied, as the sole test of product misuse. Hardball bats can be used for softball; (some) chairs can be used for standing; and hair shampoo can get into a consumer's eyes. Yet, bats are not hammers; chairs are not car

[1] Fields v. Volkswagen of America, 555 P.2d 48 (Okla. 1976).

jacks; and shampoo is not a soft drink. The precise limits of product use and the size of the margin of error about its central core will vary from case to case. This issue, like so many in the law of products liability, will often require individual adjudication. The matter is at bottom one of implied representations and shared expectations about which further precision is not possible.

The recognition that normal and proper product use has some sensible give at the margins should not, however, lead courts to the further conclusion that "abnormal" or improper product use begins only where such is not "foreseeable" by the manufacturer. Standing alone, foresight does not provide the proper limits on liability. It is of course foreseeable that a teenager might drink or sniff glue, but it hardly seems appropriate to excuse him wholly from responsibility for the ensuing brain damage. It is, of course, foreseeable that workers will use machines after they fall into disrepair, but their conduct is not therefore excusable. No manufacturer could escape the consequences of making defective products by showing that consumers could reasonably foresee the possibility of product defect. The unbounded foresight requirement should not work in reverse to impose such onerous obligations upon manufacturers. There is a vast difference between the foresight of possible harm and the responsibility for harm that has come to pass. Whenever plaintiff's misconduct is at issue, the better cases look both to what the manufacturer can expect and what he has a *right* to expect. Properly understood, the issue of foresight is as much a question of entitlement as it is of prevision.

Assumption of Risk

Assumption of risk does not imply that the simple knowledge of possible harm completely bars the plaintiff's cause of action. If it did, products liability law would die before it was born, as all apparently sound products are known to be possibly defective. This possible abuse of assumption of risk, however, does not warrant its wholesale judicial abandonment. At the other extreme is the consumer who eats chocolate known to be bad; here assumption of risk is, and should be, decisive. Contributory negligence is not the issue; the conduct may be reasonable, not to say courageous, as part of an experiment to determine the effects of rotten food upon healthy people. And apportionment, however attractive in joint causation cases, is wholly inappropriate here: *all* the risk is assumed, not just some undefined portion of it.

Thus, when a consumer eats bad food, the coercion arguments can be easily dismissed. The cash invested in the purchase of the food is trivial, and will usually be refunded by the original seller. With the exception of chocolate bars necessary for survival on a desert island, the massive social institutions for mitigating losses undercut the coercion arguments at every point. The bad food just should not be eaten.

A more difficult set of problems arises in machine tool cases where the plaintiff claims that he is forced to work with equipment known to be dangerous. That claim has great attraction where the plaintiff discovers that his equipment has just failed in midstream when it is awkward, perhaps perilous, to cease work. Yet in the typical workplace case it is far less persuasive to argue that the known defect so circumscribed the plaintiff's freedom of action as to preclude the assumption of risk defense. In *Micallef v. Miehle Co.,*[2] the plaintiff, an employee of Lincoln Graphic Arts, was operating a high-speed photo-offset press manufactured by the defendant. Just before the accident, the plaintiff noticed that a "hickie" (a foreign object) had fallen on the plates where it could ruin or blemish the printed pages. The plaintiff also knew that the press was not equipped

[2] 348 N.E.2d 571 (N.Y. 1976).

with any safety guard at the point where the plate cylinder joined the ink-form roller; and he knew that he could catch his hand at that junction point if he "chased the hickie" without turning off the press. After consulting with his foreman, he did in fact chase the hickie, but from a place where it was impossible for him to reach the press's cut-off switch. He was severely injured when his hand was drawn up into the juncture of the plate and the ink-roller.

The elements of the assumption of risk defense are all present, and the question (assuming for the sake of argument that the machine, as designed, was defective) is whether there are enough indicia of implicit coercion by the defendant to let the jury pass upon the reasonableness of the plaintiff's conduct. The issue can be considered in two separate time frames. Immediately before the accident the claim of coercion is difficult to make, given the number of options open to the plaintiff. For one thing he might have requested the foreman to shut down the machine in order to make it easy to chase the hickie. If that course of conduct proved infeasible because of the lost production time involved, someone else could have manned the cut-off switch when the plaintiff positioned himself on the far side of the machine. While in some plants the employers may take a very hard-nosed attitude toward their workers, no evidence was presented here of any probable retaliation against the plaintiff if he had made that simple request for assistance.

The case against implicit coercion by the manufacturer becomes even stronger if the time frame of decision is shifted further back. The defect was open and obvious, and the plaintiff knew about the hazards when he began employment and at all times thereafter. If he was unsatisfied with the conditions of labor, he might have chosen to work elsewhere. The defendant did not make him use the press. The fact that he chose to work suggests that he accepted the risks that were routinely incident to his employment in order to obtain the financial and other benefits of that employment. The various economic pressures of the labor market do not stem from the defendant manufacturer, but from the employers with whom the plaintiff does or might do business. The workers' compensation laws and the labor laws were designed to respond to those pressures, and there is no reason to modify the products liability law to make manufacturers responsible for the possible sins of employers. While there are cases in which a known defective product is one of several effective constraints placed upon the injured party, such is not the usual case.

Part III

Products Liability Within Other Legal Domains

Products liability is widely understood to be the progeny of tort and contract ancestors. Principles of responsibility for accidental harm give the doctrine its torts flavor, and a heritage of contract law conveys the requirement of a commercial setting—which is one of the very few defining criteria of a products liability case. The injurious product stands for both tortious conduct and the betrayal of a promise. These normative themes imply that products liability is also related to some of the purposes and the ambit of criminal law.

William Prosser's classic piece is an early adumbration of strict liability in tort. Going further, William Powers argues that strict liability cannot be separated from fault. Going still further, Powers argued in a later article (not reprinted here) that strict products liability ought to be abandoned altogether, in favor of negligence, and Malcolm Wheeler sounds the same theme. A practicing litigator, Wheeler builds his case out of doctrinal illustrations. The three pieces offer a triptych of strict liability in tort, as applied to products cases.

The contracts heritage of products liability is illustrated by three very different works. In his crisp and distinctive prose, Prosser explains the warranty of merchantability. George Priest reinterprets the consumer warranty in economics terms, as both a conscious allocation of risks and a scheme of intelligent promises. Grant Gilmore uses contract generally as an ironic counterpoint to modern, economics-tinged products liability law, and comments in passing on the impact of social context on law.

The criminal-law essays also offer contrasting perspectives. Michael Metzger canvasses the pros and cons of corporate criminal liability and individual criminal liability for corporate officials. In contrast to Metzger's moderation, Miles Lord invokes the wrath of God, directed at businessmen who marketed the Dalkon Shield. David Owen believes punitive damages—a device that partakes of the criminal law—ought to remain available, but questions whether doctrine fits the reality of manufacturer and victim behavior. Michael Rustad's empirically-based endorsement of punitive damages is summarized in the conclusion of his article, from which this excerpt is drawn.

A. Tort Law

William L. Prosser, *The Assault Upon The Citadel (Strict Liability to the Consumer)*, 69 YALE L.J. 1099 (1960)*

"The assault upon the citadel of privity is proceeding in these days apace." So said Cardozo in 1931, and has been much quoted since. With the passage of nearly thirty years, a goodly part of the citadel still holds out; but the assault goes on with unabated vigor. It is the purpose of this article to inquire, how goes the battle, in one very important and more or less separate area of the fight, where the seller of chattels defends against the ultimate consumer, with whom he stands in no privity of contract.

The Arguments

One may well ask at the outset, why is not liability for negligence enough? Why do the plaintiffs want strict liability; and have they any valid claim to it?

Where the action is against the manufacturer of the product, an honest estimate might very well be that there is not one case in a hundred in which strict liability would result in recovery where negligence does not. When a negligence action is brought against a manufacturer, the plaintiff is faced with two initial tasks. One is to prove that his injury has been caused by a defect in the product. The other is to prove that the defect existed when the product left the hands of the defendant. For neither of these is strict liability of any aid to him whatever. It cannot prove the causation; and it cannot trace that cause to the defendant. Once over these two hurdles, the plaintiff has a third task, to prove that the defect was there because of the defendant's negligence. This is by far the easiest of the three, and it is one in which the plaintiff almost never fails.

It is true that he has the burden of proof on the issue of negligence. It is true also that he seldom, if ever, has any direct evidence of what went on in the defendant's plant. But in every jurisdiction, he is aided by the doctrine of *res ipsa loquitur*, or by its practical equivalent. In all jurisdictions this at least gives rise to a permissible inference of the defendant's negligence, which gets the plaintiff to the jury. And in cases against manufacturers, once the cause of the harm is laid at their doorstep, a jury verdict for the defendant on the negligence issue is virtually unknown.

It is true that there have been occasional cases in which the defect has been of such a character that it could not have been prevented by any ordinary care, and the application of *res ipsa* has been denied. But such cases are so extremely rare as to be almost negligible, and over many years very few of them have appeared in the books. It is also true that it is open to the defendant to rebut the inference of negligence by proof of his own due care. But, again with very rare exceptions, the courts are agreed that such evidence does not entitle the defendant to a directed verdict, and raises only an issue for the jury. And again it must be repeated, once the cause of the injury is proved to lie with the defendant, once it is brought home to his plant, the jury finds for the plaintiff. Why, then, do the plaintiffs and their cohorts clamor so loudly for strict liability of the manufacturer, and why are the defendants equally vociferous in their opposition?

---

*Used by permission.

No writer seems to have suggested that the answer lies in the preparation for trial, the negotiations for settlement, and the amount of the verdict. So long as the negligence issue remains in the case, it must be litigated, and plaintiff's counsel must be prepared to examine and to cross-examine witnesses, including even experts. He may even be forced to look up a little law, which is a thing from which some personal injury lawyers notoriously shrink. So long as there is the possibility that negligence may not be found, the defendant is encouraged by vain hopes, and the plaintiff gnawed by lingering doubts; and a case which *can* be decided for the defendant is worth less, in terms of settlement, than one which can not. And so long as the defendant can introduce evidence of his own due care, the possibility remains that it may influence the size of the verdict, as jurymen impressed with it stubbornly hold out for no liability, or a smaller sum.

All this, however, is but half of the picture. There are other sellers than the manufacturer of the product. It will pass through the hands of a whole line of other dealers, and the plaintiff may have good reason to sue any or all of them. The manufacturer is often beyond the jurisdiction. He may even, in some cases, be unknown. If he is identified and can be sued, it is very often impossible to pin the liability upon him. Even where there is a proved defect which speaks of obvious negligence on the part of some one, it may still not be possible to prove that it was on the part of the maker. The cracked Coca Cola bottle may have been cracked long after it left his plant. And even when the cause can be fixed upon the manufacturer, he may turn out, in these days of chain stores and large supply houses, to be a small concern, operating on a shoestring, and financially the least responsible person in the whole chain of distribution. If the plaintiff is to recover at all, he must often look to the wholesaler, the jobber, and the retailer.

It is here that negligence liability breaks down. The wholesaler, the jobber, and the retailer normally are simply not negligent. They are under no duty to test or inspect the chattel, and they do not do so; and when, as is usually the case today, it comes to them in a sealed container, examination becomes impossible without destroying marketability. No inference of negligence can arise against these sellers, and *res ipsa loquitur* is of no use at all.

It is true that against the retailer, the consumer who buys for himself and is injured can rely, in all but a few states, upon the old sales warranties of merchantable quality and fitness for the purpose. But so long as the privity wall stands firm, these warranties are of no avail against the wholesaler; nor do they protect the buyer's wife or child, his employee, his guest, his donee, or his subpurchaser. The result has been such utterly preposterous decisions at those holding that the wife who buys the sausage, handles it, cooks it, eats it, and is poisoned by it, cannot recover because she was merely buying as the agent of her husband, who was to pay the bill and so is regarded as the contracting party, whereas the husband, who never saw the food, can recover on a warranty for the loss of her services. The arrant folly of this has led to some remarkable legal gymnastics, in the form of contradictory presumptions or holdings as to agency, and to specific provisions that extend the retailer's warranty to all members of the buyer's household.

Such are the plaintiff's grievances, and such his claim to redress. When we come to the arguments adduced in support of his claim, we are confronted with more than a few which have a specious and unconvincing sound, and would appear to have been concocted in the heads of professors rather than based upon any realities of the situation. It is said, for example, that strict liability will provide a healthy and highly desirable incentive for producers to make their products safe. A skeptic may well question whether the callous manufacturer, who is unmoved by the prospect of negligence liability, plus *res ipsa loquitur*, and by the effect of any injury whatever upon the reputation of his goods, will really be stimulated by the relatively slight increase in possible liability to take additional precautions against defects which cannot be prevented by only reasonable care.

It is said that it is the practice of reputable makers expressly to warrant their products, or to make good their deficiencies without such a warranty; and that the strict-liability rule merely enforces what the best companies already do. Undoubtedly the practice exists, on a large scale; but it is limited, on the part of almost every one, to replacement, repair, or return of the purchase price to make good the original bargain; and it does not extend to compensation for injuries to the person of the buyer, or his other property. It is said, again, that the doctrine of *res ipsa loquitur* is applied, in many cases, to impose liability upon defendants who in reality have not been negligent at all; and that the strict liability merely formulates, as a general rule, what goes on all the time in fact. They hypothesis is very likely true, although it is not capable of proof, and the number of instances in which it has occurred is probably far smaller than the proponents would have us believe; but the conclusion does not follow. One might as well say that because circumstantial evidence sometimes results in the conviction of the innocent, all criminal defendants should be found guilty; or that, because skid marks on the pavement may now and then permit the jury to find against defendants who in fact have exercised all due care, all automobile drivers should be held liable without fault.

Entitled to more respect is the ''risk-spreading'' argument, which maintains that the manufacturers, as a group and an industry, should absorb the inevitable losses which must result in a complex civilization from the use of their products, because they are in the better position to do so, and through their prices to pass such losses on to the community at large. This contention has become identified with the concurring opinion of Justice Traynor of California in *Escola v. Coca Cola Bottling Co.*, because of the following language:

> Those who suffer injury from defective products are unprepared to meet its consequences. The cost of an injury and the loss of time or health may be an overwhelming misfortune to the person injured, and a needless one, for the risk of injury can be insured by the manufacturer and distributed among the public as a cost of doing business. It is to the public interest to discourage the marketing of products having defects that are a menace to the public. If such products nevertheless find their way into the market it is to the public interest to place the responsibility for whatever injury they may cause upon the manufacturer, who, even if he is not negligent in the manufacture of the product, is responsible for its reaching the market. However intermittently such injuries may occur and however haphazardly they may strike, the risk of their occurrence is a constant risk and a general one. Against such a risk there should be general and constant protection and the manufacturer is best situated to afford such protection.

Dean Pound once denounced this as a major step in the direction of socialism. Assuming that we are not nowadays disposed to flee shrieking in terror from the prospect of a spot of socialism in our law when the public interest demands it, the question remains whether our courts, our legislators, and public sentiment in general, are yet ready to adopt so sweeping a legal philosophy, and to impose so heavy a burden abruptly and all at once upon all producers. Thus far there has been relatively little indication that the time is yet ripe for what may very possibly be the law of fifty years ahead. As in the case of the related agitation for strict liability on the part of all automobile drivers, there are too many vested interests in the way, and the sudden change is likely to be regarded as too radical and disruptive; and progress in the direction of any such broad general rule cannot be expected to be rapid.

Dedicated writers have laid great stress upon liability insurance as the controlling and decisive factor in this situation. It seems very significant that, except for the casual reference in the lone opinion of Justice Traynor in the passage quote above, no court, so far as can be discovered, ever has so much as mentioned insurance in a products-liability case. What insurance can do, of course, is to distribute losses proportionately among a group who are to bear them. What it cannot and should not do is to determine whether the group shall bear them in the first instance—and whether, for example, consumers shall be compelled to accept substantial price increases on everything they buy in order to compensate others for their misfortunes. Even the distribution of the losses through insurance may be a process that has its flaws. Until we develop, by analogy to workmen's compensation, a comprehensive system of compulsory insurance with rigidly limited damages—which no one as yet seems to have proposed specifically in this particular field-there will always be uninsured defendants, there will always be liability in excess of coverage, and there will be members of the group whose competitive situation does not permit them to pass on the cost of the insurance to their customers. Liability insurance is obviously not to be ignored; but it is a makeweight, and not the heart and soul of the problem.

No more impressive are some of the arguments advanced in behalf of the defendant. One is that strict liability will deter producers who seek to improve their products from adopting new methods. The short answer is that if they are not already deterred by existing liabilities, they are not likely to be. Another is that strict liability will expose the defendants to a deluge of false claims based upon fictitious defects and fake injuries. Undoubtedly there are, and will be, false claims, and it may be true that the rats of Hamlin were as nought in comparison with that horde of mice which has sought refreshment within Coca-Cola bottles and died of a happy surfeit. But the assumption apparently is that the fraudulent claimant, when he is inventing a defect in the product, will by choice invent one which does not indicate any negligence. This speaks for itself. It is also said that liability should *never* rest upon anything but fault, which is a position certainly out of date in this day and generation; and that only the legislature should make any such changes, which is the cry invariably raised against anything new whatever in the law.

All this aside, the arguments which have proved convincing to the courts which have accepted the strict liability are three:

1. The public interest in human life, health and safety demands the maximum possible protection that the law can give against dangerous defects in products which consumers must buy, and against which they are helpless to protect themselves; and it justifies the imposition, upon all suppliers of such products, of full responsibility for the harm they cause, even though the supplier has not been negligent. This argument, which in the last analysis rests upon public sentiment, has had its greatest force in the cases of food, where there was once popular outcry against an evil industry, and injuries and actions have multiplied, and public feeling is most obvious. It is now being advanced as to other products for bodily use, such as cosmetics. It suggests that as to still other products, distinctions may yet be drawn according to the probable danger, the frequency of injury, and what the public reasonably and rightfully expects.

2. The supplier, by placing the goods upon the market, represents to the public that they are suitable and safe for use; and by packaging, advertising or otherwise, he does everything that he can to induce that belief. He intends and expects that the product will be purchased and used in reliance upon this assurance of safety; and it is in fact so purchased and used. The middleman is no more than conduit, a mere mechanical device, through whom the thing sold is to reach the ultimate user. The supplier has invited and solicited the use; and when it leads to disaster, he should not be permitted to avoid the responsibility by saying that he has made no contract with the consumer.

3. It is already possible to enforce strict liability by resort to a series of actions, in which the retailer is first held liable on a warranty to his purchaser, and indemnity on a warranty is

then sought successively from other suppliers, until the manufacturer finally pays the damages, with the added costs of repeated litigation. This is an expensive, time-consuming, and wasteful process, and it may be interrupted by insolvency, lack of jurisdiction, disclaimers, or the statute of limitations, anywhere along the line. What is needed is a blanket rule which makes any supplier in the chain liable directly to the ultimate user, and so short-circuits the whole unwieldy process. This is in the interest, not only of the consumer, but of the courts, and even on occasion of the suppliers themselves.

Conclusion

The assault upon the citadel of privity is proceeding in these days apace.

William C. Powers, Jr., *The Persistence of Fault in Products Liability,* 61 TEX. L. REV. 777 (1983)*

The concept of fault has clung tenaciously to the law of products liability. For two decades courts have attempted to design a theory of liability for products cases that is distinct from both negligence and breach of warranty. Although courts have been reasonably able to distinguish strict products liability from warranty law, they have not succeeded in purging negligence principles from strict products liability. Courts have had difficulty deciding not only whether strict products liability should be distinct from negligence, but also whether such a distinction is even possible.

There are a number of reasons why the effort to purge fault from strict products liability has not been entirely successful. First, courts have not always articulated clearly the distinctions they have attempted to draw between negligence and strict products liability, often because they have been concerned primarily with distinguishing strict products liability from warranty law and have neglected to explain the difference between strict products liability and negligence. Second, fault's persistence in strict products liability may stem from our ambivalence toward the competing moral, economic, and political values underlying the debate about negligence and strict liability. Courts may be attempting to reconcile a desire to protect consumers with a desire to avoid fettering business, or to balance the goal of spreading losses against the unfairness of penalizing a defendant whose conduct has been faultless. The ebb and flow of these and other competing values may account partially for the shifting mixture of negligence and strict liability in products cases.

Finally, fault's tenacity may be a product of lawyers' familiarity with the analytical tools of negligence. It is not surprising that courts resolve difficult conceptual problems by relying on the familiar analytical concepts of negligence, not merely for the values they embody, but because they are familiar and have been shown to be coherent and workable. Even the proponents of strict products liability have relied on analogies to the shop-worn analytical tools of negligence.

The problem of fault in strict products liability arises primarily at three doctrinal points. First, courts often rely on negligence concepts to determine whether a product is defective. Sometimes

*Used by permission.

courts openly apply a negligence standard to a specific type of defect. At other times, however, they introduce fault subtly by evaluating a product according to its risks only as they were known at the time of sale or by using the state of the art defense. In these cases, courts hide an evaluation of the propriety of the defendant's conduct beneath the guise of a determination of defectiveness. Second, courts have had difficulty avoiding fault when they have attempted to apportion a loss among various parties, either between a culpable plaintiff and a defendant or among multiple defendants, some of whom have been negligent. For example, consumer misconduct defenses and requests for contribution have raised problems concerning the role of fault in strict products liability. Third, the problem of fault's persistence arises in the issue of proximate causation; some courts have relied on foreseeability to define proximate causation in products liability and thereby have inserted fault into the analysis.

The Requirement of Defectiveness

Although courts speak of strict liability, a plaintiff must prove more than that his injury was caused by the defendant's product. Even in its earliest formulations, strict products liability purported to apply only to defective products; it has never been synonymous with absolute or enterprise liability. Thus, an automobile manufacturer is not liable to all victims of accidents involving its automobiles, even though the accidents would not have occurred but for their availability. In order to recover, a plaintiff also must prove that the automobile was defective and that the defect caused the injury.

Although many of the policy arguments favoring strict products liability are applicable even when a product is not defective, the propriety of a requirement that the plaintiff prove defectiveness has rarely been questioned. The specific contours of defectiveness, however, have spawned more debate and litigation than any other doctrinal aspect of products liability, and one pervasive problem has been whether defectiveness can be defined without reference to the defendant's conduct and fault.

Tests of Defectiveness. Defects generally are classified in three categories: flaws or manufacturing defects, design defects, and warning or informational defects. Manufacturing defects or flaws are variations that occur when a product deviates from the manufacturer's specifications and therefore is unintentionally different from other products in the line. A design defect is a feature that conforms to the specifications of a product (and therefore is similar to other products in its line) but imposes an inappropriate risk of injury. An informational or warning defect is presented when a product imposes an inappropriate risk of injury because it is marketed with faulty or inadequate information, such as insufficient warnings or instructions for use.

Courts have not applied a uniform concept of defectiveness to all types of defects. Flaws have usually been considered to be per se defective, warnings defects have normally been judged explicitly by a negligence standard, and design defects have been judged by a variety of complex standards.

Much of the debate concerning the definition of defectiveness has focused on two basic approaches. One approach, reflecting the warranty heritage of strict products liability, provides that a product is defective if it is "dangerous to an extent beyond that which would be contemplated by the ordinary consumer." A second approach, reflecting the tort heritage of strict products liability, provides that a product is defective if it is unreasonably dangerous—that is, it possesses features whose risks outweigh their benefits. Under this risk-utility test, a manufacturer may attempt to justify a product's risks by referring to the social benefits derived from imposing them.

Of the two basic approaches to defining defectiveness, the risk-utility test has most seriously obscured the theoretical distinction between defectiveness and negligence and, consequently, has hampered the effort to purge strict products liability of fault. The risk-utility test evaluates the reasonableness of a product's risks by balancing the magnitude of those risks against the benefits of imposing them. Since this balancing test is similar to Learned Hand's famous B<PL formula for evaluating reasonable care in negligence, it tends to undermine the distinction between defectiveness and reasonable care.

Proponents of the risk-utility approach to defectiveness have argued that the concept of defectiveness is distinct from negligence because it centers on evaluation of the product rather than on the conduct of the manufacturer and, consequently, avoids an evaluation of the defendant's fault. This distinction between negligence and defectiveness often turns on the role of foreseeability in each theory: to ascertain whether a manufacturer has been negligent, a court considers only those risks that were reasonably foreseeable when the manufacturer engaged in the allegedly negligent conduct. To determine whether a product is defective, however, a court might evaluate a product's actual risks, even those that could not or need not have been foreseen at the time of sale. A product could therefore be defective even though the manufacturer behaved reasonably, and although both theories use a risk-benefit approach to reasonableness, only negligence relies on the concept of fault by evaluating the propriety of the defendant's conduct.

But the analytical distinction between evaluating a product and evaluating a manufacturer's conduct is itself tenuous. Without the addition of arbitrary distinctions, defectiveness under the risk-utility approach is merely an evaluation of a manufacturer's conduct in the guise of an evaluation of the product. Only tenuous distinctions prevent a manufacturer from using the same arguments to justify a product under the risk-utility test of defectiveness as to justify its conduct under negligence.

Every product imposes some risks, and nearly every product could be made safer. Most products are not defective, however, since they impose risks that are socially worthwhile. For example, automobiles impose risks, but they provide a valuable means of transportation. This balancing is the essence of the risk-utility test of defectiveness.

A risk is often justifiable because it is a concomitant of a socially desirable feature of a product. The speed of automobiles and the sharpness of knives provide concomitant risks and benefits. Sometimes, however, a risk is acceptable because a product that avoided it would be inordinately expensive. Consequently, courts have considered product cost to be an appropriate factor in a risk-utility balance. If they ignored product cost, every product that imposes risks would be defective, because nearly every product could be made safer at some cost. Product cost, however, is merely a reflection of the product's manufacturing process; therefore, a court's consideration of product cost represents an evaluation of the manufacturer's conduct. Including product cost to determine defectiveness thus intrinsically undermines the distinction between defectiveness and negligence.

Consider the case of a compact automobile that imposes a greater risk of injury during a crash than a larger sedan. Under the risk-utility test of defectiveness, a manufacturer could argue that the risks presented by small cars are outweighed by benefits such as fuel economy and ease of handling. The manufacturer could also argue that small cars are less expensive to build because they require less labor and materials. Since even the cost of materials reflects the labor necessary to produce the material, a risk-utility justification for compact cars based on cost is largely based on labor savings. The risk-utility test provides no justification for excluding labor costs from its ambit.

The problem is that foreseeability—a cornerstone in the distinction between analyzing a product to determine defectiveness and analyzing a manufacturer's conduct to determine negligence—is also reflected in a product's cost. Almost any risk is foreseeable if a product is tested sufficiently. But the issue in negligence is whether a risk is reasonably foreseeable, an issue that depends on the reasonableness of the decision to forego further testing. If a reasonably prudent person would believe that additional research would not be cost-effective, a decision to forego the research would be reasonable, and the risks it would have disclosed would not have been reasonably foreseeable.

Risks that are not reasonably foreseeable do not count against a manufacturer in a cost-benefit analysis to determine negligence.

We do not eliminate the problem of foreseeability by shifting the analysis to defectiveness and an evaluation of the product. Research and development expenses are as much an attribute of a product's costs as labor and material expenses. Decisions to forego further testing as well as decisions that save other labor and material make compact cars cheaper. Since product cost is a factor in the risk-utility test for determining defectiveness, the burden of testing should be considered precisely to the same extent in strict products liability as it would in an evaluation of the manufacturer's conduct to determine negligence. Product cost simply reflects the manufacturing process; the distinction between evaluating a product and evaluating the manufacturer's conduct is illusory.

Comparative Allocation

In products liability cases comparative allocation is difficult to apply because the objects of comparison are unclear. Actual causation cannot be compared because the causal contribution of each party to an injury is logically unapportionable. Fault cannot be compared because there is no requirement that the defendant be blameworthy.

Comparing the fault of a plaintiff or negligent defendant with the culpability of a strictly liable defendant seems as impossible as a comparison of apples and oranges. Opponents of comparative allocation in products liability have argued that juries asked to make such a comparison will assign percentages to each party, but they will do so either arbitrarily or by making a sub rosa appraisal of the defendant's fault. These responses would render comparative allocation of loss either arbitrary or incompatible with the nonfault basis of strict products liability. This argument is powerful as a pragmatic flag of caution, but it does not demonstrate an intrinsic incompatibility of comparative allocation and strict products liability.

We routinely compare apples and oranges by using one of two methods. One method of comparison focuses on a shared feature, such as weight, volume, juice content, or calories. The other method refers to an overreaching value system, such as price or preference, which incorporates subordinate values that appear at first glance to be incommensurate. Similar methods could be used to compare fault with the culpability of a strict products liability defendant.

The first method requires a common feature shared by the two objects of comparison. Negligence and the risk-utility version of defectiveness share such a common feature because they both reflect evaluations of a risk-utility imbalance. It is true that the risk-utility imbalance in negligence concerns the defendant's conduct while the imbalance in defectiveness supposedly concerns the product, but the relative magnitudes of these risk- utility imbalances could be compared nevertheless. The second method of comparison uses an overreaching value that adjudicates among seemingly incommensurate subordinate values. This method could be used to compare any divergent theories of responsibility, not just those involving risk-utility imbalances. It could, for example, be used in cases involving common-law strict liability, voluntary assumption of a reasonable risk, or reasonable product misuse.

We often allocate resources by balancing apparently incommensurate values. For example, we balance the competing needs of national defense and social programs without conflating the competing considerations. Even though the arguments for strengthening national defense differ from the arguments for mitigating poverty, they are made commensurate by referring to an overarching conception of a good society, based on some value like fairness or utility. On a personal level, we similarly make a choice between taking a vacation and buying a new car. The overarching values involved in these decisions may be vague and controversial, but we commonly choose among competing alternatives as though we can refer to those values.

Similarly, we could evaluate the strength of the policies favoring recovery in a specific case and compare it with the strength of either the policies embodied in a specific defense or the policies that support liability for another defendant. Courts could measure the strength of these competing policies according to some overarching motivational standard, such as fairness or utility, even though the specific policies were different. We may be fooling ourselves to believe there is an overarching standard by which we can adjudicate among competing concerns, but we commonly act as though such a standard exists in a wide variety of social and personal problems. At least the problem of establishing an overreaching value system is not unique to comparative allocation in strict products liability. It is just as significant a problem anytime we allocate resources among competing social concerns.

The theoretical possibility of comparative apportionment between a blameworthy party and a nonblameworthy party does not solve the significant practical problems such a system would impose. To implement this sort of system, jurors would have to understand, either intuitively or through instruction, the disparate rationales reflected in the various theories of recovery. We should be skeptical about a juror's ability to understand these complex factors and make a comparative allocation that is not based solely on fault. It is very likely that jurors asked to implement such a scheme would do so either arbitrarily or by making a sub rosa comparison of fault. An attractive aspect of negligence generally, and of comparative fault specifically, is that it turns on values with which jurors are likely to be familiar. Indeed, the likely persistence of fault in jurors' minds should tell us something about theories that eschew fault.

Proximate Cause

Some courts also have relied on foreseeability to define proximate causation in strict products liability cases. This approach seriously undermines the nonfault basis of strict products liability. It would be anomalous to conclude that a product is defective even though its risks were unforeseeable, but then to deny recovery under the rubric of proximate causation because of that same unforeseeability. For example, superabsorbent tampons that cause toxic shock syndrome may be defective even though the manufacturer could not anticipate this side effect when the tampons were sold. A finding of defectiveness would be meaningless to the plaintiff, however, if a court denied liability on the ground that the injury—toxic shock syndrome—was unforeseeable and therefore not proximately caused by the defect. A conception of proximate causation based on foreseeability is simply incompatible with strict products liability as a nonfault theory of recovery.

Nevertheless, there is no intrinsic reason proximate causation should insert foreseeability into strict products liability. One method of purging foreseeability from proximate cause can be derived from jurisdictions that reject the risk rule in negligence. A few courts use the directness test, which provides that a result is proximately caused by a defendant's negligence even if it was not foreseeable, so long as it was a direct, natural, and probable result that was not remote in time and space. The directness test in negligence can be criticized because it extends liability beyond the scope of the defendant's culpability, which in negligence is limited by foreseeability. The test might be supported, however, because, although it imposes liability beyond the scope of a defendant's culpability, even a slightly culpable defendant better deserves to bear a loss than an innocent victim.

Although nearly every American jurisdiction has rejected the directness test in negligence in favor of the risk rule, the underpinnings of the directness test are not implausible. The directness test provides a coherent, workable limitation on damages without relying on the faultladen notion of foreseeability. Some courts have employed a similar test in products cases, even though they also use the risk rule in negligence cases. Texas, for example, avoids foreseeability by using producing cause in strict products liability cases, even though foreseeability is the backbone of its conception of proximate cause in negligence.

Even the basic structure of the risk rule could be used in products liability without relying on foreseeability. The risk rule relies on foreseeability to limit liability in negligence because foreseeability is a factor in determining whether a defendant's conduct has been negligent. Since culpability in negligence depends on foreseeability, proximate causation based on foreseeability harmonizes with the underlying theory of liability by limiting recovery to the extent of culpability.

An analogy to the risk rule would limit liability in strict products liability to the types of risks that cause us to consider a product defective. Since we generally include unforeseeable as well as foreseeable risks in determining defectiveness, foreseeability would not normally be a factor in proximate cause. In cases in which courts rely on foreseeability to determine defectiveness, however, foreseeability would be an appropriate aspect of proximate cause. This would not itself inject fault into the analysis since the court had already done so in its determination of defectiveness. In such a case, proximate causation would simply reflect the underlying theory of liability.

Proximate cause is a doctrinal device that reflects a variety of policies concerning the extent of a defendant's liability. The doctrine of proximate cause appropriately limits liability in negligence cases on the basis of policies that underlie negligence recovery. Since fault is a basis for recovery in negligence, foreseeability forms the backbone of proximate cause. Other important policies also support liability in negligence, however, and proximate causation reflects these values as well as foreseeability. For example, the exclusion from negligence recovery of purely economic harm reflects different attitudes about the necessity of legal protection for economic rather than personal interests. This exclusion is difficult to explain on the basis of foreseeability.

Strict products liability purports to shift losses for reasons other than fault, such as to spread risks among a product's consumers. Consequently, proximate cause should limit liability in accordance with those policies, rather than on the basis of foreseeability. But the exclusion of foreseeability from proximate causation in products cases does not require the exclusion of a wide range of other policy factors. Courts that have purged foreseeability from proximate cause in strict products liability still must decide what to do with intervening human causes and recoverability for emotional distress. To the extent that negligence precedents on these issues reflect values other than foreseeability, they can and should be applied in products cases without undermining the nonfault basis of recovery.

As in the case of comparative allocation, jurors may not be competent to make these policy judgments. Jurors are undoubtedly less familiar with the policies underlying strict products liability than they are with fault, and courts that want to implement the former may be required to do so with doctrinal rules. This state of affairs is not unique to products liability, however. It is also characteristic of negligence, especially in the cases in which policies other than foreseeability define the scope of liability. Whether we delegate these decisions to juries and trial judges or implement them with doctrinal rules developed at the appellate level, it is at least possible to limit liability by referring to the underlying reasons why a product is defective, and do so without relying on fault and foreseeability.

Appraising the Advantages of a Fault-Based System of Products Liability

Negligence theory would provide courts with sufficient flexibility to preserve certain desirable aspects of current law. For example, product flaws could be deemed negligence per se. Courts often evaluate the reasonableness of a defendant's conduct within a narrow context. A surgeon who slips with a scalpel or sews a sponge in a patient may not normally claim that his procedures prevent these accidents in all but a very few cases. A motorist who changes lanes without looking may not escape liability in negligence merely because his driving habits permit this to happen only rarely. Similarly, a court could conclude that a manufacturer's deviation from its own specifications is negligent, even though quality control procedures usually prevent such an occurrence. This may be a deviation from a fault standard, but no more than in the case of the surgeon or the motorist. The negligence system has been flexible enough to accommodate those situations.

Moreover, the doctrine that holds experts to a standard of care commensurate with their superior skills and knowledge could be used to hold manufacturers to an appropriately stringent standard of anticipating and guarding against risks. Indeed, this feature of negligence would permit courts to make distinctions among different industries, distinctions that are difficult to justify under current notions of defectiveness. For example, foodstuffs or drugs may present situations where we demand extra care or make special allowances depending on expertise.

Although an explicit recognition of fault as the basis of products liability would not eliminate many sensible features of current law (especially if it were accompanied by shifting the burden of proof in appropriate categories of cases to mitigate special problems of proof), it would alleviate some of the problems courts face under the present system. Many of these problems stem from the attempt to coordinate a fault-based system with a nonfault system in personal injury litigation. The problems could be avoided by applying a uniform system to all cases. The potential for linguistic confusion that arises from the application of comparative allocation and proximate cause principles to strict products cases could be alleviated if negligence were explicitly recognized as the underlying theory of products liability. Moreover, problems encountered at the boundary of products cases, such as the issue of whether negligence or strict liability governs hybrid sales-service transactions, real estate transactions, and leases or other nonsale arrangements, could be avoided. Maintaining the boundary between negligence and strict liability creates tension that could be resolved with an explicit recognition of fault in products cases.

Jury instructions would also be easier to develop if courts were explicitly to recognize fault in products cases. Not only would such a recognition avoid the danger of jurors conflating defectiveness with negligence, but it would also permit courts to use the expertise jurors have with regard to the values that underlie fault based liability. In many cases, comparative defenses and proximate cause would once again be based on values within the province of jury expertise.

An explicit recognition of fault in strict products liability would also mitigate problems raised by the selective application of negligence principles within products liability itself. Furthermore, an explicit recognition of fault in products cases would permit courts to engage in reasoned and principled adjudication by removing some of the arbitrary distinctions made under current law. In short, it would reduce the confusion caused by, and the time and energy spent on, coordinating a liability system that purports to eschew fault with the negligence system in which it is embedded.

Conclusion

Fault's tenacity in products cases is not merely a reflection of the courts' attraction to familiar concepts or their political unwillingness to abandon fault. Fault is deeply embedded in the doctrinal structure of strict products liability itself, specifically in the concept of defectiveness. This article suggests arguments that support an explicit recognition of fault as the basis of liability in products cases. Such a recognition would alleviate some of the problems courts have encountered coordinating strict products liability with negligence, without preventing courts from flexibly responding to specific problems, such as the difficulty of proof, that face victims of product accidents. Moreover, courts could base liability on a representational theory where consumer expectations are sufficiently specific to warrant recovery.

Regardless of the merits of these arguments, however, fault is analytically implicit in current products liability law and cannot be purged simply by a careful use of language. The notion that defectiveness differs from negligence, because it does not evaluate a manufacturer's conduct, rests on an illusory distinction between product costs and manufacturing burdens. As long as courts permit manufacturers to justify products with reference to cost, fault is analytically embedded in strict products liability law whether we like it or not.

MALCOLM WHEELER, *The Need for Narrow Tort Reform: Abolishing Strict Product Liability, in* PRODUCT LIABILITY REFORM: DEBATING THE ISSUES (Kenneth L. Chilton ed. 1990)*

Surely there are few participants in our product liability system who do not consider tort reform, either statutory or common law, desirable. The real issue is, "What type of reform is desirable?" For members of society, including members on each side of the bar, the answer should be, "Reform that will improve the quality of justice in the tort system. Reform should promote logical consistency among the various substantive, procedural and evidentiary rules, improve predictability and consistency of outcomes, reduce the societal cost of tort litigation, and, in general, better serve the compensatory and deterrent purposes of the tort law." With this last answer in mind, I suggest that the most vitally necessary product liability reform is nationwide abolition of strict product liability claims in design-defect and inadequate-warning litigation (which together constitute what I call product-line litigation).

The salient characteristic of strict product liability law is that the body of law developed for that purpose remains intellectually and morally indefensible. Strict liability in product-line litigation arbitrarily carves out a limited set of actors—manufacturers and sellers of products—and subjects them to a set of rules far harsher than those that govern most other actors. The lack of justification for this discrimination can be shown in several ways. The one I will use here is a brief summary of a variety of decisions in which courts and legislatures have struggled with the metaphysics of what is a "product," and therefore subject to strict product liability rules, and what is not.

Plasma and Blood Products

In California, at least, plasma and other blood products sold to medical patients are not products. Never mind that these are precisely what most of us think of when we hear the word "product": tangible items processed and packaged for human use. The California Legislature has enacted a statute declaring that the sale of those items is the sale of services, not of products, "for any purpose or purposes whatsoever."

Like Humpty-Dumpty in Wonderland, a legislature can make words mean what the legislature wants them to mean. But why should blood products be exempt from strict product liability, when hundreds of other life-saving products, such as medical machines, artificial heart valves, and pharmaceutical drugs, generally are not?

*Used by permission.

Sales by Pharmacists

In *Murphy v. E. R. Squibb and Sons, Inc.*,[1] the California Supreme Court had to decide whether, when a pharmacist sells a prescription medicine to a customer, the pharmacist sells a "service" or a "product." The court first looked at the nature of the transaction to determine whether the "dominant role" of a pharmacist in supplying a prescription medicine is one of performing a service or selling a product. Understandably, the court found it to be a "hybrid," combining the performance of services with a product sale. The court then concluded that the overall nature of the transaction was "essentially" a service, and strict product liability therefore did not apply. The dissent argued that it was "abundantly clear" that the sale aspects of the transaction predominated.

None of the justices, however, asked, much less attempted to answer, the question that would have revealed that the product liability emperor has been wearing no clothes for a quarter century: "Why does the sale of *any* service, much less *all* services, deserve more protection from litigation than the sale of *any* product, much less *all* products?" No member of the court identified any public policy that could justify such a distinction. No one explained why a pharmacist's sale of prescription medicine is "hybrid," while the same pharmacist's advice to buy, and her subsequent sale of, over-the-counter aspirin is not "hybrid" or why an audio-equipment store that provides listening rooms, demonstrations, literature, and advice when selling amplifiers and tape decks does not sell a "hybrid" of services and products.

Electricity

The judicial pronouncements on the metaphysics of "product" have been even more Delphic in decisions in which courts have decided whether electricity is a product. In *United Pacific Insurance Co. v. Southern California Edison Co.*,[2] for example, the plaintiff sued a utility for damages that had resulted from a fire that had occurred when a kite had become entangled in high-tension wires. The kite string had pulled the conductors on the utility pole so close that an arc of electricity had occurred, which had caused the emission of molten aluminum, which in turn had ignited a brush fire that eventually had destroyed some 200 homes. The plaintiff alleged that the cable system had been defectively designed. The court ruled that strict product liability could not apply.

The court relied in part on cases from other jurisdictions holding that electricity is not in a marketable state or in the "stream of commerce" until actually delivered to the consumer. The court did not state where that delivery occurs—for example, when the cable first enters the consumer's land, when the cable first enters the consumer's home, or when the electricity enters an appliance in the consumer's home or on the consumer's land. The court also opined that utilities were sufficiently regulated by statute, that no broader risk-spreading liability should be imposed on them absent a further statement from the legislature. Other than this one question-begging assertion, however, the court provided no basis for giving utilities more protection than is given to manufacturers. The court did not ask whether utilities may be better able than many manufacturers to spread risk, to compensate for defects, or to prevent injuries from defects. The court did not ask whether the safety regulations for utilities were more or less comprehensive than those for pharmaceuticals, medical devices, automobiles, airplanes, and other products that are subject to federal and state regulations, yet receive no exemption from strict product liability.

---

[1] 710 P.2d 247 (Cal. 1985).

[2] 163 Cal. App.3d 700, 209 Cal. Rptr. 819 (1985).

The court in *Fong v. Pacific Gas & Electric Co.*[3] followed *United Pacific* and held that an electric utility was not strictly liable for damage allegedly caused by defective insulation on the utility's incoming power lines at the point above a garage where they were attached to the plaintiffs' wires. The plaintiffs contended that, as a result of the defective insulation, electric current had arced between the utility's wires, which had caused them to drip molten aluminum onto the garage roof and start a fire.

The court held that the alleged defect was located in power lines owned and controlled by the utility and was therefore outside the "stream of commerce." The court ruled that electricity does not become a product, or enter the "stream of commerce," until it has passed through the customer's meter. Because the fire started at a point along the transmission lines before the electricity passed through the meter, strict product liability did not apply.

In *Pierce v. Pacific Gas & Electric Co.*,[4] on the other hand, the court was faced with a plaintiff who had received an electrical shock when electricity had reached her home at a dangerously high voltage following the defendant's replacement of a storm-damaged transformer with a defective transformer. A "power surge" somewhere in the system had caused 7,000 volts of electricity to reach her home. The plaintiff contended that household electricity must be considered a product for strict liability purposes and that, because it had reached her residence at nearly sixty times its intended voltage, it was defective. The court agreed, holding that, by the time the electricity had reached her house, it had been sufficiently in the "stream of commerce" for her to have had a reasonable expectation that it would be at marketable voltage.

After the decision in *Pierce,* the plaintiff in *Thibos v. Pacific Gas & Electric Co.*[5] attempted to amend his complaint to allege strict product liability against the same utility. He had been struck by a car while crossing a street over which hung a street light that the defendant had installed and maintained and that had burned out, leaving the roadway dark.

The *Thibos* court rejected the plaintiff's strict product liability claim for two reasons. The essence of his claim was that the utility had put a product into the stream of commerce by placing the light bulb into the light fixture. The court disagreed, quoting the language of the contract between the utility and the City of Concord, which was a contract for "street and highway *lighting* and consistently refers to what is being provided as a *service.*" Further, the court found that *Pierce* militated against finding that the defendant had placed any product on the market, because *Pierce* distinguished between faulty electricity, for which the utility could be held liable, and a faulty transformer manufactured by someone other than the utility, for which it could not. The *Thibos* plaintiff did not claim that faulty electricity had caused the bulb to burn out. Consequently, the court found, the utility was the consumer of the product, not its manufacturer or distributor.

Animals

In Oregon a pet skunk is a product. In Illinois it is not. In *Sease v. Taylor's Pets, Inc.*,[6] the plaintiffs came into contact with a rabid skunk and had to undergo rabies vaccine treatments. They sued the pet shop where they had purchased the skunk and the farm on which it had been raised for sale. The court had to decide whether a live animal was a product, and held that it was. The

[3] 199 Cal. App.3d 30, 245 Cal. Rptr. 436 (1988).
[4] 166 Cal. App.3d 68, 212 Cal. Rptr. 283 (1985).
[5] 187 Cal. App.3d 337, 232 Cal. Rptr. 11 (1986).
[6] 700 P.2d 1054 (Or. 1985).

court focused upon and rejected the defendants' contention that animals are not products because of their "mutability." In *Anderson v. Farmers Hybrid Cos., Inc.*,[7] however, an Illinois court held that the changeable nature and health of living creatures and the effects of circumstances outside sellers' control militated against finding them to be products.

Buildings

Courts have held that builders of mass-produced houses are subject to strict product liability, but builders of small numbers of houses are not. That distinction is tenuous enough. California courts have taken it a step further.

In 1985, the California Supreme Court expanded strict product liability to include leased premises, holding that a landlord engaged in the business of leasing apartments was strictly liable for injuries resulting from a latent defect in the premises when the defect existed at the time the premises were let to the tenant. In *Becker v. IRM Corp.*[8] the plaintiff tenant had been injured by falling through an untempered glass shower door in his rented apartment. It was undisputed that the risk of injury would have been substantially reduced if the shower door had been made of tempered, rather than untempered, glass. It also was undisputed that, except for a small mark in the corner of each piece of glass, it would have been impossible for a lay person to distinguish between tempered and untempered glass shower doors in the apartment.

The court concluded that a landlord "sells" rental housing as a "product," just as a builder of mass-produced homes sells residences. The court held that strict product liability should apply because "the paramount policy of the strict product liability rule remains the spreading throughout society of the cost of compensating otherwise defenseless victims of manufacturing defects."

Given the rationale offered in *Becker,* it was understandable that a plaintiff would attempt to extend strict product liability to lessors of space in commercial buildings. In *Muro v. Superior Court*[9] the employee of a commercial tenant brought a strict product liability action against her employer's landlord after having fallen on a stairway on the premises. The appellate court held that *Becker* extended strict product liability only to lessors of residential premises.

The court attempted to distinguish *Becker* by noting that its rationale in part "reflects a view that no one should be allowed or forced to live in unsafe and unhealthy housing." The court also suggested that commercial lessees, unlike the paradigmatic hapless "consumer" of goods and residential property were sophisticated, had greater bargaining power, and so could "protect" themselves from harms against which consumers were powerless to act.

* * *

Conclusion

Strict product liability in product-line litigation should be abolished. I would prefer to see this done by the individual states, but that is unlikely to occur. The mistaken notion that if we have strict product liability in manufacturing defect cases, we must have it in design-defect cases and inadequate-warning cases seems too firmly entrenched to allow such a major reversal by piecemeal action. The very persistence of strict product liability in product-line litigation in the face of a quarter century of massive judicial and scholarly criticism of each substantive test that has been tried shows a profound judicial reluctance to admit that the experiment has been a failure.

---

[7] 408 N.E.2d 1194 (1980).

[8] 698 P.2d 116 (Cal. 1985).

[9] 184 Cal. App.3d 1089, 229 Cal. Rptr. 383 (1986).

B. Contract Law

William L. Prosser, *The Implied Warranty of Merchantable Quality,* 27 MINN. L. REV. 117 (1943)*

Section 15 (2) of the Uniform Sales Act reads as follows:

> **Where the goods are bought by description from a seller who deals in goods of that description (whether he be the grower or manufacturer or not), there is an implied warranty that the goods shall be of merchantable quality.**

This section was copied almost verbatim from the English Sale of Goods Act of 1894, which was itself a restatement and codification of the common law of England as it existed at that date. As it is stated in the American act, the section undoubtedly represents the more prevalent, and certainly the better, holdings of our courts at common law. If our standard warranty exists, it must be found in this section and the construction which has been placed upon it.

History

In its inception, breach of warranty was a tort. The action was upon the case, for breach of an assumed duty, and the wrong was conceived to be a form of misrepresentation, in the nature of deceit and not at all clearly distinguished from deceit. Even after Lord Holt's decisions made it clear that the action would lie for a mere affirmation of fact by the seller even though he made it innocently and without any knowledge of its falsity, the action was still in tort; and as late as 1797 we find Lord Kenyon talking of breach of warranty as a form of "fraud."

Warranty has never entirely lost this tort character which it had in the beginning; and this may have important consequences at the present day. For one thing, it is generally agreed that a tort form of action, as on the case, may still be maintained for the breach, without any proof of either intentional misrepresentation or even negligence. In addition, the tort element involved may permit damages not recoverable for mere breach of contract, such as wrongful death, or the application of a different statute of limitations; and it has served as a strong argument for those who seek to extend implied warranties of quality from the producer to the ultimate consumer, in the absence of any privity of contract between the two. Furthermore, it has continued to color the substantive law of warranty itself, by introducing some idea of misrepresentation of fact, however innocent, and of reliance on the part of the buyer upon the seller's knowledge, skill or judgment, or some implied assertion concerning the character of the goods sold.

Shortly after 1750, an express warranty began to be recognized as a term of the contract of sale, and attorneys adopted the practice of declaring on the contract. In *Stuart v. Wilkins,* in 1778, the practice was sanctioned by a decision that assumpsit would lie for a breach of warranty if it were express. In the course of argument with counsel there seems to have been a lively discussion, not reported in the case, as to whether this might be true of an implied warranty also; and Lord Mansfield was of the opinion that that at least was still exclusively a matter of tort. Evidently the reference was to the implied warranty of title, the only one recognized at the time. By 1810,

*Used by permission.

however, when implied warranties of quality were first established, a whole generation of lawyers had been taught to regard any warranty as a contract, and the assumpsit action was accepted as a matter of course.

The leading case is *Gardiner v. Gray,* at nisi prius in 1815. The buyer declared on a contract for the sale of a quantity of "waste silk" imported from the continent. Neither buyer nor seller had seen the goods, although samples had been forwarded and shown by the seller to the buyer's agent. Lord Ellenborough stated the fundamental principle of the implied warranty of merchantable quality:

> "I am of opinion, however, that under such circumstances, the purchaser has a right to expect a saleable article answering the description in the contract. Without any particular warranty, this is an implied term in every such contract. Where there is no opportunity to inspect the commodity, the maxim of *caveat emptor* does not apply. He cannot without a warranty insist that it shall be of any particular quality or fineness, but the intention of both parties must be taken to be, that it shall be saleable in the market under the denomination mentioned in the contract between them. The purchaser cannot be supposed to buy goods to lay them on a dunghill. The question then is, whether the commodity purchased by the plaintiff be of such a quality as can be reasonably brought into the market to be sold as *waste silk?* The witnesses describe it as unfit for the purposes of waste silk, and of such a quality that it cannot be sold under that denomination."

Observe that here is no mention of misrepresentation, conscious or otherwise, or of any reliance by the buyer upon the seller's knowledge or judgment. The ground of the decision is merely that the seller has contracted to deliver one thing and has delivered another; effect is given to the "intention of both parties" as the contract they have made is interpreted; it is breach of contract, pure and simple.

A long line of later cases rounded out the picture. The seller's warranty, as a matter of contract, was held to mean not only that the goods delivered must be genuine according to the name, kind or description specified, but that they must be of a quality to pass in the market under that description, and this in turn to mean that they must be reasonably fit for the ordinary uses to which such goods are put. The warranty was recognized as a dealer's warranty only, and trade usage must be taken into account. The implied warranty of fitness for the buyer's "particular" purpose developed, and was recognized as something separate and distinct from that of merchantable quality, although the two might, and often did, overlap. Finally in 1868, the whole matter was summed up in *Jones v. Just,* the famous case of the Manila hemp, which Jelf, rather over-enthusiastically, listed as one of his "Fifteen Decisive Battles of the Law;" and the warranty of merchantable quality was stated in terms which have passed, in substance, into the Sales Act section quoted above.

At about the same time, if not earlier, the idea began to make its appearance that warranties arose by implication "of law" from what had been said and done, and were independent of any intent on the part of the seller to contract with regard to them, or to be bound by them. This idea, now generally accepted as to express warranties, was carried over all the more readily into those "implied," where it became involved with the development of modern notions of policy, based upon the increasing practice of reputable sellers to assume responsibility for defective goods sold, together with the feeling that such responsibility is best placed upon the seller as a cost of his business, which he may distribute to the public at large as a part of the price. As a result, it is often said that implied warranties of quality arise by operation of law and are independent of any intention to agree upon their terms as a matter of fact; and there are many cases, at least, in which to hold that the warranty is a term of the contract is "to speak the language of pure fiction."

Implied Warranty

When the ordinary lawyer, or court for that matter, says that a warranty is "implied," what seems to be meant is merely that it is not expressed. There has been surprisingly little discussion of just how, or why, the implication arises. Both as a matter of history and at the present day, however, there are three distinct theories to be discerned as the basis of implied warranties of quality.

1. *The warranty is a misrepresentation of fact.* The seller has asserted, whether expressly or by his conduct, that the goods are of a particular kind, quality or character, and the buyer has purchased in reliance upon that assertion. This is obviously a tort theory, closely allied to the cases of deceit; and it differs from deceit only in that it imposes strict liability for innocent misrepresentations, in the absence of any "scienter" in the form of knowledge of their falsity or lack of belief in their truth. Logically, however, it does require reasonable reliance on the part of the buyer upon some supposed information of the seller concerning the truth of the assertion; and if the seller does not purport to have such information it should follow that the buyer does not reasonably rely upon it, and no implied warranty is to be found. In many cases where the seller obviously knows nothing about the goods, as in the case of a sale by a retailer of beans sealed in a can, the courts have refused to imply a warranty for lack of such reliance.

2. *The warranty has in fact been agreed upon by the parties as an unexpressed term of the contract of sale.* The seller has contracted to deliver described goods, and it is understood that they are to have certain qualities; but that understanding has not been embodied in the agreement. Nevertheless the court, by interpreting the language used, the conduct of the parties and the circumstances of the case, finds that it is there. Such a contract term "implied in fact" differs from an express agreement only in that it is circumstantially proved. Any difficulties arising from the parol evidence rule usually have been met by saying that the description of the goods appearing in the contract is open to interpretation or explanation in the light of the circumstances of the case.

Obviously this theory is pure contract. It arose only after warranties had been held to be enforceable in a contract action; and the first case in which it appeared was one in which the seller did not know what the goods were, and the buyer knew that he did not know and never had seen them. It does not rest upon any belief on the part of the buyer that the seller has superior information, or any information at all about the goods; and the seller's innocence or ignorance or inability to deliver what he has contracted to deliver will no more excuse him than in any other breach of contract. Any "reliance" of the buyer upon the seller becomes important only in so far as it bears upon his actual understanding of what the latter has undertaken to deliver.

3. *The warranty is imposed by the law.* It is read into the contract by the law without regard to whether the parties intended it in fact; it arises merely because the goods have been sold at all. This theory is of course one of policy. The loss due to defective goods is placed upon the seller because he is best able to bear it and distribute it to the public, and because it is considered that the buyer is entitled to protection at the seller's expense. It is perhaps idle to inquire whether the basis of such as liability in contract or tort. It partakes of the nature of both, and in either case it is liability without fault. It is not often that "implication of law" is differentiated clearly from

''implied in fact;'' but the question of the policy involved is seldom absent from warranty cases, and there are a respectable number in which it appears to have controlled the decision.

If it be asked which of these three theories is the basis of the law of implied warranties in general, it can only be answered: all three. It is seldom that it makes any difference which is adopted; but when the occasion arises, the courts have flitted cheerfully from one to another as the facts may demand, always tending to an increasing extent to favor the buyer and find the warranty. When lack of ''reliance'' of the buyer upon the seller's information becomes an obstacle, the first is abandoned in favor of the second; when it is necessary to avoid the effect of disclaimers or the parol evidence rule, the second is forsaken for the third; and when it is desired to extend the warranty to one not in ''privity of contract'' with the seller, there is a return to the first. So far as the warranty of merchantable quality is concerned, however, the second theory, that of agreement ''implied in fact'' and actually understood but not expressed, has predominated from the beginning; and with few exceptions, it explains the decisions.

Merchantable Quality

Before considering when the warranty arises, it is well to determine what it means when it does arise. Professor Llewellyn has said that there is no more puzzling question than what ''merchantable'' means under the Sales Act. Certainly it has meant a variety of things; but an array of several hundred cases, reasonably consistent in their approach, will at least permit some general conclusions. When a seller undertakes, expressly or by implication, to deliver merchantable goods, the extent of his obligation is at least as follows:

1. *Genuine according to name, kind and description.* Nothing is more elementary in all the law of contract than that an agreement to deliver a horse is not satisfied by delivery of a cow. Accordingly, it was held quite early that a contract calling for ''scarlet cuttings,'' or ''prime bacon,'' or ''Skirving's Swedes seeds,'' or for that matter a foreign bill of exchange, necessarily implied an agreement, or condition or warranty, that the thing sold should answer the name or kind described. Such a description is of course a matter of express language; and it has been held frequently enough that it amounts to an express warranty in itself. The earlier cases, however, treated the understanding that the goods should conform to the description as an ''inference'' or implication of fact; and both the English Sales of Goods Act and the Uniform Sales Act contain a section, substantially identical in the two, which states the warranty as one ''implied.'' Whether it is to be called express or implied is ordinarily of no importance; it appears to be both, and the courts have treated it more or less indiscriminately as one or the other.

The connection with merchantable quality arises from the fact that when goods are bought from a dealer, the description obviously must be construed to call for the kind of goods usually sold by that name by such dealer, and the usages of the trade become part of the understanding of the parties. It follows that what is sold as ''waste silk'' must be something known to the trade and capable of passing in the market as waste silk; a ''copper-fastened vessel'' must have a sufficient amount of copper to conform to trade understanding of the term; ''oxalic acid'' must be the oxalic acid of commerce; ''foreign refined rape oil'' and ''Calcutta linseed'' must be pure enough to be accepted under that name by the trade; and ''Manila hemp'' must not be so wetted by sea-water that it can only be sold as defective goods. Out of a very long list of decisions implying such a warranty of genuineness, there is space to mention only a few.

2. *Saleable in the market under the designation.* Upon this foundation of genuineness according to trade understanding was built the second requirement, that the goods must be capable of passing

in the market under the name or description by which they are sold. It is not enough that they be merely something which can be called by the name; they must be of the kind or quality commonly sold in the market. This involves two elements. The buyer—who in the earlier cases was himself a dealer—must be assured the possibility of resale if he so desires; and here it seems clear that the warranty of merchantable quality overlaps its twin implied warranty of fitness for the buyer's particular purpose. Or, if he buys for use, he is still assured that he is receiving what dealers customarily sell, and what he might buy elsewhere under the same name.

It is not enough that the goods are capable of sale to somebody at some price; they must be acceptable generally on the market under the same name or description. Nor, of course, is it enough that they would pass in the first instance on their appearance, with their defects concealed; they must be marketable with their true character known, and the fact that the buyer's customers return them to him after purchase is at least strong evidence that they are not of merchantable quality. "Saleable" in the market means not only that the goods themselves are of passable quality, but also that they are not improperly packed or labeled so as to interfere with their resale under the same description; that they are not in dangerous containers; that they have no unnecessary unpleasant odor; that their sale or resale in the same market does not violate any applicable statute; and even that the resale will not subject the buyer to liability for infringement of another's trade mark, or require him to pay a license tax not necessary for the goods as described.

Apparently, so far as the warranty of merchantable quality is concerned, all that the buyer can demand is that the goods shall be saleable in the market in which he buys. If he seeks an assurance that they can be sold elsewhere, he must exact an express warranty, or look to the implied warranty of fitness for his "particular" purpose. Likewise the time as of which merchantable quality is to be invoked is that of the passage of title, and if goods are to be shipped there is ordinarily no implication that they will stand shipment, or continue merchantable for any period after sale. Again, however, the "particular" purpose may require goods of a quality or condition to stand shipment when shipped, and if title is to pass at destination, the goods must of course be merchantable when they arrive.

3. *Fit for the ordinary uses and purposes of such goods.* It was recognized quite early that goods cannot be expected to pass on the market, and hence are not of merchantable quality, unless they are reasonably fit for the ordinary uses to which goods of that kind are put. The purchaser cannot be supposed to buy goods to lay them on a dunghill; nor do dealers customarily offer useless goods to their trade. It follows that when a dealer contracts to sell a barge, he is understood to be selling something reasonably fit for ordinary use as a barge, and the same is true of an automobile, a piano, a hot water bottle, milk, fertilizer, food, clothing, furniture, or any other marketed commodity. On this purely contractual basis of an understanding implied in fact, it has long been recognized that merchantable quality is reflected in use value as well as exchange value, and that the two are inseparably linked. Goods are not merchantable if they cannot be used; and merchantable quality necessarily includes some reasonable fitness for the ordinary purposes for which such goods are intended, designed and sold.

4. *Free from defects interfering with sale or ordinary use.* Frequently the warranty of merchantable quality is stated in terms of freedom from defects: the goods must "not have any remarkable defect," or any defect rendering them unmarketable. Obviously what is meant is any defect which would interfere with sale or ordinary use. "Unmarketable" is too strong a word, since a very trivial defect, such as a broken glass over the dial of an expensive computing scale, which might be repaired for 30 cents, may still prevent its sale. It is of course not necessary that the defect be

an obvious one, and any latent condition, such as a pin inside of a loaf of bread, which would prevent the purchase if it were known, is enough. But trifling deficiencies, obviously of no consequence to anyone, such as the fact that a single screw or bolt in a machine is not new, are not to be taken into account. The usages of the trade and the liberality of customers must of course be considered; and the precise percentage of sand which the public will tolerate in its sugar, the amount of checking it will accept in the finish of a piano, or the quantity of alloy which will pass in a gold watch, may very well be questions for the jury.

5. *Quality and price.* Obviously some minimum standard of quality is called for by a merchantable article. Sometimes this is expressed by saying that the seller warrants good materials and workmanship; more often, merely that the goods must pass in the market and be suitable for ordinary use. As to anything over and above this, unless the contract itself calls for a particular quality or grade, it is well settled that the buyer has no right to expect it. The "medium quality" proposed in an early New York case has been rejected, since obviously some goods will be merchantable that are less than the mean. The "fair average" quality recommended by the draft of the Revised Uniform Sales Act seems to set too lofty a standard, if "fair average" is construed, as it might conceivably be, to mean the average of all that are made or sold. There are clearly goods of the name of so poor a quality that they cannot be sold readily on the market, and these the buyer is not required to accept; but above this merchantable minimum, unless he exacts an express warranty or relies on fitness for his particular purpose disclosed to the seller, he is not entitled to any particular grade or fineness.

The price paid by the buyer has had little consideration in the cases. There was an old doctrine of French law, that "a sound price warrants a sound article," which has passed into the law of South Carolina and Louisiana. Because of the doctrine that consideration need not be adequate, the English courts rejected it quite early, and other American jurisdictions continue to repeat that it is not accepted. Yet it is difficult to escape the conviction that the price cannot be left out of account. It has been held that a price materially below apparent value shows that the buyer understands that he is receiving low-grade or defective goods; and if this is true, the converse would seem to follow. Certainly jewelry sold at Tiffany's is understood by both parties to be something better than that sold at Woolworth's, although both no doubt are merchantable as "jewelry." If there are ten grades of sardines on the market, a buyer who pays the market price of the first can scarcely be supposed to be contracting for the tenth; and the fact that off-grade goods circulate freely at a discount should not, in reason, affect the bargain in a sale by a reputable dealer at full price. There are a few rather vague indications that the price paid bears upon what the seller undertakes in the way of merchantable quality; and when the issue is squarely presented, it may be expected that the buyer will be held entitled, not to the value of his money, but at least to a grade not entirely and hopelessly out of line with what he has paid.

Conclusion

From the simple proposition, first announced by Lord Ellenborough in 1815, that a dealer who contracts to sell goods of a particular description is understood to agree that he will deliver what is commonly sold in the market under that description, the courts have developed the implied warranty of merchantable quality. It has grown, by degrees to include not only genuineness according to the description and saleability in the market, but also fitness for the ordinary uses and purposes for which such goods are made and sold, and freedom from all defects which will interfere with sale or use. The time may yet come when it will be extended to include a grade or quality not totally inconsistent with the price. It has grown to include all dealers, even the retailer and the restaurant keeper, and to cover specific goods which are in the presence of the buyer and under his inspection when he agrees to buy. On all three fronts, although there are decisions which still lag behind, the battle is now virtually won for the buyer. The warranty includes all dealer sales in which the buyer is given to understand that he is to receive goods of a particular description, which means all but a negligible few. In short, it has become a standard dealer's warranty, presumed to exist, in practice and effect if not technically in law, in every sale made by one who deals in goods of the kind and description required by the contract, and defeated only by words or circumstances amounting to an express or implied disclaimer.

The implied warranty of merchantable quality is the most powerful weapon at the buyer's command. It has lain under the double shadow of the ancient tort origin of warranty, with its emphasis upon misrepresentation of a fact which the seller purports to know, and of the companion warranty of fitness for the particular purpose. Both have led many courts, in the past, to insist upon some reliance upon the seller's skill, or judgment, or supposed information. The warranty of merchantable quality does not rest, and from the beginning did not rest, upon any such basis. It is a matter of contract, of interpretation of the language used in the light of the fact that the seller is a dealer, and dealers deal in merchantable goods.

George L. Priest, *A Theory of the Consumer Product Warranty*, 90 YALE L.J. 1297 (1981)*

Imagine that consumers are perfectly informed about the likelihood of a product defect and about the losses that will be suffered should a product become defective. Imagine also that consumers somehow make their preferences regarding warranty terms known to manufacturers and that manufacturers are responsive to those preferences. Imagine that warranty contracts are standardized *only* to reduce negotiation costs and thus that the standardized form itself does not affect the substantive obligations of consumers relative to manufacturers. Finally, imagine that all products are manufactured under conditions of perfect competition, so that each characteristic of a product—including warranty terms—serves to optimize the welfare of some dominant class of consumers. What would be the terms of product warranties?

In the common view, a warranty serves as both an insurance policy and a repair contract. As an insurance policy, a warranty provides that if, within a certain period, the product or some part of the product becomes defective, the manufacturer will compensate the buyer for the loss by repair, replacement, or refund of the purchase price. As a repair contract, a warranty fixes an obligation upon the manufacturer for some period of time to provide, without charge, services necessary to repair a defect in order to prolong the useful capacity of the product.

A warranty operates as an insurance policy to the extent that the occurrence of a product defect is probabilistic. To insure for a loss is to redistribute wealth from periods in which no losses are suffered to the period in which the loss occurs. A manufacturer can redistribute wealth in this

*Used by permission.

manner by collecting a premium in the sale price from a broad set of consumers for whom the prospects of loss during any single period are unrelated. The market insurance premium reflects both the expected loss for the period and some share of the costs to the insurer of aggregating these unrelated contingencies, called loading costs. A consumer may prefer, however, some personal form of temporal wealth redistribution in the face of a loss. A consumer self-insures for product losses by accumulating savings for the replacement of defective products, by reserving future time for product repair, or, more simply, by expecting to tolerate a defect once it occurs. These methods of self-insurance, of course, also involve costs of transaction. As a general proposition, therefore, we may expect to observe market insurance in a warranty only where the sum of the expected loss and loading costs of market insurance is less than the sum of the expected loss and transaction costs of self-insurance.

As a repair contract, a warranty reflects the respective costs to the consumer and the manufacturer of repair services. Repair by the consumer and manufacturer are substitutes, and the consumer can be expected to purchase repair services as part of the warranty wherever the manufacturer's price is less than the consumer's cost of providing the repair himself. Obviously, a consumer can (and frequently does) provide many repair services more cheaply than a manufacturer. It is plausible, for example, that where shelves fall in a refrigerator, repair by the consumer is cheaper. Of course, since the consumer and manufacturer are always free after the purchase of the good to negotiate for the provision of services of this kind, the warranty itself is valuable only if it reduces transaction costs for future agreements. Thus, a warranty may be expected to allocate responsibility to the manufacturer for those types of repairs that most frequently are difficult or burdensome for consumers to provide themselves.

Although the above example, as well as most uses of the word "repair," refers to investments designed to return a product to a condition it enjoyed at some previous period of time, it is worthwhile to consider "repair service" to a product more broadly as any investment designed to optimize the performance of the product over time. Viewed in this light, for example, restraining young children from swinging on a refrigerator door represents an investment in a form of "repair" that may well be less costly than hiring a serviceman at a later date to install new hinges. Similarly, a manufacturer may anticipate future repair services by technological investments in the design of the product that make its operation less susceptible to interruption—designing brackets to hold refrigerator shelves more securely, for example—or by investments to control a consistent quality of production.

With respect to repair investments of this nature, however, a warranty serves a role beyond that of reducing transaction costs. The warranty promise establishes and enforces the obligation of the manufacturer to make investments in the design of the good or in quality control. Such an agreement between the parties subsequent to the sale could not achieve the same result as easily, so that there are advantages to "tying" the warranty to the sale of the product. The warranty in this regard operates as a performance bond of the manufacturer. The value of the bond is equal to the costs to the manufacturer of defective product claims. As long as the manufacturer makes appropriate investments, the bond will not be forfeited. The decision to allocate repair investments of this nature between the manufacturer and consumer, however, is identical to the decision of who should bear typical repair costs. As before, we would expect the parties to allocate between themselves, according to relative costs, all investments in "repair," whether in the form of direct reconditioning services, of product design, or of a consumer's care for or maintenance of the product so as to extend its useful life.

It is evident that the various activities described as repair are substitutes for insurance. Repair, like insurance, is a means of reducing the magnitude of a loss from an unexpected event such as a defect. It is important now, however, to depart from the common view of the warranty and to distinguish more clearly between repair as a redistribution of wealth over time, like insurance, and repair as an allocative investment which alters the productive capacity of the good. The first example of repair—the reinstallation of the refrigerator shelves by the consumer—is a form of self-insurance for the loss. The owner bears the full cost of time and energy necessary to replace the shelves after the event occurs, which, in this case, appears to be cheaper than buying market insurance requiring the manufacturer to replace the shelves. But neither repair by the consumer nor by the manufacturer directly alters the probability of the loss occurring and, thus, is like insurance. The second example—restraining the child from swinging on the refrigerator door—is an allocative investment by a consumer that extends the useful life of the product by reducing the probability of a future loss. Certainly, the burdens of a parent increase as the discipline of children becomes more strict or specific. But, again, it may well be cheaper for a consumer to restrain his child than either to buy market insurance for repair of the door or to pay the manufacturer to design a refrigerator with hinges as sturdy as playground equipment.

Thus, in this terminology, a consumer's decision to accommodate himself to a scratch in the surface of an appliance is an example of self-insurance of the defect. The consumer's earlier efforts to reduce the likelihood of the scratch, for example, by increasing the level of his care or by isolating the appliance, is an allocative investment by the consumer. The manufacturer's promise in a warranty to repair the scratch after it occurs is market insurance. And the manufacturer's production decision to make the surface more resistant to abrasion is an example of an allocative investment by the manufacturer.

Self-insurance, market insurance, and allocative investments by consumers and manufacturers, therefore, are each substitute methods of reducing losses in order to optimize productive services. A consumer selects among these methods according to the relative prices and marginal productivities of each with respect to expected elements of product loss. As the price of market insurance rises, other things equal, the quantity of it demanded will decline, and the demand for self-insurance and for manufacturer or consumer allocative investments will increase. Similarly, as the cost of an allocative investment by the consumer rises—say, in our second example, by the addition of a child to the consumer's family, which makes it more difficult to reduce the probability of loss—the relative attractiveness of market insurance, self-insurance, or an allocative investment by the manufacturer is enhanced. These various ways of reducing product losses, however, may not be perfect substitutes. An individual is likely to select some combination of these four methods to optimize expected utility. For example, as the value of a consumer product or of the consumer's life increases—and, as a result, the potential risk from a defect increases—the consumer may increase consumption of each of the four.

Most discussions of product defects in the economics literature and most legal decisions involving warranties regard the probability of loss from a defect as inherent in the nature of the product and independent of actions of the consumer. According to this approach, allocative investments by a consumer which serve to reduce the probability of losses are nonexistent, and the only relevant consumer and public policy choice is between consumer self-insurance and manufacturer liability, whether leading to an allocative investment or insurance. Often these analyses are qualified by a reference to consumer behavior, although seldom by more than an acknowledgement that in some cases a consumer may actively misuse a product. The implicit conclusion of each of these discussions is that allocative investments by a consumer are empirically unimportant to the optimization of the productive life of the good.

Of course, there is no theoretical justification for disregarding allocative investments by consumers. A more important implication of the theory, however, is that there is no meaningful way to consider a product defect independently of a consumer's allocative investments. Investments to reduce the probability of losses may take very subtle forms. I have alluded earlier to the control of children and the placement of an appliance—as it affects the number of times the appliance is scratched or jarred—as representing allocative investments.

As a more general proposition, however, two forms of investment by consumers will affect the likelihood of defects in any consumer product. The first is the consumer's selection of a product suitable for his expected needs. Warranty claims are likely to be more frequent, for example, where a washing machine is undersized or a vacuum cleaner underpowered, or where there occurs some unexpected increase in the demands that the consumer makes on the product. If the consumer accurately anticipates his uses, and if he selects a product designed most appropriately for those uses, the productive capacity of the good is more likely to be preserved. The second form of investment is the consumer's decision about the extent to which he will use the product. A consumer who operates an appliance infrequently may be said to be preserving the life of the product by choosing to store rather than to use it.

Initially, this conception may seem foreign because it is common to infer from personal experience some "normal" use of a product. Indeed, the law requires judges and juries to make inferences of "normal" use by implying in product sales a warranty of merchantability that a product is "of fair average quality" and is "fit for the ordinary purposes for which such goods are used." If it were possible to infer some "normal" use of a good, then the decision of an individual consumer to use or not to use the good would be analytically irrelevant.

But preferences regarding the frequency of use of a product differ among consumers. The preferences of the particular set of consumers for whom the product has been designed in order to optimize sales cannot be determined by inference. Where the dominant set of purchasers operates the good infrequently and, thus, where the "normal" use of the good is storage, the level of the consumers' allocative investments in preservation of the product is high. As a consequence, the level of the manufacturer's allocative investment in product design or in insurance that optimizes productive services may be very low. In such a case, the design or manner of production of the product may be optimal even though the product appears grossly defective when operated with greater frequency, which is to say, when operated with lower allocative investments in care by consumers.

A warranty in this view is the instrument that expresses consumer preferences for allocative or insurance investments. It is a contract that divides responsibility for allocative investments and insurance between the consumer and the manufacturer. The content of the contract is determined by the respective costs to the two parties of allocative investments or insurance. According to this approach, a manufacturer makes investments to prolong product life up to the point at which the marginal cost of such investments equals the marginal benefit. A manufacturer, then, offers market insurance for those losses or items of service for which market insurance is less costly than insurance or allocative investments by the consumer himself.

* * *

Optimal Warranty Provisions

The task of defining optimal warranty provisions resembles the task of defining optimal rate classes in insurance contracts. In all insurance contexts, it is advantageous for an insurer to segregate applicants according to the level of risks added to the insurance pool. If the risk of loss of an individual can be predicted, then the insurance premium can be tailored to reflect the likelihood of future payouts. In particular, insurance coverage can be offered at a lower premium to an individual for whom the risk of loss is relatively low.

For most types of insurance, of course, it is prohibitively costly either to predict exactly the risk that an individual brings to a pool or to charge individual premiums. As a consequence, an insurer is forced to lump individuals into separate classes or, sometimes, into a single class. The premium charged each member of the class must reflect the average level of risk of the class. Thus, the premium undercharges relatively high-risk individuals and overcharges relatively low-risk individuals. At the margin, some low-risk individuals are likely to find that the cost of market insurance exceeds the benefit, and will shift to allocative investments that reduce the likelihood of the loss or to self-insurance. In the context of consumer products, these individuals will shift their purchases to products sold without, or with less, warranty coverage. The more precisely the insurer is able to construct classes comprising individuals with relatively similar levels of risk, however, the smaller the discrepancy will be between the premium and the value of insurance to the lower risk members of the pool. Thus, the lower risk members become less inclined to substitute self-insurance for market insurance. As a general proposition, therefore, discrimination that reduces differences in risk between members of a given insurance class optimizes the sale of insurance.

It is common for life, medical, accident, and home insurers to obtain information about applicants prior to making contracts in order to place applicants in appropriate insurance classes. Insurers routinely solicit information about age, sex, property location and value, as well as medical records and driving histories in order to construct rate classes. Some insurers make it possible for individuals with characteristics that tend to be correlated with low levels of risk, such as abstemious smoking and drinking habits, to identify themselves in order to qualify for lower premiums. Analogues to these methods of discrimination, however, are not immediately apparent in the context of consumer product insurance. Typically, insurance policies for consumer product losses are tied to the sale of the product itself, so that the insurance pool invariably consists of all consumers who have purchased the product.

Consumers may differ in two general ways with respect to risk under a product warranty. First, the amount of use of a product during the period of warranty coverage may vary considerably between consumers. Compare, for example, the expected service costs to a washing machine manufacturer from a family with many children and from a family with only a single child. The costs of service to the large family will almost certainly be greater. If the manufacturer could define warranty coverage in terms of number of washloads, however, as an automobile manufacturer defines coverage in terms of mileage, then the expected costs from the two families to the manufacturer might be similar. But for washing machines, as well as for most other consumer appliances, the least costly measure of use appears to be duration of ownership. As a consequence, no matter what the period of coverage, the amount of use of the machine by the two families is likely to differ greatly. The insurance premium must be set to cover all expected costs of service. Thus, smaller families at the margin may find warranty protection to be worth less than its cost.

Second, the risk of loss may differ between consumers with respect to what I will call the "intensity" of product use. Compare now for the large and small families, the expected service costs to a television manufacturer. The amount of use of the television—that is, the number of viewing hours—might be identical for the two families. Nonetheless, the probability of a warranty claim is likely to be higher for the larger family, because of the greater number of individuals operating the set, because of the greater frequency of channel changes, and because of the greater risk in a large family that the set will be jostled, that the antenna will be struck, or that the machine will otherwise be treated roughly.

"Intensity" of use is inversely related to the marginal cost to the consumer of "care" for the machine, that is, the cost of allocative investments to reduce the probability of a loss. The cost of monitoring the activities of children is likely to increase as the number of children increases. Thus, the family with many children is more likely than the family with a single child to substitute recovery under a warranty for allocative investments in care of the machine. As a consequence, the cost to the manufacturer of warranty coverage will be greater for the machine sold to the larger family. Again, at the margin, consumers with smaller families may find it advantageous to shift their purchases to machines sold without, or with less, warranty coverage.

Although product insurers do not directly acquire information about consumers prior to sale, a variety of subtle methods can enable them to segregate consumers. For example, a manufacturer can develop models of a product that differ with respect to characteristics related to differences in intensities or amounts of consumer use. A manufacturer of washing machines may produce models that differ in motor size or washbasket volume that are differentially convenient to families of different sizes. If these product characteristics segregate consumers according to the extent or intensity of use, then the manufacturer can offer, for each individual model, different allocative investments and levels of warranty coverage determined by the expected warranty claims for each model.

This technique, however, may achieve only partial success. The advantage to a manufacturer of culling out higher intensity or higher volume consumers from a particular insurance pool is to enable it to offer warranty coverage at a relatively lower premium, or greater coverage at the same premium, of models designed for lower volume or intensity uses. A lower premium or more extended coverage, however, makes those machines relatively more attractive to all consumers, including those who expect to use the machine with greater intensity or in higher volume. At the margin, some of these consumers can be expected to purchase machines undersized for their needs. Such purchases substitute the extended warranty coverage of the lower volume machine for the mechanical superiority of the higher volume machine. This adverse selection by higher volume or intensity consumers will force manufacturers to reduce the extended coverage of the lower volume machine or to charge a higher premium for it. Either reaction will reduce the attractiveness of the lower volume machine to the lower risk members of the pool.

A separate but closely related method of segregating consumers is to offer warranty contracts with different terms at different premiums in conjunction with the sale of a given product. For example, automobile manufacturers have introduced insurance policies for separate fees extending coverage for periods beyond the basic period of the warranty. The optional service contract of many appliances is similar. These contracts segregate consumers according to the amount of insurance coverage they wish to buy. The warranty provides a term of basic coverage demanded by the lowest risk members of the pool. Those consumers for whom the risk is greater, however, can purchase more extensive coverage. Because relatively high-risk consumers are more likely to select such contracts, their premiums are likely to be proportionally higher for a given duration of coverage than the premiums of the basic warranty included in the sale price.

A more subtle method of differentiating consumers is the offer by many retailers of warranty coverage that is separate from and, typically, more extensive than the coverage offered by the product manufacturers themselves. This additional coverage need not be explicit. It may take the form only of a more liberal or courteous return or exchange policy. It is not uncommon, however, for retailers to announce and, thus, to make contractual a guarantee of consumer "satisfaction" that far exceeds the typical manufacturer warranty. This practice enables consumers to segregate themselves according to the level of protection each desires. Those consumers who value their time highly and who avoid allocative investments in care and maintenance or insurance investments in self-repair of products, may seek out retailers with liberal policies, although the products can be purchased at lower retail prices elsewhere. Dealers who offer more extensive warranty coverage are undoubtedly fully compensated for doing so, but their customers are less likely to be those for whom the costs of allocative investments or self-insurance are relatively low.

Finally, a manufacturer may segregate consumers by means of explicit contractual provisions in the warranty. A manufacturer, for example, may exclude warranty coverage for a particular use of a product or specific class of consumers for which the volume or intensity of use is relatively high. The common provision that excludes coverage of commercial use is an obvious example. This provision narrows the class of those insured to domestic users of the product and may be incorporated to enforce a manufacturer's segregation of domestic and commercial purchasers by model design.

Some elements of product loss, however, may be excluded from coverage in the warranties of all product models. A common example is the exclusion of liability for consequential damages. The unavailability of any coverage of some loss, nonetheless, may be related to the reduction of differences in risk between members of the insurance pool. Where consumers differ substantially in the incidence or magnitude of a loss, such as consequential damages, there may be no single premium attractive to a sufficient number to justify offering coverage. Put another way, the increase in the premium required for coverage of such losses may be greater than the benefit of coverage to large numbers of consumers. If so, the sale of product insurance may be optimized by excluding coverage altogether.

Warranty exclusions are a form of product standardization. An exclusion of some element of loss is indistinguishable analytically from the exclusion of, say, magenta and acquamarine as product colors. If the number of consumers willing to purchase machines of unusual colors is very small, it may not be worth the cost for the manufacturer to introduce the colors into the product line. Similarly, if the incidence or magnitude of an element of loss differs greatly between consumers of a product, the market for insurance may not be sufficiently large to justify offering insurance. Such a warranty exclusion enables the manufacturer to offer, for losses not excluded, either more extensive or less costly warranty coverage than if no exclusion were made, just as the production of appliances in a limited range of colors lowers price by reducing the costs of production and distribution. In this respect, consumers of the product may be said to have demanded the exclusions.

The segregation of consumers by explicit contractual provisions, however, is effective only to the extent that the manufacturer can identify prior to sale those consumers, product uses, or elements of loss for which differences in risk across the set of potential consumers are great. All those not identified and segregated must be lumped into a common pool, high-risk and low-risk alike. The terms of the standard warranty, then, establish the minimum level of coverage that is demanded uniformly by each member of the large class of purchasers; that is, a base level that can be supplemented in the variety of ways suggested above by those consumers desiring more extensive protection. The standard level of coverage comprises the minimum performance bond necessary to encourage appropriate investments by manufacturers in the design or mechanical qualities of the product and the minimum insurance coverage demanded by the lowest risk members of the consumer pool.

Grant Gilmore, *Products Liability: A Commentary*, 38 U. CHI. L. REV. 103 (1970)*

To the extent that we make use of the model hypothesized by the Coase theorem in making judgments about what we should do in the real world, the exercise leads us to conclude that we should do nothing; we should go no further; we should stop where we are. But I see no relationship between Professor Coase's world in which there are no transaction costs and all exchanges are voluntary, and a world in which there are always transaction costs and few, if any, exchanges that are voluntary. I am not persuaded by economic analysis to say to the world: "Stop"—even if I thought that was a sensible thing to say to a world so irrevocably caught up in its gravitational system. Nor am I persuaded that we would all be as happy as larks if we could somehow get back to *Winterbottom v. Wright*—although I hasten to add that I am sure that *Winterbottom* was quite as sensible a case in England in 1842 as *Goldberg v. Kollsman Instrument Corp.* was in New York in 1963. It may be that what had changed between 1842 and 1963 was not so much the law as the societies which the law reflects.

My point is that most cases—perhaps all cases—are sensibly, or even "correctly," decided as of their own time and place. Exploring this point, I will indulge myself in a brief digression on a landmark of the common law which takes us back two centuries before *Winterbottom v. Wright*—a case called *Chandelor v. Lopus,* which was decided by the Exchequer Chamber in 1625. A goldsmith had sold for £100 a stone which he "affirmed" to be a bezoar. The stone turned out not to be a bezoar. The disappointed buyer, who had presumably paid the price for a true bezoar, brought an action to recover damages for, as we should say, breach of warranty. Judgment for the goldsmith-seller: he had merely "affirmed" that the stone was a bezoar without "warranting" it to be one wherefore the buyer's action did not lie. For several hundred years the case has been cited, with approval or with scorn, as illustrative of the extremely narrow scope of liability which seventeenth-century law placed on sellers for the quality of the goods they sold.

The report of the case does not bother to explain what a bezoar was—presumably everybody knew what a bezoar was, just as we all know what a diamond is. It occurred to me one day, in thinking about the case, that I for one had no idea what a bezoar might be. The Oxford Dictionary proved to be illuminating. A bezoar (or "bezar") was, descriptively, "a calculus or concretion found in the stomachs of some animals, chiefly ruminants, formed of concentric layers of animal matter deposited round some foreign substance, which serves as a nucleus." That explains everything except why a bezoar would have been worth £100 in the early seventeenth-century. The true value of a bezoar, it appears, lay in its magic or, as we should say, medicinal properties: application of the bezoar to a diseased part of the body cured the disease. "Everything that frees the body of any ailment," it was said, "is called the Bezoar of that ailment." And the East India Company had reported in 1618 that: "On the island of Borneo, diamonds, bezoar stones and gold might be obtained."

Now that we know more about bezoars than we did, we may begin to wonder whether our initial reaction to the holding in *Chandelor v. Lopus* was, historically, correct—or even relevant to the case. It was generally known that there were true, or magic, bezoars. It must also have

*Used by permission.

been a matter of common knowledge that it was extremely difficult, if not impossible, to tell a true bezoar from a false one. And no doubt the attitude of the user counted for something: if I believed in my bezoar it might indeed preserve me from the plague, while the same stone in the hands of a skeptical rationalist would be worthless. Under such circumstances a court might hesitate to impose liability on a seller who had merely said that, to the best of his knowledge, he believed (or affirmed) the stone to be a bezoar, but did not warrant it. It may be that the seventeenth-century concept of liability was not as narrow as we have supposed it to be. This digression, at all events, goes to the point that law cases—and rules of law—are really not abstract propositions, although we like to phrase them, and talk about them, as if they were. The cases and the rules—and indeed the codifying statutes—are merely particular responses to particular states of fact (assumed to be true whether or not they are). The law is, and I dare say always will be, *ad hoc* and *ad hominem* to a fault.

Just as everyone accepts the Coase theorem, so everybody accepts the proposition that in the course of the past hundred years there has been a notable expansion of seller's (and particularly manufacturer's) liability toward the buyers (or users) of goods sold. The allocation of the risks inherent in the use of the goods has tended to shift from the buyer-user to the seller-manufacturer. Professor McKean cautions us that "the *magnitude* of the shift in liability assignment *so far* has not been dramatic. The main thing that has happened lately is a further modest increase in the probability that injured persons will be compensated by the producer." [Roland N. McKean, *Products Liability—Trends and Implications,* 38 U. Chi. L. Rev. 3, 21-22 (1970)]. As he points out, no court has ("so far") imposed truly strict liability—that is, allowed recovery where all that the injured plaintiff proved was that his injury resulted from his use of the goods. To date even the most "advanced" or "humanitarian" courts have insisted that the plaintiff prove, additionally, that the goods, whose use caused the injury, were, in some sense, "defective." And "defective," as Professor McKean argues, can be taken to mean approximately the same thing that "fault" or "negligence" meant in the old cases—so that there has been at most a "modest," not a "dramatic," realignment of liabilities.

And yet I am inclined to wonder whether there may not be more in the terminological switch from "negligence" to "defective" than meets the eye. A rose, we have been told on good authority, by any other name would smell as sweet. And yet, if we start calling a rose by some other name, something important has obviously happened: our conception or perception of the rose has fundamentally changed—otherwise we would still call it a rose. We now think differently about what we used to call roses—which may affect not only ourselves but also the roses (or ex-roses). Quite possibly the rose will go on smelling as sweet as it does only so long as we go on calling it a rose. Professor McKean is obviously in the right when he says that "defective" can be made to bear the same freight of meaning that "negligence" used to bear. But I am not at all sure that things will work out, or have been working out, that way: if that was in the cards, I think we would have gone on saying "negligence."

I will, therefore, mildly object to Professor McKean's downgrading of the revolution: there has been not a "modest" but a dramatic shift in the allocation of liability. Whether the shift has been modest or dramatic is irrelevant to Professor McKean's argument, on his own premises. But it is the prerogative of any commentator to switch the premises, without warning, which is what I now propose to do.

"Products Liability" is a term that has come into use only in recent years. Lawyers used to talk, more cumbersomely, of liability for breach of warranty, without bothering to make clear whether they were talking about liability in contract or liability in tort. Warranty law indeed has always had one foot in contract and the other foot in tort and this ambiguous straddle over the great legal divide has done a great deal to keep the legal discussion open-ended. Whenever a particular state of doctrine on one side or the other of the divide has seemed to present a roadblock to further progress, it has been possible to get around the obstacle by pointing out that the action is really in tort (if the roadblock is on the contract side) or really in contract (if the roadblock is on the tort side). In days when the courts took the concept of "negligence" more seriously than they do now, the escape from carrying the burden of proof on that issue was to emphasize the absolute promissory nature of contract warranties; in the course of that demonstration there developed the vast and intricate structure of the law of implied warranties. In this century the roadblocks have been located mostly on the contract side—the defenses of privity of contract, of disclaimer, of the plaintiff's failure to give timely notice of the defect—so that we have become accustomed to thinking of tort as providing the escape route. But if the going were to become rough in tort—if, for example, by judicial reversal or statutory reform, a meaningful concept of fault as a condition of recovery in the tort action were reintroduced—we would no doubt revert almost instinctively to emphasizing the contract nature of the action.

It will be noted that "Products Liability" identifies a field of law much more narrowly circumscribed than what would be included if we followed the older usage and said "liability for breach of warranty." The warranty concept covers transfers not only of goods but of real property and, for that matter, negotiable instruments and intangible claims. Even if we restrict ourselves to goods, the concept covers not only the products of a complex technology but, indifferently, the farmer's horse or crop of hay or stock of firewood. And throughout most of our history we have not differentiated, as to warranty liability, between the simple and the complex. The coming into use of such a term as "Products Liability" suggests that we are beginning to make such a differentiation—or at least that those who use the term think that we ought to make such a differentiation. The liability of one who furnishes a "product"—which obviously means a complex artifact—should be thought about differently from the liability of one who furnishes a simple thing like a horse or a haystack or a cord of firewood.

This identification of a new field of law, by way of narrowing or subdividing a previous, broader field, is a recurrent phenomenon in our legal history. For example, there are no references, much before 1800, to a law of sales of goods, conceived as a branch of law separate and distinct from the law of sales of property in general. The new field organized itself, with astonishing rapidity, within half a century following the Industrial Revolution of the eighteenth-century. In much the same way the law of insurance in the nineteenth-century and labor law in this century split off, or were divorced from, the undifferentiated law of general or simple contracts. The appearance of a new "field" or "branch" of law is always a matter of great interest: it teaches us that something new and important has taken place and gives us, as it were, a new fix on the elephant. Thus the recent surfacing of something called Products Liability, with the suggestion that the time may have come for differentiating the law of complex artifacts from the law of simple goods, is something with a claim to be taken seriously. And, as the spate of law review articles over the past ten years shows, it is being taken seriously.

And yet, in the understandable excitement of realizing that we may have come on something new—Products Liability—we are, I think, in danger of putting ourselves in blinkers by concentrating too narrowly on what appears to be going on in our newly discovered landfall. I will suggest, at all events, that we can profitably broaden our discussion. I will put forward this proposition: that the expansion of seller's or manufacturer's liability for the use of goods manufactured or sold is by no means an isolated development in the newly discovered area of Products Liability; a comparable expansion of liability has been going on, notably since 1900, over the whole spectrum of our law of civil obligations, alike in contract and in tort.

This proposition obviously does not rise to the dignity of a theorem: I could not prove it if I were, like Gibbon, to scribble on for the rest of my natural life. But let us assume, arguendo, that my proposition expresses at least one of the many possible faces of truth—that what has been going on in Products Liability is merely a special instance of what has been going on over a much broader front. If that is so, we would be at fault, as lawyers or as economists, in dealing with the special instance as if it were an isolated, or isolatable, phenomenon. In trying to understand it or explain it or criticize it—or even clarify our thought about it—we should at least make an attempt to see it in the broader context.

In our legal system we have—largely as the result of historical accident—split the whole field of civil obligation into contract obligations and tort obligations. Essentially the distinction is that the typical contract obligation is one that was voluntarily assumed (or at least the transaction that gave rise to the obligation was voluntarily entered into) whereas the typical tort obligation is one that was blundered or stumbled into through accident, negligence or fraud. The categories merge or blur at the edges: we have come to speak of a no man's land between contract and tort as quasi-contract although we might just as well have called it quasi-tort.

In most situations of this type we can identify an active and a passive party. In tort there is the tortfeasor and his victim. In contract there is typically one party who has undertaken to provide goods, services or whatever to another party whose only duty is to pay for what he receives. We will speak of performing parties (*e.g.*, sellers) and paying parties (*e.g.*, buyers).

Our law of contract is almost entirely a nineteenth-century construct—there is little or nothing (except for some antiquarian embroidery) whose roots go back in time beyond the Industrial Revolution. Indeed the first authoritative formulations of our theory of contractual obligation came late in the nineteenth-century, with Langdell, Holmes and Williston in this country and Pollock in England. These writers put together, from bits and pieces of then fairly recent case law, a comprehensive theory of contract in much the same way that the staff of a natural history museum might reconstruct a dinosaur from a tooth or two and a few odd scraps of bone. It is impossible not to conceive the greatest admiration for the ingenuity of their construction; it is equally impossible to escape the conclusion that they achieved their results by overstating their cases and by erecting monumental hypotheses based on the flimsiest substructure of evidence or fact. What came out was no doubt responsive to the spirit and ethos of the time: we get not only the governments but also the theories we deserve.

As we look back, the nineteenth-century construct seems to have favored the active or performing over the passive or paying party to a degree that we now find difficult to comprehend. It may be that a society which had not yet learned to think of itself as affluent and in which the remembered threat of famine and scarcity still weighed more heavily on the mind of man than present visions of glut and abundance treasured any form of social action—particularly any form of action which would increase the aggregate production of manufactured goods. Such action should be encouraged in all possible ways—it received indeed, in addition to the unqualified blessing of press and pulpit, the weighty approval of the best, or at least the most respectable, economic theorists. One of the ways in which it was sought to be encouraged was by the prompt provision of a legal structure which cast the risks of enterprise or action on the passive recipients of its bounty and insulated the actor from the incidentally harmful consequences of his socially useful activity.

During the past seventy-five years or so the legal rules and doctrines which successfully immunized actors or enterprisers from liability have been in process of breakdown. The process could, with equal facility, be traced on either the tort or the contract side. I shall, impressionistically and without any attempt to document my statements, describe some of the things that have been going on in contract during this century.

Under the rules of offer and acceptance, as they came to be formulated in the late nineteenth century, no contractual obligation could be imposed until the last *i* had been dotted and the last *t* crossed. Courts, it was said, did not make contracts for the parties; the undotted *i* or the uncrossed *t* was fatal and the courts would do nothing about it. Nor was any duty recognized to deal fairly or in good faith with the other party during what may be called the pre-contractual period while negotiations are going on but the deal has not yet been worked out to its last detail. Until the contractual trap was sprung, I could lead you on and keep you in play as long as I wanted (or was able) to without coming under any liability to you if at the last minute I decided to cut you loose. And if, without the protection of a binding contract, you incurred expenses, in reliance on my presumed good faith, the resulting loss was yours, not mine. These rules, were, of course, stated as two-way streets: either party could take advantage of them. Factually it was the enterpriser, the performing party, who could manipulate the rules to his own advantage and delay binding himself while being in a position to spring the trap on the other party whenever he pleased.

Just as the rules made it extremely difficult to get into a contract in the first place, so they made it extremely difficult to escape from a contractual obligation once imposed. The rules of discharge, like the rules of offer and acceptance, were stated in terms of even-handed justice: nothing short of absolute impossibility or the act of God would discharge either party to a contract. The way this worked out, for example, between sellers and buyers, was this: buyers were never discharged, no matter how catastrophically the contract had turned against them, while sellers were discharged with great liberality. As to buyers: it is never impossible, the courts explained, to pay money. As to sellers: if the goods which the seller has contracted to sell are destroyed before they have been transferred to the buyer, or if the source of supply from which the seller expected to obtain the goods becomes unavailable, it is, "obviously," strictly impossible for him to perform the contract—wherefore he is discharged. And, some courts suggested, if the case is that the seller can still perform the contract but only at a cost greatly in excess of the contract price, there too he should be discharged on a theory of "economic impossibility."

Damages for breach of contract, we have been told for a hundred years, are meant to be compensatory—no more, no less. What is compensatory? When a buyer breaches a contract, it is hard to imagine a case where the seller's damage claim can exceed the contract price; under nineteenth-century sales law seller, on buyer's breach, was almost routinely entitled to recover the full price. When a seller breaches a contract, the losses which the buyer may suffer as the direct result of the breach need not be limited to the contract price and may largely exceed it. The whole structure of the nineteenth-century damage law seems to have been dedicated to the proposition that the buyer should get no more than a token recovery. The buyer could almost never get the goods in any form of action; he was remitted to his action in damages and in that action what he was entitled to was the differential between the contract price and the (higher) market price at the time and place when the seller ought to have delivered them. For a buyer to recover any more than that differential was about as easy as it is thought to be for a camel to pass through the needle's eye. (Larger damages—for injury to person or property—were recoverable in the action for breach of warranty, but of course that action was cribbed, cabined and confined by the many available contract defenses that Professor McKean has described for us.)

I have briefly suggested three aspects of nineteenth-century contract doctrine which worked in favor of sellers against buyers or of performing parties against paying parties. At the cost of another dozen pages, I could add a dozen more examples—which, however, I will not burden you with. I should add that I have been describing the overt or received doctrines of the period. It is entirely possible to demonstrate, by a sophisticated analysis, that sometimes or frequently or even most of the time what the courts did in fact did not jibe with what they said they were doing. But, jurisprudentially, what the courts say they are doing is at least as interesting as what they do—particularly when they say one thing and do another. That line of thought, however, would take us into uncomfortably deep waters and I will not further pursue it.

An observer of the current contract scene, as contrasted with the one I have been describing, could only conclude that a revolution must have taken place. Indeed, as we all know, a revolution has taken place and it would be surprising if it had not left its traces on our law of contract. The old offer and acceptance rules have quite broken down. Courts do indeed make contracts for the parties, dotting any number of *i*'s and crossing any number of *t*'s; they have indeed been directed to do so by statute. The idea of a pre-contractual duty of good faith and fair dealing has come to the surface; maybe it was there, hidden, all the time but now, for the first time, it is being talked about openly in the respectable columns of the *Harvard Law Review*. The old law of strict impossibility has given way to the so-called doctrine of frustration: if a party's purpose in entering into a contract has been "frustrated" by an untoward turn of events, he should be discharged. Under this approach buyers are now discharged quite as liberally as sellers ever were. While the seller's right to recover the price on buyer's breach has been severely cut back, the buyer's right to get the goods, on seller's refusal to deliver them, has been correspondingly expanded. And one of the most dramatic events of the past thirty years or so has been the rewriting of the law of damages in favor of buyers claiming large recoveries and the rapid development of the idea that reliance losses should be reimbursed even when they are incurred without the protection of a binding contract.

The point of the foregoing discussion is that the same reversal of risks, which Professor McKean has documented in the Products Liability cases, has been going on all over the place. It has been, no doubt, all part and parcel of the great shift, so bitterly lamented in many quarters, from laissez-faire to the Welfare State and beyond. We falsify and distort our discussion if we isolate for analysis one particular ripple in the tidal wave—at least we falsify and distort if we end up arguing that our chosen ripple ought to have gone this way even though the rest of the wave went that way.

There is no point in arguing with a revolution. It may be that whatever can be pulled down ought to be pulled down; if it is no longer strong enough to withstand assault, it should be replaced by something that is. In this sense any successful revolution is self-justifying: by its success it has revealed the inadequacies of what it has replaced. We may have a romantic attachment to the old regime but we should not let it cloud our thought about present reality.

I do not for a moment dispute or deny the great value of abstract theoretical analysis or the pure delight of engaging in it. I doubt that it gives us, or is meant to give us, guidance in handling real problems in the real world. It is entirely within the realm of possibility that the forces which have determined the shift in risk allocation which has been going on for the better part of a hundred years will cease to operate and that we will reverse our course or set out in a new direction never before dreamed of. But that, if it were to happen, would have nothing to do with the fact that we had at last learned to think clearly about what was going on. The wit of man is from the start overmatched by the weight of circumstance and, except in the simplest situations, thinking clearly and acting sensibly really have nothing to do with each other.

C. Crime and Punishment

Michael B. Metzger, *Corporate Criminal Liability for Defective Products: Policies, Problems, and Prospects,* 73 Geo. L.J. 1 (1984)*

With properly drafted legislation, criminal liability for defective products can readily be imposed on corporations. To say a thing *can* be done, however, is not to say it *should* be done.

Individual Criminal Liability

Many observers have argued that focusing criminal penalties on responsible individuals within the corporation provides better deterrence without unfairly stigmatizing the firm or its innocent officers and employees or punishing innocent shareholders and consumers. Corporate officers, like other white-collar criminals, are seen as uniquely susceptible to the deterrent effect of the threat of criminal sanctions: they are particularly sensitive to the stigma associated with a criminal conviction, dread the prospect of incarceration, and can rationally calculate the risks associated with their criminal behavior. Subjecting corporate officers to the threat of criminal sanctions may also provide corporations with additional incentives to comply with the law, because such corporations might otherwise be inclined to treat financial penalties as nothing more than a cost of doing business.

Imposing personal liability on corporate officers may serve other preventive aims by reinforcing notions of personal responsibility in the organizational context and strengthening employees' incentives to resist corporate pressures to violate the law. Holding corporate executives criminally responsible under some form of vicarious liability standard for offenses originating from corporate operations over which they have formal authority may encourage them to ensure that they have knowledge of, and exercise actual control over, activities that could lead to a criminal conviction. Applying the criminal sanction to corporate executives may also be necessary to mitigate the public perception that white-collar offenders are treated differently from the perpetrators of street crime and to shift the present public attitude that corporate crime is not therefore as morally blameworthy. Finally, punishing individual corporate officers may also punish the corporate entity itself, because the conviction and incarceration of experienced managers may hurt corporate profitability and tarnish a corporation's public image.

Despite its myriad theoretical advantages, however, imposing individual criminal liability in the corporate context is often exceedingly difficult, particularly if we adhere to traditional notions of moral culpability. The realities of the corporate decisionmaking process make pinpointing responsible individuals within the firm expensive and problematic. Organizations are unlikely to cooperate with investigators seeking to ascribe responsibility to their employees.

Also, since corporate decisionmaking and corporate action tend to be collective in nature, a given corporate offense may be attributable to the actions of numerous individuals in various levels of the corporate hierarchy. Moreover, the diffusion of responsibility that characterizes the modern

*Used by permission.

large corporation often can make ascription of individual responsibility exceedingly difficult, if not impossible. These problems place difficult and costly burdens on prosecutorial resources.

These realities converge with particular force upon attempts to impose individual liability on upper-level executives who, from a deterrence standpoint, are probably the most desirable targets of sanctions and who may have created the very policies or pressures that led to the violation. It is often difficult to prove that upper-level corporate executives possess knowledge of corporate offenses sufficient to ascribe responsibility to them. Complex organizational structures and gaps in internal control and communication systems can insulate them from such knowledge. Lower-level employees may also prevent "bad news" from reaching their superiors, in part because they may perceive that their superiors "don't want to hear about" it. Upper-level executives may also deliberately avoid acquiring such knowledge and may operate by a system of informal communication that makes their role in corporate decisionmaking difficult to prove. Finally, subordinates may anticipate their supervisors' desires and act accordingly without advance authorization of any kind.

The result is that a wrong may not be attributable to any culpable individual, either because organizational complexity obscures individual responsibility or because the source of the wrong was internal bureaucratic failures rather than the deliberate act of any particular corporate employee or employees. When culpable individuals can be identified, they often tend to be middle managers who carry out corporate policy, rather than the upper-level executives who formulate it. This causes obvious problems for deterrence, because prosecutors may hesitate to indict, and juries to convict, subordinate employees whom they perceive as "taking the rap" for an unidentified superior or as innocent victims of an evil system rather than morally responsible actors. Also, if middle-level managers become, in effect, the sole targets, firms may be encouraged to view them as fungible scapegoats, easily replaced. Nor would imposing vicarious criminal liability on upper-level corporate executives necessarily result either in deterrence or in punishing the morally culpable. Because actual authority may not correspond with formal authority, the individual who is formally responsible for the operations that generated the wrongful act may not have made the decisions or created the policies which culminated in the wrong.

Even if responsible individuals can be identified with an acceptable degree of certainty, there are still significant obstacles to bringing against them the deterrent force of criminal sanctions. They may have died, retired, moved on to another company, or have been transferred beyond the reach of the jurisdiction in which the wrong occurred. Convicted white-collar offenders are likely to get a fine, probation, or a suspended sentence. When incarceration is imposed, the sentences tend to be short, parole before the offender has fully served his sentence is highly likely, and the offender is likely to be sent to a "country club" institution.

The reluctance to incarcerate white-collar defendants is usually attributed to the favorable public image these defendants possess and to the public perception that most white-collar offenses are not morally blameworthy. Meaningful incarceration threats thus are likely to be achieved only if the public perceives that committing a white-collar offense involves significant moral culpability. Yet significant increases in the incarceration of convicted executives are probably unrealistic. Even where sufficient culpability can be demonstrated to warrant tough sentences, it is doubtful whether we, as a society, are willing to pay the price necessary to eliminate white-collar crime.

Imposing fines on white-collar defendants is an equally unpromising deterrent. At present, fines imposed on white-collar defendants tend to be quite small. Imposing higher maximum fines in order to increase deterrence may be ineffective, however, if the corporate employees who are fined are indemnified by their employers. Although the convicted white-collar criminal who avoids incarceration and whose fine is reimbursed by his employer may nonetheless suffer the stigma associated with a criminal conviction, convicted executives appear to get significant peer support and to suffer little career damage. Moreover, fines could reach only those corporate officers who had significant financial resources.

Other proposals to improve the effectiveness of individual sanctions include increasing criminal prosecutions by administrative agencies and statutorily designating the corporate executive responsible for assuring compliance. Administrative agencies, however, are unlikely to press for criminal convictions unless they believe such convictions will be secured and will result in meaningful sanctions. In addition, legislative designation of responsible parties within the corporate hierarchy, without more, will not necessarily result in the targeted individuals having the actual authority, and thus the moral culpability, required in order to impose severe sanctions.

The manifest difficulties in bringing conventional criminal penalties against white-collar defendants have led to less conventional suggestions. One proposal would bar convicted defendants from holding corporate positions for a fixed period. Other proposals include probationary dispositions utilizing the deprivation of leisure time and personal-service restitution to victims of corporate offenses. If we conclude that individual liability, either standing alone or in conjunction with corporate liability, is a desirable method for dealing with corporate crime, these alternative approaches may offer the best hope for consistent and meaningful punishment of white-collar criminals because they are not so draconian as to inhibit judges and juries from regularly imposing them.

Ultimately, an inquiring policymaker needs to consider what other social costs might result from a well-conceived, vigorously waged campaign to impose individual criminal liability on corporate officers. This effort might limit individual initiative, stifle innovation, and sacrifice growth. Individual liability could harm corporate efficiency by diverting employee attention away from legitimate corporate concerns like quality control, product durability, and efficiency because engineers and managers would be unwilling to approve new product designs involving unknown risks or risks that might later be considered unacceptable. Whether, and to what degree, these costs would result, and whether they would be offset by gains flowing from the imposition of individual liability, are plainly matters of judgment.

A prevention strategy based exclusively on individual liability may be less than desirable for many other reasons. If the corporation is immune from prosecution, the entity may stand to gain rather than to lose from the offenses of its employees. Individual liability, unlike corporate liability, does not force the corporation to remit the profits that may flow from an offense, and thus may not counter illicit profit motives at their source or give corporate executives sufficient incentives to try to prevent violations by subordinates. Of course, the profit motive may not be the genesis of many socially undesirable corporate acts, and civil products liability cases arguably can force the organization to disgorge ill-gotten gains. But when the source of the offense is institutional, individual liability coupled with organizational immunity is unlikely to reduce significantly the incidence of corporate offenses. Individuals are ordinarily dispensable in large bureaucratic organizations. Unless internal structural changes to the organizations are effected, individual corporate officers who are incarcerated or otherwise removed from the organization will be replaced by others likely to respond in a similar fashion. Only corporate-entity liability offers the prospect of structural modification.

Numerous other assertions have been made on behalf of corporate liability. In a group-based society, it may simply be more efficient to deal with groups rather than with their individual human components. Holding organizations responsible focuses on the *corporate* aspects of corporate crime, presents fewer prosecutorial problems, and punishes the organization in circumstances where it may be unjust to punish individuals. Corporate liability may be necessary in order to avoid punishing only officers of small corporations, which are less effective than large corporations at shielding individual responsibility. Individual liability could thus result in conferring de facto immunity upon officers of large corporations, a factor that could make it more difficult for smaller firms to attract and hold good executives. Corporate liability may also encourage employees and officers to see the larger *res publica*, rather than the corporation, as the primary source of rules of social obligation. But imposing criminal penalties on corporate entities remains far from ideal in conception and application.

The Efficacy and Desirability of Corporate Criminal Liability

The major purpose advanced for corporate criminal liability is preventive: the hope that the *in terrorem* effect of criminal sanctions aimed at the corporation will deter illegal acts by corporate agents. These sanctions may prompt corporations to undertake internal disciplinary measures aimed at avoiding liability. This approach theoretically offers certain efficiency gains by augmenting the state's limited investigative and enforcement resources with internal corporate resources. It may be easier for corporations to detect internal misbehavior than for the state to do so, since corporations have a better idea of where to look for violations, are not bound by fourth or fifth amendment restrictions on searches and seizures or self-incrimination, and can dismiss employees for behavior and on evidence that would not suffice to prove guilt beyond a reasonable doubt. The corporate employer and the employment environment may have a stronger, more immediate influence over employee behavior than the more remote threat of criminal sanctions aimed at employees. Rules of conduct formulated by those concerned with their daily implementation offer a more refined system of control than that which can be achieved solely by external regulation. Possible positive corporate responses to the threat of criminal sanctions include training, supervisory, and disciplinary efforts aimed at preventing future violations, and organizational changes that clarify internal responsibility and encourage employees to act lawfully. Also, if internal discipline, training, and supervision inculcate individuals to form law-abiding routines, the state is able efficiently to achieve the more general preventive effects of habitual individual compliance with legal norms.

Corporate criminal liability has also been justified on the grounds that it can serve remedial ends like compensation, restitution, and restoration. Some types of corporate wrongs may unjustly enrich the corporation without resulting in losses that are recoverable by private parties. Remedial fines imposed as a condition of avoidance of prosecution, or of probation, discharge, or deferment or reduction of sentence can take up some of the "remedial slack" in such cases. Statutes imposing corporate criminal liability could also create a private right to recovery, thereby augmenting the enforcement resources of the state by utilizing private attorneys general. These arguments appear relatively inapposite in civil products liability, however, where potentially dramatic punitive damages are already available for the kinds of corporate behavior which would be the proper subject for criminal liability. While technical rules may hinder the civil recovery of certain plaintiffs, a strong case could be made that reducing vagaries in the availability of civil remedies would be less problematic than imposing criminal sanctions, particularly if our aim is remedial.

Corporate criminal liability may serve retributive ends, as well. Immunizing corporate entities from criminal liability suggests a tolerance of corporate deviance which may legitimize deviance from civil norms elsewhere in the community and which consequently may erode the moral base of the legal system. Imposing criminal sanctions in the corporate context thus may serve retributive ends by helping to retain public confidence in the rule of law.

The publicity associated with the prosecution of a corporate defendant can provide the public with information that counters undeservedly good corporate reputations and lessens public ignorance about the nature and extent of harms perpetrated by corporations. Publicity can also warn those who may suffer harm as a result of a corporation's acts, provide investors and consumers with relevant information, and alert those who have already suffered harm to the possibility of filing private actions. Adverse publicity can tarnish the image that employees, shareholders, suppliers, customers, and potential customers have of the firm. An adverse public image can thus affect a firm's sales volume, its management recruiting, the prestige enjoyed by its management, and perhaps its ability to attract capital. Indeed, the threat of negative publicity may carry more deterrent force than the threat of fines as presently applied.

Stigmatizing a legal fiction remains problematic, however. Conceiving of corporations as "criminals" may be difficult for the average person, resulting in less damage to the corporate image than anticipated. Widespread publicity is a prerequisite before a corporation's public image is significantly sullied, but media coverage of corporate crime appears less than adequate. Media attention appears to be directed principally at corporate wrongdoing that results in personal injury or death—conduct that is like the harm conventionally associated with criminality, and for which punitive damages are available. Given that it is the nature of the injury, not the nature of the sanction, that creates newsworthiness, one wonders whether a well-publicized criminal conviction would diminish a corporation's image in a manner substantially different, either qualitatively or quantitatively, from a well-publicized punitive damages award. Finally, is it just or fair to stigmatize indirectly all officers, directors, and employees of a corporation by convicting the corporation for an offense that may have resulted from the acts of only a few individuals?

The traditional sanction imposed on convicted corporate criminal defendants is the monetary fine. Criminal fines are not tax deductible, and represent an obvious threat to corporate profits. Fines can remove the profit motive for corporate crime by forcing convicted corporations to disgorge profits that would otherwise flow from a violation.

Observers have argued that criminal fines, as presently administered, are incapable of serving a preventive function. The fines imposed on corporations tend to be too small to affect corporate profits significantly, and thus may be treated by offenders and potential offenders as a cost of doing business. The most common solutions offered to augment the deterrent force of fines involve increasing the amount of statutorily authorized fines and persuading courts to impose maximum fines. These proposals possess obvious intuitive appeal, for fines of sufficient size would arguably make an impression even on firms that are not profit-maximizers or that respond to their environments in a nonrational fashion.

Increased cash fines raise a significant ethical concern, however. Corporate fines cannot truly "punish" the corporation; they really punish, either directly or indirectly, particular individuals who receive benefits from the corporation. Such punishment inevitably affects the innocent as well as the guilty, and thus has about it an unpleasant air of randomness. These ethical arguments do not impress proponents of corporate criminal liability. Commentators commonly note that shareholders' losses cannot exceed equity. Moreover, losses from criminal fines are indistinguishable from losses resulting from corporate civil liability or from mismanagement, and thus should be considered simply another investment risk.

However one resolves these issues, it is apparent that dramatic increases in corporate fines would simply exacerbate the problem. Fines of sufficient size to threaten corporate solvency may be required for meaningful special deterrence, since large corporations can easily absorb even relatively large fines. Extraordinarily severe penalties may also be required for general deterrence, because rational actors will discount the expected punishment by the likelihood of apprehension, prosecution, conviction, and meaningful punishment. Yet fines of that magnitude would aggravate injury to shareholders, and would probably produce large-scale layoffs of innocent employees who derived little, if any, benefit from the violation, with consequent negative impact on local communities, suppliers, and customers. Huge fines probably are not politically feasible, however, and even if they were, there is considerable doubt whether courts would actually impose them, since courts may fear the spillover effect on innocent parties. Massive fines also raise efficiency issues: enforcement costs tend to rise with penalty levels, and, more seriously, high penalty levels heighten the risk of overdeterrence.

* * *

Interventionist and Noninterventionist Proposals

Several existing noninterventionist devices could augment the threat of fines. Allowing private plaintiffs as private attorneys general to file class actions or to recover treble damages would dramatically enhance the corporation's risk of detection and of eventual financial loss. Private enforcers, however, may misrepresent their injury, and, unlike public enforcers, have no interest in the development of a rational body of law. In addition, the combination of high potential damages and private enforcement may force defendants to settle civil suits or enter *nolo contendere* pleas, even if convinced of their innocence, in order to avoid potentially catastrophic liability. Finally, to the extent that private enforcement ultimately results in the imposition of dramatic monetary penalties upon target corporations, spillover problems similar to those associated with massive fines inevitably occur, although perhaps with some additional justification derived from the compensatory aspects of class actions and treble damages.

A more novel approach to fashioning effective financial threats against corporations is Professor John Coffee's suggestion that a convicted corporation be forced to issue equity securities to a state-administered victim-compensation fund. "Equity fines" would allow the imposition of higher penalties than a corporation could pay in cash, would pose a less immediate threat to a corporation's future than would a large cash fine, and would serve compensatory as well as deterrent ends. Equity fines would also pose a significant threat to corporate management, not only because managers' self-interest is identified with the value of corporate stock, but also because such fines could represent a threat to corporate control. Equity fines may also minimize the externalities associated with large cash fines because their effect would be concentrated on shareholders, they would be less likely to be passed on to consumers, and they would pose little threat to corporate creditors since they could not result in insolvency.

The impact of equity fines on innocent shareholders raises issues similar to those associated with cash fines, however. While lower-level corporate employees would probably not face the loss of employment that could accompany a large cash fine, they may nonetheless be hurt by the dilution in value of corporate stock held in, for example, pension plans or profit-sharing plans. The widespread use of equity fines could cause an anticipatory decline in the share value of companies perceived as operating in "risky areas." Policymakers must ponder the equities of so punishing the shareholders of all such companies and the effect on the economy as a whole if investors were to shun perceived high-risk industries. Ultimately, equity fines, while an improvement over cash fines, share the same fundamental flaw: they are largely noninterventionist in character. Only in rare instances would an equity fine result in the sort of internal restructuring that may be necessary to prevent future corporate violations.

For a truly interventionist approach to corporate control, one must turn to corporate probation. Probation can serve both remedial and preventive ends by ordering convicted corporations to make restitution for harms or to terminate operations in areas susceptible to future violations. More importantly, the imaginative use of probation can provide both a better understanding of the internal factors that contributed to a violation and a device for ordering internal restructuring. Corporate defendants could be required to conduct self-studies, or to hire outside counsel or consultants who would conduct investigations, in order to identify the cause of misconduct and propose appropriate probation conditions. If such a study, or the state's investigation, indicates that bureaucratic failures caused or contributed to the offense, the court could, as a condition of probation, order the restructuring of limited, discrete corporate decisionmaking procedures. This approach is similar to that employed in recent years by courts in cases involving prisons, mental-health facilities, and schools, and by various regulatory-agency consent decrees. Restructuring represents rehabilitation in the corporate context, and would vary depending upon the particular case.

Judicially ordered restructuring offers several advantages over financial threats. Rather than treating the corporation as a "black box," restructuring imposes direct and selective restraints on the organization's handling of its internal problems. Restructuring can enhance individual accountability within the organization by clarifying individual responsibility, by assuring that identified officers have the information necessary to hold them liable for future violations, and by reducing the costs of identification and prosecution in the event of a violation. The threat of restructuring may also have a deterrent impact on managers who fear both the loss of autonomy and the additional burdens of compliance associated with judicial intervention. Restructuring also may prevent violations caused by bureaucratic flaws like defective standard operating procedures. In addition, judicially ordered restructuring appears less costly than fines, with a consequently minimal spillover on innocent parties.

Numerous criticisms can be made of court-ordered restructuring, however. Restructuring would constitute another governmental intrusion into the private sector and, unless carefully limited, could develop into "a system of judicial socialism with courts and probation officers running most public corporations." Restructuring runs counter to arguments for market superiority which hold that those whose well-being is tied to the corporation are best able to avoid legal penalties in the most cost-efficient manner, and that firms that fail to respond efficiently will incur competitive disadvantages that will ultimately lead to their decline. Some observers have also argued that the courts are not well suited to organizational intervention: courts are incapable of collecting the data necessary to determine whether and how to alter internal organizational processes, and judges may not have the expertise to evaluate the evidence they do receive. Finally, there is a very real risk that the organization will informally subvert the formal structural modifications dictated by judicial intervention.

Several rejoinders are available. Restructuring is certainly less intrusive than corporate reform proposals aimed at restructuring a board of directors in the name of securing more socially responsible corporate behavior, and is apt to have less disastrous social consequences than do massive cash fines. Furthermore, courts are likely to tread warily in the uncharted territory of judicial intervention into corporate operations—as well they should. The dangers of "judicial socialism" are probably exaggerated. Judicial shortcomings in information gathering and evaluation can be ameliorated by, for example, appointing special masters or using expert witnesses and consultants.

Judicially mandated restructuring appears particularly appropriate for large corporations that have committed serious offenses, especially offenses of the "structural" variety. A corporate history of similar offenses involving different personnel indicates that organizational factors may be encouraging violations, and also calls into question the presumption that corporate managers have superior abilities to design measures calculated to avoid future violations. The threat of such an intrusion sanction for a second violation might motivate some corporations to restructure voluntarily. Furthermore, limiting restructuring to corporate recidivists is consistent with the basic thrust of our sentencing law in favor of harsher treatment for repeat offenders.

Judicially mandated restructuring will no doubt encounter organizational resistance and, like any new legal device, will stimulate new forms of cheating. Courts that employ probationary restructuring must appreciate the unique characteristics of a convicted corporation. This will entail understanding the organization's sense of "mission" and analyzing its power structure so that likely internal supporters of judicial intervention can be given leadership roles in implementing the court's orders. Courts also have numerous means for policing the implementation of court orders during the probationary period, including contempt sentences for corporate officers who shirk their assigned duties, fines for probationary violations, post-decree compliance reporting, and continued resort to independent consultants for monitoring.

To the assertion that the novelty of corporate probation renders its presumed advantages conjectural, only one answer is possible: More conventional approaches are woefully ineffective. Probationary approaches appear more consistent with our knowledge of organizational reality and offer a realistic hope for corporate rehabilitation.

The criminal-law approach most likely to yield success in controlling corporate behavior should include a wide range of sanctions aimed at both corporate entities and their employees. Criminal sanctions, properly employed, may enjoy significant advantages over punitive damages as a means for controlling especially reprehensible manufacturer misconduct. Criminal law, unlike civil law, can strike directly at the managers who make corporate decisions. Using judicially mandated restructuring, courts can pierce the corporate veil and reform the internal corporate processes that produced misconduct. Restructuring thus may afford a level of prevention that is unobtainable via punitive damages, which rely upon the hope of inducing corporate reform indirectly, through financial punishment. In addition, individual liability and restructuring afford prevention without the aggravated spillover effects common to punitive damages and to criminal fines. Even where a court eschews restructuring—either out of a belief that a defendant corporation is likely to respond properly to the more traditional criminal fine, or because the defendant corporation is a first-time violator—the amount of the fine will be limited by statute and determined by the court, not by an excitable jury. Moreover, the fine will inure to the public treasury, not to the private purse.

Before any ultimate conclusions may be drawn on the merits of the criminal sanction versus punitive damages, however, inquiry must be made into the particular problems associated with utilizing criminal penalties in the products liability context.

The Desired Dimensions of Criminal Products Liability

Courts could employ existing criminal statutes, assuming these were properly worded or sympathetically interpreted, to assess criminal penalties in the manufacturing context. Reckless conduct that causes the death of a human being supports an involuntary-manslaughter or reckless-homicide prosecution in most states. And while most states require more than ordinary tort negligence for manslaughter, a few states have defined manslaughter as negligently causing the death of another. Products that produce nonfatal injuries could also give rise to criminal liability, because reckless or negligent conduct that causes bodily harm supports a battery indictment in most jurisdictions. Indeed, actual harm is not always a necessary predicate to corporate criminal liability, since some jurisdictions have passed "endangerment" statutes which make criminal the reckless creation of a risk of harm to others and which could arguably be used against manufacturers of products that embody such a risk.

Using traditional criminal statutes appears less than desirable, however. The most obvious problem is the *ex post facto* application of traditional criminal statutes in a new context. Certainly it is questionable whether legislatures ever intended criminal statutes to apply in the manufacturing context. Doing so arguably contravenes basic criminal-law principles of *nullem crimen sine lege* and *nulla poena sine lege*. Novel application of broadly worded, traditional statutes would afford prosecutors undue discretion in deciding which cases to prosecute. A traditional statute provides no express guidance about how to resolve the many difficult issues of, *inter alia*, manufacturing costs, technological feasibility, and safety choices inherent in product-related cases, and would create the risk of ''lawless'' verdicts on jury antipathy. The jury might also find it difficult to apply traditional criminal-law terms like ''reckless'' or ''negligent'' to new situations. Defendants would have with little or no guidance concerning courses of conduct that would minimize their chances of future liability. A further difficulty is that general criminal statutes furnish no guidance on whether compliance with federal regulatory standards should provide a defense against liability. There are significant due process concerns about the ability of the state to punish a manufacturer for conduct that has conformed to such standards.

Product-related prosecutions under existing criminal statutes also raise disturbing problems of multiple punishment similar to those encountered in civil cases. Although multiple prosecutions for the ''same offense'' violate the fifth amendment's double jeopardy clause, multiple prosecutions for similar product-related offenses appear to be possible. Individuals within the corporate hierarchy could thus conceivably face multiple indictments for one allegedly wrong product decision. Manufacturers exposed to multiple prosecutions would face the prospect of multiple cash, or perhaps equity, fines, or the daunting prospect of several courts ordering disparate internal structural reforms under judicially imposed restructuring.

It seems obvious that criminal statues drafted expressly for regulating the products area are required. What should such statutes look like? The first question concerns what kinds of product-related behavior considered appropriate for punitive damages—concealing known dangers associated with a product, grossly deficient product-testing or quality-control procedures, knowing violation of legislative or administrative product-safety standards, failure to warn customers about or to reduce nonobvious dangers, and failure to warn consumers about or to take steps to remedy product dangers discovered after a product has been marked—evidences sufficient culpability to merit the criminal sanction.

Whether we should also require that the proscribed behavior produce some tangible harm before criminal liability attaches is a more difficult question. Certainly a statute could be drafted imposing liability when the conduct creates a risk of death or serious bodily injury. Moral culpability, and hence the need to deter, rehabilitate, or punish the offender, does not vary with the degree of harm the behavior actually produces. Making criminal ''dangerous'' behavior in the absence of harm has been criticized on moral grounds as ''cowardice,'' however. On utilitarian grounds, it appears that the public will more readily accept corporate criminality if the harms resulting therefrom resemble those resulting from traditional criminal behavior. The desire for retribution probably increases with the magnitude of the harm associated with a wrongdoer's conduct, and therefore restricting liability to conduct involving serious harm is likely to assure greater prosecutorial interest and to enhance the possibilities of a stern reaction by judges and juries. Also, limiting corporate criminal liability to conduct that causes serious harm can minimize the potential for multiple prosecutions that endangerment statutes would pose. Finally, given the nature of the product risks at issue and the large number of persons exposed thereto, it is unlikely that a manufacturer will fortuitously avoid punishment because the product failed to produce sufficient harm. Good reasons therefore exist to suggest that at least initial excursions into the uncharted realm of criminal products liability be confined to making criminal behavior that has produced demonstrable and serious harm.

Another issue in criminal products liability is the level of intent required for liability. Difficulties of proof have led to suggestions that some form of strict or vicarious liability may be necessary to achieve adequate deterrence. Both strict liability and vicarious liability represent dramatic departures from the criminal law's traditional insistence on proof of personal culpability. Dispensing with proof of individual culpability has encountered significant resistance from the commentators as well as the courts. Critics convincingly argue that making morally neutral conduct criminal will not necessarily enhance deterrence. The greater procedural protections afforded criminal defendants and the higher burden of proof that the state must bear make enforcement and conviction more difficult to achieve under criminal law than under civil. In addition, making morally neutral conduct criminal dilutes the moral impact of the criminal sanction, with a consequent loss of deterrent force. Certainly juries and courts are unlikely to impose meaningful sanctions on defendants whose behavior fails to demonstrate significant culpability. Linking liability to culpability may also maximize deterrence because potential defendants are then aware that they are committing an offense. Thus, despite the difficult burdens of proof, neither prevention nor retribution appear to be adequately served by dispensing with proof of culpability as a prerequisite for liability.

Numerous other culpability issues unique to the product-manufacturing context should be addressed by any well-considered criminal products liability statute. For example, unless the statute expressly addresses the issue of cost-benefit analysis by manufacturers, there is every reason to suppose that evidence of this activity will be introduced to prove manufacturer culpability. A statute should provide that a manufacturer's use of cost-benefit analysis, standing alone, is not a basis for liability. Only when the manufacturer's analysis or the conclusions drawn therefrom are so distorted as to evidence a "flagrant indifference to public safety" should liability be imposed.

Likewise, a statute should explicitly address the effect, if any, of a product's compliance with applicable administrative or legislative standards. At a minimum, compliance with standards should create a defense to liability, unless the prosecution can prove that the defendant knew or should have known that the standard was grossly inadequate. In a related vein, a criminal products liability statute should address the issue of good-faith corporate efforts to prevent violations.

A criminal products liability statute should also expressly address the disturbing potential for multiple prosecutions. While the prospect of multiple prosecutions for each distinct harm resulting from behavior traditionally adjudged as criminal may not be offensive, the prospect of multiple prosecutions, whether of individuals or of their corporate employers, for behavior that may amount only to serious errors of judgment is considerably more daunting. Many states, however, are likely to eschew exercising their sovereign right to prosecute conduct that is actionable under state law merely because a defendant has already been convicted for the same act in another jurisdiction. Thus it would be desirable that Congress preempt state efforts by enacting a federal criminal products liability statute.

Finally, if the criminal sanction is to intrude into the realm of products liability we must also address the relationship between criminal and civil products liability. This involves looking at not only the effect that criminal liability should have on the availability of punitive damages, but also at the offensive collateral estoppel effect that a criminal conviction should have in subsequent civil cases where compensatory damages are at issue. Although in the past the courts have rarely given criminal judgments collateral estoppel effects in subsequent civil suits, of courts are now willing to do so. This development may have a potentially dramatic impact on products liability cases. The criminal conviction of a manufacturer based on a defective design, for example, could trigger a multitude of civil suits. Plaintiffs' chances of recovery in these suits would be significantly enhanced if they were freed from the challenging task of proving that the product was defectively designed.

There are reasons to give to criminal convictions stemming from trials collateral estoppel effect in subsequent civil litigation. Defendants in criminal trials receive procedural protections beyond those afforded to civil litigants and therefore cannot readily question either the adequacy of their opportunity to litigate the issues or the reliability of the resultant determination. Also, criminal defendants normally have sufficient incentives to mount a vigorous defense to the charges against them. A conviction under a well-drafted criminal products liability statute would likely be more useful to civil plaintiffs in subsequent civil suits than would a conviction under a general criminal statute: A plaintiff could prove with relative ease that critical issues like defectiveness of design were necessarily decided against that defendant in a trial brought under a criminal products liability statute. Giving collateral estoppel effect to criminal convictions may encourage civil suits by plaintiffs who otherwise would not have pursued a remedy, and may facilitate recovery by some plaintiffs who might otherwise have been denied recovery. Collateral estoppel could thus significantly augment the deterrent potential of criminal statutes and further reduce the need for punitive damages.

Although recent developments have made it easier for plaintiffs to use collateral estoppel offensively in civil contexts, however, there apparently exists a countertrend of judicial reluctance to apply collateral estoppel in products liability cases. This countertrend probably results both from troubling aspects of collateral estoppel in general and from special problems inherent in its application to products liability. First, offensive, nonmutual collateral estoppel may encourage some plaintiffs to bring suits that otherwise would not have been brought, while encouraging others to delay filing suit rather than to intervene in existing suits. Thus the judicial-economy rationale often used to support collateral estoppel does not necessarily justify offensive collateral estoppel. A more grave consideration is that giving a prior judgment offensive collateral estoppel effect in future cases involving the same product design could result in a single jury, sitting in review of certain limited facts fashioning a verdict which would establish safety standards for a given product for the entire country. Yet given the complex nature of products liability issues, there may be a particularly great risk that the first jury verdict was erroneous. For these reasons it is probably desirable that judgments under a criminal products liability statute not be given offensive, nonmutual collateral estoppel effect in subsequent civil litigation.

* * *

Conclusion

Both punitive damages and the criminal sanction, the two most prominent means of punishing corporations, are less efficient than is desirable, due to our misconceptions concerning the nature of the behavior they seek to regulate. The criminal sanction, properly informed by an understanding of the nature of organizational behavior, appears to offer the best hope for enhancing prevention at a lower social cost, however. Criminal sanctions can directly reach the managers who formulate corporate policy. When applied to corporate entities, criminal sanctions in the form of judicially mandated restructuring offer hope for corporate rehabilitation while largely avoiding the spillover effects of punitive damages.

Applying the criminal sanction to product-related behavior also entails costs, both known and unknown. The most obvious of these is the diversion of scarce law-enforcement resources away from the tasks to which they are already devoted. A less obvious cost is overdeterrence or other counterproductive behavior that will reduce economic efficiency. In addition, utilizing novel sanction approaches will undoubtedly produce new enforcement dilemmas and behavioral responses whose costs will become apparent only with increased experience.

If our policymakers conclude that the deficiencies of the present products liability system are sufficiently great as to justify the risks associated with imposing criminal sanctions on manufacturers, they must recognize that the unique problems presented by criminal products liability require special criminal products liability statutes. In particular, criminal statutes must address the question of multiple criminal liability for multiple harms associated with a single product line or product-related decision, the possible defenses of compliance with regulatory standards or of general good-faith efforts, and the interrelationship between criminal and civil liability. A proper statute would include sanctions for both corporate entities and their employees. Finally, a well-drafted statute would make criminal only behavior that manifests a significant level of moral culpability.

Ultimately, the question of gaining enhanced control over corporate behavior in the products-manufacturing context is a small part of the much larger social question of how to gain more effective control over the large organizations that dominate the nation's economy. Our currently primitive understanding of organizational behavior limits our ability to engage successfully in organizational control. The degree of success attained here and elsewhere depends largely upon our ability to extend the horizons of our knowledge in this critical area of human behavior.

Revised Annotated Reprimand by Chief Judge Miles W. Lord, 9 HAMLINE L. REV. 7 (1986)*

[*Editor's note:* This is the text of the reprimand Miles Lord delivered in court on February 29, 1984, to A.H. Robins corporate officers E. Claiborne Robins, Jr., William A. Forrest, Jr., and Dr. Carl D. Lunsford. The statement was delivered five days after the parties had entered into a settlement agreement.]

Mr. Robins, Mr. Forrest, and Dr. Lunsford, after months of reflecting, study and cogitation and no small amount of prayer I have concluded it perfectly appropriate to make to you this statement, which will constitute my plea to you to seek new horizons in corporate consciousness and a new sense of personal responsibility for the activities of those who work under you in the name of A.H. Robins Company. It is not enough to say, "I did not know," "It was not me," "Look elsewhere." Time and time again each of you have used this kind of argument in refusing to acknowledge your responsibility and pretending to the world that the chief officers and directors of your gigantic multinational corporation have no responsibility for the company's acts and omissions.

In a speech I made several years ago—the document which I have just asked you to read—I suggested to hundreds of ministers of the Gospel, who constitute the Minnesota Council of Churches, that the accumulation of corporate wrongs is in my mind a manifestation of individual sin.

You, Mr. Robins, Jr., have been heard to boast many times that the growth and prosperity of this company is a direct result of its having been in the Robins family for three generations,

*Used by permission.

the stamp of the Robins family is upon it, the corporation is built in the image of the Robins mentality.

You, Dr. Lunsford, as director of the company's most sensitive and important subdivision, the medical division, have violated every ethical precept to which every doctor under your supervision must pledge as he gives the oath of Hippocrates and assumes the mantle of one who would cure and nurture unto the physical needs of the populace.

You, Mr. Forrest, are a lawyer who, upon finding his client in trouble, should counsel and guide him along a course which will comport with the legal and moral and ethical principles which must bind us all. You have not brought honor to your profession, Mr. Forrest.

Gentlemen, the result of these activities and attitudes on your part have been catastrophic. Today, as you sit here, attempting once more to extricate yourselves from the legal consequences of your acts, none of you have faced up to the fact that more than 9,000 women have made claims that they gave a part of their womanhood so that your company might prosper. It is alleged that others gave their lives so you might prosper. And there stand behind legions more who have been injured but who have not sought relief in the courts of this land. I dread to think what would have been the consequences if your victims had been men rather than women, women who seem through some strange quirk of our society's mores to be expected to suffer pain, suffering and humiliation.

If one poor young man were by some act of his, without authority or consent, to inflict such damage upon one woman, he would be jailed for a good portion for the rest of his life. And yet your company, without warning to women, invaded their bodies by the millions and caused them injuries by the thousands. And when the time came for these women to make their claims against your company, you attacked their characters, you inquired into their sexual practices and into the identity of their sex partners. You exposed these women and ruined families and reputations and careers in order to intimidate those who would raise their voices against you. You introduced issues that had no relationship whatsoever to the fact that you planted in the bodies of these women instruments of death, mutilation, and of disease.

Gentlemen, you state that your company has suffered enough, that the infliction of further punishment in a form of punitive damages will cause harm to your ongoing business, will punish innocent shareholders and, conceivably, depress your profits to the point where you would not survive as a competitor in this industry. Well, when the poor and downtrodden in this country commit crimes, they too plead that these are crimes of survival and that they should be excused for illegal acts which helped them escape desperate economic straits. On a few occasions when these excuses are made and a contrite and remorseful defendant promises to mend his ways, courts will give heed to such a plea. But no court would heed this plea when the individual denies the wrongful nature of his deed and gives no indication that he will mend his ways. Your company in the face of overwhelming evidence denies its guilt and continues its monstrous mischief.

Mr. Forrest, you have told me that you are working with members of the Congress of the United States to ask them to find a way of forgiving you for punitive damages which might otherwise be imposed. Yet the profits of your company continue to mount. Your last financial report boasts of new records for sales and earnings with a profit of more than fifty-eight million in 1983. And all the while, insofar as this Court is able to determine, you three men and your company still engage in the same course of wrongdoing on which you originally commenced.

Until such time as your company indicates that it is willing to cease and desist this deception and seek out and advise victims, your remonstrances to Congress and to the courts of this country are indeed hollow and cynical.

The company has not suffered, nor have you men personally. You are collectively being enriched by millions of dollars each year. There is as yet no evidence that your company has suffered any penalty whatsoever for these litigations. In fact the evidence is to the contrary.

The case law indicates that the purpose of punitive damages is to make an award which will punish a defendant for his wrongdoing. Punishment traditionally involves the principles of revenge, rehabilitation and deterrence. There is no evidence I have been able to find, in my review of these cases, to indicate that any one of these factors has been accomplished.

Mr. Robins, Mr. Forrest, Dr. Lunsford, you have not been rehabilitated by the punitive damage awards that have been made so far. In fact, I don't think one of them has ever been paid yet, up until this settlement. Under your direction your company has in fact continued to allow women, tens of thousands of them, to wear this device, a deadly depth charge in their wombs, ready to explode at any time. Your attorney, Mr. Alexander Slaughter, denies that tens of thousands of these devices are still in the bodies of women. But I submit to you that Mr. Slaughter has no more basis for his denial than the plaintiffs for stating it as a truth—because we simply do not know how many women are still wearing these devices; and your company, run by you three men, is not willing to find out.

The only conceivable reasons you have not recalled this product are that it would hurt your balance sheet and alert women, who already have been harmed, that you may be liable for their injuries. As I said before, and out of context, you have taken the bottom line as your guiding beacon and the low road as your route. This is corporate irresponsibility at its meanest.

Rehabilitation involves an admission of guilt, a certain contrition, an acknowledgment of wrongdoing, and a resolution to take a new course towards a better life. I find none of this in the instance of you and your corporation.

Confession is good for the soul, gentlemen. Face up to your misdeeds. Acknowledge the responsibility that you have for the activities of those who work under you. Rectify this evil situation. Warn the potential future victim and recompense those who have already been harmed.

Mr. Robins, Mr. Forrest, Dr. Lunsford, I see little in the history of this case that would deter others from partaking of like acts. The policy of delay and obfuscation practiced by your lawyers in courts throughout this country has made it possible for your insurance company and you, the Aetna Casualty and Assurance Company and the A.H. Robins Corporation, to delay the payment of these claims for such a long period that the interest you earn in the interim covers the costs of these cases. You in essence, assuming you owe something at the time the harm came, pay nothing out of your pocket to settle these cases. What other corporate officials anywhere could possibly learn a lesson from this? The only lesson could be that it pays to delay compensating victims, and to intimidate, harass and shame your victims, the injured parties.

Mr. Forrest, Mr. Robins and Dr. Lunsford, you gentlemen have consistently denied any knowledge of the deeds of the company you control. You, Mr. Robins, Jr., I read your deposition. Many times you state that your management style was such as to delegate work and responsibility to other employees in matters involving the most important aspects of this nation's health.

Judge Frank Theis, who presided over the discovery of these cases during the Multi-District Litigation proceedings, noted this phenomenon in a recent opinion:

> The project manager for Dalkon Shield explains that a particular question should have gone to the medical department. The medical department representative explains that the

question was really the bailiwick of the quality control department. The quality control department representative explains that the project manager was the one with the authority to make a decision on that question.

Under these circumstances, Judge Theis noted, it is not at all unusual for the hard questions posed in Dalkon Shield cases to be unanswerable by anyone from Robins.

Your company seeks and has sought to segment and fragment litigation of these cases nationwide. The courts of this country are now burdened with more than 3,000 Dalkon Shield cases. The sheer number of claims and the dilatory tactics used by your company's attorneys clog court calendars and consume vast amounts of judicial and jury time. Your company settles those cases in which it finds itself in an uncomfortable position, a handy device for avoiding any proceeding which would give continuity or cohesiveness to this nationwide problem. The decision as to which cases to try rests almost solely at the whim and discretion of the A.H. Robins Company.

In order that no plaintiff or group of plaintiffs might assert a sustained assault upon your system, evasion, and avoidance, you have time after time demanded that able lawyers who have knowledge of the facts must, as a price of settling their cases, agree to never again take a Dalkon Shield case nor to help any less experienced lawyers with their cases against your company. Minnesota lawyers have filed cases in this jurisdiction for women from throughout the United States. The cases of these women have waited on the calendar of this Court for as many as three years.

Until such time as this settlement came about, the evidence that the women were to present was simply their own testimony or that of their doctor, usually taken by deposition, and then the generic evidence concerning the company's actions—which is as easy to produce in Minnesota as anywhere else. Yet your company's attorneys were persisting in asking that these cases be transferred to other jurisdictions and to other judges unfamiliar with the cases, there to wait at the bottom of the calendar for additional months and years before they could have their day in Court. Another of your callous legal tactics is to force women of little means to withstand the onslaught of your well-financed nationwide team of attorneys, and to default if they cannot keep up with the pace. Your worst tactics were reserved for the meek and the poor.

Despite your company's protestations, it is evident that these thousands of cases cannot be viewed in isolation, and that is one of the main reasons why I feel free to make this statement here today. If every judge is terminated as soon as he catches on to what's going on, if you settle the case and flee the jurisdiction, that leaves no one to follow up to make any cohesiveness to this.

The multi-district litigation panel of the Federal District Court found these cases to have sufficient similarity on issues of law and fact to warrant their reference to a single Judge who, for varying periods of time, conducted discovery depositions and proceedings designed to devise an efficient method of handling these cases. Yet I find, as I previously indicated, from the report of the Masters—as late as this morning—that the Multi-District Litigation Unit was only given about a third of the documents, and the most relevant documents are in the hands of the lawyers for the defendant. So that is twelve years of delay.

If a judge were to wait until all the cases were over before he spoke out on the evils he sees inherent in the system and in the trial tactics, then no one would ever speak out. There is a time when measures must be taken, when steps must be taken to see that fair play and ethical standards apply to the disposition of all the cases that are to come in the future, regardless of what might have happened in the past. These litigations must be viewed as a whole.

Were these women to be gathered together with their injuries in one location, this matter would be denominated a disaster of highest magnitude. The mere fact that these women are separated by geography blurs the total picture. Here we have thousands of victims, present and potential whose injuries arise from the same series of operative facts. You three gentlemen have made no effort whatsoever to locate them and bring them together to seek a common solution to their plight.

If this were a case in equity, I would order that your company make an effort to locate each and every woman who still wears this device, and to recall your product. I would order you now to take to the Food and Drug Administration a correct and proper report on what's happened with these devices. If I did that, they would order you to recall.

So while the governmental agencies are set up to protect the public, there is evidence here that you didn't tell the truth to the governmental agencies. I believe that evidence; I've made judgment on it. These matters of which I speak are not matters about which I speculate. They are matters contained in the evidence that has gone before me in the briefs of counsel, in the admissions and in the documents—some of which I have seen and no lawyer has seen—but I haven't disclosed anything about them except my conclusion about the matters about which I here spoke.

I do not have the power to order you to do this. I must therefore resort to moral persuasion and a personal appeal to each of you. Would you believe it, gentlemen, I am not angry with you. I don't dislike you personally. I am not happy with some of things you have done. I would really like to try to talk you into doing this.

It's just awful, and you can't get hung up in that corporate thing, you can't worry about whether or not the stocks are going to drop. You've got lives out there, people, women, wives, moms, and some who will never be moms. Can't you move in on this thing now? You are the people with the power to recall. You are the corporate conscience. Please, in the name of humanity, lift your eyes above the bottom line.

You, the men in charge, must surely—I know you have hearts and souls and consciences—and I am not a great "Bible pounder," but this almost takes you into a Biblical reference, you can only explain it in that way. If the thought of facing up to your transgressions is so unbearable to you—and I think it will be difficult for you—you might confess to your Maker and beg forgiveness and mend your ways.

The options are few. Either you go along stonewalling it, like you are going, or you face up to what you have done, and then you have to start thinking about how you might make amends for that.

Please, gentlemen, give consideration to tracing down the victims and sparing them the agony that will surely be theirs. And I just want to say I love you. I am not mad at you.

* * * *

[*Editor's postscript.* Robins responded not with "repentance" but by filing misconduct proceedings against Lord, alleging that in making this reprimand the judge had acted without authority and had violated the due process rights of the three officers. Former attorney general and former chief justice of the Fifth Circuit, Griffin Bell, represented Robins in these proceedings. In a unanimous decision, the Eighth Circuit accepted the due process argument and ordered the reprimand expunged from the record.

Later in 1984, Robins announced that it would pay for the removal of Dalkon Shields that were still being worn. Lord said in an interview that he hoped that his exhortations had lead Robins to make the recall decision, but he still disapproved of the company's lack of contrition. *See* MORTON MINTZ, AT ANY COST: CORPORATE GREED, WOMEN, AND THE DALKON SHIELD 235 (1985).]

David G. Owen, *Problems In Assessing Punitive Damages Against Manufacturers of Defective Products*, 49 U. Chi. L. Rev. 1 (1982)*

Punitive damages have been the subject of substantial criticisms by some courts and commentators for many years. In addition to the absence of criminal law procedural safeguards in their application, such damages are criticized generally for being inconsistent with the civil law's focus on providing compensation for losses, for giving plaintiffs undeserved windfalls, for having no objective standard for determining their propriety or amount in individual cases (which may make them largely unpredictable and effectively nonreviewable), and for being designed to deter misconduct when there is no good proof that they do. Yet punitive damages awards are a fixture of the civil law, dating back at least to the Code of Hammurabi of 2000 B.C., and criticisms notwithstanding they appear likely to remain in general use for some time.

Products liability cases present a variety of problems that complicate the application of the traditional punitive damages rules.

Juror Limitations and Attitudes

A jury trial presents difficulties for the fair administration of a complex products liability case, and the problems are aggravated by the presence in the case of a punitive damages claim. Plaintiffs do not by any means win all products liability cases, even for compensatory damages, and in fact the odds at present appear to favor the manufacturer when such cases go to trial. Yet a full explanation of the manufacturer's decisionmaking process (which is on trial in a punitive damages case) is necessarily complex and somewhat dull, and jurors easily can become confused and bored by the technical evidence. Cases often drag on for weeks or even months, with one expert witness following another, and the interest, attention, and comprehension of many jurors often are left far behind. The engineering complexity of the typical design case is multiplied considerably by the difficult concepts and issues of value added by the allegation of flagrant manufacturer misbehavior. The desirability of jury trial in other types of complex civil litigation presently is under reconsideration by some courts and commentators; it may be that the debate should be broadened to include complex products liability cases, particularly those involving claims for punitive damages.

In addition to problems of comprehension, jurors have a natural sympathy for a seriously injured person that is reinforced when the defendant is a manufacturer, for many persons are hostile toward major institutions in general and big business in particular. Some jurors may thus be tempted to resort to simplistic explanations of the issue (such as that the defendant callously traded lives for dollars) that comport with their preconceived notions of manufacturers' oppression of consumers.

Such preconceptions may generally be tolerable in determining compensatory liability. Because most companies are insured against such losses, and because they have greater access to much of the crucial evidence and greater financial resources with which to defend their cases, a little bias in favor of compensating the injured user of a product may in fact be good. For

---

*Used by permission.

even if a close-call case is wrongly rendered for the plaintiff, his suffering will be lessened, and the institutional suffering of the manufacturer will be limited to the amount of the plaintiff's actual loss, his compensatory damages. Only infrequently, and only in a few jurisdictions, will such wrong decisions against a manufacturer reach one million dollars. We thus may wish to tolerate, and perhaps be able to afford, a little such compassion at the expense of some efficiency. The stakes are increased considerably, however, in both principle and amount, when claims are made for punitive damages. The presence of such claims places a premium on the oratorical and other trial skills of counsel in products cases, raising a special risk of tapping juror bias that may test the limits of fair adjudication.

Changing Social Values and Economic Conditions Over Time

A product may be designed in one decade, manufactured and sold in the next, and produce injury in another; a suit involving the product may go to trial in the next decade, and perhaps not be reviewed on appeal until yet another decade has begun. Before the case is finally resolved, an entire generation may have passed. Nor are substantial time delays uncommon in products litigation; a case where the design and final appeal both take place in the same decade may today be more the exception than the rule.

The problem, of course, is that society's values concerning safety and corporate responsibility have been evolving rapidly in recent years. It is one thing to judge according to today's higher standards the safety or defectiveness of a product that was made when concern for safety was much less, and to compensate a victim accordingly for losses actually suffered. It is quite another to exact enormous punishment from an enterprise, acting on our greater social consciousness of today, for decisions that were made pursuant to business ethics of times past by men and women who since have left the company and perhaps this life. In our zeal to punish abuses discovered today, we must be cautious not to overlook the prevailing moral and business standards of the time involved.

Problems with Punishing a Manufacturing Entity

Punitive damages were developed largely as a punishment and deterrent for trespassers, oxen thieves and other such human malefactors. When the device is transferred to the complex bureaucracy of a modern manufacturing concern, the fit is awkward in many respects. Final decisions concerning a complex product are often the result of a splintered, bureaucratic process involving a complicated combination of human judgments made by scores of persons at different levels in the hierarchy who pass on different aspects of the problem at different times. Various engineers may have to rely upon the work of research chemists, physicists, and other scientists; input from the financial and marketing arms of the enterprise must be factored in along the way. The entire process may take years. Each of these human actors makes decisions based on his own motives and on different types and amounts of information, and even the responsible executive at the end of the decisional line can possess only a small bit of the total information involved. Moreover, the corporate owners of the enterprise are usually far removed from most decisions of even the top executives.

This is not to say that institutional safety procedures cannot be put in place and monitored to ensure that safety gets its day in the manufacturer's decisional court, and the modern company without procedures of this type should be held to some account. Yet we must remember that the concepts of moral responsibility, punishment, and deterrence can mean vastly different things when judging the conduct of an institution rather than of a human being.

The problem in capsule form is simply this: humans are clearly culpable when they act to gain a minor advantage in a way they know will be likely to kill or injure others. Thus, we usually punish a person who deliberately or recklessly kills or maims another without good reason. Yet manufacturers of hazardous products such as automobiles (which kill and maim thousands every year) must design them in many different ways they know with virtual certainty will result in harm or death at some time to a certain number of unfortunate, statistical persons. In a sense, then, such manufacturers always act intentionally in derogation of human life, yet surely punishment is inappropriate for simply being in the business of making high speed machines.

Documentation of Design Process Decisions

The key to winning a punitive damages case against a manufacturer is often said to lie in finding a smoking gun in the defendant's files. The powder keg memorandum, for example, was pivotal in the *Gryc* flammable fabrics case [297 N.W.2d 727 (Minn.), *cert. denied*, 449 U.S. 921 (1980)], as was Ford's cost-feasibility memorandum—examining various design improvements for the Pinto fuel system—in the *Grimshaw* case [119 Cal. App. 3d 757 (1981)]. On rare occasions such documents may in themselves prove a callous disregard by corporate executives of human health or safety.

In many cases, however, there are significant dangers of abuse in the manipulation of documentary evidence. Manufacturers necessarily create massive documentation of their design and production processes, sometimes amounting to millions of pages of notes, memoranda, and correspondence over the life of a product. Especially during the initial design of the product, but also as information returns on the product's performance in the field, reports of many instances of one problem or another will be documented, acted upon, and filed away. In fact, the more a manufacturer is truly concerned about its product's safety, the more it will encourage self-criticism and negative analyses of the product within the company. For example, it often is desirable during the initial stages of a product's design to test it to its limits to discover what those limits are: cars may thus be crash-tested until their gas tanks burst, and rats may be injected with a drug in ever higher doses until some die. Documentary evidence (especially films) of such tests can later return to haunt the manufacturer, as they did in the *Grimshaw* Pinto case. Such a manufacturer, constantly striving to uncover sources of weakness in and dissatisfaction with its products to produce an every better product for the public, may thereby create the documentary seeds for a punitive damages claim in a future products suit.

Measuring Wealth and Poverty

Because the defendant's wealth is a relevant factor in determining the amount of punitive damages, one must inquire what wealth really means in the case of a manufacturing entity. Basic financial sheet data such as sales, profits, and net worth most often have been regarded as the relevant indicators of a corporation's wealth. Yet figures on a company's sales are often largely unrelated to a company's true financial prosperity, for very little of the gross earnings remains—even when times are good—after deducting the costs of materials, labor, sales, administration, taxes, and, increasingly, the cost of capital. Even profits after taxes are plainly not idle wealth, because the enterprise will fail if the owners do not receive a fair return on their investment. And even after the payment of dividends, although such retained profits may travel to the balance sheet adding to net worth, the remaining dollars hardly represent a pot of idle gold, ripe for plucking by the plaintiff and his lawyer, for usually they will be reinvested in plant, equipment, salaries, and other future costs of operation—the costs of staying in business. Moreover, a large assessment of punitive damages against an enterprise will affect at least to some extent its earnings, and hence, most likely, the value of its stock.

These are difficult notions for juries to understand, and the sophistication of many judges on such matters also leaves much to be desired. The difficult job of education will fall squarely upon the shoulders of the defendant's financial experts, and the trial court will have to hold a tight rein on evidence and argument in this area where prejudice follows error with special ease. Yet even when the evidence and argument on these matters are beyond reproach, the multi-million (sometimes billion) dollar figures discussed at trial may all begin to blur in the minds of many jurors. If such be true, a typical juror may well be receptive to an argument that anything less than $1 million would be but a drop in the bucket and that much more than that would be required to catch the attention of the company's executives and to teach them a lesson.

The Basis of Liability

Cost-benefit analysis is fundamental to the design engineer's trade. The depth of the rubber on an automobile's bumper forever may be increased by another one-tenth inch. One more crossbeam always may be added to protect the occupants in certain types of collisions. The configuration of crossbeams may be changed to increase their strength; thicker or harder steel may be used in the beams; perhaps they may be made of another metal, or perhaps even of a form of plastic. Many hundreds of such choices are made by design engineers in the production of a single complex product, and each such decision involves a range of trade-offs between cost, weight, appearance, performance capabilities (for separate functions in varying environments), and safety in one type of accident versus another. A steel beam that protects an occupant in one type of accident may endanger him in another, as by rendering that portion of the vehicle less energy absorbent, and may endanger pedestrians and the occupants of other vehicles as well. Although much of this decisionmaking involves the application of proven scientific principles, much is art, and some by its nature can be little more than trial and error.

There is an increasing appreciation among courts and commentators of the inherent difficulties in judging the adequacy of such complex design decisions in determining liability for compensatory damages. The courts must be even more vigilant to prevent punitive awards from intruding too deeply into the heart of American industry. Many of our most important products, from airplanes, cars, and tires, to guns, drugs, pesticides, and other chemicals, are daily productive of injury, death, or disease. Surely we should demand of their manufacturers that all reasonable steps be taken to protect us against harm where feasible and affordable curative measures will not diminish unduly the usefulness of the products, and in some circumstances we may fairly hold the manufacturers strictly to account for their failure to protect us. Moreover, when a manufacturer knowingly sacrifices the public's greater safety interests to reap a profit that it knows is worth much less, punitive damages are in order. Yet many useful products must be placed on the market with risks of unknown type or extent, and manufacturers must be protected scrupulously against punishment for their good faith decisions to market such products, even if they contain substantial risks.

Because much in both resources and principle is at stake in cases of quasi-criminal punishment against manufacturers, they and the public generally are entitled to much fuller explanation by the courts of why punitive awards should stand or fall. Once the courts and commentators fight through the emotion and maze of words that tend to dominate such cases, we may expect to see a healthy clarification of legal principles being to emerge. And even if we probably can never find a set of rules that are precise and clear, detailed explanations of judicial results in such cases will give better insight into the true nature of a manufacturer's responsibilities to the public.

Michael Rustad, *In Defense of Punitive Damages in Products Liability: Testing Tort Anecdotes With Empirical Data,* 78 Iowa L. Rev. 1 (1992)*

Social Functions of Punitive Damages

[Rustad's conclusions follow a lengthy exposition of his empirical findings.]

Many of the large-scale risks in products liability cases that punitive damages seek to prevent are not defined or recognized as crimes, even though this corporate misbehavior may create a far more substantial public danger than many actions labelled as criminal. Even when product failure cases result in criminal penalties, the penalties are too insignificant to effectively deter corporate misbehavior. If punitive damages were stricken from the legal landscape, the states and federal government would need to assume the burden of punishing and aggressively deterring manufacturers which recklessly endanger the public interest.

In order to spearhead a criminal-law effort against reckless and callous manufacturers, it would be necessary to create specialized and expensive new "crim-tort" units, a step not feasible during a period of state budget deficits. Can prosecutors and the police spare the resources to prosecute complex workplace risks, such as the careless use of chemical mutagens? Law enforcement personnel are simply not prepared to hire the experts necessary to detect and prosecute companies risking the public safety.

My study indicates that the regulatory agencies, too, have generally failed to adequately protect the public in cases where punitive damages are awarded. Professor Richard Stewart has noted that private remedies protect the right of the public when the government fails. One might argue that truly conservative audiences would prefer a private remedy to government regulation. This is the appropriate role of punitive damages in products liability cases.

The rationale behind punitive damages in products liability cases is based on a simple model of punishment and deterrence. Fear is a particularly effective deterrent when the penalty is indeterminate. The remedy of punitive damages serves the useful purpose of expressing society's disapproval of conduct which leads to intolerable rates of injuries and deaths. To the extent that the remedy frightens corporate executives, it performs its historic function as an effective social control device. Fixed civil fines would have to be so large as to paralyze small- and medium-sized manufacturers if they were to be of sufficient magnitude to deter Fortune 500 firms.

Punitive damages not only punish and deter, they create an even playing field by depriving unethical corporations the opportunity to gain a competitive advantage by shortchanging on safety. The social policy behind the remedy is to prevent a "race to the bottom" as manufacturers are forced to forgo the public's safety in order to compete in the marketplace. In the modern period, punitive damages constrain conduct that is on the boundary between crime and tort, that would go unpunished if not for this system of private attorneys general. Society is safer as a result.

The data gathered for this study permit the first overview of how the punitive damages remedy works. The data allowed examination of the overall patterns of punitive damages awards in American products liability cases rather than a misplaced focus on a few extreme, often atypical, cases. No legal remedy is expected to perform perfectly. One can almost always find some example of

---

*Used by permission.

injustice or absurdity in any branch of the law. Tort reform proponents have the more difficult burden of establishing systematic evidence of the widespread misuse of the remedy. This study uncovered no such evidence.

Contrary to the claims of Vice President Quayle and other tort reformers, this study suggests that punitive damages are being appropriately applied. In the majority of the cases studied, the manufacturer's conduct was beyond the level of ordinary negligence. Manufacturers which made a profit-motivated decision not to test, warn, redesign, or recall their products knowing that they were endangering the consuming public were deservedly punished. There is certainly no crisis justifying immediate revamping of the remedy.

Reformers argue that punitive damages have impeded product innovation, but this study suggests that punitive damages have also encouraged innovation. Dangerously defective small aircraft have been redesigned or removed from the market. Unsafe birth control devices have been replaced with superior technology. Those who come into contact with asbestos are now protected from its hazards. Football helmets that cannot withstand foreseeable collisions have been redesigned to protect against head injuries. Infant formula is now regulated by a federal agency. Awards were correlated with these changes and have stimulated greater preventive measures.

To the extent that safety sells, these improvements have also increased competitiveness. It is absurd to argue that American firms which recklessly produce unsafe products need to be protected in a safe harbor, immune from the threat of punitive damages. Even if punitive damages were eliminated, it is doubtful whether competitiveness could be significantly affected because these cases are so rare and so modest in size. Japanese auto companies did not become preeminent because they sold the cheapest cars; they prevailed because they paid attention to the desires of their customers and employees. Sweden carved out a market by advertising their cars as the safest. Today, Chrysler is regaining sales by advertising its extensive use of airbags.

Modern society is full of consumer risk. However, as consumers, we must believe that products will meet our reasonable expectations. When we walk past a construction site, we must believe that the pulley will not fail and cause the wrecking ball to fall on us. We cannot live with the constant fear that our car will spontaneously shift from neutral to reverse. Yet, over the past quarter century, these unthinkable product failures have happened.

Even so, punitive damages awards are not about simple product failures; they are about corporations that know about risk and sometimes, for profit-oriented reasons, fail to take safety steps. Tort reformers seem concerned with only the protection of those few producers which trade safety for profits. It is even more crucial that manufacturers take every possible step to produce safe products. Corporations must not be allowed to externalize the costs of safety by allowing workers and consumers to be hurt. The threat of punitive damages is one of the few effective instruments of social control because the potential penalty, in terms of dollars or bad publicity, is usually enough to convince corporations not to trade the public interest for their own self-interest. Punitive damages awards in products liability cases help to make consumer products more trustworthy. The vast majority of American companies have received the message that safety sells.

Punitive damages also function to clarify society's values. The remedy induces conformity by controlling deviance through punishment, which signals a moral message to others who consider breaking the law. When a jury awards punitive damages, it sets the boundaries for a community's approved moral code and thus functions as an educator as well. As Clarence Morris describes the remedy, it involves extreme circumstances that deserve punishment, "both as an expression of society's disfavor of their action and as an example so that others may be deterred from the commission of similar acts."

Part IV
The Collective Goals of Products Liability

Products liability, following the Traynor concurrence in *Escola v. Coca Cola Bottling Co. of Fresno*, 150 P.2d 436 (Cal. 1944), has been defended as a source of safety and insurance. The works that follow both challenge and endorse this assertion. George Priest, skeptical about the safety claim, surveys accident data, some of which are included in this excerpt. Peter Huber argues that liability actually impedes safety. Stephen Teret and Michael Jacobs, both lawyers and both epidemiologists, are more optimistic about the effect of liability on safety.

Victor Schwartz and Liberty Mahshigian offer a pointed perspective on the insurance-compensation rationale in their much-cited article about the National Childhood Vaccine Injury Act of 1986. Schwartz and Mahshigian write that the insurance function of liability requires a healthy market and the ability of firms to spread the costs of injuries chargeable to their product. When these conditions are absent, the tension between liability and insurance is exposed. The Vaccine Injury Act confronted this tension, and chose to curb liability in order to increase insurance. George Priest also considers the failure of liability to provide effective insurance. The section concludes with an essay by Ernest Weinrib criticizing Traynor's introduction of insurance principles into the common law.

A. Safety

George L. Priest, *Products Liability Law and the Accident Rate, in* LIABILITY: PERSPECTIVES AND POLICY (Robert E. Litan & Clifford L. Winston eds. 1988)*

Within the past three decades, products liability law has been transformed from a minor subfield of commercial law and negligence litigation to an exceptionally rich and diverse set of doctrines that constitutes perhaps the most prominent feature of modern civil jurisprudence. There is little need today to plead the importance of products liability law. No one conscious of the dwindling budget and meager accomplishments of the Consumer Product Safety Commission can pretend that the United States makes a serious effort to regulate product quality directly. Instead, our society relies

*Used by permission.

on liability actions to police the manufacturing process. The prospect of liability judgments affects design and production decisions of all manufacturers, foreign and domestic, that sell to U.S. consumers. And increasing numbers of corporate bankruptcies and reorganizations stem from such judgments. As recently as a decade ago, insurance for products liability was subsumed in general commercial liability coverage, of insufficient importance for separate categorization. Today it is a growing component of commercial underwriting—indeed growing at such a rate that foreign and domestic reinsurers have recently been frightened into withdrawing further coverage.

Along with medical malpractice law, products liability law is widely viewed as the most egregious source of modern legal uncertainty. Within the past two years, efforts to reduce these uncertainties and, more generally, the extent of liability have generated extraordinarily vituperative legislative battles among manufacturers, insurers, consumers, and trial lawyers seeking to change the law or to preserve it. Yet despite the tremendous controversy over modern products liability law, its goals have been uncontroversial.

Virtually all courts and commentators have embraced the goals of accident reduction and insurance that correspond to the principal economic effects of the law. There are only two important economic effects of any legal rule: a rule can provide incentives to reduce the accident rate and, for accidents that cannot be prevented, a legal rule can provide a form of victim compensation insurance tied to product sales. Although there are occasional references to fairness and equity, courts in products cases have largely focused on these two economic goals alone in their elaboration of the law.

The current controversy instead stems from disagreement over whether the expansion of products liability law successfully achieves these objectives of deterrence and providing compensation insurance. Until recently, the debate has not been well focused on the goals the courts are striving to achieve. Critics of the law, including product manufacturers, have condemned the extent to which the law has disrupted their activities, but they have not shown that increased manufacturing costs and insurance premiums are inappropriate results of a demand for safer products. Consumer advocates have championed the higher levels of compensation awarded to injured consumers, but they have not shown that higher compensation is essential for obtaining safer products or that the compensation provided by litigation offers insurance that would not otherwise be available. A separate group of academic analysts, led by prominent law and economics scholars, has argued that modern products liability law promotes accident reduction efficiently, but the scholars have supported the claim only with models and have provided no empirical confirmation of any sort.

Here I evaluate the other of the two goals of modern products liability law—the effect of the law on product safety—through a study of data concerning trends in products liability claims and judgments and in product-related accidents.

Trends in Products Liability Litigation and in Accident Rates and Their (Questionable) Implications for Evaluation of the Law

Much of the severe disagreement over the ultimate effects of the expansion of modem products liability stems from differing interpretations of changes in the volume of products liability litigation. Products liability filings in federal courts have increased from 1,579 in 1974 to 13,595 in 1986. It is this 861 percent growth in twelve years that suggests the great increase in the effect of products liability law on manufacturing operations. Annual filing rates increased substantially in 1975 and 1976, again in 1979 and 1980, and in 1985. Curiously, the volume of filings remained virtually constant between 1985 and 1986.

One study assessed changes in products liability jury trials and judgments since 1960 in Cook County, Illinois, and San Francisco. The absolute number of jury trials and the proportion of products liability trials in civil litigation increased rapidly in both jurisdictions from 1970 to 1974 but have been declining since. Regardless of number, the mean plaintiff judgment in these trials has skyrocketed, with extraordinary increases in Cook County in 1970–74 and 1980–84 and in San Francisco in 1975–79 and 1980–84. Judgments in the largest cases have been the primary influence on the increase in the average award. As a percentage of total trial judgment dollars awarded, products liability awards expanded in Cook County and San Francisco, respectively, from a relatively insignificant 6.4 percent and 6 percent of judgment dollars in 1960–64 to nearly 24 percent and 14 percent of judgment dollars in 1975–79. From 1980 to 1984, however, this proportion dropped substantially in Cook County (to 10 percent), although it increased in San Francisco (to more than 16 percent).

It might be thought at first glance that the data concerning litigation trends for the past decade are contradictory, since they show large increases in filings and trial judgments yet decreases in the number and proportion of products liability trials and in the proportion of trial awards. All trial statistics, however, must be interpreted with the influence of litigants' settlement decisions in mind. Only 4 to 5 percent of all claims are ultimately litigated to trial; thus 95 to 96 percent are settled without entering public records. Indeed, products liability defendants have strong incentives to settle suits because adverse judgments will affect manufacturing operations beyond the award's dollar amount.

Increases in the average judgment and, presumably, in the likelihood of a plaintiff's success because of the expansion of manufacturer liability may very well lead to an increase in suits filed. Defendants, however, are likely to have greater interests in settling these suits to avoid the larger impact of adverse judgments. Indeed, as the implications of adverse judgments become broader and more far-reaching, manufacturers' incentives to settle increase. Thus the decline in the number and proportion of trials and trial dollars, coupled with an increase in filings and in average awards, may well reflect a substantial rise in the rate of products liability settlements.

The relationship between this litigation data and accident data is complex. If the expansion of products liability has had an important impact on product safety, we should observe a decrease in the injury rate in the years after the expansion.

The greatest growth in products liability trials occurred between 1965 and 1974. If this litigation were stimulated by an increase in the injury rate, one should observe the increase between 1962 and 1970, given the typical three- to five-year delay between accident and trial. Trial volume declined after 1974. If the decline reflected an increase in product safety rather than in settlement behavior, the product-related injury rate should have dropped after 1970. Indeed, given the substantial increase in median awards after 1969, the injury rate should have dropped rapidly after 1970 if the decline in trial volume reflects an increase in product safety.

Tables A, B, and C report accidental death and injury rates in the United States, of which, of course, deaths or injuries that are the consequence of products constitute only some proportion. Table A presents accidental death rates by the context of the accident. Death rates in almost all accident categories have been declining steadily but not sharply since 1950. There is little evidence of a sharp decrease in accident rates after 1970 that might be attributed to the deterrent effect of products liability law. The substantial decline in the death rate between 1970 and 1975 in the motor vehicle category can be more confidently attributed to the increase in gasoline prices and adoption of the fifty-five mile per hour speed limit than to products liability law. Moreover, the rate of auto deaths rose between 1975 and 1980, a finding inconsistent with any deterrent effect of expanding products liability law. There was also a sharp decline between 1965 and 1970 in the death rate attributed to poisoning by "other substances," but this occurs too early to be the result of products law. Similarly, the decline in this category between 1975 and 1980 is isolated. From these data it is difficult to credit the expansion of products liability with much deterrent effect.

Table B shows death and disabling injury rates for workers. Again, the data do not indicate the proportion of injuries caused by products, although it is well known that injuries on the job form a very large component of total products liability claims. Worker death rates have declined steadily since 1945, although the rate of decline seems to have slowed after 1960. The rate of disabling injuries has been far more variable, increasing from 1960 through 1973 and remaining roughly constant from 1974 through 1981. Although it declined somewhat in 1982, even in 1982 and 1983 it was only slightly less than the rate in 1950.

Table C shows work injuries by industry calculated against worker hours rather than against the size of the work force. The results are mixed. The injury rate declined between 1965 and 1970 in only four industries: lumber and wood products, coal mining, contract construction, and wholesale and retail trade. For all others the rate has increased progressively since 1960, although in many it had been decreasing from 1950 to 1960. In the few industries in which there were declines, the declines were modest. There is no evidence in either table B or table C of a reduction in the injury rate of a magnitude corresponding with the expansion of products liability.

Finally, table D shows the annual number of product-related injuries requiring hospital emergency room treatment. These data present the most detailed correlation of injuries according to specific product type, but they show only the absolute number of injuries rather than injury rates adjusted according to the number of products in use, the number of users, or the extent of use. In addition, they are vastly overinclusive for my purposes because they report all injuries related to products, not just those related to product manufacture or design features that are affected by the law. Thus, for example, according to the full reports of the Consumer Product Safety Commission, the nation's most injurious consumer product is stairs (662,000 injuries in 1980), followed by bicycles (526,000), baseball equipment (432,000), and football equipment (425,000). Even beds generate more injuries a year (168,000) than any of the products reported in table D. I have therefore culled from the complete tables those products for which injuries are most likely to be the consequence of technological design or manufacturing features affected by the expansion of products liability.

Table D shows that for most products and most years, the number of injuries increased steadily between 1974 and 1981. As is evident, declines are infrequent (sixteen of a possible seventy-seven). If products liability had remained constant over the period, one might expect that the number of injuries would increase as product use increased in a growing economy and would decline as technological advances made products safer (see, in particular, tables C and D). Given the expansion of products liability litigation over this period and the increase in damages awarded, it is surprising that there is no evidence of a systematic decrease in product-related injuries. Indeed, these data present no evidence of even a slowing in the growth rates of these injuries.

What do these statistics tell us about the effects of the expansion of products liability litigation? Little more than the obvious: that there has been an enormous expansion of products liability. They cannot tell us whether the expansion has been beneficial or harmful.

The injury and death statistics in tables A through D are mysterious. Although they are admittedly crude, they provide no evidence that the expansion of litigation has affected the injury or death rate. This conclusion corresponds to findings of the small number of careful empirical studies of specific products, each of which shows little accident-reduction effect of either expanded products liability litigation or greater direct regulation of product quality.

If this conclusion is accurate, it is disquieting. The expansion of products liability has led to the withdrawal of large numbers of products from consumer markets and large increases generally in product prices. Most commentators presume that products withdrawn from the market are relatively more risky than others and that product prices have been increased in response to greater manufacturer investments in product safety. Both effects, however, should result in sharp reductions in the injury rate, reductions that appear not to have occurred. The quality of empirical data is so poor, however, that no confident conclusion can be reached about the success of products liability law in establishing incentives for the manufacture of safer products. The law appears to have had no significant effect, but more careful research on the issue is needed.

Table A. *Deaths per 100,000 Resident Population, by Accident Type, Selected Years, 1950–80*

Accident type	*1950*[a]	*1955*[a]	*1960*	*1965*	*1970*	*1975*	*1980*
Possibly product related							
Motor vehicle	23.1	23.4	21.4	25.4	26.9	21.3	23.5
Railway	1.4	0.8	0.6	0.5	0.4	0.3	0.3
Fires and flames	4.3	3.9	4.3	3.8	3.3	2.8	2.6
Firearms	1.4	1.3	1.3	1.2	1.2	1.1	0.9
Explosive material	n.a.	n.a.	n.a.	n.a.	0.3	0.2	0.1
Hot substances, corrosive liquids	0.6	0.5	0.2	0.2	0.1	0.1	0.1
Poisoning by drugs and medicines	n.a.	n.a.	n.a.	n.a.	1.2	1.5	1.1
Poisoning by other substances	1.1	0.9	0.9	1.1	0.6	0.7	0.3
Poisoning by gases	1.2	0.7	0.7	0.8	0.8	0.7	0.5
Medical procedures	0.4	0.5	0.6	0.8	1.8	1.5	1.1
Nonproduct related accidental falls	13.8	12.3	10.6	10.3	8.3	6.9	5.9
Accidental drowning	3.2	3.1	2.9	2.8	3.1	3.1	2.7
All other accidents	10.1	9.5	8.9	8.8	8.4	7.6	7.6
Total	60.6	56.9	52.3	55.7	56.4	47.8	46.7

Source: U.S. Bureau of the Census, *Statistical Abstract of the United States, various issues.*

n.a. Not available.

[a] Excludes Alaska and Hawaii.

Table B. *Worker Job Deaths per 100,000 Workers and Total Disabilities, Selected Years, 1945–83*

Year	*Deaths*	*Disabling injuries (millions)*	*Year*	*Deaths*	*Disabling injuries (millions)*
1945	33	2.00	1976	14	2.20
1950	27	1.95	1977	14	2.30
1955	24	1.95	1978	14	2.20
1960	21	1.95	1979	13	2.30
1965	20	2.10	1980	13	2.20
1970	18	2.20	1981	12	2.10
1973	17	2.50	1982	12	1.90
1974	16	2.30	1983	11	1.90
1975	15	2.20			

Source: U.S. Bureau of the Census, *Statistical Abstract of the United States,* 1985 p. 425.

Table C. *Disabling Work Injuries per Million Employee Hours, by Selected Industry, Selected Years, 1950–70*

Industry	*1950*[a]	*1955*[a]	*1960*	*1965*	*1970*
Manufacturing					
Food products	18.9	18.6	21.1	23.4	28.8
Textile mill products	11.0	9.7	9.2	9.6	10.4
Lumber and wood products	50.2	40.5	38.0	36.0	34.1
Chemicals	11.1	8.0	7.4	7.5	8.5
Petroleum products	9.3	6.5	6.8	8.6	11.3
Fabricated metal products	19.0	15.4	15.4	18.1	22.4
Machinery (excluding electrical)	13.8	11.1	10.8	11.9	14.0
Coal mining	n.a.	n.a.	42.5	44.7	41.6
Contract construction	41.0	34.5	31.5	28.3	28.0
Transportation and public utilities					
Local rail and bus	n.a.	11.8	14.3	15.8	23.9
Trucking	34.5	28.7	32.3	29.2	35.3
Electric and gas	13.8	8.2	6.2	5.3	6.6
Wholesale and retail trade	12.3	12.6	n.a.	11.8	11.3
State government hospitals	n.a.	n.a.	16.3	21.0	21.4

Source: U.S. Bureau of the Census, *Statistical Abstract of the United States, 1960, p.232* and *1972, p.239.*

n.a. Not available.

a. Excludes Alaska and Hawaii.

Table D. *U.S. Product-Related Injuries Requiring Hospital Emergency Room Treatment, Fiscal Years 1974–81*

Thousands

Product	*1974*	*1975*	*1976*	*1977*	*1978*	*1979*	*1980*	*1981*[a]
Playground equipment	140	143	158	164	151[b]	165	162[b]	178
Ladders	61	73	81	85	83[b]	98	89[b]	98
Power lawn mowers	56	63	57[b]	61	69	74	63[b]	71
Swimming pools	53	56	69	68[b]	68	89	116	124
Power saws	41	58	59	60	68	71	73	79
Cleaning agents	35	36	40	35[b]	40	38[b]	32[b]	38
Electrical fixtures	25	22[b]	26	28	26[b]	34	32	41
Chain saws	23	27	28	35	48	51	62	64
Space heaters	20	7[c]	8	10	10	16	23	25
Electric power tools	13	13[b]	16	16	14[b]	22	25	28
Tractors	6	7	7	10	9[b]	10	13	13

Sources: *Annual Report of the Consumer Product Safety Commission,* various issues.

[a]Calendar Year.

[b]Indicates reduction from previous year.

[c]CPSC begins to differentiate among three heater categories.

Peter W. Huber, *Safety and the Second Best: The Hazards of Public Risk Management in the Courts*, 85 COLUM. L. REV. 277 (1985)*

The standard diagnosis in many judicial opinions and in much of our scholarly legal literature has been that our society produces too much "public" risk, through its excessive or unwise use of dangerous new technology and the tools of mass production. The standard prescription has been for lawyers to do something about it. But this diagnosis is probably wrong, and the prescription should certainly be rejected.

The legal debate about risks is very much a debate about "public" risks. These are threats to human health or safety that are centrally or mass-produced, broadly distributed, and largely outside the individual risk bearer's direct understanding and control. Public risks usually derive from new or especially complex technology—they are the hazards of large-scale electric power plants, air transport in jumbo jets, mass-produced vaccines, chemical additives and contaminants in food, or recombinant-DNA technology. For many lawyers, "advancements" such as these arouse deep suspicion and concern. "Private risks," by contrast, are discretely produced, localized, personally controlled, or of natural origin. They are the risks of cottage industries, wood stoves, transportation by car, or exposure to natural toxins or pathogens. Typically, private risks arouse little anxiety among legal commentators.

The legal system's almost obsessive preoccupation with public risks is, in my view, entirely misguided. I wish to develop this argument soberly; there can be no technological arrogance in the shadow of Bhopal. But the facts and the regulatory arguments seem plain nonetheless. First, public risks are progressive—they improve the overall state of our risk environment—whenever the incremental risk created is smaller than the quantum of existing privately-created risk that is displaced. The point may seem obvious, but the fact that a large number of judges and legal commentators ignore it suggests otherwise.

Second, the judicial system is, for a variety of reasons, incapable of engaging in the aggregative calculus of risk created and risk averted that progressive public-risk management requires. While it is not my goal to replace an absolutist's aversion to public risk with an absolutist's embrace of it, I will argue that the judicial role sought (and achieved) by many commentators is imprudently biased against many progressive, risk-reducing (though still risky) technologies. This bias significantly hinders our progress towards a healthier, safer environment.

* * *

Excess Public Risk

Life is already unacceptably hazardous, and likely to grow more so as the result of excessively rapid and overwhelming technological change. This is the common starting point in much of the legal commentary. How is the point to be proved? First, by referring to the public's aversion to public risks. Second, by reciting the myriad public terrors already in our midst. Third, by developing the microeconomic and philosophical underpinnings of a case against means of production that entail public hazards.

*Used by permission.

Lawyers opposed to public risks are in good company. The public consensus, if there is one, seems to be that risk-taking, like abortion, religion, travel, or marriage, should be a private affair. Indeed, consumer hostility to public risk is matched only by consumer affection for private risk.

Illustrations of this division of preferences abound. The aerial spraying of malathion in a California program to combat the Mediterranean fruit fly provokes passionate opposition, but consumers eagerly spray tens of thousands of gallons of the same pesticide in their own, private gardens. A proposal to vent small amounts of radioactive gas and water from the damaged nuclear reactor at Three Mile Island in the course of cleaning up that facility—a comparatively minuscule investment in public risk with clear risk-reducing benefits—causes panic. But a proposal to ban saccharin—a proposal to curtail, as these things go, a fairly substantial investment in comparatively "private" patterns of risk taking—precipitates what was described in the New York Times as panic buying of the sweetener. Mass aircraft accidents arouse great concern, and the mandatory use of seat belts in planes is accepted without a murmur. But in the much more hazardous private-risk environment of automobile travel, seat belt interlock systems or mandatory seat belt laws encounter vociferous consumer opposition. Mandatory vaccination programs are vigorously attacked in the courts, but individuals also come to court to insist on their right to be treated with medical quackery of every description, apricot pits providing a recent and much-publicized example.

Panic, protest, and organized resistance thus greet almost every venture that entails new public risk. Meanwhile, efforts to restrain private risk-taking are denounced as grave attacks on personal freedom. Some litigants have seriously maintained—and some courts have agreed—that the Constitution itself enshrines both the right to bear a private risk and the right not to be exposed to a public one. In short, shared risks, like shared goods, are thought to be almost un-American—a collectivist affront to individual autonomy and self reliance.

The layperson's aversion to public risks is shared by much of the legal community. Lawyers, for the most part, are convinced that there is too much public risk out there, and they generally begin their indictment of public risks by citing some that they especially dislike. Professor Yellin, for example, uses as his paradigm case the hazards of generating nuclear power, but he also points to chemical pesticides, air and water pollution, occupational hazards, and "complex environmental decisions" of every description—the "ominous, not yet fully understood risks to public health [that] involve decisions that may seriously alter our physical environment." Professor Rosenberg's concern centers on similar targets: the risks accompanying "the production, distribution, marketing, consumption, and disposal of toxic agents." He lists as examples "asbestos, Agent Orange and Agent White, Three-Mile Island, dioxin, and a string of acronyms—DES, PCB, PBB and IUD," drugs, and aircraft disasters. Numerous other commentators have similar lists of concerns, and all supply citations to cases in which judges and juries have echoed these fears.

To the lawyer *qua* economist, risk is a cost—the cost of confining, disposing of, or simply coexisting with hazardous matter or energy. The cost can, of course, vary enormously, depending on how wisely a particular hazard is managed. It is nevertheless ascertainable. As with all other costs, the lawyer-economist will contend, the creator of a risk must shoulder it if markets are to operate "efficiently." A producer of risk who is not held strictly accountable for the unconsented-to consequences of that risk will generate risk in socially undesirable amounts. The result will be a market failure. Or so the story goes.

The lawyer *qua* philosopher may reach similar conclusions about public risks on somewhat different grounds. Our libertarian, individualistic political ideal forbids one person from imposing unconsented-to burdens on another. Burdens that take the form of external threats to health or safety are especially objectionable intrusions on the risk bearer's private space and personal autonomy. Like the lawyer-economist, the lawyer-philosopher is therefore opposed to external risk. The mass producer of a dangerous good, or the operator of a hazardous power plant, acts antisocially. Her conduct is worse than economically inefficient—it is morally wrong. Or so the story goes.

Arguments along these lines are wheeled out, with pedestrian regularity, by those opposed to everything from nuclear power to synthetic sweeteners. Absent the risk bearer's individual, fully informed, and entirely free consent, any activity that creates public risk is, pro tanto, both a threat to market efficiency and an infringement on the just entitlements of the risk bearer. Public risks are an absolute bad. We want as few of them as possible.

* * *

The Relative Safety of Old and New

Life has been growing steadily safer in this country, and at a rapid pace. The reasons are undoubtedly complex, but the trend strongly suggests a first rule of thumb for prudent risk management: new technologies, new chemicals, new consumer products, and new industrial processes, though hazardous in themselves, are on average much safer than the old hazards they displace.

There is hardly a product in use today—a car, plane, boiler, municipal water system, drug, vaccine, or hypodermic syringe—that is not many times safer than its counterpart of a generation or even a decade ago. The net change that results from any particular risk exchange may be difficult to evaluate. But actuarial tables strongly suggest that the aggregate change in our risk environment wrought by new technology has been inexorably and swiftly progressive. Innovation and technological change, one must presume, reduce risk. Nothing else satisfactorily explains the steady decrease in aggregate background risk in the past several centuries of technological transformation.

The Hazards of Technological Stasis

Our working assumption in public risk management, I have argued, must be that new risks are, on average, less serious than the old ones they will displace. The first hazard in delaying the introduction of new risks is that the old ones are proliferating. The second hazard involves the risks of opportunities not taken. The gravity of this hazard is measured not by the deterioration of the human risk environment that inevitably follows technological stasis, but by the established risks of living that are potentially within our power to avoid.

The problem is well illustrated by the tale of two sweeteners: saccharin, a century-old dietetic sweetener, and aspartame, a reasonably close substitute. Aspartame was discovered over a decade ago, but it took the FDA eight years to determine that the sweetener should be approved. Now, the biological workings of synthetic sweeteners, we must concede, involve scientific questions as complex, and hazards as potentially devastating and irreversible, as those of any other product of new technology. So perhaps another eight years of delay are in order, while federal judges are consulted on the safety of the sweetener. There are, indeed, public interest groups demanding precisely that, and they have met with some success. The FDA Administrator was obliged to bypass the findings of his own Scientific Board of Inquiry to approve the licensing of aspartame. There are surely reasonable prospects of finding some federal judge who can detect something wrong in this administrative record.

Some in the legal community may see much virtue in an unhurried judicial hard look before 100 million Americans are permitted to begin consuming aspartame in their soft drinks. But a word is in order about the other side of the risk picture. By some estimates saccharin causes 2000 cases of bladder cancer per year. Aspartame's risks are still not altogether clear, but available evidence suggests that aspartame is safer. If aspartame is only half as risky as saccharin, and can be used to displace about half of all saccharin consumption, the eight year regulatory delay imposed by the FDA already has cost the public 4000 cancers; additional years of review by the courts would have kept the risk meter ticking at 500 cancers per year. My figures (other than for saccharin's risks) are entirely hypothetical, but the conclusion they suggest is not. Delay in approving safer substitutes can involve countable bodies.

The lesson should be clear: while we wait for a judicial pronouncement on each new risk, the old ones already in our midst continue unabated. Aspartame is certainly not the only example to be found. The FDA—which on its own initiative has already raised caution to the levels Professor Yellin advocates—sometimes approves new and beneficial drugs for use in this country only years after they are approved elsewhere. The risk costs of delay by the Nuclear Regulatory Commission in approving new nuclear plants include the costs of acid rain and urban air pollution; air pollution, in turn, causes an estimated 50,000 deaths per year. In addition, each day's delay in approving a "new source" of air pollution can translate into an additional day's operation of an older—and dirtier—one. A delay in approving a new hazardous waste-disposal site diverts yet another shipment of wastes to the older and even more dangerous alternative site already in existence.

Lengthy judicial review can only aggravate these hazards of delay. And it is most certain to have regressive risk consequences when it delays the introduction of new technology that has already received administrative approval. Here the "second opinion" comes after a favorable first opinion from an expert agency—that is, after the experts have already concluded that in comparison with existing alternatives the new technology represents a sound risk investment. This is precisely when a languorous second look by the courts is likely to entail the greatest cost in lost risk-reducing opportunity.

Lawyers cling to the regulatory ideal of preserving the status quo at all cost. But judicial delay in the introduction of new sources of risk is a regulatory strategy built on the Panglossian belief that we already reside in the safest of all possible worlds, and the Malthusian conviction that the future has nothing to offer but a snake. In the second-safest of worlds that we in fact occupy, the superior regulatory policy is to license the new snake-venom antidote with reasonable dispatch, even if the drug is not perfectly safe. When things start less than perfect, haste pays haste. With interminable judicial review of new technology, leisure surely answers leisure.

* * *

Risk Regulation in the Courts

Retrospective risk regulation in the courts is governed by somewhat more varied (though equally unsatisfactory) criteria: "luridness" is perhaps the best one-word summary of the dominant judicial risk-selection standard here. First, rare, exotic risks tend to be discovered earlier than common ones, for the simple reason that they stand out against the otherwise grey background of ubiquitous hazard. A new product, safer than its old and widely used substitutes, will be attacked quickly if it causes a distinct and readily identifiable type of harm; existing substitutes will escape attention if they are entrenched and so widely used that the risks they cause are already counted as part of the "background" incidence of accident or disease.

Second, the operation of the existing administrative regulatory system adds to the likelihood that the tort system will not focus primarily on relatively grave hazards within particular risk markets. New sources of risk are routinely subjected to more intensive administrative scrutiny than older ones. Statutory mandates commonly focus particular attention on new sources of hazard, and agencies recognize that improper approval of new risks are politically much less acceptable than the improper neglect of old ones. But the result, surprisingly enough, is that the amount of information regarding relatively new risks is usually much greater than the amount of information regarding old ones, notwithstanding the fact that the newer substitutes have arrived on the scene more recently and are, more often than not, less hazardous.

It is equally certain that "natural" selection of tort litigation—controlled largely by the mass-exposure plaintiffs' bar—fails to operate as a rational ordering device for selecting among good and bad public risks. First, the mass-exposure lawyer wastes little time thinking about the substitute risk of the disease when suing the vaccine manufacturer, or about the risks of sugar when suing the saccharin manufacturer. Nature's risks, grave or mild, are of no concern whatsoever to the litigator; her overwhelming financial imperative is to exact from man what is man's, and leave God's risks to God. The tort lawyer selects her risk targets with complete indifference to the risks Nature may have to offer once the human producers are driven out of the market. But as we have seen, "natural" life is much more dangerous than the technological cocoon.

For similar reasons, the mass exposure lawyer will take her defendant as she finds him. She will be unlikely to spend much time worrying about precisely which among substitute manmade goods are more dangerous. A mass-exposure lawyer is a traditional saleswoman; the customer is the jury. And as with most saleswomen, the actual quality of the product will often be of much less interest than its saleability. For the plaintiff's bar, the most attractive risks are those for which the evidence is the most unusual and lurid, the class to be represented the largest, and the problems of proof the lowest. According to these criteria, the risks that happen to land at the top of the list are not likely to be those that would be selected by risk experts engaged in a sober examination of the competing sources of risk in a market filled with a rich variety of hazardous substitutes.

Finally, tort liability is a poor vehicle for choosing risks because judges and juries have little capacity to make risk choices wisely. First, judges and juries, like most people unfamiliar with the quantitative aspects of risk, routinely assume that new and less familiar hazards are graver than they really are, and that older, more common ones are less severe. The risk-creator's conduct inevitably looks very much more reasonable when it produces familiar and entrenched hazards than when it creates novel ones. Age, familiarity, and ubiquity are the most powerful legitimizing forces known to the legal system.

Furthermore, jury liberality with the resources of the deep-pocket defendant is such a well-known phenomenon that it scarcely deserves mention. Juries have been known to answer special interrogatories so as to absolve the large corporate defendant from any possible liability and then to award damages to the plaintiff anyway. Juries tilt heavily against public risks created by wealthy defendants. But the wealth of the risk producer is not a good surrogate for ranking substitute risks in order of relative severity.

To recapitulate, a risk selection system in which risks are simply ranked according to the volume, luridness, or distinctiveness of risk information that plaintiffs' lawyers find comprehensible and judicially saleable is likely to be heavily biased against relatively new and mass-produced sources of risk; beyond that, it is likely to be largely random in its choice of risk targets. It is plain that random regulation entails social costs without commensurate benefits, and as I have discussed, novelty and mass production represent risk solutions much more often than they represent risk problems.

* * *

Private Injury and Public Safety: The Courts and the Agencies

My discussion brings me to two conclusions. First, governmental control of public risks is both necessary and useful. Many public risks should be excluded if they are not yet a part of our environment, or controlled if they already are. Government regulation, moreover, is also needed to fulfill the second half of the regulatory function—to supply our collective consent to public risks that are judged to be good risk investments. Second, the courts are institutionally predisposed to favor regressive public risk choices. The courts systematically prefer old risks to new ones and discretely produced or natural hazards to mass-produced substitutes, and have neither the inclination nor the expertise to distinguish sources of truly "excess" risk from their risky yet risk-reducing counterparts.

Who then should decide how much public risk we will accept and in what areas?

The answer is painfully obvious to almost everyone outside the legal community: expert administrative agencies, not lawyers. To make life safer, faster, we need not more scientists in the legal process, but fewer lawyers in the scientific one. The legal system has no special competence to assess and compare public risks, and the legal process is not designed or equipped to conduct the broad-ranging, aggregative inquiries on which sensible public-risk choices are built. Expert administrative agencies, troubled and erratic though they may be, remain best able to regulate public risks in a manner calculated to advance the public health and welfare.

* * *

Conclusion

In keeping with a pattern set by most other legal commentators, I come out of the public risk debate more or less where I went into it. Some measure of public risk in our economy advances the public health and safety. Frugality in risk expenditures is certainly a virtue. Yet if we are too miserly with public risk, life will grow more dangerous, or at best remain less safe than it might be.

It is difficult to say for certain whether we currently accept the right ratio of public to private risk. But what is clear is that in the extremely safe society we already inhabit the unfavorable rate of exchange that attends the privatization of public risks is overlooked much too often. We will be able to move forward aggressively to conquer the residual hazards of our existence only when we cross the psychological barrier of risk choice, and learn to accept that a little unfamiliar risk is the price of much of our familiar safety.

We can only speculate what publicly risky yet risk-reducing possibilities may lie ahead, for it is in the nature of highly profitable investments that they are difficult to identify at the outset. Recombinant DNA research creates some new risks—and may also hold the key to curing cancer. Should the courts set up a Legal-Scientific Commission and call a moratorium on research while we await a pronouncement from the judicial oracle? Or should the plaintiffs' bar perhaps sue Genentech at once, charging it with whatever proportional-risk premium a lay jury deems reasonable? If we do, the lawyers will surely win; the public at large will probably lose. There is even louder opposition to the technology that could provide abundant and cheap electric power. Yet now that we have overcome the problems of supplying abundant, safe food and water, our next best risk investment is almost certainly in energy. The high-tech world of information processing is risky too—there is some concern for example, about the hazards of video display terminals that are standard equipment on most computers. But the information revolution also makes possible robotics, which may soon lower a final curtain on the sordid hazards of the nineteenth-century factory.

And what of Bhopal? Our response must be a rational, progressive one. The engineering lesson must be learned. There will most certainly be other, equally tragic, industrial accidents, but this one, at least, must not be repeated. And the chemical industry in India, as in this country, must be allowed—indeed encouraged—to develop and grow. The Bhopal victims cannot be brought back to life but their surviving parents, children, and siblings can be fed and sustained. In a country that has hovered for many years on the brink of mass starvation, this will not be possible without agricultural pesticides.

The greatest vanity of the legal profession—a profession with more than a few vanities—is its conviction that there are no limits to the contributions lawyers can make to the public safety. The natural, self-aggrandizing instinct of altogether too many lawyers and judges is to stand up and do something—anything at all—when any aspect of life seems less than perfect. But the reality is that life has grown safer not because of the legal system but despite it. The technological community, far from ushering in an endless series of new terrors, can rightfully claim full credit for the extraordinarily safe society it has built. Pesticides and vaccines save lives, although they also create some risks of their own. It is undoubtedly futile to curse the darkness of starvation and disease. But it is insane to snuff out with legal paper those who would light the candle of a cure.

The path to a safer existence lies in fewer, not more legal constraints on those whose genius allows for the replacement of old and grave risks with less grave new ones—scientists, engineers, the mass-manufacturers of drugs, pesticides, and consumer products, the suppliers of water, food, energy, and transportation. Public risk investments still hold out the promise of large, risk-reducing returns. Hotspur was right. It is out of the nettle, danger, that we pluck the flower, safety.

Stephen P. Teret & Michael Jacobs, *Prevention and Torts: The Role of Litigation in Injury Control,* 17 LAW, MED. & HEALTH CARE 17 (1985)*

Those who study, teach, and practice in the field of injury epidemiology and prevention often compare injuries to diseases; to do so enhances the understanding that injuries, like diseases, have etiologic agents that act within particular environments to affect predictable hosts. It is important to stress the scientific underpinnings of injury control, so that injuries will not continue to be seen as randomly occurring events that strike the unlucky, who have little or no preventive opportunity available to them. Those within the field argue that injury prevention, like disease prevention, when approached with the proper scientific method, holds the prospect of saving thousands of lives per year in the United States.

The comparison of injuries to diseases, however, can distract attention from some crucial aspects of injury prevention. Infectious disease control is the story of man's battle with living organisms that often do their damage to hosts at the cellular or sub-cellular level. The pathways of those diseases can be difficult to discern, and some mysteries are yet to be solved. Injuries, on the other hand, do their initial damage on a more visible level. Their etiologic events are often apparent,

*Used by permission.

and do not require epidemiologic or biochemical detective work for an understanding of the causes of injury.

Moreover, the prevention of injuries often requires a different strategy than the prevention of diseases. With diseases, an elusive agent, borne by a vector that is difficult to control, may indicate that the best prevention technique is to immunize the potential host. With injuries, immunization may be impossible. But the agent (the transfer of energy) is obvious, and the vehicle that delivers the agent to the host is most often a manmade product. Frequently, it is the failure of the product that creates the injury.

Prevention of injuries, then, deals with man's control over his own creations. It deals with providing incentives or requirements for product makers and others to anticipate hazards and to reduce them to the extent feasible. These incentives and requirements are usually created through the legal system. They can come in the form of legislation, regulation, or litigation. This article examines the role that litigation plays in injury prevention.

As a category of litigation, product liability suits are relatively new. It is only in the past few decades that product liability law has blossomed and has had a measurable impact on the course of injury prevention. Typically, the use of product liability suits as a tool for injury prevention is the last step in a process that goes as follows: First, there is the discovery that a particular product is dangerous in some respect and is causing substantial numbers of injuries; this discovery is followed by efforts to persuade the manufacturer to make its product safer; if those efforts fail, there is then an attempt by injury prevention advocates to achieve through legislation or regulation a modification of the dangerous product or a means to make it less dangerous; if legislation and regulation do not succeed, finally, there is a lawsuit, usually well-publicized, that finds the manufacturer of the product liable and that awards compensation to the plaintiff. The lawsuit brings in its wake the threat of other lawsuits, and ultimately, a change in the marketing of the product or in the product itself that will result in fewer injuries.

The history of air bag litigation in this country provides a good example of this process. Since the late 1960s there has been overwhelming evidence that many thousands of lives could be saved each year in the United States if all cars were equipped with air bags. Car manufacturers knew this, but failed to make the product available. The federal government knew this, but was unable to enact and sustain effective legislation or regulation requiring automatic protection, largely because of opposition by car makers. From 1969, when the federal government first suggested that it would require the installation of air bags in cars, until 1983, failed regulatory efforts followed one upon another. Because of these repeated legislative and regulatory failures, the plaintiff's trial bar was urged to litigate to protect the public's health.

In 1983 a suit was brought on behalf of Rebecca Burgess who, at the age of 18, was a front seat passenger in a Ford Pinto struck by another car, and was rendered a severely brain-damaged quadriplegic as a result of the crash. She sued Ford Motor Company for failing to have provided an air bag in the car, a failing that made her injuries much more severe. After 10 days of trial, Ford settled the case for $1.8 million, a settlement that received wide publicity both within professional circles and among the public generally. This publicity, in turn, spawned more air bag cases; and in November 1985, Ford announced that it would offer air bags as optional equipment on some 1987 models.

The air bag case is a good example of the customary pattern: injuries, failed efforts at informal change, failed efforts at legislative or regulatory change, a successful private lawsuit, publicity, the threat of more lawsuits, and, finally, product modification. As slow as it is, this pattern of action for the modification of products has been successful on many occasions, and can clearly result in the prevention of injuries.

Another example of the use of product liability suits for the reduction of motor vehicle injuries deals with shoulder harnesses in the rear-seat positions. In 1986, the National Transportation Safety Board stated that it has been "widely recognized for many years" that a lap-shoulder combination belt provides "better overall crash protection, and less inherent hazard, than lap belts." Despite this evidence, American automobiles and federal regulators have failed to require that rearseat shoulder belts be standard equipment in new cars. The car manufacturers claim, on the one hand, that lap belts are safe enough and, on the other, that adding rear shoulder harnesses presents "a challenging technical problem." The regulatory authorities say that the extra safety benefits provided by the combination belts would not be worth their costs, an estimated $12 per car.

In the past few years, a dozen or so lap-belt injury suits have been filed against the major auto companies. As these suits come to be tried or settled, it seems clear that the large amounts of damages paid by the auto manufacturers in these cases will constitute a strong incentive for change.

In September 1986, General Motors Corporation paid $5 million to settle the claim of Sabrina Phillips, a nine-year old who is now a quadriplegic as a result of injuries allegedly sustained from the lap belt she was wearing in the rear seat of a GM car involved in a crash. In January 1987, American Honda Motor Co. paid $2 million to settle the case of John Rosario, a 22-year old paralyzed from the waist down allegedly as a result of a rear seat lap belt. And in December of 1987, in one of the first lap-belt cases to be tried, a federal jury in Baltimore awarded $3.3 million to James Garrett and his family for damages sustained by Garrett as a rear-seat passenger in a Ford Escort, when his lap belt broke one of his vertebra during an accident, paralyzing him from the waist down.

In the *Garrett* case, the Escort in which Garrett was a passenger had no rear seat shoulder harness. Plaintiffs argued to the jury that the absence of such a rear harness was responsible in part for Garrett's injuries, and that the injuries were also due partly from a design defect in the Escort's rear seat lap belt. An elastic strap used to keep the rear belt from slipping down into the back seat tended to pull the belt up over the hips and onto the waist, positioning it to cause serious internal injuries in some crashes and, in particular, causing it to break one of Garrett's vertebrae. Ford disputes the jury's findings and is in the process of deciding whether to appeal.

Prior to the *Garrett* verdict and the settlements described above, automobile manufacturers had little incentive to install rear seat shoulder harnesses in the United States. Although General Motors has offered the back seat harnesses as an option since the 1960s, although Ford has included them in some of its European-made models since 1972 and although some European car makers have included them as standard equipment in the U.S. since the mid-1970s, the lack of any government regulation on the matter, the relatively low level of seat belt usage until recently—especially in the rear seat—and the absence of any effective litigation, permitted the car makers to argue that the harnesses were not really necessary and that their $12 per car cost would discourage some potential car buyers.

* * *

Successful product liability suits have several effects, some intended, others not. The most obvious intended effect is to secure for the plaintiff, the injured party, adequate compensation for injuries. Successful lawsuits—those that result in large settlements or jury awards—have the additional effect of causing the maker of the dangerous or defective product in question to modify the product to make it safer. Once a manufacturer has been found liable for damages caused by a dangerous or defective product, the specter of additional lawsuits and of more money to be paid out—a specter made vivid by the publicity gained in plaintiff's lawyers' circles by a large verdict—acts as a great incentive for the manufacturer to eliminate the dangerous or defective aspects of its product. These two effects, the compensatory and the preventive, are intended and anticipated consequences of successful product liability cases, and are generally seen as beneficial to consumers and to the public health in general.

Occasionally, however, successful product liability actions can arguably result in unintentional consequences detrimental to consumers and to public health. For example, in the past several years manufacturers of children's car seats have been named as defendants in dozens of product liability actions which cumulatively seek damages in excess of the manufacturers' combined net worth. According to "Passenger Protection Report," the large number of these lawsuits—said to be related more to "the litigious attitude of society today" than to product defects—has caused product liability insurance rates for the industry to climb 2000–5000 percent in one year. The report states that coverage limits have been dramatically reduced, deductibles greatly increased and companies forced to pay such high premiums ($1.6 million for $2 million in coverage, in one case) that "two manufacturers have already stopped making car seats entirely and three-fourths of the others are considering eliminating them from their product lines."

The extent to which increased liability insurance premiums in this industry (and others) represent a rational response to successful lawsuits or an overreaction by insurance companies to one or two large verdicts is unclear. What is clear, however, is that successful product liability actions, and even the threat of such actions, can in certain circumstances place in jeopardy the continuation of entire product lines, some of which—such as child car seats—play an extremely important role in injury prevention. What is also clear from the child car seat example is the relatively unnoticed but powerful role that insurance companies can play in the world of injury prevention: By raising liability premiums for truly dangerous or defective products, insurance companies can create significant economic disincentives for the manufacture and distribution of those products while encouraging the development of safer ones.

* * *

Conclusion

The legal system was not designed with an eye toward evaluations of the effect that lawsuits have on society. The incidence of specific types of lawsuits is difficult to measure, information on certain lawsuits is often unobtainable, and the responses of defendants to litigation are most frequently not discussed. Therefore, an analysis of the preventive effects of tort litigation, by force, takes on an anecdotal tone. Unfortunately, the anecdotes that receive attention are too often the horror stories, obscuring many instances in which lawsuits successfully fulfill their compensation and deterrent potentials. The weight of evidence is strong that the health and safety of the public can be enhanced by tort litigation.

Those who advocate tort reform argue that levels of compensation obtained through tort litigation are often excessive, and therefore the tort system must be changed by capping recoverable amounts and otherwise limiting litigation. These arguments fail to take into account the preventive importance of tort litigation. An abridgment of the legal opportunities to fully compensate injuries would, in some situations, make it cheaper to produce dangerous products. If, through litigation, the costs of injuries caused by an unsafe product are factored into the cost of the product itself, manufacturers and retailers are provided with an important incentive to protect the public's health.

B. Insurance

Victor E. Schwartz and Liberty Mahshigian, *National Childhood Vaccine Injury Act of 1986: An Ad Hoc Remedy or a Window For the Future?*, 48 OHIO ST. L.J. 387 (1987)*

In 1986, Congress enacted legislation creating an innovative method of resolving claims for childhood vaccine injuries. It establishes a mandatory no-fault compensation system for persons injured through childhood vaccines. After the no-fault proceedings, the claimant has the option of accepting the compensation awarded, if the injury were found to be vaccine-related, or bringing a civil action against the vaccine manufacturer in which several limitations on the manufacturer's tort liability would apply.

The legislation responded to two concerns: (1) liability for these injuries was causing United States manufacturers to stop producing vaccines, and (2) children injured by vaccines were often without a source of payment or compensation for their medical and rehabilitative needs, leading to greater resort to the tort system for some form of financial relief.

The approach Congress took in the National Childhood Vaccine Injury Act of 1986—which on the one hand sets up a no-fault compensation system and on the other hand modifies the tort law rules for injured persons who choose not to accept compensation through that system—could be viewed as either a panacea for the vaccine liability problem or as precedent for an approach that Congress could take in addressing the broader product liability problem. Here we explain that the dual compensation system/tort reform approach was a response to a unique situation with childhood vaccines, and that this type of approach would not work in a broad product liability bill.

Childhood Vaccine Crisis

The National Childhood Vaccine Injury Act addressed a crisis situation that existed for products that provide tremendous societal benefits. Vaccines to protect against serious and life-threatening diseases such as pertussis (whooping cough), diphtheria, tetanus, measles, mumps, rubella, polio, and small pox, are, without doubt, vital products. An increase in tort lawsuits for injuries associated with vaccines, however, caused a number of United States vaccine manufacturers to withdraw from the market. Faced with a dwindling vaccine supply and the imminent scarcity of a much-needed product, Congress stepped in. The House Energy and Commerce Committee noted:

> The loss of any of the existing manufacturers of childhood vaccines at this time could create a genuine public health hazard in this country. Currently, there is only one manufacturer of the polio vaccine, one manufacturer of the measles, mumps, rubella (MMR) vaccine, and two manufacturers of the DPT vaccine. Two States, Michigan and Massachusetts, produce their own DPT vaccine. Despite Congressional support, Federal vaccine stockpiles maintained by the Centers for Disease Control (CDC) have never reached CDC's recommended level

---

*Used by permission.

of six-months' supply. Thus, the withdrawal of even a single manufacturer would present the very real possibility of vaccine shortages, and, in turn, increasing numbers of unimmunized children, and, perhaps, a resurgence of preventable diseases.

Childhood Vaccine Compensation Program

The National Childhood Vaccine Injury Act of 1986 establishes a two-tiered system for obtaining compensation for injuries resulting from immunizations that state governments require children to receive as a condition of entry into school—vaccines for polio, diphtheria-pertussis-tetanus (DPT), and measles-mumps-rubella (MMR). The first tier is a mandatory no-fault system under which compensation for specific injuries related to childhood immunizations, listed in the Vaccine Injury Table, is to be paid out of a Trust Fund established by the Act. The Trust Fund is to be financed with the proceeds of an excise tax imposed on each dose of the covered childhood vaccines.

If a person has been injured by a vaccine covered by the Act, a claim must first be brought through this no-fault compensation system before a tort lawsuit may be filed against a vaccine manufacturer. The Act's objective is to provide a more speedy and more certain compensation alternative to the tort system, so that litigation is the last resort.

A claim for compensation is made by filing a petition with a United States district court. The petition must contain a variety of materials necessary to make a finding as to whether compensation is to be made, including evidence that the person received a vaccine listed in the Vaccine Injury Table of the Act or contracted polio from a recipient of an oral polio vaccine, and that the person sustained or had significantly aggravated an injury listed in the Table and within the time periods specified in the Table.

If the petitioner's injury is listed in the Table, and occurred within the time period set forth in the Table, there is a presumption that the injury was caused by the vaccine. This presumption can be overcome by preponderance of the evidence, submitted by the Secretary of Health and Human Services or a vaccine manufacturer, that a particular petitioner's injury is not vaccine-related. Evidence that may be submitted to overcome the presumption includes proof of other infections, traumas or conditions, but does not include speculative or hypothetical matters or explanations. Petitioners may also seek to prove that an injury not covered by the Table was caused by a vaccine. The entire proceeding, from date of filing through special master proceedings and court review, is to take place as expeditiously as possible and, in no case, should take more than one year.

If the district court determines that an injury is vaccine-related, it will award compensation to be paid from the Trust Fund established by the Act. Compensation is made for actual, unreimbursable medical expenses, rehabilitation costs, and lost wages. The award is to include an amount to provide for reasonable attorneys' fees and other costs incurred in proceedings on the petition. The court may, in its discretion, make an award for attorneys' fees and costs even if it does not award compensation on a petition, if it determines that the action was brought in good faith and that there was a reasonable basis for the claim for which the action was brought. In addition, the court may award compensation for pain and suffering up to $250,000. In the case of death, a fixed award of $250,000 is made. Compensation under the program may not include punitive or exemplary damages or any form of compensation, other than death benefits or lost earnings, that is not for the health, education, or welfare of the injured person.

After the judgment of the district court regarding the petition for compensation has become final, the petitioner may, within 90 days from that date, decide in writing either to accept the court's judgment or to file a tort action for damages for the vaccine-related injury or death. The petitioner's decision must be filed in writing even if the court has refused to award compensation.

If the petitioner fails to file a decision in writing within the 90-day period, he or she will be deemed to have accepted the court's judgment.

In sum, the compensation proceeding is relatively simple. There is no discovery, cross-examination, pleadings, or trial. The power of the special master to require evidence, submission of information, and require testimony, is intended to replace the usual rules of discovery in civil actions in federal courts. The only issues relevant to the compensation proceedings are whether the petitioner suffered a compensable injury and, if so, the extent of compensable damages. Congress structured the Act so as to encourage persons to take advantage of the compensation system by making it (1) mandatory, (2) not based on proving fault for a vaccine-related injury, (3) speedy, and (4) fair in terms of the amount of compensation.

As a trade-off for the certainty of no-fault compensation and as an added incentive to have less resort to the tort system, the Act modifies tort law for vaccine injury suits in several respects. Except to the extent that the Act has established a rule of law for such actions, tort actions for vaccine-related injuries will be governed by applicable state law. Thus, tort litigation under these modifications of law is the secondary system of recovery for vaccine injuries.

First, the Act adopts the principle contained in comment *k* of section 402A of the *Restatement (Second) of Torts*, that a vaccine manufacturer should not be liable for injuries or deaths resulting from unavoidable side effects if its products are properly prepared and accompanied by adequate directions and warnings. Under the Act, a vaccine is presumed to be accompanied by proper directions and warnings if the manufacturer demonstrates that the directions and warnings comply in all material respects with relevant federal law governing the approval and labeling of the vaccine. This presumption may be overcome if the claimant shows that the manufacturer engaged in fraudulent conduct or intentionally or unlawfully withheld information in obtaining pre-market approval for the vaccine from the Federal Food and Drug Administration, or if the claimant shows by clear and convincing evidence that the manufacturer failed to exercise due care notwithstanding its compliance with Federal Food and Drug Administration requirements.

Second, vaccine manufacturers may not be held liable in tort lawsuits for their failure to provide warnings directly to the vaccine recipient, rather than physicians. This provision overrules several court decisions that have held drug manufacturers liable for failure to provide direct warnings to the patient rather than to an intermediary such as a doctor, nurse, or pharmacist who can be expected to know about the product and its risks, and who is responsible for informing the patient.

Third, a vaccine manufacturer will be protected against punitive damages in a tort lawsuit if it shows that its product complied with applicable requirements under the Federal Food, Drug and Cosmetic Act and specified provisions of the Public Health Service Act.

A Solution to the Vaccine Liability Problem?

The approach Congress took to address the children's vaccine liability problem, which creates a no-fault system as the primary method of compensation, is, undeniably, a response to a unique problem.

First, children's vaccines are unlike other products. Children are required by law in every state to be immunized in order to attend public school. The fact that state governments require children to undergo a risk in order to protect society as a whole, was seen by Congress as justification for development of a national fund to compensate children who are injured because of these risks.

Second, unlike some other products, the incidence of serious injury with children's vaccines is very low. Thus, a vaccine compensation system can be self-funding by adding a very small excise tax to the price of vaccines. It would not be as easy to finance a compensation system for other products which have higher incidences of serious injury and, therefore, would require funding from outside sources, such as general revenues.

Third, the children's vaccine liability insurance situation was more widely felt than the liability crisis that exists with most other products. Most of the vaccine manufacturers in the United States have withdrawn from the market. The loss of even one more manufacturer could mean that some children would be unable to receive vaccines, which would create a very serious public health problem.

Based on these justifications for having a no-fault compensation system for vaccines, Congress set out to achieve two objectives: to provide an expeditious method of compensating children who are injured because of vaccines and to make liability for vaccine manufacturers more predictable so that the supply of vaccines in the United States will be adequate.

The first of Congress' objectives, to create an efficient method of providing adequate compensation for vaccine-injured persons, can be achieved only if the compensation proceedings are not abused. The overriding guideline of those proceedings is simplification. The burden will be on the district courts and the appointed special masters to administer the compensation program within these guidelines. Attempts by either side to interject discovery into these proceedings or to raise issues other than causation of the injury and the extent of damages, will defeat this objective.

The second objective, to make vaccine liability more predictable, will be accomplished only if the no-fault compensation program becomes the primary means of redress for vaccine-related injuries, meaning that the majority of claims that otherwise would be resolved in the tort system are resolved in the compensation system. Congress could have more greatly assured this result by making the no-fault compensation system the exclusive remedy for persons injured by vaccines. Instead, Congress attempted to make the compensation program an appealing alternative to tort litigation and to reduce incentives for persons to choose tort suits as a means for resolving vaccine injury claims.

Congress may have decided to retain the tort system for vaccine injury claims, at the expense of greater predictability, as a means of providing incentives for the manufacture of safe vaccines. For example, under the Act, vaccine manufacturers will be subject to liability in tort lawsuits if vaccines are not properly prepared or are not accompanied by adequate directions or warnings. It could be argued that under a no-fault compensation program, particularly where compensation derives from a general fund and is not linked to individual responsibility, expeditious and certain compensation is provided for at the expense of removing those incentives. The argument would be that the absence of a linkage between fault and payment for injuries removes incentives for vaccine manufacturers to act safely. Interestingly, representatives of professional consumer groups and trial attorneys have consistently opposed the establishment of fault standards of liability in federal products liability legislation proposed in Congress, on the theory that absolute liability is the greatest incentive for safety. A fundamental principle of tort theory, however, is that placing liability on persons who act wrongfully creates incentives for safety. For this reason, it could be argued that an exclusive no-fault compensation system might not provide safety incentives.

In order to accomplish this objective within the framework of an exclusive no-fault compensation system, other methods of penalizing unsafe conduct and rewarding safe conduct could be developed. For example, instead of funding the program through an excise tax, some method could be developed for making assessments on vaccine manufacturers in accordance to the incidences of injuries related to their products.

A Window for the Future?

By enacting this legislation Congress recognized its responsibility for major products liability problems. Congress has in the past acknowledged its interstate commerce responsibility for products by enacting legislation regulating product safety—the Consumer Product Safety Act, the Federal Food, Drug, and Cosmetic Act, the National Traffic and Motor Vehicle Safety Act, and so on—but this step into products liability is a groundbreaker.

But this approach to the vaccine liability problem is unlikely to be followed on a broader basis. The mandatory nature of childhood immunizations and the ability to fund a compensation program without outside sources may have motivated Congress to take this approach. For this product, harms are capable of being listed on a Vaccine Injury Table, but outside this context, the inability to define an objective trigger would thwart development of a broad product-injury compensation program.

The bottom line—this particular approach to liability problems is unlikely to be a window for the future.

George L. Priest, *The Current Insurance Crisis and Modern Tort Law*, 96 YALE L.J. 1521 (1987)*

Modern Tort Law and Its Economic Effects

Since the early 1960s, courts have steadily expanded tort liability for injuries suffered in the context of product and service use. These changes in the law result from the acceptance of a coherent and powerful theory that justifies the use of tort law to compensate injured parties, a theory its founders called enterprise liability. According to the theory, expanded provider liability serves three important functions: to establish incentives for injury prevention; to provide insurance for injuries that cannot be prevented; and to modulate levels of activity by internalizing costs, including injury costs.

The second feature of the theory—the importance of providing insurance for unpreventable losses—is most crucial for understanding our current insurance crisis. According to enterprise liability theory, expanded legal liability does more than achieve optimal control of accident and activity rates. Expanded tort liability improves social welfare, in addition, because it provides a form of compensation insurance to consumers. A provider, especially a corporate provider, is in a substantially better position than a consumer to obtain insurance for product- or service-related losses, because a provider can either self-insure or can enter one insurance contract covering all consumers—in comparison to the thousands of insurance contracts the set of consumers would need—and can easily pass the proportionate insurance premium along in the product or service price. Most importantly, to tie insurance to the sale of the product or service will provide insurance coverage to consumers who might not otherwise obtain first-party coverage, in particular the poor or low-income among the consuming population.

*Used by permission.

The insurance rationale was central to the first judicial adoption of enterprise liability theory, by the California Supreme Court in *Greenman v. Yuba Power Products*. The approach was rapidly extended across the various state jurisdictions, first in the products liability field and, later, in other areas of tort law. Enterprise liability theory has justified both restrictions in available legal defenses and expansion of substantive liability standards.

As examples, since the mid-1960s, courts have invoked the insurance rationale to limit the defenses of contributory negligence, assumption of risk, and consumer product misuse; to eliminate defenses related to the status of the victim (as in actions brought by licensees and trespassers against property owners); and to restrict the effectiveness of statutes of limitation. At the same time, the theory has supported the affirmative extension of liability through the adoption of standards of strict liability, retrospective liability, and unreasonably dangerous per se, relaxation of causation requirements, and, more generally, through the near-universal acceptance of comparative negligence, which permits a jury to render judgments against defendants even if they are responsible only in some small proportion for a plaintiff's injury.

These legal changes have particularly affected insurers because courts have simultaneously expanded the scope of the insurance contract. Again, under the influence of enterprise liability theory, courts have adopted the maximization of insurance coverage as the principal interpretive objective in insurance contract disputes. Thus, courts have interpreted policy coverage provisions broadly and policy exclusions narrowly to achieve the compensation goal.

As a result of these doctrinal developments, both the range of defendants against whom a plaintiff might collect a judgment and the range of plaintiffs to whom a corporate defendant might ultimately be liable, have expanded. Courts have also expanded the range of losses for which compensation might be sought, chiefly by allowing increased recovery of emotional and other non-economic losses.

* * *

How Insurance Works

Imagine an insurer asked to write a products liability policy for a single manufacturer of a unique product. Putting aside other insurer skills, the insurer has no comparative advantage to a single manufacturer in establishing reserves against future expected losses. If the insurer, however, can also write products liability policies for other manufacturers of unique products, the insurer can create an effect similar to that of the law of large numbers. As long as the risks of the individual manufacturers are independent, the level of total risk will be less than the sum of the individual risks. Thus, the risk that all products will be designed defectively is less than the sum of the risks that any one product will be designed defectively. If the risks faced by the insurer, however, are highly correlated and not independent—such as the socio-legal risk that the legal standard for proving defective design will be relaxed—the benefits from aggregation are defeated. Total risk will equal the sum of the individual risks, and the insurer has no comparative advantage to the insureds themselves.

It is a well-established implication of this approach that the more narrowly risk pools can be defined, the more broadly insurance can be offered in the society. A legislature or court that wanted to maximize the availability of insurance within the society would adopt policies that facilitated the segregation of risks into the narrowest possible pools. Competition among insurers serves this objective. Insurers try to lure an insured away from competitors by offering membership in a pool for which the premium is closer to the insured's expected loss, because of the more discrete definition of the pool. In essence, the insurers are competing over the relatively low-risk insureds of any risk pool, who are likely to select that insurer most precisely able to price the risk the insured brings to the pool. Such competition increases total insurance availability. Unfortunately, much of modern insurance regulation is designed to thwart such efforts. As we shall see, much of modern tort law (and, incidentally, much of the modern judicial approach toward the interpretation of insurance contracts) also impairs the ability of insurers to define narrow risk pools in order to extend insurance availability.

We never observe individuals purchasing insurance for pain and suffering or other emotional losses. However severe the pain, a larger bank account is an imperfect anesthetic. As a consequence, there is no market for pain and suffering insurance in any society in the world. Indeed, if the pain is especially severe, individuals may prefer a form of reverse or anti-insurance: more assets available to enjoy before the accident than after. Of course, there are very limited situations in which anti-insurance of this nature can be arranged.

The lack of consumer demand for insurance for pain and suffering losses is certainly also a consequence of adverse selection problems. Individuals may differ substantially in the level of pain and suffering that they experience or can tolerate. If so, offering coverage for pain and suffering will increase the variance of risks brought to an insurance pool. As before, if the variance in expected risks is sufficiently great, the risks will be uninsurable because the low-risk members will successively drop out of the pool.

Pain and suffering may also involve moral hazard. Moral hazard refers to the effect of the existence of insurance itself on the level of insurance claims made by the insured. Moral hazard can occur either ex ante or ex post the occurrence of the loss. Ex ante moral hazard is the reduction in precautions taken by the insured to prevent the loss, because of the existence of insurance. Ex post moral hazard is the increase in claims against the insurance policy beyond the services the claimant would purchase if not insured. In the context of medical insurance, for example, ex post moral hazard includes excessive (at full-price) visits to doctors, longer hospital stays, and more elaborate and expensive methods of treatment. In this context, a person who might, ex ante, choose one level of care, may ex post, choose more care, because the costs of the care are paid by the insurer. Full insurance reduces the price of future purchases of medical care to zero, and so a person is likely to choose a greater level of care than he or she would choose if charged for the care at marginal cost.

Moral hazard, in part, is a particular source of the adverse selection problem. Where insureds, ex post, can affect the level of claimed losses, the variance in expected risks increases. Those individuals who are less likely to gain from exaggerated visits to doctors or from more extensive hospitalization will drop out of the pool if full coverage is offered.

For these reasons, market insurance universally incorporates deductibles and coinsurance where the extent of the loss can be influenced by insureds' ex ante or ex post decisions. A deductible is a condition in an insurance contract that requires an insured filing an insurance claim to pay a fixed sum unrelated to the magnitude of the claim. Coinsurance requires the insured to pay some fraction of the amount of each claim. Deductibles and coinsurance reduce indifference to preventive investments, and they reduce the incentive to consume what, from an ex ante view, are excessive levels of the service for which insurance has been purchased. They reduce differences in risks brought to insurance pools.

The discussion to this point has addressed only first-party insurance. Tort law, of course, provides insurance through a third-party mechanism: the insurer pays money to the victim through the medium of the product or service provider who purchases the insurance policy. Although third-party institutional arrangements are somewhat more complex than first-party arrangements, the determinants of the insurance function are the same.

In third-party insurance, there are two sets of risk pools. Consumers of products or services comprise one set of risk pools. To consumers, the insurance policy and the premium are tied to the sale of the product. It is advantageous to define risk pools narrowly for consumers in third-party contexts for exactly the same reasons that it is advantageous to define risk pools narrowly in typical first-party insurance contexts. Defining consumer risk pools narrowly increases product sales, because the premium added to the price of the product more closely approximates the consumer's expected loss.

Manufacturers, for example, will attempt to segregate consumers into risk pools by product design and by advertising and marketing techniques. A chain-saw manufacturer, for example, may design one model appropriate for industrial use and a second model appropriate for occasional gathering of firewood. Of course, such design differences may also be related to different consumer preferences for product features—in this example, features related to safety. But the point is that, if the demand for chain saw injury insurance coverage differs between the professional and the weekender, both consumers and the manufacturer will gain if the manufacturer can design products that differentiate the two markets. In this example, market differentiation would reduce one very broad risk pool into two more narrow risk pools. Narrowing the pools allows the manufacturer to charge different insurance premiums to the two markets and to increase product sales.

Similarly, the accident insurance premium added to the price of an airline ticket from the United States to Europe will be greater on, say, the Concorde than on low-budget or charter lines. The risk of an accident among the various airlines may be the same, but the accident payout risks brought into the pool by passengers on the Concorde are likely to be much greater than the risks brought by charter passengers, if only because of their greater expected future income. The third-party insurance premium must be adjusted in response. In this respect, the qualitative differences between the Concorde and the charters in terms of accident insurance are no different than qualitative differences in meals, time of transit, or other amenities. Indeed, much of the attraction of the charters derives exactly from the ability of these firms to narrow the pool of consumers of their product. Those passengers who travel on low-fare flights are those who prefer or are willing to tolerate lower levels of amenities in return for a lower ticket price.

The second set of risk pools within third-party insurance contexts includes the service and product providers themselves. Providers of products and services purchase market insurance for the same purposes as any first-party insured: to equalize monetary returns over time in the face of some probabilistic chance of loss. Providers will choose market insurance if its costs are lower than the costs of alternatives.

The costs a provider faces by deciding not to purchase insurance depend upon diversification within the provider firm or the provider's ability to diversify risk by other means. As suggested above, marketing different models of a product is a form of diversification, if the risks of loss attending sales of the respective models are uncorrelated. Of course, organization in the conglomerate form or investing retained earnings in diversified assets are other ways in which providers can self-insure.

Insurance companies, however, can (and do) compete for the custom of providers by trying to define narrow risk pools that make market insurance more attractive than self-insurance alternatives. Insurers attempt to aggregate within a pool a set of providers whose risks are uncorrelated, and will set individual premiums for the firms according to the risk each brings to the pool. The insurer's diversification of risk, again, can be achieved either by aggregating a very disparate pool, by holding other assets whose riskiness is uncorrelated, or by reinsuring—hiring another insurer to provide meta-diversification.

These simple insurance principles seem very general, but they provide an explanation for the insurance crisis we are currently observing.

How Contemporary Tort Law Affects Insurance Markets

As discussed earlier, over the past two decades, courts have expanded corporate liability in order to provide compensation insurance to injured persons through tort recoveries. The expansion of corporate liability has progressively undermined the insurance function by increasing the variance (coefficient of variation) of existing insurance risk pools. As described previously, increasing the variance of a risk pool endangers the pool because it increases the likelihood that the pool will unravel as low-risk members drop out, either by self-insuring or by ceasing to engage in the potentially injury-related activity. These effects are present in both consumer and provider risk pools. Thus, contemporary tort law has restricted rather than expanded insurance availability. The parties that have been most adversely affected are the low-income and poor who, in terms of tort recoveries, are the low-risk members of the consuming population.

It is helpful at the outset to describe forms of expanding liability that will not affect insurance markets. The [Reagan] Justice Department has argued that the insurance crisis is the result of increases in the level of damage judgments over the past ten years, emphasizing increases in average tort judgments in medical malpractice and products liability cases, in particular. I have challenged the Department's empirical substantiation of its claim (as have many others), but a stronger criticism should be made. Other things equal, a scalar (proportionately equal) increase in the level of tort judgments and settlements will not affect the degree of insurability of any risk. A scalar increase in tort payouts, other things equal, does not affect the marginal benefit of insurance to any insured because it will not change the ratio of the premium to an insured's expected loss. The premium set equal to the average risk brought to the pool will increase by exactly the same proportion as will the expected loss to the insured.

Of course, modern tort law has changed in dimensions beyond the average damage judgment. I have described how modern tort law has expanded the range of plaintiffs to whom corporate enterprises are liable, the range of provider defendants against whom injured persons may bring suit, and the range of activities for which corporate enterprises have become subject to liability, changes which, obviously, expand commercial liability risk pools. The Justice Department, in addition, has suggested that increases in tort filings and in million dollar judgments have contributed to the crisis. I believe that these developments, in fact, have undermined commercial casualty insurance markets. But the exact mechanism that generates the effect is not immediately obvious. As a consequence, simple proposals, such as those of the Justice Department, to no more than retrench corporate liability are not immediately compelling. Increased corporate liability may surely increase corporate insurance costs, but why does it lead to a breakdown of the insurance function?

The question is especially puzzling because of the curious empirical context of the recent crisis. Two phenomena, in particular, are important here. First, there is no evidence of increase in the rate or severity of accidents for the principal set of activities affected by the crisis. Of course, in recent years some products have been newly discovered to be harmful (for example, the Dalkon Shield), generating substantial liability. But the insurance crisis has not been dominated by products of this nature; there have been no claims of previously unknown toxic damage from diving boards or slides in public parks.

Moreover, the extension of tort liability on insurance grounds has not generated totally new insurance coverage. Today, the vast majority of Americans possess health, disability, and life insurance coverage, either through private first-party sources or through government supported Medicaid, Medicare, veterans' benefits, and the like. Here, too, there are exceptions: chiefly occasional workers, such as migrant laborers, actors, artists; and the marginally poor, those who remain above the social service qualifying level while healthy and injured, but who are likely to qualify for social service insurance after they suffer an injury. Yet, again, no one claims that the insurance crisis has been generated by tort recoveries of occasional workers and the marginally poor. These individuals consume less and thus are less likely to be involved in product- or service-related injuries. More importantly, because these individuals have low levels of both current and prospective income, the damage judgments they recover are typically insubstantial. It follows that both past increases in tort judgments and expected future increases in tort judgments derive, in the largest part, from the claims of individuals already possessing first-party insurance coverage.

These facts redefine the issue to be analyzed. If there has been no increase in the accident rate and if the largest majority of tort law claimants already possess first-party insurance, then the expansion of corporate legal liability has chiefly shifted coverage from (private and government) first-party sources to corporate defendant third-party sources. The question, then, is why the shift from first- to third-party insurance sources has led to a breakdown in insurance markets?

I believe that there are very clear insurance reasons why the shift towards third-party coverage has undermined the commercial casualty insurance industry, generating the crisis. In comparison to first-party insurance, third-party tort law insurance provides coverage in excessive amounts, in a manner that substantially restricts risk segregation, and at costs that far exceed the costs of first-party insurance. For both consumer and provider risk pools, these differences will increase the correlation of risks within existing pools and, as a consequence, increase the extent of adverse selection, leading to the breakdown of the pools.

Why Consumer Risk Pools Have Unraveled

Provider tort law insurance coverage differs substantially from first-party insurance coverage. One of the objectives of the tort system is to create incentives for appropriate investments in preventing injury. To obtain optimal incentives for injury prevention, a party that has violated a legal standard must pay full losses to the victim, including both pecuniary and non-pecuniary losses.

The award of both pecuniary and non-pecuniary losses, however, is inappropriate for providing optimal insurance for unpreventable losses. The effort to extend insurance coverage through modern tort law represents a confusion of incentive objectives with insurance objectives. Third-party insurance payments administered through the tort system differ from first-party insurance payments in two ways. First, no first-party insurance market provides coverage of non-pecuniary losses. Non-pecuniary losses do not affect the marginal value of wealth across states of the world. In addition, moral hazard and adverse selection problems make coverage of these losses exceedingly costly. Losses representing pain and suffering or other emotional effects of an injury, therefore, are never insured in first-party markets because it is not worthwhile for consumers to pay the premiums necessary to support coverage of them.

Secondly, deductibles and co-insurance are features of every first-party insurance contract. Third-party insurance through the tort system, in contrast, never incorporates deductibles or co-insurance to control victim moral hazard. Yet victim moral hazard is as serious a problem in a third-party context as in a first-party context. Preferences for extra visits to a doctor, prolonged hospitalization, or more advanced forms of medical treatment do not diminish because the source of the injury is a third-party defendant.

These two differences mean that, for the same injury, first-party insurance coverage—which corresponds to what consumers are willing to purchase—is substantially different in magnitude than the third-party insurance coverage provided through tort law. First, awards for pain and suffering and other non-pecuniary losses are known to comprise a large portion of tort damages: the most commonly mentioned figure is 25% to 50%. More detailed empirical studies of trial awards—studies of awards in Cook County, Illinois—show that non-pecuniary losses comprise 47.2% of total tort damages. Thus, to approximate, out of the median products liability judgment of $187,000 in Cook County (1980–84), $88,264 represents pain and suffering against which the typical consumer would not choose to insure.

The remaining portion of the average damage judgment represents compensation for pecuniary losses, chiefly lost income and medical expenses. Recoveries for these losses in an active first-party insurance market, however, are also likely to be significantly more modest than under third-party tort law insurance. For example, virtually all United States workers are covered by state workers' compensation plans that provide coverage for lost wages subject to a strict income ceiling. In Illinois, for example, the maximum weekly benefit is $376.33 (for fifty-two weeks, $19,569), which corresponds to a $30,000 annual income. Even for workers with incomes equal to or below $30,000, the precise coinsurance level is difficult to determine since workers' compensation benefits (like the lost income component of tort judgments) are net of income taxes. Workers' compensation plans also provide for lump-sum payments for different forms of permanent disability. In sum, the best recent estimate is that net workers' compensation benefits provide .835 income replacement. Lost income, on average, constitutes slightly over half of pecuniary damages. The lost income component of the median Cook County product liability judgment, then, would be roughly $49,368 of which the victim, under workers' compensation, would receive $41,222 and suffer individually $8,146.

Similarly, with respect to medical expenses, the typical Blue Cross-Blue Shield policies provide an average deductible of $1000 (per member) and coverage of 80% of service costs. Similarly, the typical Blue Cross major medical plan covers only 80% of charges. Thus, under a typical first-party medical plan the victim would be reimbursed $38,694 of the approximate $49,368 medical expense component of the median Cook County product liability judgment and would pay $10,674.

Even this crude estimate of the value of deductibles and co-insurance, however, fails to measure the effect of these payments on the level and character of medical care chosen by insureds. All first-party medical plans incorporate detailed limitations on the nature of available care and on the extent of specific forms of care. Blue Cross-Blue Shield plans, for example, limit coverage to semi-private room accommodations, limit coverage of hospitalization or of skilled nursing facility care to 120 days, and exclude coverage altogether of services such as "custodial care designed to assist an individual in meeting activities of daily life." Of course all consumers would prefer more coverage to less, but these limitations—though they force consumers sometimes to make difficult decisions about medical treatment—represent the best accommodation with the insurance premiums consumers are willing to pay. Because of moral hazard, additional medical services would require increases in insurance premiums beyond their value to consumers.

In contrast, under third-party insurance provided through tort law, there is little reason for the beneficiary of the insurance—the tort plaintiff—to engage in difficult decisions about appropriate levels of medical treatment. Both because of the specific policy care limitations and because every first-party insurance claimant must pay a not-insubstantial portion of medical costs, he or she must consider very carefully which medical procedures will be most effective as well as whether, and the extent to which, extended care is needed. The tort plaintiff, on the other hand, loses nothing by requesting (or asserting as essential) all available advanced methods of medical treatment regardless of cost.

Tort law claimants do encounter costs not faced by first-party insurance claimants, though estimating their magnitude is difficult. Tort law claimants must pay attorneys' fees. In addition, in the vast majority of cases, tort claimants settle prior to trial for amounts less than the highest possible judgment. Regardless of settlement, some tort judgments are reduced under comparative negligence standards. There are analogues to these costs, however, under first-party insurance coverage. If the first-party insurer contests the claim, the first-party claimant must pay attorneys' fees. Similarly, many first-party claims involve negotiation and settlement at some figure less than the full amount demanded by the claimant.

Some might regard the additional level of insurance coverage provided by tort law to be beneficial to consumers because it affords them greater compensation for the injuries they suffer. But this view misunderstands the consumer interest in insurance. Of course, after an injury has been suffered, the victim would prefer a greater to a lesser award. But the ex ante interest of the victim is an award tied to the victim's pecuniary losses, not an award greater than these losses. Where the victim is the product or service purchaser, the victim must pay for the insurance in advance. To compel insurance greater than the amount demanded by the purchaser reduces, rather than increases, his or her welfare. To illustrate: if my $100,000 home burns down, I of course would be happier if my insurer gave me $234,000 rather than the $100,000 of coverage I purchased. But, I would object strongly if I were compelled in advance of the fire to purchase $234,000 coverage since I could replace the home in its entirety for an amount in the range of $100,000. A similar concern for optimal insurance extends to contexts involving pure third-party injuries—for example, when bystanders are harmed by the product or service use of others. In modern society, all of us are at once product and service purchasers and bystanders of products and services used by others. Again, in terms solely of insurance, each of us ex ante prefers that the optimal level of insurance be provided by tort law, the level that optimizes insurance coverage subject to insurance costs.

The provision of insurance coverage through tort law in amounts greater than consumers would willingly purchase has additional effects that implicate the recent crisis. An increase of 64% to 134% in the level of insurance coverage under tort law will not operate as a scalar, but will increase consumer risk pool variance and will lead to the unraveling of consumer risk pools.

The increase in the level of insurance coverage from the shift to the third-party tort mechanism is not likely to be uniform over all cases. The empirical observation that pain and suffering awards constitute 47% of total damages is an average figure. Pain and suffering and other non-pecuniary amounts comprise a much higher proportion of large damage judgments. For this reason, risk pool variance is likely to be greater under third-party tort insurance than under first-party insurance.

More importantly, segregating risks into narrow risk pools is substantially more difficult in third-party than in first-party insurance contexts. First-party insurers, by using insurance applications, can distinguish insureds by age, income, occupation, the level of coverage desired, and other personal characteristics related to levels of risk brought to the insurance pool. Moreover, the administration of first-party insurance allows the insurer to distinguish insureds by past loss experience. The collection of these data allows a first-party insurer to define risk pools of very narrow scope, increasing the likelihood that low-risk individuals will find insurance attractive. Narrow risk differentiation maximizes the availability of insurance.

Very little information about individual risks, however, is available to third-party insurers. A product manufacturer, for example, may design and market a product with reference to characteristics of discrete sets of average consumers. But the manufacturer must sell the product on equivalent terms to all who wish to buy it, and cannot distinguish among consumers with respect to the insurance policy provided in the product price.

Some products, of course, will attract relatively homogeneous sets of consumers. A very wide range of products, however, are accessible to and are purchased by consumers of different income levels. Studies of consumers of individual products show that, for virtually all products, the income levels and personal characteristics of consumers of the product differ widely.

The difficulty of segregating risk pools in third-party contexts means that third-party tort insurance pools are likely to be substantially broader than first-party pools even without the effects, described above, of levels of coverage. Compare, for example, the risks of non-preventable injuries from auto use. The first-party insurer can create separate driver pools for teenagers and other age groups; it can segregate insureds by levels of driving, total mileage, distance from home to office, and car type; and it can rate the policies by accident experience and by moving violations within previous time periods. It can allow the insured to choose whether to purchase medical expense and disability coverage in the auto policy or to rely on separate medical and disability policy coverage set according to the deductible the insured prefers and according to the insured's income level. Each of these techniques helps keep premiums low for the low-risk drivers of the consuming population—those who drive little, are very skilled or careful, or generate small claims because of low expected income losses.

In contrast, the auto manufacturer—that must buy third-party liability insurance for all those injured in its cars and pass on the premiums in vehicle prices—can implement none of these distinctions. Some auto models may be more or less attractive to commuters, to teenagers, or to the very wealthy, but, except for these crude distinctions, the auto manufacturer must provide insurance to all who buy the model, high-risk and low-risk alike. Consequently, the variance in the insurance pool is vastly greater in the third-party context, and the premium is commensurately higher—even if the same level of coverage is offered. Of course, given the greater amount of coverage provided under a third-party policy, the variance and the premium are higher yet.

One of the most seriously deleterious effects of lumping consumers into undifferentiated third-party risk pools is glaringly inconsistent with the judicial objective of aiding the poor. That is the regressive redistributional effect of third-party insurance. The largest items of damages in most third-party personal injury contexts, especially those involving permanent disability, are lost income and pain and suffering, which are highly correlated with individuals' expected future income streams. As a consequence, these damage elements constitute the largest component of the third-party insurance premium tied to the sale of any product or service.

The third-party premium is set with reference to average expected loss. Thus, the high correlation of total awards with income means that premiums reflect the average income of the population of consumers. The implication of charging each consumer a premium related to average income is that consumers with high incomes are charged a premium lower than their expected loss, and consumers with low incomes are charged a premium higher than their expected loss. Third-party insurance thus requires low-income consumers to subsidize high-income consumers.

Moreover, third-party insurance requires low-income individuals to subsidize both pecuniary and non-pecuniary losses of high-income individuals. Compare the insurance premium that a low-income consumer would pay in a first-party auto, product, or disability policy to the premium tied to the product or service in a third-party provider policy that includes coverage to the high-income consumer. The auto or product manufacturer cannot charge the low-income consumer a lower price based on the lower dollar risk the consumer brings to the risk pool. The first-party casualty or disability carrier can do so, and thus can increase the availability of insurance.

As a consequence, the disadvantages of third-party insurance coverage are substantial. Courts justified third-party insurance coverage based on how easy it seemed to be for manufacturers or service providers to aggregate risks by adding an insurance premium to the price of the product or service. Whatever comparative advantage providers enjoy in risk aggregation, however, is overwhelmed by the disadvantages of excessive coverage, the inability to segregate risks in third-party contexts, and regressive distributive effects.

* * *

The Effect of Increased Variance on Consumer Risk Pools

Adverse selection in consumer risk pools occurs when some group of consumers chooses not to pay increased prices that include the higher level of third-party insurance. These consumers decline to purchase the product or service and, thus, drop out of the existing risk pool. The consumers most likely to drop out are the low-risk within the pool. In general, within any pool there will be two low-risk sets: those systematically less likely to suffer injuries at all and those whose injuries systematically generate lower real costs.

Consumers who systematically face a lower injury probability are likely to find the insurance provided with the product or service not worth its added premium. Many commentators have tended to view product- or service-related injuries as occurring randomly, generating an equal injury probability to each consumer. Many product- and service-related injuries, however, are systematically associated with particular product uses. Most modern products can be employed in a wide range of diverse activities. Those consumers who use products in typically less, rather than more, risky ways are likely to drop out of the consumer pool if tort law requires the manufacturer to insure all consumer uses. These consumers will shift to alternative products or services that cannot be used in equally risky ways—products which, as a consequence, will be cheaper because of the lower attendant insurance premiums.

A familiar modern example is consumers of four-wheel drive vehicles. In recent years, the liability of manufacturers of such vehicles has been expanded under design defect and warning law and, more generally, as courts have limited the defenses of contributory negligence, misuse, and assumption of risk. Manufacturers have been held liable, for example, for injuries suffered when these vehicles have rolled or flipped in contexts of extreme mountain driving on grounds that the manufacturer could either design the product to better protect the consumer or insure the consumer for the loss.

Manufacturers must respond to this increased liability either by changing product design to protect drivers in extreme conditions or by increasing insurance coverage for the consumer set as a whole. Whether the manufacturer changes the design or merely increases insurance coverage, product costs will increase and the product price will increase. The price increase, of course, may seem desirable for consumers who drive in extreme backroad conditions. But consumers who purchase four-wheel drive vehicles for other purposes—say, easier driving on snowy or muddy roads—may not find the increased price worthwhile. These consumers could be lured away if they were offered a four-wheel drive vehicle suitable for snow and mud, but not for extreme grades which, if only because of the lower attendant insurance premium, could be offered at a lower price. It is not surprising that many manufacturers have begun offering van and station wagon models with a four-wheel drive option.

This process is adverse selection in the product market. Prior to the expansion of manufacturer liability, the vehicle was sold without insurance for losses resulting from flips or rolls. Consumers who enjoyed backcountry travel insured themselves for such losses in first-party insurance markets. The expansion of manufacturer liability shifted the insurance source to the third-party mechanism. Because the manufacturer was prohibited by product liability law from making this additional insurance optional, low-risk consumers within the pool—those not intending to expose themselves to backcountry risks—dropped out of the pool, either by shifting to domestic four-wheels, or by declining to buy the product at all. When low-risk consumers drop out, the insurance premium added to the price of backcountry four-wheels must be increased by an ever greater amount.

The second set of low-risk consumers affected by the expansion of provider liability are the low-income or poor, who bring low risks to a liability insurance pool because of the lower damages they will receive because of their lower income and poorer future employment prospects. As the insurance premiums tied to products and services increase, these consumers also drop out because the price they must pay is increasingly greater than the value received. Such consumers will shift to substitute products for which the consumer set is more homogeneous in terms of income or for which the underlying risk level is lower. Of course, an income effect is also likely to be important here: Such consumers will discontinue buying products with large insurance premiums because, given their available resources, they cannot continue to afford them. Again, as this set of low-risk consumers drops out, the attendant insurance premiums must be commensurately increased.

Adverse selection in consumer risk pools explains why the increase in insurance premiums has been extreme for products and services in recent years. It also provides the only explanation of why increases in corporate tort liability compel providers to withdraw products and services from markets altogether. Again, if there were no adverse selection, increases in insurance premiums or self-insurance costs could largely be passed on to consumers. Sales may decline, as must be expected from any price increase, but there would be no reason to withdraw products from the market. There is a different effect, however, where a price increase derives from increasing risk pool variance. Increasing variance generates adverse selection by low-risk consumers who successively drop out of the pool. The pool, as a consequence, unravels. At some point, demand for the product sold with the necessary insurance premium simply disappears. There remains no set of identifiable consumers to whom the product or service is worth its price.

It is difficult for others than industry experts to distinguish insurance from consumer preference grounds for product differentiation, but there is some strong evidence of this trend at least with respect to more extreme risks. Some bus companies, for example, are reported to have terminated charter transit to ski areas because of the relatively higher risks of icy roads. In addition, as noted earlier, one New York vineyard has terminated or severely curtailed wine-tasting from fear of host liability for alcohol-related injuries. Public parks that have removed playground equipment or school districts that have removed diving boards from swimming pools are other examples of the effect. By excluding such services, these entities reduce the variance of risks related to the services they continue to provide.

The large number of products and services that have been totally withdrawn from markets demonstrate the severity of the effects of contemporary tort law's shift to the third-party insurance mechanism. Except for a few particularly notorious examples, product and service withdrawal tends to be effected silently, ignored as consumers shift to alternative sources that are higher priced or less convenient for their needs. It has been reported, however, that vaccines and pharmaceuticals have been withdrawn, despite prior FDA approval. Cessna Aircraft terminated several small plane models because insurance costs (estimated at $75,000 per plane) had pushed prices beyond the reach of its consumers. Similarly, the G.D. Searle Co. terminated sales of intrauterine devices in U.S. markets. Searle's annual sales volume for the devices was $11 million, but it spent $375,000 defending each product liability action brought by users of the IUDs. Litigation costs of this dimension are not likely to persist once the novel liability issues with respect to the product are resolved. But even a dramatic reduction in litigation costs per case may not make the intrauterine device price-competitive with other means of birth control.

Product and service withdrawal, however, has extended far beyond the limited examples reported in the press. Very recently, a Conference Board survey of the nation's 500 largest corporations showed that twenty-five percent had removed products or services from markets. Oddly, this datum was reported amidst the author's conclusion that the deleterious impact of the insurance crisis was exaggerated because firms were still profiting from sales of products they had not been forced to withdraw. The author confuses the existence of corporate profits with consumer welfare. Consumers do not benefit from having fewer products and service choices (any more, from a broader view, than do corporations), even if quarterly corporate earnings exceed zero. Of course, it is even more difficult to estimate the extent to which new products and services were never introduced because of the expansion of liability.

* * *

Who has suffered most from these developments? It is clear in my mind that the greatest harm from the expansion of tort liability and the consequent shift from first- to third-party tort insurance coverage has been suffered by the poor and low-income within the consuming population. The increase in market insurance and self-insurance costs leads to increases in the price level of virtually all commodities. In some cases, these increases will effectively price low-income consumers out of the market for the product altogether. Increases in product prices shrink the purchasing dollar and, in proportionate terms, shrink it more severely for the poor.

The increase in insurance costs reduces the availability of products or services for the poor in still more ways. The unwillingness of obstetricians to perform normal deliveries for less than $1200, noted earlier, more severely affects those individuals for whose deliveries Medicare will pay $507 than those consumers able to pay the full cost by private negotiation with the doctor. Similarly, the termination of midwife services because of the absence of insurance is relatively less troublesome to those who can afford to substitute licensed physicians or full-priced obstetricians.

More generally, even if the low-income are able to continue to pay the insurance-enhanced prices of products, they are harmed. The poor and low-income are much more likely to be paying a premium that exceeds the risk they bring to the pool under third-party than under first-party insurance coverage, because of the difficulty providers face in segregating risk pools. No one today would seriously propose that all citizens pay an identical life insurance premium where some of the beneficiaries—the high-income—would receive greater total benefits. No one would urge that all individuals pay the same disability premium regardless of expected income. No one would seriously propose that all homeowners pay the same fire premium regardless of home value, or that all drivers pay the same auto premium regardless of car value. Yet this is exactly the regime of life and disability insurance provided by modern tort law. Modern tort law forces all consumers to pay the same third-party insurance premium for product- and service-related coverage for losses leading to injury, disability and death.

Ernest J. Weinrib, *The Insurance Justification and Private Law*, 14 J. Legal Stud. 681 (1985)*

I

In this comment I wish to outline the significance for private law of using insurance as a basis for liability. My focus will be Justice Traynor's statement in *Escola v. Coca-Cola Bottling Co.* that "the cost of an injury and the loss of time or health may be an overwhelming misfortune to the person injured, and a needless one, for the risk of injury can be insured by the manufacturer and distributed among the public as a cost of doing business."[1] Whether the insurance justification is regarded as essential or supernumerary, it is part of a conception of law that is now dominant in the United States, especially in the products liability field. This conception can be contrasted with another that is still regnant elsewhere.

Strict product liability and its attendant justifications are now solidly entrenched in American law and academic discourse, and distant indeed in that seemingly dark era when the forces of barbarism were clinging to the shrinking citadel of privity, when the fall of each outpost of the old dispensation was celebrated in the country's leading law reviews. Yet it is worth recalling that in the common-law world, only the United States has witnessed the judicial creation of a regime of strict products liability. Unlike so many American ideas, this one has not inspired imitation. In Canada, for instance, the courts' tailoring of liability rules to the operation of insurance would be regarded as bizarre, and there is no judicial pronouncement similar in impact to Justice Traynor's statement in *Escola*.

The peculiarity of the American position on the significance of insurance can perhaps best be appreciated in the contrast between Traynor's statement and that of Mr. Justice Stephen of the High Court of Australia. In a judgment dealing with liability for negligently inflicted economic loss, Mr. Justice Stephen disposed of the consideration of insurance as follows:

> In any reference to the writings on this topic, and articles abound in the law journals of the last fifteen years in the common law countries, frequent mention will be found of the important role to be played by insurance and of the significance which judicial policy consideration should accord to it and to what has come to be known as "loss spreading." . . . I have myself avoided reference to either of these two factors and I should explain my reasons for doing so. If loss-inflicting consequences of an act are reasonably foreseeable and the necessary proximity is shown to exist, the present state of the law of torts, unreformed by any fundamental departure from fault liability, suggests no reason why the tortfeasor should not bear the consequences of his conduct. The task of the courts remains that of loss fixing rather than loss spreading and if this is to be altered it is, in my view, a matter for direct legislative action rather than for the courts. It should be undertaken, if at all, openly and after adequate public inquiry and parliamentary debate and not worked towards covertly, in the course of judicial decision, by the adoption of policy factors which assume its desirability as a goal and operate to further its attainment. . . [T]here is, I think, no justification for the courts, when deciding actions in tort between private litigants, to make use of such views as policy determinants in the absence of any independent opportunity

*Used by permission.

[1] 24 Cal.2d 453, 462, 150 P.2d 436, 441 (1944).

> to test their soundness and without parliamentary sanction for the departure from pre-existing goals of the law of torts which their espousal involves.[2]

This statement sets out the conception of tort law that is prevalent in non-American common-law jurisdictions. Their relegation of insurance is not a consequence of lack of sophistication concerning fortuities or of antipathy toward loss spreading as a social goal. The path-breaking compensation schemes that have originated in the Commonwealth—from the Saskatchewan no-fault automobile plan of 1946 to the more recent accident compensation legislation in New Zealand—belie explanation of that kind.

Rather, Stephen's statement embodies a conception of the relationship between insurance and tort liability. Liability insurance is triggered by a judgment or settlement of tort liability; the liability is therefore antecedent to the operation of the insurance. But if the likelihood of insurance becomes a factor in the process of assigning liability, this sequence is reversed. The presence of insurance is transformed into a means for creating the liability to which it is supposed to respond.

But I wish to concentrate on a further point. The priority of liability to liability insurance is required if liability is to be a judgment on human interaction and not a tax on activity. The preservation of this priority is an element in the preservation of private law itself. Stephen indicates as much by invoking a constellation of considerations that are characteristic of private law: the fault standard, the disavowal of instrumental policy factors, and the distinction between legislative and adjudicative functions. As Stephen says, his ultimate theme is what counts as "justification for the courts, when deciding actions in tort between private litigants."

The difference between Stephen's treatment of insurance and Traynor's thus ties into a very broad issue concerning the nature of private law. Although loss spreading through insurance may be an appealing goal, Stephen's conception of tort law excludes it. What, then, is this conception, and why is it unreceptive to basing liability on insurance?

II

In the common-law world generally, tort law treats the two litigants as connected one with the other through an immediate personal interaction as doer and sufferer of the same harm. Tort law's conceptual apparatus of cause, duty, standard of care, and fault provides the signposts for the judicial articulation of this immediate interaction. Attention to activity and passivity in the context of a given harm precludes consideration of the litigants' wealth, virtue, or need: whatever the relevance of these factors for distribution or moral assessment, they are not elements in the parties' immediate interaction as such.

Now the invoking of insurance undermines this conception of tort law by draining the parties' relationship of its immediacy. Attention is no longer confined to the interaction of doer and sufferer. The status of one of the parties as an injured assumes paramount importance, and insurance becomes the lens through which the relationship between the litigants is refracted.

When a mediating factor is interposed between litigants, their juridical relationship takes on an instrumental aspect. Implicit in the use of this factor is the claim that the parties' relationship can be understood with reference to it. But since the factor in question is not an element in the interaction as immediately conceived—if it were, it would not be a mediating factor—its presence is alien. Explication of the litigants relationship in terms of this extrinsic factor implies that the former stands to the latter as a means to an end. In strict products liability, the operation of insurance becomes a measure of the validity of the plaintiff's claim, and some consequence of insurance—

---

[2] Caltex Oil (Australia) Pty. Ltd. v. The Dredger "Willemstad" (1976), 136 C.L.R. 529, 580.

loss spreading, the maximization of the parties' joint welfare, general deterrence, redistributing wealth from the deeper pocket—is considered to be a desirable goal.

The instrumentalism arising from the mediation of the litigants' relationship also implies a distinctive role for the state and for positive law. Insurance is only one mediating possibility among many, and the several goals it promotes are not always consistent. Since all mediating factors are alien to the parties' immediate interaction, none is spontaneously valid with respect to it. The diversity of possible objectives necessitates the exercise of the paradigmatically legislative function of selecting the collective goal. Here political and technical considerations play a large role. The recognition of any goal as decisive thus depends on its authoritative incorporation into the schedule of collectively approved aims. In this respect legislation differs from adjudication, which presupposes that juridical relations are intelligible prior to the authoritative declarations that retrospectively make this intelligibility explicit.

Deploying insurance considerations to resolve tort disputes thus entails an instrumentalist and legislative conception of law. The difference between American products liability law and that of the rest of the commonlaw world is not, therefore, a difference of doctrine alone. In refusing to follow the American example, other courts of the common-law world are viewing law as a realm of immediate relationships, resistant to the instrumentalist and legislative coloration insurance introduces. In other words, they are maintaining a conception of tort law as essentially private.

Now one must not think that private law is concerned with a different subject matter from public law; nor does the distinction between private and public raise issues analogous to those of the division of powers in a federal system. The private character of tort law does not point to a range of inherently private matters: since tort law deals with the harms one person inflicts on another, such harms cannot pertain to a single individual. Tort law is private in that the immediate interactions it governs are intelligible without recourse to legislative instrumentalism. Private law in this conception is not instrumental, because it does not orient the parties' relationship toward an extrinsic purpose. In working out the meaning of interaction it recognizes that each party acts for its own purposes, and it does not stamp the relationship from without with a further purpose. Similarly, private law is not legislative, since a court does not direct the relationship toward a substantive policy of its choosing but rather discloses the considerations that make the relationship intelligible on its own account. As the judicial practice of retroactively enunciating tort duties shows, this intelligibility is independent of legislative fiat. The spelling out of the implications of activity and passivity is an exercise of cognition and not of creation.

This conception of a truly private law may, to Americans, appear outmoded or fantastic. But the eccentricity of the insurance justification and the dispute about its soundness underscore the parochialism of this reaction. No doubt the peculiar American position that allows the courts to function as instruments of political change has its own historical conditions: the ineffectiveness of the legislative process, the consciousness of the revolutionary origins of legal order, the modeling of adjudication on the interpretation of a constitution continually beset by crisis. Conversely, the survival of a more pristine conception of private law in Canada was perhaps facilitated by the sustained liberal and even social democratic influence on the political process and by a conservative tradition that encouraged the realization of the common good through state action. When the pressures of change can thus be channelled through public law, there is perhaps less need for courts to trench on and tamper with the domain of private right.

III

Skepticism about the coherence of a noninstrumental and nonlegislative conception of law is the legacy of the American Realists, who supposedly destroyed forever the conceptualism that must undergird it. The orthodoxy that the Realists attacked asserted the possibility of a legal science based on an inductive ordering of the mass of decided cases. To the extent that the existing case law was the ultimate point of reference for this orthodoxy, its foundations were positivistic. But the lances of the Realist attack would be broken against a conception of juridical relations that is prior to positive law and that positive law actualizes.

In the natural law tradition, private law is understood as an ordering that makes explicit the immanent rationality of the transactions it governs. Aristotle called this rationality corrective justice, thereby distinguishing it from the rationality of mediated interaction, which he termed distributive justice. By contrasting the structure of a bilateral transaction with that of distribution among an indefinite number, Aristotle's accordingly, not a substantive principle that the adjudicator weighs against other substantive considerations. It is rather the justificatory structure—of which adjudication is itself a part—through which private law makes good its claim to rationality.

Corrective justice regards the interaction between the plaintiff and defendant as an integrated whole in which both litigants have an equal standing. Goals such as compensation or deterrence, which subordinate the relationship between the parties to a factor peculiar to one of them, are excluded, because this integrated relationship of equals cannot be grasped as an aggregate of one-sided functions. Corrective justice is the understanding of interaction in terms of itself and not in terms of an extrinsically devised purpose: the only function of the law of torts is to be the law of torts.

In corrective justice the litigants are equal despite their inequality in wealth, virtue, or station. These attributes are not part of the interaction as such, and therefore corrective justice abstracts from them to the formal equality that all actors have as actors. The construal of interaction as immediate thus presupposes the Kantian notion of action, according to which the self-conscious ego exercises its freedom through its capacity to abstract from the particularity of its situation. For Kant, and for Hegel after him, private law is the most primitive expression in external relationships of the internal freedom that marks self-conscious and self-determining beings. Inasmuch as private law orders the interaction of self-determining actors, it cannot admit an instrumentalism that subjects the actor to an exogenous end.

The rise of insurance as a factor in tort litigation is a harbinger of the attenuation of the hold of private law as a ruling component of the American legal experience. Now an assertion of the integrity of private law supplies no ground for preferring private to public law: both modes of ordering can have their own integrity. Affirmation of the coherence of private law in terms of corrective justice is in no way inconsistent with the advocacy of the replacement of tort law by a comprehensive compensation scheme on the New Zealand model.

Even those who favor the extension of the scope of public law or who construe law in essentially public terms should, however, feel some disquiet at the intrusion of a mediating factor such as insurance into the plaintiff's claim against the defendant. A coherent pattern of state action hardly seems likely to emerge from the judicial grafting of a public purpose onto a series of fortuitous relationships between pairs of litigants. Public law does not require the existence of private law as a positive reality of the legal system, but the *intelligibility* of public law requires at least the recognition that private law too must have the status of, in Kant's words, an idea of reason. This is because public law inasmuch as it *is* law, must no less than private law actualize freedom in man's external relationships, and the freedom that law actualizes—the recognition of a person's status as a self-determining enity—is the same for law in both its public and its private aspects. Orientation of the plaintiff's suit to an extrinsic purpose reflects badly on that commitment of legal institutions to the ideal of law they supposedly serve. Proponents of public law have no reason to rejoice in the warping of the realm of private right.

C. An Assessment

W. Kip Viscusi, *Toward a Diminished Role for Tort Liability: Social Insurance, Government Regulation, and Contemporary Risks to Health and Safety*, 6 YALE J. REG. 65 (1989)*

Society approaches health and safety risks in a piecemeal fashion. Regulators attempt to control the risks in their domain as if regulations were the only factor preventing injuries at home, in the workplace, and on the highways. Similarly, the courts address accidents with rules that not only discourage, but sometimes also forbid, consideration of norms and institutions outside the tort system. Academic commentators share this blind spot, focusing on only one method of managing risks and recommending, for example, an optimal tort liability structure or an appropriate level of stringency for an administrative regulation.

These methods and analyses are valuable, but they do not consider the complexities arising from the overlap of market forces, tort law, social insurance, and government regulation. Each of these four institutions influences the management of risks in important ways. And each has effects that, when combined, create dissonance between risks and societal responses. Without coordination of these risk-reduction systems, society will rarely invest optimally to achieve the goals of creating efficient incentives and providing appropriate compensation to injured parties. Further, even if society is not over- or under-responsive to risks as a whole, it may still react inefficiently to certain large risks. The solution to the problem lies in finding an appropriate mix of market incentives, tort liability, social insurance, and regulation.

The recent increase in the number of mass product liability suits and toxic tort claims arising from exposure to carcinogens and other harmful substances makes more evident the necessity of finding the appropriate mix of risk-management institutions. The tort system does not address these accidents as well as the ones it has traditionally encountered.

The optimal mix of risk-reduction institutions requires a diminished role for the tort system. Markets and government regulations generally can create more efficient risk-reduction incentives; social insurance generally provides more appropriate compensation to the injured. There are good reasons to retain the tort system, but its role should diminish as risks to health and safety increase in number, duration, and complexity. The new practical and analytical question about tort liability is how to make it an effective adjunct to more efficient regulatory and insurance schemes.

Markets

The current approach to risk management generally limits markets to addressing injuries resulting from voluntary transactions. Although parties do not explicitly trade health and safety risks, they do so implicitly because these risks are attributes of market-traded commodities. For example, workers accept potentially hazardous jobs only if there are compensating factors that make the job as attractive as safer alternatives. Such offsetting advantages include higher wages and compensation for income loss due to injuries.

Although most of the literature on market premiums for risk focuses on wage rates and occupa-

*Used by permission.

tional risks, similar differentials accompany other hazards implicitly traded in markets. For example, consumers demand some offsetting advantage to smaller automobiles, such as greater fuel economy, to compensate for the cars' lower crashworthiness. Depending upon consumer preferences, these tradeoffs may be substantial.

Perfect markets for risk provide efficient compensation and incentives to operate safely. However, markets often do not operate in an ideal fashion. The strongest departure from a perfect market occurs when even implicit markets for risk do not exist. For example, the current depletion of the ozone layer in the atmosphere imposes risks on future generations. Although our descendants might be willing to pay us to alter our behavior, there is no means for them to do so.

The inadequacy of the insurance market aggravates the effects of the lack of implicit risk markets. A number of factors impede the development of efficient insurance agreements. First, adverse selection, whereby only high-risk customers purchase insurance, can prevent the emergence of any insurance coverage for important classes of risk. Second, adverse incentives, or moral hazard, can impede the growth of insurance markets by reducing incentives to avoid injuries. Third, even when insurance markets do exist, the premiums charged are actuarially unfair because they necessarily include a reasonable profit for insurers.

Finally, inaccuracies in risk perception also impede the development of efficient markets. People tend to overestimate low probability risks, such as the chance that a child might be poisoned from household chemical products, or that someone might have tampered with a bottle of medicine. When individuals overestimate a risk, the price they demand to engage the risk is too high. Conversely, if they underestimate a risk, the price they demand is too low. In both cases, the imperfect market produces inefficient incentives to reduce risk and inappropriate compensation to those engaging the risk.

Tort Liability

Whereas the market's inability to affect anything other than voluntary transactions limits its use as a risk-management institution, the tort system's relative inflexibility restricts the reach of that institution as well. The tort system requires injured parties to comply with formal legal rules before they receive any compensation. For example, under the broad theory of negligence, the plaintiff has the burden of proving by a "preponderance of the evidence" that the defendant's "negligent conduct" was the "legal cause" of the "injury" suffered by the plaintiff. Similarly, in an action based on a theory of strict liability, the plaintiff has the burden of proving that the "defective product" in question was the "legal cause" of plaintiff's injuries. In both of these formulations, every word and phrase is filled with meanings and interpretations that act as hurdles in the plaintiff's effort to receive compensation. Therefore, the tort system provides compensation for only a subset of all injuries: those that meet these restrictive criteria. In contrast, market forces generate compensating differentials for all additional risks imposed by particular products or activities. Plaintiffs can often experience extreme difficulty demonstrating that a particular defendant caused an injury, especially for injuries with multiple potential causes that pose long-term health risks. Furthermore, even if causal relationships are fully understood, which is seldom the case, the history of individual exposures to the diverse causes of a disease is rarely known. The tort system can handle only hazards with discrete, easily traceable causes.

Social Insurance

The scope of social insurance is potentially all-inclusive. Except for scarcity of funding, there is no inherent barrier to providing general coverage of risks. For example, compensation for

Table 1
The Cost of Regulations Per Life Saved

Proposed (P) or Final (F) Regulation	Year	Agency	Thousands of Dollars (1984) Per Life Saved
Steering Column (F)	1967	NHTSA	$100
Passive Restraints (F)	1984	NHTSA	300
Children's Sleepwear Flammability (F)	1973	CPSC	1,300
Asbestos (F)	1972	OSHA	7,400
Acrylonitrile (F)	1978	OSHA	37,600
Asbestos (P)	1986	OSHA	89,300
Arsenic (F)	1978	OSHA	92,500
Asbestos (P)	1986	EPA	104,200
Benzene/Storage (P)	1984	EPA	202,000
Land Disposal (P)	1986	EPA	3,500,000
Formaldehyde (P)	1985	OSHA	72,000,000

disability under the Social Security program is extensive, but the level of benefits is low due to the program's comprehensiveness and its limited resources. Targeted social insurance programs, such as workers' compensation, share some of the tort system's impediments to coverage. To receive compensation, the claimant must show "by a preponderance of the evidence" that an injury occurred and that the injury arose "out of and in the course of employment." In contrast to tort liability, however, social insurance programs award benefits regardless of fault.

Regulation

The potential scope of regulation is limited only by the imaginations of regulators. The government can influence a range of outcomes that supplements or displaces both the market, which operates largely *ex ante,* and tort liability, which operates *ex post.*

Current regulatory efforts differ in their scope of coverage. The National Highway Traffic Safety Administration (NHTSA) and the Nuclear Regulatory Commission (NRC) can regulate only particular activities, whereas the Environmental Protection Agency (EPA) has a broader mandate encompassing a wide range of hazards. The form of the regulations promulgated reflects the flexibility of the administrative apparatus. For example, most government regulations focus on design aspects of technologies or on externalities that the regulated activity generates. In some cases, however, regulations emphasize defective aspects of the initial design or defects arising from errors in the manufacturing process. This flexibility gives regulation the broadest potential scope of any of the risk-management institutions, combining the coverage of the market with that of tort liability.

* * *

The danger of poorly designed regulations was exposed in a study of the cost-effectiveness of forty-four proposed or enacted health and safety standards. Table 1 demonstrates the range of variation in the cost of saving a life under some of the regulations.

The study generally shows that many regulations save lives at a cost that is greater than the

Table 2
Summary of Effects of Regulation

Class of Regulations (Investigator)	General Conclusion
Product Safety	
1. CPSC—General (Viscusi)	Few standards and no significant beneficial effects on safety.
2. CPSC—Mattresses (Linneman)	No significant beneficial effect on safety.
3. CPSC—Safety Caps (Viscusi)	No significant beneficial effect on safety due to offsetting behavioral response.
4. NHTSA—Seatbelts (Peltzman)	No significant beneficial effect on safety due to offsetting behavioral response.
5. NHTSA—Seatbelts (Crandall & Graham)	Offsetting response to seatbelts exists but does not negate their beneficial effects.
6. FDA—Pharmaceuticals (Grabowski & Vernon)	Excessively stringent drug screening leads to lag in obtaining health-enhancing drugs.
7. Prescription Drugs (Peltzman)	No significant health benefits of prescription requirement.
8. FDA—Food Additives (Lave)	Need to set priorities and promulgate more balanced regulations.
Worker Safety	
9. OSHA (Viscusi)	Weak enforcement. No significant effects until 1980s, when small effects are observed.
Environmental Risks	
10. EPA—Air (Crandall)	Improvements are needed in enforcement; a market-based pollution tax should be implemented.
11. EPA—Water (Magat & Viscusi)	Frequent enforcement and substantial effect on pollution by pulp and paper mills.
12. NRC—Nuclear (Wood)	Need to reorganize entire agency and streamline licensing process.
Hazard Warnings	
13. Worker and consumer (Viscusi & Magat)	''Educational'' efforts that provide no new information are unsuccessful, but warnings that convey new knowledge can be effective.

private valuation of life. This means that if efficient control of risks is the sole objective of a risk-management system, then regulations are far too stringent in many cases. The study also shows that when technological change is not very costly, as with steering column controls, regulation can save lives quite inexpensively. However, when products do not have inexpensive substitutes, as is the case with land disposal facilities, the cost of saving lives can be extremely expensive. Regulation is most efficient when directed at industries that can respond quickly and when information and technological changes are less costly.

Table 2 provides a summary of various studies concerned with the efficacy and effects of a variety of regulations.

The studies included in Table 2 indicate that a regulatory regime must surmount three main difficulties to become an attractive policy alternative: (1) inadequate regulatory design; (2) ineffective and shoddy enforcement of efficient regulations; and (3) offsetting behavior of workers and consumers that counteracts some of the salutary effects of regulation.

The first major problem with regulations is that they may not enhance safety even if they are effectively enforced. For example, of the few regulations that the CPSC has promulgated, almost none is strongly related to safety. In the case of prescription medicine requirements, restrictions on access to drugs have not had the expected benefits in terms of safer drug use. In the case of workplace safety, OSHA's standards may be less effective than performance-oriented alternatives.

A second and more pervasive problem with regulations is that entities empowered to enforce them may not do so. Proper enforcement is a function of information, monitoring costs, and sanctions for violations. In some instances, agencies enforce standards strictly; for example, FDA must approve new pharmaceuticals before they can be sold. These regulations are associated with full compliance, as are requirements that cars have seatbelts and that medicine bottles have safety caps. Similarly, EPA water pollution regulations have reasonably high rates of compliance because they require firms to submit monthly reports regarding their discharges and EPA to inspect firms roughly once a year. Thus, if information and monitoring costs are relatively low, compliance rates tend to be quite high.

Weak enforcement sanctions compound the problems created by monitoring difficulties, hampering regulatory performance even further. OSHA regulations only modestly reduce worker injuries because they require only rare inspections and because their sanctions for noncompliance are usually inconsequential. Other classes of regulations that lack strong enforcement provisions include those governing the dumping of toxic wastes, where the injuring party often cannot be identified. In these and other instances in which enforcement is not effective, regulations are inefficient.

A third difficulty with regulations is that they cause offsetting behavioral responses by consumers that counteract beneficial regulatory effects. For example, in the case of seatbelt regulations, the use of belts reduces the risk-reduction incentives that drivers might otherwise face. Wearing a seatbelt may decrease the likelihood of safe driving, leading some analysts to conclude that drivers wearing seatbelts cause additional injuries to pedestrians and motorcyclists. Safety cap regulations also induce a potentially counterproductive behavioral response: some individuals now leave bottles open because it is so difficult to grapple with the caps. Moreover, caps have lulled some parents into a false sense of security, causing them unintentionally to increase their children's access to the products. As a result, the number of analgesic poisonings has increased, offsetting the expected beneficial effects of safety caps.

But none of these problems, except perhaps occasional offsetting behavioral responses, is intractable. Society can establish whatever health and safety standards it believes are appropriate, with the only concerns being the cost of providing the increased safety and the value of the increased safety to society. For risk regulation to realize its potential, however, regulatory design and enforcement must improve. Society can resolve these problems more easily than the problems associated with both tort liability and social insurance. In addition, once an agency promulgates regulations, social costs need not be incurred again. In this sense, regulation is a larger investment in a more permanent solution than the ones offered by insurance or tort liability.

* * *

Conclusion

The tort system can promote risk-reduction incentives and provide adequate compensation for accident victims in simple cases involving only financial losses. Although other institutions may still have competitive advantages, tort liability could be the foundation of an effective effort to manage some risky activity in these kinds of cases.

The efficacy of the tort system diminishes considerably in the context of mass product liability suits. Many of the deficiencies of tort liability stem from its individualized nature. Small-scale tort actions lack the economies of scale necessary to provide the risk-reduction incentives and compensation that mass product liability claims require. Although class actions remove some inefficiencies, the tort system tends to function poorly in these situations.

The recent explosion of toxic tort cases has created even more fundamental difficulties because of the courts' inability to determine linkages between producers' actions and victims' health status. In addition to the intrinsic uncertainties involved, the courts lack the scientific expertise to develop the necessary doctrines and causation rules relevant to multiple and probabilistic causation. In these cases, government regulation is the best institution to create efficient risk-reduction incentives and social insurance is the best institution to provide appropriate compensation.

The superiority of regulation and social insurance in these types of cases does not mean that tort liability cannot play a constructive role in managing risks. Rather, it implies that the role of the tort system should be subsidiary to the other institutions. Tort liability can create significant risk-reduction incentives and compensate some of those who are injured.

In addition, the tort system provides a useful forum for identifying potential targets for regulation and for addressing idiosyncratic risks not covered by broadly based regulations. However, tort reform proposals should recognize the subsidiary role that tort liability must play in the future and focus on achieving the traditional goals of the tort system through increased use of government regulation and social insurance.

Part V
The Products Liability Crisis

A. What Crisis?

Products liability is associated, perhaps indelibly, with the term "crisis." Tort reformers included products liability in their 1980s criticisms of the American legal system. This section offers differing perspectives on the debate. An association of more than a hundred manufacturers, suppliers, and service providers presented their consensus in an article prepared in their behalf by the Chicago law firm Sidley & Austin. A few years later, James Henderson and Theodore Eisenberg published their empirical investigation of how products liability claims were faring in the courts; their conclusion—that an earlier trend in favor of plaintiffs and expanded liability had been reversed—drew much attention. Richard Abel goes quite a distance further, arguing that the true crisis consists of an inadequate number of injury claims.

Sidley & Austin, *The Need for Legislative Reform of the Tort System: A Report on the Liability Crisis From Affected Organizations,* 10 Hamline L. Rev. 2 (1987)*

The purpose of this article is to focus on, and advance, the emerging national debate about the need for legislative reform of the tort system as one solution to America's liability insurance crisis. The article has been endorsed by 140 organizations, covering a broad spectrum of American life and representing public and non-profit associations, the professions, small businesses, international corporations and the insurance industry. That these diverse groups endorse this report and call for legislatively enacted tort reform is itself significant. Tort reform is not a partisan issue, and the problems created by the tort system affect all of this nation's citizens. From the experience of their members across the nation, these groups agree on certain key propositions, which are covered in more detail in the body of this article.

---

*Used by permission.

The Tort System is a Significant Cause of the Liability Crisis

Developments in the legal system for compensating personal or economic injury—the tort system—have contributed to the sharply increasing problems relating to the availability, affordability, and adequacy of liability insurance. These developments are driving up liability costs, creating uncertainty about their future costs. Three dimensions of the tort system are of particular significance in this regard:

First, the concept of fault has been eroded by judges and juries, in general, through imposition of damages on those with deep pockets, regardless of their fault, and in particular, through changes in the doctrine of joint and several liability, rejection of state of the art defenses, weakening of the concept of causation, and the creation of new causes of action that may be tenuously related to the concept of fault.

Second, the size of damage awards has been increasing significantly and unpredictably, especially those components relating to noneconomic damages and punitive damages.

Third, appropriate sanctions for frivolous suits may not exist, and the possibility of windfall contingency fees for plaintiffs' lawyers is an incentive encouraging litigation and discouraging reasonable settlements.

The Liability Crisis is Having a Widespread Impact on Society

Citizens are generally finding that the costs of private sector products and services are increasing as insurance costs are passed on and in some cases are discovering that access to products and services is denied as liability insurance is cancelled.

State and local governments and the taxpayers in those jurisdictions, may have to bear the increased costs of insuring public services, or forego those services that cannot be insured.

Employees may have decreased growth in income as the costs of insurance reduce the amount of available resources for real wages. Employees may also lose jobs to overseas competition which does not have to bear liability insurance costs equivalent to those borne by American businesses.

Businesses, of course, also have to bear increased costs, thus reducing competitiveness in an international economy. Moreover, the huge potential costs of liability insurance create disincentives to innovate. Excessive insurance costs also reduce income available for investment aimed at increasing productivity.

Professionals, such as physicians, accountants, engineers and architects, face sharply increased premium costs and may leave their practices altogether. Furthermore, client encounters are strained by increasingly adversarial relations, and professionals are forced to employ costly and unnecessary defensive practices. Insurance companies, facing significant unpredictability in the legal system, have difficulty in pricing liability insurance, or providing it at all.

Finally, self-insured entities, like physicians' groups and cities, are facing great unpredictability in determining how, in the absence of insurance, to best guard against the rising costs of liability.

Tort Reform is Only One Solution to the Liability Crisis

The organizations endorsing this article clearly recognize that the liability crisis has multiple causes and thus multiple solutions. In addition to tort reform, it would help solve the liability crisis if professional organizations more rigorously policed themselves. Professional groups must devote more resources to policing their members. The states and the federal government, where appropriate, should authorize professional self-regulation in a manner that protects such activity from liability under the federal antitrust laws. Businesses and other entities should improve risk management efforts and devote more resources to the rehabilitation of those injured. Citizens must recognize that no society is risk-free. Accidents happen, and not all harms in life are the result of fault or are fully compensable through litigation. The insurance industry must recognize its duty to continue to provide the public with complete and accurate information explaining how and why premiums fluctuate over time and must make every effort to insure necessary public and private activities.

Nonetheless, we are convinced that problems with the tort system—especially rising liability costs and increasing unpredictability—have contributed significantly to the liability crisis, and it is that conviction which has led to this article. That other causes also need to be addressed is not a reason to ignore the effects arising out of the tort system.

Precise data does not exist, at present, with which one could ''prove'' the precise relationship between changes in the tort system and the increasing costs, or unavailability, of insurance. Nor can the ultimate impact of the sharp increase in insurance costs and sharp reduction in insurance availability be fully known yet. Major study groups at both the state and federal levels have concluded that the tort system contributes in a significant way to the problems of adequacy, affordability and availability of insurance.

The kinds of fundamental changes that have occurred in the tort system necessarily have far-reaching impact, as discussed below. The impact is being felt now by the groups and organizations endorsing this report, and the impact of the liability crisis is likely to increase in the future. Thus, even if the precise magnitude of the crisis cannot be measured now, its existence is agreed upon by the groups endorsing this report.

Harms to Citizens Generally

Because the adjudicative process is inherently unwieldy, judicial developments that significantly expand liability will have consequences beyond their effects on the specific parties to litigation. At the most basic level, it seems clear that costs of the tort system are being felt by the average citizen. As the costs of liability increase, the citizen consumer will be asked to pay for these costs in increased prices for the product, service, or entity that is subject to potential tort litigation. Of course, ultimately, consumers pay for any increased insurance costs.

Moreover, when costs of insurance rise to a sufficient level, citizens may simply lose access to a service or the opportunity to purchase a particular product because the provider or manufacturer withdraws from the market. This problem of access is very real. Significant numbers of physicians already have stopped delivering babies because of the costs of insurance and the potential for litigation arising out of a particular medical procedure. Similarly, the city of St. Joseph, Missouri shut down the only public transportation system in that community of more than 75,000, for eight days, because the city's insurance company went bankrupt, and the City could not afford to self-insure the system. These are examples of a significant trend—the withdrawal of products and services because the cost of liability, and insurance against liability, has become too high.

* * *

Harms to Business and Professional Innovation Generally

The most obvious effect of the tort system on these groups is the increased cost of doing business and remaining insured. This effect is not the most damaging to society. We already have mentioned the phenomenon of businesses not producing certain products and professionals not performing certain services. The tort system also almost certainly decreases these groups' incentives to pursue innovation in products and services. New products and methods may carry unforeseeable risks to consumers. If substantial liability can be imposed no matter how carefully the new product or service is produced and delivered to the consumer, then risk adverse individuals and businesses will choose not to pursue these new techniques. The fact that businesses will face significant problems acquiring insurance for their new products or services will further deter interest in development. The effect is that the nation as a whole suffers from the lost benefits that come from technological and methodological innovation. This effect, in time, could have a significant adverse effect on the general quality of life in this country and on our nation's ability to compete internationally.

* * *

Recommendations

Restoration of the Concept of Fault. A basic problem with the tort system which affects all of the undersigned groups is that the judicial system has been eroding the historic fault-based underpinnings for imposing liability on defendants in tort actions. This erosion has come about in a variety of ways. Substantively, courts have expanded almost every potential tort defendant's exposure to liability through the development of new causes of action based more on the judicial decision that a defendant should pay for harm than on a determination of the defendant's fault.

Until relatively recently, fault was clearly the dominant basis of the common law tort system. While imposition of strict liability has long been recognized as appropriate for defendants engaging in unusual and ultrahazardous activities, such as keeping wild animals or engaging in blasting within a city, these limited rules were readily justified as imposing upon the person who is engaged in obviously abnormal activity the risk that his or her actions will cause harm. However, the judicial system has adopted strict liability for conduct that traditionally would have been regarded as appropriate for scrutiny under a fault system. This shift from negligence to strict liability inevitably increases the likelihood that plaintiffs will receive compensation for their injuries, regardless of any fault by defendants. This impulse to use tort law as a surrogate system of social insurance is in part responsible for the current problems in the tort system.

Of course, while strict liability yields gains in terms of achieving the goal of compensation, what is lost by shifting liability away from a fault based concept is a meaningful system of deterrence. When a person's conduct is found to be unreasonable within the meaning of the negligence standards, that finding creates a basis for other individuals to conform their conduct to certain norms. When a product is found to be defective because someone was injured, even though the maker of the product could not reasonably have anticipated the problem, meaningful deterrence is diminished. Most rational producers will continue to operate their businesses based on what they foresee to be realistic liability problems. If they go in search of unlikely problems, they will tend to waste their resources. The tort system works with the benefit of hindsight; whereas businesses, governments, and professionals must operate on the basis of current knowledge.

In deciding specific cases courts have stretched existing doctrines and have approved new and far-reaching causes of action to justify granting recovery for injured plaintiffs. For instance, in efforts to compensate victims of manufactured products, courts have imposed liability on manufacturers for failing to warn users of unknowable risks (beyond what the manufacturer should have known at the time), if it would have been negligent to sell the product without a warning if the risk were known. In one case the jury found no negligence by the defendant concerning its warning for flammable chemicals, and plaintiff's expert testified that no fire would have occurred if the plaintiff had heeded the warning. Nevertheless, the New Jersey Supreme Court reversed the judgment for the defendant because the jury was not given a strict liability instruction which would make clear liability was appropriate "even if the product is perfectly inspected, designed, and manufactured," and that the scope of the duty to warn is "without regard to prevailing industry standards."[1]

Judicial expansion of liability for breach of a duty to warn constitutes a significant problem. As the Attorney General's Tort Policy Working Group observed:

> The duty to warn has been a particularly fertile ground for such after-the-fact compensation oriented findings of fault. It is all too easy after the occurrence of an injury to postulate a warning that might have influenced the plaintiff to be more careful or to reconsider his action, no matter how fanciful or unreasonable such a warning might appear prior to the injury.

The duty to warn problem has two components. First, some courts impose strict liability upon manufacturers for both failure to warn and for manufacturing defects. Thus, one court has held that "the foreseeability of the dangers involved in the use of the product are [sic] not relevant to the strict tort theory. . . ." This doctrine is obviously far removed from any notion of fault. In addition, courts and juries frequently find, with the benefit of hindsight, that a particular warning might have prevented an accident or that actual warnings did not fully inform a consumer of the nature or extent of the possible risk. Because of this trend in the law, the City of Chicago reportedly paid $1.5 million in a case where a two-year old child was permanently and severely injured when he fell off an eleven-foot sliding board at a playground maintained by the park district. Although it seems inconceivable that the child's parent was not basically at fault for failing to supervise the child's play, the city was sued, in part, for failure to give an adequate warning against use of the slide by small children. Rather than risking a jury's finding of liability under the broad duty to warn doctrine, the city settled the case. Thus, even though the city by all appearances was not "at fault" for the tragic accident involving the child, it paid a significant judgment and is presently in the process of removing sliding boards from all city-managed parks.

Legislatures should thus consider two broad areas of reform designed to return the adjudicatory system to its traditional focus on the determination of fault. First, the judge-made law described above, which has weakened the concept of fault as the basis for liability in individual cases, should be carefully examined and appropriately modified. Judicially developed doctrines such as expanded joint and several liability, expanded concepts of duty, extensions of strict liability, use of national rather than local standards of conduct regarding professionals, retroactive application of contemporary standards of care, loose standards of causation and foreseeability—to name the more salient doctrines relating to determinations of "fault"—require systematic legislative examination. Second, to the extent that modifications of legal doctrines used by courts mean that certain categories or types of injuries will not be compensated by the tort system, then legislatures should consider alternative statutory schemes for compensating harm

[1] Freund v. Cellofilm Properties, Inc., 432 A.2d 925, 932 (N.J. 1981).

when such injuries are a cost of innovation or other desirable activity that society, not the individual or a blameless defendant, should bear. Such cost-spreading determinations should be made by legislators elected by all citizens.

Structuring Damage Awards That Bear a Predictable and Reasonable Relationship to Economic Injury. The undersigned groups and organizations are unanimous in their agreement that economic injury caused by fault should be fully compensated. What has caused the enormous fluctuation and unpredictability in tort damages is the size of awards for pain and suffering and, to a lesser extent, awards of punitive damages. Compensation for pain and suffering and for grossly negligent or intentional torts has a legitimate place in our system of remedies. However, legislatures must examine whether those damage awards bear a reasonable and appropriate relationship to actual injury or whether they amount to unwarranted windfalls to plaintiffs that should be reduced. It appears likely that the unpredictability of such awards has contributed significantly to the increased cost and reduction in availability of liability insurance.

These organizations strongly believe that a second broad area of tort reform should include a serious consideration of a statute establishing either fixed or proportional limits on noneconomic damages. In other words, awards for pain and suffering and punitive damages should either have upper dollar limits or should be fixed in proportion to the underlying economic injury. Such fixed or proportional limits have been used historically in criminal law, antitrust law, and numerous compensatory schemes established by federal and state statutes.

Deterring Frivolous Litigation and Preventing Unfair, Windfall Fees for Plaintiffs' Lawyers. Access to the legal system, especially for the individual plaintiff, is essential to our system of civil justice. But no individual has a right to bring a frivolous suit in the hope of securing a settlement from a defendant who wishes to avoid the higher costs of litigating a case to conclusion. Furthermore, no attorney has the right to windfall legal fees far beyond reasonable compensation for his or her time and effort.

Accordingly, a third area of tort reform should include the development of effective measures to deter frivolous suits and to limit contingency fees. State legislatures should consider, as a possible basis for legislation, recent modifications in the Federal Rules of Civil Procedure imposing sanctions, including payment of defendants' legal fees, on plaintiffs who file frivolous suits.

Limiting plaintiffs' attorneys' fees to reasonable amounts is well established under numerous federal civil rights statutes where some incentive for the activities of "private attorneys general" is necessary to vindicate important national policies. Unlimited windfall fees for tort actions appear to encourage continuation of litigation in cases which might otherwise be settled and to contribute to the "roulette" aspect of the current tort system, as attorneys take greater risks in bringing less meritorious lawsuits in certain situations because of the potentially great financial rewards. Although abolition of contingency fees would be improper because it would deprive individuals of modest means of their day in court, preventing windfall fees should not impair access of legitimate claims to the legal system. Limiting fees to compensatory amounts would encourage settlements and reduce the costs to society of both plaintiff and defense lawyers.

As noted at the outset, reforms in the tort system are only part of the solution to the current liability crisis. All of the undersigned groups and organizations have significant responsibilities of their own in ameliorating this threat to reasonable cost and needed access to many of our nation's services and products. The ultimate purpose of all these efforts must be to reduce fault to a minimum, compensate victims of fault fairly and quickly, and deter wrongdoers while minimizing the tremendous and increasing adverse side effects which the current tort system is imposing upon us all.

James A. Henderson, Jr. & Theodore Eisenberg, *The Quiet Revolution in Products Liability: An Empirical Study of Legal Change,* 37 UCLA L. Rev. 479 (1990)*

Most revolutions are noisy, tumultuous affairs. This is as true of significant shifts in legal doctrine as it is of shifts of political power through force of arms. The pro-plaintiff revolution in products liability in the early 1960s will forever be associated with heroic, martial images, epitomized in Prosser's description of the assault upon, and fall of, the fortressed citadel of privity. The same sort of terminology could be aptly used to describe the last five or ten years of state legislative reform activity. Reacting to what many see as "crises" brought on by courts extending liability too far, state legislatures have enacted breathtakingly large numbers of changes in products liability law, ranging from the trivial to the drastic to the draconian. For anyone who follows products liability, these developments bring to mind the ancient Chinese curse: "May you live in interesting times."

In contrast to these noisy, exuberant events, the revolution to which we refer has gone all but unnoticed. In fact, some followers of the products liability wars will find our hypothesis so contrary to currently shared wisdom as to warrant its summary rejection. This quiet revolution is a significant turn in the direction of judicial decisionmaking away from extending the boundaries of products liability and toward placing significant limitations on plaintiffs' rights to recover in tort for product-related injuries. These changes are quite recent. Looking back on these events in years to come, scholars are likely to trace the turn in judicial lawmaking to the early to mid-1980s. Although some who follow products liability cases closely have begun to sense change, even those who track products developments will be surprised to find the roots of the trend in the early 1980s.

Our objective in this article is to show that changes in judicial decisionmaking are occurring and that current trends favor defendants. The endeavor is important for two reasons. First, this study shows that since the early to mid-1980s policymakers and industry leaders have been operating from questionable, if not false, premises. Industry leaders have characterized products liability lawyers and clients as a "plague of locusts," who "have brought a blood bath for U.S. business and are distorting our traditional values." Reacting, one hopes, to somewhat less extreme descriptions of products reality, several federal proposals for products liability reform have been introduced, and many states have enacted limiting legislation. The overall impression is one of an area of judge-made law on the rise, threatening to engulf the legal system, harming industry, and requiring legislative reaction to reign in judges. This article shows, however, that even before many of the reforms were in effect, products liability had turned an important corner. The judges whom state legislatures sought to reign in had already begun a trend of doctrinal change favoring defendants. This trend is evident in an increasing percentage of published opinions, both routine and groundbreaking, favoring defendants. At the trial court level, at a time when plaintiffs' likelihood of success in products cases is said by many to be increasing, it has been moving in quite the opposite direction.

[*Editor's note:* For their data, Henderson and Eisenberg both published opinions of state and federal courts and material prepared by the Administrative Office of the United States Courts.]

*Used by permission.

* * *

THE QUIET REVOLUTION REFLECTED IN AN ANECDOTAL SAMPLING OF PUBLISHED COURT DECISIONS

The Background: Judicial Decisionmaking from the Mid-1960s to the Mid-1980s

To set the scene for the unusual court decisions of recent years, we briefly describe decisions that epitomized the decades preceding our sampling. After the citadel of privity had fallen in most American jurisdictions by the mid-to late 1960s, courts let the plaintiffs' bar take full advantage of its victory. Other single-factor barriers to recovery, such as the patent danger rule and the bystander rule, fell in the decade that followed. After the elimination of those gatekeeper barriers to reaching the jury, more significant prizes waited to be won. Courts steadily extended the formal boundaries of strict products liability to include an impressive array of new types of transactions and categories of defendants. Partly through expansions of doctrine and partly through improvements in trial techniques and tactics, plaintiffs found if increasingly easy to reach juries with product defect claims. Failure-to-warn cases also blossomed during this period to the point that by the mid-1980s, pleadings and rhetoric practically replaced proof as the major prerequisites to recovery. The last great frontier to be crossed was liability for defective product design. From the beginning, manufacturers had been held liable for faulty, self-defeating product designs. But courts generally were reluctant, until the mid-1970s, to impose liability for harm caused by product designs that performed exactly as they were intended to perform. For example, when a driver of an automobile inadvertently crashed into a tree, courts traditionally refused to consider seriously the argument that the vehicle should have been designed to prevent or reduce injury to its occupants. Notwithstanding predictions of doom from some quarters, courts gradually overcame their reluctance and by the late 1970s and the early 1980s they routinely imposed liability for harm caused by manufacturer's conscious design choices. Indeed, courts in the various jurisdictions seemed to compete with each other to see who could make it easiest for plaintiffs to reach juries with claims of defective product design.

As the decade of the 1980s arrived, the products liability agenda of the plaintiff's bar was ambitious, but appeared to be well within its grasp. Extending product design liability continued to offer the greatest promise for significant gains. At the head of most plaintiffs' wish lists was persuading courts to review, and condemn as defective, entire categories of product designs, including handguns, cigarettes, alcoholic beverages, swimming pools, electricity, and off-road, all terrain vehicles. With an indefatigable determination that would have made Dean Prosser proud, plaintiffs stormed the barriers that traditionally prevented recovery in such cases. They met with enough success to create the reasonable expectation that it was just a matter of time before those citadels fell in turn.

Liability for harm caused by prescription drugs, another area of traditionally pro-defendant products liability doctrine, was under heavy siege in the late 1970s and early 1980s. Traditionally, drug companies have escaped strict liability if they complied with FDA regulations and acted reasonably in warning prescribing physicians of product-related risks. Courts would not review the designs of prescription drugs, refusing to second-guess the medical profession, the FDA, or the pharmaceutical industry. Plaintiffs attacked this traditional approach on at least three broad fronts: first, they argued that drug companies brainwash doctors so forcefully through advertising that warnings are useless; second, they insisted that the drug companies should also warn patient-consumers directly; and third, they urged courts to review the reasonableness of drug designs independently of whether adequate warnings were supplied. Again, sufficient numbers of plaintiffs succeeded on these three fronts by the early 1980s to suggest that a new regime, much more liberal toward plaintiffs, would govern liability for prescription drugs in the not too distant future.

Other areas of potential judicial expansion that looked promising from the plaintiff's point of view in the late 1970s and early 1980s included the following: The imposition of liability on distributors of prescription drugs and other toxic substances based solely on epidemiological evidence of causal links between those products and plaintiffs' injuries; the imposition of strict liability for so-called "long tail" risks that were not scientifically knowable at the time of original distribution by defendant; liability for the failure (by virtually every foreign and domestic auto maker) to replace seat belts with passive air bag restraints, extension of industry-or market-wide liability theories beyond cases involving the prescription drug DES to include most, if not all, cases in which plaintiffs cannot identify which defendants distributed the product unit(s) that caused injury; adoption of increasingly pro-plaintiff rules holding successor corporations liable for harm caused by defective products distributed earlier by their corporate predecessors; expansion of the size and frequency of punitive damage awards; and increases in the extent to which responsibility for product-related workplace injuries are shifted from admittedly negligent employers to manufacturers and distributors of the products causing injury.

That plaintiffs' efforts in these regards had already begun to succeed in the late 1970s and early 1980s is reflected not only in published decisions but also in the rising levels of alarm voiced by business concerns in the popular media and in the extent to which state legislatures began to consider and enact statutes aimed at undoing these expansionary trends in judicial lawmaking. Taken together, the body of case law from mid-1960s to the mid-1980s reflects an attitude, widely shared among judges, that our products liability system plays an important social insurance role in making America a safer, better place in which to live and work.

The early 1980s seemed to foreshadow a decade of courts and legislatures locked in power struggles borne of fundamental differences in outlook. Judges would push the products liability boundaries further and further, and legislatures would try to contain such activity by statute. Judges, in turn, could be expected to scrutinize the new legislation carefully and to set it aside frequently as being antithetical to the values reflected in the state constitutions. Even when reform statutes passed constitutional muster, courts could be expected to circumvent them, devising even more expansionary liability theories with which to meet the pressing social needs of injured plaintiffs.

Judicial Decisionmaking in the Mid- to Late 1980s

Judicial opinions in products liability cases of the mid- to late 1980s depart from prior trends in two important ways. First, several cases are outright retreats from prior pro-plaintiff stances. Courts effectively are taking away what they previously have given or, in matters of first impression within a jurisdiction, are refusing to follow the lead of other courts that had earlier adopted a pro-plaintiff rule. Second, in an area that developed for plaintiffs as rapidly as did products liability, refusals to extend doctrine are almost as significant as withdrawals from earlier holdings. The opinions show that courts now exhibit a novel reluctance to expand established products doctrine to benefit plaintiffs.

In nearly every significant area of products liability litigation, courts in recent years have sent unambiguous signals that they are ready to rethink and pull back on earlier commitments to extend the liability frontiers. Many courts have become tougher on plaintiffs who seek to prove that a manufacturing defect, originating with the defendant, caused their injuries. Perhaps the most striking example is a decision by the Ohio Supreme Court. The plaintiff attempted to show that an original defect in the automobile manufactured and sold by the defendant caused a fire that destroyed an automobile and damaged the plaintiff's home. The auto was relatively new and had manifested electrical wiring difficulties several times before the fire. The fire occurred in the plaintiff's garage while the auto was parked there during the night. An expert testified for the plaintiff that "the cause of the fire was electrical, to a reasonable degree of scientific probability," and eliminated causes other than an electrical fire under the dashboard of the auto. Another of plaintiff's experts also traced the problem to electrical problems under the dash. It was undenied that the day before the fire, plaintiff had asked the dealer from whom he had bought the car for a replacement vehicle while wiring repairs were effected. When the dealer refused, plaintiff said, angrily, "If this car burns it is your fault because I brought it in here to you."

On the facts of this case, it is inconceivable that a state high court five or ten years ago would have refused to allow this case to reach the jury. However, that is exactly the conclusion reached unanimously by the Ohio Supreme Court. Pointing to the possibility that the fire might have been caused by, or the defect might have arisen from, other sources not specifically excluded by the plaintiff's witnesses, the court concluded that "it is the plaintiff's burden to respond with evidence which will permit a jury to go beyond speculation and render a judgment in accordance with law. Manufacturers are not insurers of their products."

Even if this decision stood alone it is an important signal of a shift in judicial temperament. But it does not stand alone. It is only one of several similar decisions imposing tougher standards on plaintiffs' circumstantial proof of manufacturing defects.

In earlier cases regarding liability for harm caused by prescription drugs, several courts had moved toward imposing liability on drug companies for dangerous drug designs notwithstanding that the defendants had given full and adequate warnings of the relevant risks. The Supreme Court of California heard arguments early in 1988 in a case involving just that issue. Given that California in years past has been in the forefront of extending the boundaries of products liability for defective designs, most observers expected that court to take the lead in moving American products liability to a new, more generous-to-plaintiffs approach to prescription drug liability. To almost everyone's surprise the California high court not only refused unanimously to review prescription drug designs as a general matter, but also refused, again unanimously, to adopt a halfway position embraced by other jurisdictions.

Successor liability was a particularly "hot" products liability topic at the end of the 1970s and the beginning of the 1980s. It seemed to be moving ahead confidently in favor of injured plaintiffs, with courts increasingly willing to allow recovery against successor firms for injuries caused by products manufactured and distributed by predecessor corporations prior to the latter firms being taken over, At the beginning of the 1980s, it appeared to many observers that the so-called "product line" extension of vicarious successor liability, first adopted by the California Supreme Court and clearly the most pro-plaintiff approach to the problem, would carry the day. Decisions in the late 1980s, however, make clear that the early predictions were wrong. The "product line" exception to traditional no-liability rules for successor corporations has been flatly rejected by no fewer than six of the highest state courts in recent years. Indeed, in the period 1983-1989, the score in all courts stands 18 to 3 in favor of rejecting the "product line" approach.

Practically the identical fate has befallen efforts by the plaintiffs' bar to extend market-wide liability to cases involving products other than DES. When the plaintiffs' bar first succeeded in convincing courts to accept market-wide liability in the late 1970s in the DES cases, many believed that within a short time the market-share approach would spread to a wide range of other product categories. In fact, no such developments have occurred. In the last several years decisions in a number of jurisdictions clearly indicate that courts are in no mood to extend that expansionary doctrine any further. Indeed, a 1989 decision in the New York Court of Appeals explicitly limits the market-share approach to a range of products so narrow as to appear, at first glance, arbitrarily selected.

Another recent significant shift in judicial attitudes should be noted. Traditionally, courts have pushed responsibility for product-related workplace injuries over onto the manufacturers of the products causing injury, notwithstanding large elements of irresponsibility on the parts of the employers who control the work environments. Because worker compensation statutes prevent employees from suing their employers in tort, courts apparently believed that the next best solution, clearly superior to leaving the employees to their limited worker compensation remedies, is to allow recovery in tort against the product manufacturers. No attitude seemed more entrenched and less likely to change than the courts' commitment to allow injured workers to circumvent the worker compensation tort bar by suing third parties in products liability. And yet even here, in the face of this seemingly most unshakable of commitments to helping plaintiffs, a trickle of judicial doubt has, in the last several years, turned into a stream of growing proportions.

The trend of recent products doctrine extends beyond courts changing their own view or refusing to adopt pro-plaintiff positions that other courts have embraced. There is a new reluctance to apply old pro-plaintiff products liability reasoning to new situations. For example, recent decisions indicate that the prospect of courts labelling entire categories of product designs defective has all but disappeared. It is now quite clear, as it was not five years ago, that American courts are reluctant to condemn as inherently defective handguns, cigarettes, alcoholic beverages, swimming pools, electricity, off-road vehicles, or any other broad category of product design.

With respect to the narrower but equally important issue of the alleged defectiveness of particular examples of product designs within these broad categories, no evidence suggests that courts generally are beginning to turn significantly in the direction of more pro-defendant approaches. But neither have courts shown any inclination to extend the availability of markedly pro-plaintiff defectiveness standards. And one line of cases that held great promise for the plaintiffs' bar air bag auto design cases—appears to have received a fatal blow in a 1988 decision in the U.S. Court of Appeals for the First Circuit. A decision by the U.S. Supreme Court effectively bars states from further developing pro-plaintiff caselaw in another significant class of products liability cases: federal government contractor liability.

Therefore, on balance, in the last several years courts have been in a holding pattern regarding liability for allegedly defective product designs. They appear to be digesting what has happened over the last decade or so, showing indications of increased awareness of what the real problems are and how to deal with them. Compared with almost any other period dating back to the early 1970s, the past two or three years on the product design front of the liability war have been peaceful and unexciting.

Viewing the products area as a whole, this tally of important recent developments suggests a clear trend. From cars bursting into flame, to deformed children, to exploding gas cylinders, the products field has not run out of plaintiffs with plausible claims that command sympathy. Courts once favorably inclined to break new ground and to discard doctrine blocking recoveries now are inclined to reflect more cautiously on the implications of their decisions. Courts continue to break new ground and discard doctrine in ways that favor plaintiffs. But they are increasingly apt to change the law to preclude liability rather than to promote it.

* * *

Conclusion

American courts deciding products liability cases are in the midst of a significant revolution. After decades of extending the boundaries of liability, both appellate and trial judges are reaching decisions favoring products defendants in unprecedented numbers. Although it is difficult to pinpoint exactly when this legal change began, we trace its origins to the early to mid-1980s. Clearly, it has been in full swing for the past several years. Unlike most revolutions, legal and nonlegal, this one has been amazingly quiet. Other writers have observed that some recent claims of "crisis" in products and other areas of tort are exaggerated. And pro-defendant state legislative change has not gone unnoticed. But no one has paid systematic attention to patterns of all products decisions by courts. This article discerns, and empirically establishes, that major changes in judicial decisionmaking are occurring.

Two sources substantiate the legal change hypothesis. Viewed anecdotally and systematically, the published opinion data unambiguously point to significant shifts in direction. The federal district court data, though more ambiguous standing alone, support the conclusion that change is taking place. The shift in products decisions is driven by shifting trends in judicial decisionmaking, not by the products liability and tort reform statutes enacted in many states in the 1980s. The change is not simply part of broader pro-defendant trends in tort cases or in civil litigation generally. Furthermore, the change reflects trends in products generally, not in one or two large (and thus potentially distorting) subsets of products litigation, such as asbestos cases.

Despite our efforts to control for influential variables, important items remain to be explored. The breadth of the data on which we rely, while assuring that the detected trends are not isolated local phenomena, can mask notable subthemes. For example, the published opinion data reveal an important difference between state and federal courts. Plaintiffs' declining success in cases leading to published opinions is attributable to a decline at the state, but not the federal, level. Federal published opinions, which include trial court opinions but are dominated by appellate opinions, have not increasingly favored defendants; only state court opinions have. At the same time, federal trial court activity, as reflected in the Administrative Office data, has paralleled state court activity by increasingly favoring defendants.

Federal district courts thus seem to be faithfully applying state products law in the majority of cases, but it is something of a mystery why federal appellate opinions reveal no similar trend. Perhaps their relatively greater remoteness from state law or trends in popular attitudes causes federal judges to be less sensitive to shifts at the state level. Or perhaps federal judges are appointed based on criteria different enough from state court judges to account for the disparate responses in the published opinion data. Another issue for further inquiry is whether regional differences are detectable. For example, the spate of tort and products reform statutes may have created or may reflect local legal environments that differ widely. Distinguishing among regions based on their statutory environment is a possible fruitful area of study.

A final issue worth further inquiry is the very quietness of the revolution. In some areas of law, observers of opinions and trial court activity see different realities and one can understand why one view of reality might dominate. But the observed trends in products liability are not ambiguous. Both opinions and trial court activity tell the same story. How can knowledgeable observers have not only failed to detect a near-decade old trend, but also believed that judge-made products law was heading in the opposite direction?

Accepting the existence of the quiet revolution, what should we make of it? One question is whether the change is for the better. Liability law has tried to serve as a system of social insurance for the past few decades, a function many believe it is poorly equipped to perform. Beginning in the early 1980s, state legislatures attempted to correct what they saw to be overextensions of tort and products law. But even well-drafted and well-intended statutes cannot succeed without enlisting the willing support of the judiciary, and that support cannot be legislated. Those questioning the transformation of tort and products law into social insurance systems should view the change we describe as not only improving products liability law, but also as suggesting that the statutory reforms are likely to be given a fair chance in courts.

Common sense suggests that products liability early growth rate could not be sustained indefinitely. Changes in time and temperament realistically left room for major change in only one direction, especially since the early, pro-plaintiff developments put powerful social, industrial, and financial interests on the wrong side of innovative lawsuits. These interests have mounted massive publicity campaigns as well as enormously expensive federal and state legislative lobbying efforts. On this view, at least in the long run, the ''haves'' will come out ahead.

A second obvious question is whether reform statutes are needed any longer now that judicial change has occurred. One's answer here probably depends on one's position regarding the underlying question whether reform legislation makes sense in any event. Opponents of reform legislation will use this article as evidence that no further legislative action is necessary. Indeed, opponents of change may rely on our results to support repeal of reform statutes already enacted into law. Proponents will argue that courts at last are headed in the right direction and should be given even more legislative encouragement.

Facile use of our analysis in either fashion would, to borrow a bit of products terminology, constitute ''misuse'' of our data. The general pro-defendant trend does not mean that courts in every jurisdiction have solved, or will in the foreseeable future solve, all of the problems some perceive to have been caused by earlier expansionary trends. As observed in our anecdotal reports of recent decisions, court in some states and in some doctrinal areas continue much as they have for more than twenty years, pushing outward the boundaries of liability, Thus, in assessing whether statutory reform is required notwithstanding the change we detect, one must examine the relevant decisional law in the particular jurisdiction. If that law is judged to be inappropriate, our analysis provides no guarantee that courts in the jurisdiction will ever, on their own, improve the situation. Moreover, even if the trend we identify could somehow be expected, over time, to correct most of the perceived earlier mistakes, it could take years for those corrections to be made.

Nor do our findings mean that legislatures should now necessarily feel freer to maintain or adopt reform statutes encouraging the pro-defendant trend. In states where judicial decisions expanded the products field, and where recent developments suggest that courts are rethinking those expansions, products law may best be left to stabilize, or shrink, through the same process. And some statutes have imposed ill-conceived and draconian changes. Such statutes should be re-examined regardless of judicial trends. Each jurisdiction must assess the status of its products law in light of its judicial trends and existing statutes.

It follows that, although our analysis identifies a major shift in judicial lawmaking, it can only partly inform the decisions whether a particular statutory proposal should be enacted and whether existing statutes should be modified or repealed. In jurisdictions concerned with earlier pro-plaintiff judicial trends, our analysis offers hope that sensible statutory reform will yield results. Never in recent memory has the judicial climate in products law been more receptive to statutory reform. A legislature might choose to initiate such change, engaging in what hopefully would become a cooperative effort between legislature and courts. At the very least our findings should make legislators considering change more inclined to observe the reality of the legal products climate in which they operate. Some will be surprised by what they see.

Richard L. Abel, *The Real Tort Crisis—Too* Few *Claims,* 48 OHIO ST. L.J. 443 (1987)*

What is the tort crisis? Most commentators assert that the crisis is too much tort liability: too many claims, the extension of liability rules to new situations, the relaxation of the requirement of fault, loose notions of causation, the erosion of defenses, and the inflation of damage awards. These commentators also deplore the consequences: increased liability insurance premiums and the unavailability of insurance; the tendency for potential defendants to go bare; and the number of entrepreneurs who have left the market because they no longer can make a profit, thereby depriving consumers of valuable goods and services. There is a grain of truth in these claims, although I think they often are exaggerated.

Although I believe that the empirical evidence for a liability insurance crisis is weak and that the crisis is actually a mere reflection of an economic cycle produced by market forces, I do not wish to rest on those grounds. Instead, I want to advance three propositions. Everyone working within the generally accepted paradigm of contemporary tort law must concede the first: successful tort claims do not create liability costs, they merely shift them from victims to tortfeasors. It is the tortfeasors who create liability costs by injuring victims.

My second proposition is empirical and therefore subject to correction and refinement by further research, but I do not think it is particularly controversial. If liability costs are high, it is because injuries are frequent and serious. The United States Bureau of the Census recently found that fourteen percent of those between ages 16 and 64 and twenty-one percent of those over age 15 have significant physical disabilities (of course, not all these are the result of tortious acts). The American Bar Foundation study of legal needs found that fifty-eight percent of all men and forty-four percent of all women reported that they had incurred a serious tort problem during their lifetimes. And the investigation by the Oxford Centre for Socio-Legal Studies found that forty out of every 1,000 people had suffered at least two weeks of incapacity from an injury during the preceding twelve months.

It is my third proposition—the core of this article—that is controversial. The real tort crisis is old, not new. It is a crisis of underclaiming rather than overclaiming. The tort system does not encourage fraud or display excessive generosity but fails to compensate needy, deserving victims. It does not place undue burdens on socially valuable activities but fails to discourage unreasonable risks. And it does not censure the innocent but fails to condemn the guilty. The rhetoric of those who deplore the burden of liability and insurance costs is simply another expression of the conservative backlash of recent years. It can be summarized in a sentence: "Let's hang on to what we have, and when others seek the same privileges we'll say our society can't afford it."

Many Injury Victims Fail To Claim

My proposition that many tort victims fail to claim is empirical. Proving a negative always is difficult. Proving this negative is costly as well, for it is necessary to establish the population of injury victims who could recover tort damages before examining how many of them, and which ones, actually do so. Only a few studies attempt this rigorous task. The joint study of the legal

*Used by permission.

needs of the public by the American Bar Association and the American Bar Foundation in 1973 and 1974 found that only sixteen percent of those who reported tort problems consulted lawyers about them; the proportion ranged from thirty-four percent of those who suffered personal injury to eight percent of those who suffered property damage. Other studies have disclosed that the claims rate varies significantly by the environment within which the injury occurs. One investigator compared expert judgments about injuries caused by medical malpractice, based on the 1974 records of twenty-three California hospitals; this study found that one in every 126 patients suffered an injury due to negligence. Only a tenth of these filed a claim. And only forty percent of the claims, or four percent of the negligent injuries, resulted in payment. Even among those who suffered major permanent partial disability as a result of medical malpractice, less than seventeen percent filed claims, and only 6.5 percent received any payment. Another study of the 1972 records of two hospitals found that only one out of every fifteen significant injuries caused by malpractice led to claims (6.7 percent) and acknowledged that even this was an overestimate because not all incidents of malpractice could be detected from the records. And a third study discovered that forty percent of the malpractice incidents physicians themselves report to their insurers never result in claims.

Many workplace injuries also fail to produce claims but for different reasons: employers discourage workers from reporting or claiming, in an effort to conceal such incidents for fear of liability, increases in liability insurance premiums, greater regulatory activity, and criminal penalties. The California Supreme Court has taken the unprecedented step of holding Johns-Manville liable to its employees in tort rather than workers' compensation because, for decades, Johns-Manville concealed from workers the fact that company health records showed they were suffering from exposure to asbestos. A contemporary American study found that only about thirty-seven percent of work accident victims claim workers' compensation.

Even road accidents display significant underclaiming, despite the facts that the police generally record the event, the defendant usually is a stranger to the victim, and liability insurance coverage is very widespread. In New York City, eighty-seven percent of a random sample of those suffering slight shock or contusion in an automobile accident in 1957 had made a claim by September 1959, sixty-six percent had retained a lawyer, and sixty-four percent had obtained some compensation; but it seems likely that higher proportions of that half of the sample who could not be located failed to take each of these steps. A Michigan study in the early 1960s found that only fourteen percent of all automobile accident victims hired lawyers; but among those who suffered $500 in medical expenses, two weeks of hospitalization, permanent physical impairment or death, half of the victims or their families did so.

The Oxford Centre interviewed 1,202 individuals [located in Great Britain] who had been identified in a previous survey as having suffered at least two weeks of incapacity due to injury within a recent twelve month period. It found that 5.3 percent had incurred their injuries on the road, 8.7 percent at work, and eighty-six percent in other settings. The proportions who considered claiming, however, varied inversely with the importance of the category: forty-seven percent of road accident victims and forty-six percent of work accident victims considered claiming but only nine percent of victims in other accidents. The proportions actually obtaining damages were lower still: twenty-nine percent of road accident victims, nineteen percent of work accident victims, and only two percent of victims of other accidents. Because this last category greatly outnumbered the other two, a total of only twelve percent of all those who suffered two weeks of incapacity as a result of injury recovered any damages.

The levels of claiming in the United States and Great Britain are surprisingly similar—about half of road accident victims, somewhat fewer work accident victims, and hardly any victims of other accidents, who are by far the largest category—even though there are several reasons why victim behavior might differ. On one hand, Britain awards costs against an unsuccessful plaintiff, damages are lower, contingent fees are prohibited (although a victim's solicitor may forgive the costs of an unsuccessful claim), social insurance is more comprehensive, and cultural attitudes differ. On the other hand, legal aid is available to tort victims in Britain but not the United States, and the British rule on costs allows a successful plaintiff to keep the entire award, without the deduction of attorney's fees.

These data indicate that only a small proportion of victims take any action to redress their injuries. I am sure many readers can and will raise methodological quibbles. But in the face of such consistent findings, the burden clearly is on those who insist that there are too many tort claims to support their view with equally persuasive empirical studies.

Injured Victims Should Claim

Demonstrating empirically that many injured victims fail to claim is only half of my argument; I also must explain normatively why they should do so. We can learn by analogy from several other realms of behavior where participation is positively valued: politics, the market, cultural life, and social services.

All theories of democratic politics strongly encourage citizen participation. Indeed, we compel certain forms of public service, such as jury duty or the wartime draft. We view an informed, engaged public as the prerequisite of a healthy polity. The New England town meeting remains a nostalgic symbol of direct democracy. Readers who are lawyers or law teachers will feel a sense of obligation to participate in bar associations or faculty self-governance. Indeed, the voluntary associations that de Tocqueville characterized as the foundation of American democracy more than 150 years ago remain an essential building block of liberal pluralism. Many states have a long tradition of submitting important issues to popular referenda. Because the size of our nation makes representative institutions a necessity, we view the level of participation in electoral politics as an index of the quality of political life.

The health of a market economy, like that of a democratic polity, is measured by the degree of participation. High and rising productivity is good; unutilized productive capacity and stagnant production are bad. Full employment is good; high levels of unemployment and underemployment are bad. Consumer spending and confidence are good; underconsumption can cause a crisis. Free markets are good; anything that interferes with market activity is bad, whether it is state regulation, monopoly, or restrictive practices. Observers seeking to explain the failure of third-world economies to grow have praised the informal sector and recognized the inevitability and value of black and gray markets. Although consumers rarely complain about unsatisfactory goods and services, commentators argue that they should be encouraged to do so in order to provide producers with the information necessary to improve quality. And some retailers do welcome complaints for just this reason.

We also value participation in cultural life, encouraging it by investing substantial resources in public education and even making education compulsory. Obviously, literacy and numeracy are essential for participation in political and economic life as well. We view functional illiteracy as a national and personal tragedy. Americans are proud of their diverse cultural heritages and seek to preserve them. And even though many deplore the banality and superficiality of much popular culture, others argue that the consumption of both television and popular music is not a passive process but rather an active critical engagement.

I believe that our enthusiasm for participation in politics, the market, cultural life, and social services should extend to participation in the legal system. Litigation is an important form of political activity: courts exercise political authority, modify substantive laws, and allocate resources. Litigation also affects the economy, conveys information, alters prices, and corrects market imperfections. Litigation declares and changes fundamental cultural values. Additionally, litigants consume a vital social service, since courts (and of course legislatures) are subsidized by the state. Many commentators deplore the levels of law, lawyers, and litigation in contemporary America. We can certainly imagine and strive to create a society in which the role of law would be greatly diminished—Marx, after all, hoped that the state would wither away under communism. But it is only realistic to acknowledge that such an ideal is either utopian (in the good sense of that word) or romantically nostalgic. Our society possesses only weak historical traditions; it constantly experiences rapid change; our population is extremely heterogeneous; there are substantial inequalities among classes, races, genders, ethnic groups, and regions; monopoly capitalism enormously concentrates power; national, state, and local governments all threaten individuals. In such an environment, law is an essential ingredient of social order.

If readers have followed me this far, accepting the view that participation in the legal system is socially valuable, I still must show that injury victims should be encouraged to claim tort damages.

A tort is, among other things, a normative violation. The tortfeasor has behaved dangerously and has caused injury to another. In order to preserve and strengthen the norm against dangerous behavior it is imperative to publicize the violation and punish the wrongdoer. Our legal system does little to respond to the sense of violation and outrage experienced by victims, especially those injured seriously and permanently. Indeed, fear of liability in the particular case and of its precedential value in others often leads defendants to continue denying moral responsibility even after paying damages. Other societies, notably Japan, require the tortfeasor to apologize to the victim as part of the remedial process. And where interpersonal honor is highly valued, victims or their kin must seek revenge. There are obviously strong cultural reasons why it would be difficult, and perhaps undesirable, to incorporate apologies or feuds into our own tort process. But that does not alter the necessity of responding to legitimate hurt and anger by encouraging the victim to seek legal redress in every case. Unredressed wrongs allow resentment to fester, breeding a feeling of pervasive injustice, and sometimes leading to acts of vengeance.

* * *

Deterrence

Although tort lawyers and scholars differ about the relative virtues of negligence and strict liability, they agree that tort law must play an important role in discouraging dangerous behavior. In the absence of effective regulation, what must the tort system do? Years of research on the deterrent effect of sanctions repeatedly has confirmed that the likelihood of suffering punishment is at least as important as the severity of that punishment and probably more influential. Indeed, we cannot increase the efficacy of deterrence by raising penalties indefinitely because society grows more reluctant to impose punishment as penalties become more severe. In any case, punitive damage awards remain rare, and compensatory damages, by definition, are limited to the victim's actual loss. Therefore, critics of the tort system who would curtail punitive damages, eliminate or cap elements of compensatory damages, such as pain and suffering, and deduct collateral sources should welcome a proposal to make up for the loss of deterrent efficacy by increasing the frequency of claims.

Tort liability presumably is most effective in influencing the behavior of economically rational actors—medium or large profit-seeking enterprises in competitive markets engaged in repetitive activities and thus capable of learning how to modify their behavior as a result of tort damages imposed on themselves or others. Therefore, we probably should discount the efficacy of tort liability as a deterrent in precisely those situations where research shows that such liability is most likely, namely road accidents. And in the United States we cannot use tort liability to reduce danger at work—the environment in which victims are next most likely to claim—because workers' compensation generally is the exclusive remedy, and it consciously is designed not to reflect the full costs of accidents. Consequently, tort liability is most likely to be an effective deterrent of other accidents.

Yet our limited data strongly suggest that tort liability for other accidents fails to deter because too few victims claim. A profit-seeking entrepreneur in a competitive market would have to discount the threat of tort liability by ninety-eight percent in deciding how much to spend on safety. This is not a matter of personal callousness or indifference because it is not a matter of individual choice. An entrepreneur who fails to cut safety costs whenever the tort system allows such savings will be put out of business by a competitor who does. Thus, raising the frequency of claims is essential if tort is to play its central role in discouraging dangerous behavior.

* * *

Conclusion

I have shown that the level of claiming is extremely low. I have argued that claiming should be encouraged just as we encourage participation in political, economic, and cultural life and the consumption of social services. And I have asserted that the generally accepted theories of tort law require the highest possible level of claiming in order to strengthen norms against endangering others, relieve victims' feelings of injury, compensate victims, and generally discourage dangerous behavior. The failure to claim actually erodes norms and encourages risk. And even if one accepted the dubious deterrent theory that increasing the magnitude of the penalty could make up for its infrequency, it still is necessary to respond to the victims' hurts and needs for compensation in every case. A higher claims rate has the potential to change the functioning of the tort system more substantially than any other politically feasible change. If we could persuade all tort victims to claim, we would more than double the efficacy of the tort system in road and work accidents and increase it fiftyfold in the remaining situations, which constitute eighty-six percent of all serious accidents. No change in substantive or procedural rules could have an equivalent impact. This demonstrates the contribution that a critical sociology of law can make to social reform as well as to our theoretical understanding of the legal system.

For too long the media have disseminated, and the public uncritically has believed, the pronouncements of self-styled Jeremiahs decrying the alleged litigiousness of Americans. Their claims are unsubstantiated and false. Litigation rates are low and rising too slowly. Vast numbers of accident victims fail to seek and thus to recover any compensation whatever. The most significant reform of the tort system—far more consequential than any incremental change in substantive or procedural law—would be to make it begin to fulfill its promises by responding to a higher proportion of victims. This would strengthen the norm against dangerous behavior, relieve the anger of victims, ameliorate the financial plight of victims, and encourage safety. Of course, the reform will be opposed by many: the insurance industry; manufacturers, retailers, and other potential defendants; the medical profession; and the personal injury defense bar. But these opponents will have great difficulty justifying their hostility to the public. Proponents of the reform, by contrast, can invoke many powerful political symbols. They will be seeking to help victims and to reduce the dangers to all. They will be increasing access to the legal system and reducing bias against those disadvantaged by race, sex, and class. Most importantly, they will be assisting tort victims to serve society while seeking to help themselves. To assert a legal claim is to perform a vital civic obligation.

B. The Effect of Liability on Innovation

What relationship does liability have on innovation? Peter Huber and Robert Litan offer a summary of the debate, based on their review of papers published in their collection *The Liability Maze: The Impact of Liability Law on Safety and Innovation* (Brookings, 1991). Providing readers with the benefit of a specific case study, Robert McKenna discusses the likely effect of products liability law on the development of an AIDS vaccine.

PETER W. HUBER AND ROBERT E. LITAN, *Overview, in* THE LIABILITY MAZE: THE IMPACT OF LIABILITY LAW ON SAFETY AND INNOVATION (1991)*

It has been suggested that the broad and unpredictable sweep of U.S. liability law deters innovation. The logic here has been straightforward: when the legal costs of certain kinds of accidents are prohibitively high and unpredictable, entire sectors of enterprise shut down. Liability law will not promote anything systematically if it is imposed capriciously, if it imposes costs on superior options, or if it assesses damages that swing wildly. Such reasoning has been invoked more often in recent years to justify legislative or common law limits on liability. Given the ubiquity and scope of the U.S. liability system, it is surprising that there is little empirical research to back up assertion. Whichever side of this debate one is inclined to favor, the debate is surely important. The U.S. liability system is clearly a major force in the ordering of our affairs.

Any effects the liability system may have on innovation should have been growing more apparent as the scope of liability doctrines has expanded, the number of suits has increased, and the average size of awards has escalated. The analytical task, however, is not so straightforward. As we discuss later, an array of forces independent of the liability system exert constant pressure for improvements in both safety and innovation. Distenglanging the effects of liability from these other effects is fraught with complications. Nonetheless, the size, pervasiveness, and economic importance of the U.S. liability system require that some attempt be made to gauge its practical impact, particularly since the expansion of that system has been justified in large part on the assumption that the net effect would be beneficial.

The current literature addressing the broader social impacts of the liability system is abundant, but mostly theoretical and speculative. The most comprehensive and perhaps most widely publicized

*Used by permission.

survey on innovation was conducted by the Conference Board, a well-known business research organization, which in 1986 asked 500 chief executive officers of large U.S. corporations about the impact of the tort system on their companies. Among other things, the study reported that roughly one-third of all firms surveyed, and nearly half of those claiming "major impacts," had decided against introducing new products because of liability fears. And 58 percent of those who had experienced a major impact from liability had discontinued some of their products for the same reason.

Anecdotes about products said to have been withdrawn from the market because of liability concerns provide a second, though indirect, form of evidence. For example, Louis Lasagna cites the case of Bendectin (once widely used to alleviate pregnancy-induced nausea among women), while Robert Martin highlights the disappearance of small aircraft. Similar examples are cited in other studies. A study by the American Medical Association (AMA) on the development of new medical technologies found:

> Innovative new products are not being developed or are being withheld from the market because of liability concerns or inability to obtain adequate insurance. Certain older technologies have been removed from the market, not because of sound scientific evidence indicating lack of safety or efficacy, but because product liability suits have exposed manufacturers to unacceptable financial risks.

On the specific subject of contraceptives, the AMA notes:

> In the early 1970's, there were 13 pharmaceutical companies actively pursuing research in contraception and fertility. Now, only one U.S. company conducts contraceptive and fertility research. Unless the liability laws are drastically altered, it is very unlikely that pharmaceutical companies will aggressively pursue research in this area.

An expert advisory panel of the Food and Drug Administration (FDA), the American Academy of Pediatrics, and the Institute of Medicine have made similar statements about vaccines. Two other observers claim that "the distortions introduced by skyrocketing punitive damage claims and awards have deprived patients of significant existing therapies and have inhibited research and development concerning new therapies."

* * *

Dogs That Don't Bark

The biggest problem in making any empirical assessment of the effects of U.S. liability law lies in the nature of what must be measured. The entire debate—on both sides of the issue—revolves around things that *don't* happen. Many states have faced a similar question in connection with Good Samaritan laws, which limit liability for volunteers, rescuers, and the like. Those who oppose Good Samaritan liability limits point out that there are few cases on record of rescuers being sued. Supporters point out that the paucity of suits may simply reflect a paucity of volunteers and rescuers—the very problem that Good Samaritan laws are intended to redress. As another pair of commentators has noted, "Indirect costs . . . often defy quantification because they . . . are most frequently manifested by the absence of action. Identifying, categorizing and counting the *absence* of action in an objective, statistically valid survey clearly is not feasible using current methodologies." The challenge, in effect, is to count the dogs that don't bark in the night.

A similar census of things that don't happen is required to study innovation. One must somehow find ways to count valuable patents not sought, safe products not marketed, and needed services not supplied out of fear of liability. The inquiry is complicated by the fact that the baseline is constantly shifting.

The difficulty of discerning the connection between liability and innovation that does not occur is compounded by the reticence of those most immediately involved. Providers of goods and services have little incentive to be forthcoming about the issues. They will not care to dwell at length on the fact that they no longer sell a life-saving vaccine, or have decided not to market a safe substitute for asbestos. Providers who protest adverse effects on innovation imply that their technology is static or obsolete.

Finally, the inquiry is further complicated by the difficulty of interpreting trends that can be observed. A decline in the number of general practitioners willing to provide obstetrical services, for example, may reflect a loss of needed, safety-enhancing services. Or it may reflect inevitable and desirable specialization, which centralizes complex services in urban centers where they can be provided by the most experienced practitioners with the best available technology. The collapse of the general aviation industry almost certainly makes life more dangerous for those who continue flying in aging planes, but the overall impact on safety must also take into account those who stop flying altogether.

Summary of Findings

Expressly or by implication, most authors agree that the effects of the liability system, whatever they may be, depend on much more than the narrow question of whether liability is imposed, or on the still narrower question of what legal standard (like "negligence" or "strict liability") is applied. The authors all recognize that jury trials, contingency fees, long-tail liability, the sheer size of awards, and the stigmatizing effect of punitive damages, along with adverse publicity, market forces, and regulation are at least equally important.

Authors who study innovation have also looked to a combination of anecdotal and historical evidence to assess the impact of liability in specific industries and sectors. Viscusi and Moore performed a statistical analysis of a newly compiled data series on insurance losses for various sectors of the economy for the period 1980-84, or the years when the so-called liability crisis of the 1980s first came to public attention. They attempted to determine whether differences in liability costs across industries were related to differences in various measures of innovation. They found that for industries with relatively low liability costs the liability system appeared, if anything, to enhance innovation. But in industries such as general aviation, in which liability costs rose sharply during the early 1980s and became a significant share of total costs, liability does seem to have dampened innovation.

Expressly, or by implication, the authors of the innovation case studies generally agreed with Viscusi and Moore. All the authors focused primarily on design, rather than manufacturing, defects. Martin, for example, notes that virtually all aviation product liability cases have involved claims of defective design. Similarly, in his discussion of vaccine litigation, Lasagna notes that in the 1950s and 1960s litigation over defective vaccine designs was more common than over defective batches of particular vaccines. Few of the authors offer much comment on manufacturing defect cases, from which one may perhaps surmise that these are much less problematic.

The case studies identify some concrete instances of the liability system's negative impact on innovation. General aviation appears to have suffered broad systemic effects; some segments of the industry have almost folded, apparently in large part because of the pressure of liability. In several industries—most notably some types of pharmaceuticals and small aircraft—the combined effects of uncertainty and high awards seem to have discouraged the research, development, and marketing of entire categories of products. Laurence Tancredi and Dorothy Nelkin suggest that fear of malpractice liability has in certain areas curtailed the use of innovative medical procedures, while stimulating in other areas (especially obstetrics, with a major increase in Caesarean sections) excessive "defensive" medicine.

Several authors also discern an active, marketwide, liability-driven retreat from such things as obstetrics and the marketing of vaccines. Reiser argues that, the effects of informed consent aside, liability has transformed medical practice in ways that are fundamentally inimical to better health care. Mackay discusses various examples of auto design in which European manufacturers and consumers have either initiated or been the first to gain access to innovative design improvements. Martin presents figures on the declining rate of introduction of new light aircraft in the decades between 1950 and 1990, suggesting that this decline is a direct effect of expanding liability.

Lasagna concludes that at least for a few identifiable classes of products, liability has had a demonstrably depressive effect on innovation. On the basis of the Bendectin experience, he writes, "it seems safe to predict that never again will a manufacturer petition the FDA to approve for marketing a new prescription drug for nausea and vomiting during pregnancy." In one especially interesting case study, Lasagna revisits thalidomide, takes note of the "fascinating medical uses discovered for the drug in the years since 1961" (such as the treatment of leprosy and a dozen other rare diseases), and then briefly examines the difficulties that have been encountered in marketing the drug even for desirable uses. Tancredi and Nelkin point out how the depressive effect of liability on innovation of medical technologies, vaccines, and drugs may be reducing the quality of medical care.

Several authors observe that while manufacturers may win the great (sometimes overwhelming) majority of some kinds of cases tried, litigation costs may still be prohibitive. Martin notes that aviation manufacturers successfully prove that "in more than 80 percent of the cases brought to trial . . . there was no defect in design or manufacture which caused the accident." Lasagna notes that Merrell Dow has "won the great majority" of Bendectin claims. Nonetheless, both authors go on to describe the withdrawal of the products in question, because manufacturers concluded that even the costs of successful litigation were too high or unpredictable to shoulder.

Few of the authors have ventured specific estimates on what liability is adding to the costs of the specific goods and services they address. Martin is an exception, providing estimates that liability costs in 1987 added "from $70,000 to $100,000 per [light airplane] built and shipped during the year." Mackay estimates that the cost of the U.S. product liability system for U.S. manufacturers "runs into hundreds of dollars per car sold."

Rollin Johnson's work on the effects of liability in the chemical industry is a notable exception to the other innovation papers. Using various standard quantitative indicators of innovation—R&D expenditures and patents granted, for example—Johnson finds that innovative activity seems to be alive and well in this industry. He sees little evidence that it has been dampened by liability litigation thus far, though he warns that future litigation over the effects of toxic substances eventually could chill innovation by chemicals firms.

Policy Recommendations

The large uncertainty that remains about the effects of liability in the United States may suggest to some that no policy conclusions are possible, and that therefore no policies should be formulated. There are "virtually no solid data," Swazey noted in her discussion of the effect of liability law on drug safety, and "it is interesting to wonder how policy is made in their absence."

Interesting indeed, but the one issue beyond dispute is that legal rules are policy, and policy *will* be made, in courts if not in legislatures, with or without data. Some will suggest that the absence of solid empirical data argues for leaving the legal system alone. Others will quickly respond that the absence of empirical data on efficacy argues equally well for curtailing a system that churns more than $100 billion through the U.S. economy, entailing transactions costs of perhaps half that amount, without demonstrable benefit and with some real risk of harm.

The debate between these two views will undoubtedly continue. Nevertheless, we believe several potentially useful and important policy recommendations do emerge from the discussion in this volume. Given the clear division of views of many of the authors, we stress that these recommendations are our own, though based on the analysis and conclusions of the various chapters.

First, those who formulate tort policy should perhaps learn from the well-established tenet in the field of psychology that rewards tend to be more effective in influencing behavior than punishments. Both liability law and regulation try to induce safety-enhancing behavior by punishing or curtailing the activities of firms and individuals. Graham suggests that it is time to try rewards instead, by offering positive legal incentives to manufacturers that promptly correct design defects and experiment with safety innovations. Along these lines, judges and legislators might consider allowing manufacturers partial, if not total, defenses against liability claims if they can prove they have behaved in that fashion. At a minimum, such behavior ought to shield manufacturers from punitive damages.

Rules of evidence are also relevant in this regard. Both negligence and strict liability doctrines recognize that designing products and providing services are multifaceted undertakings, with many trade-offs among considerations of price, safety, and utility. Innovation can be a benefit in and of itself, for the individual consumer and society at large. The cutting-edge new drug or surgical procedure may offer the gravely ill patient a chance that cannot be found otherwise; society may also realize important benefits from its use even if the individual consumer does not. The legal system should be prepared to recognize such benefits, intangible though they are, and to give them serious consideration and weight in any analysis of liability in any particular case. Trying new things is always somewhat risky, but *not* trying them carries risks too. Legal rules, jury instructions, and evidentiary standards can all be crafted to give more equal weight to these symmetric considerations.

Second, a major theme that emerges is that the uncertainty of the tort system is its greatest vice, magnifying risks of liability while disconnecting them from unduly risky conduct. To a large extend, of course, uncertainty is created by factors not directly related to liability doctrines, such as wide variations in jury awards. Doctrine is nevertheless important. One we would single out relates to the ability of plaintiffs to recover for product-related injuries decades after products have been on the market and previously not been held liable for injury. The prospect that liability may nevertheless be imposed in such circumstances clearly raises the risks for manufacturers seeking to introduce new products. At the same time, such retrospective liability can have no material effects on safety. A case exists for statues of repose, at least for nontoxic products. A similarly strong case exists for shielding manufacturers from punitive damages where it is shown that product designs meet all applicable regulatory standards.

Third, legal scholars and jurists must become more willing to apply the same cost-benefit standards to the liability system that the liability system applies to doctors, drug companies, and the manufacturers of planes, chemicals, and cars. The risk-utility calculus so often applied *by* the tort law must also be applied *to* the tort law. It is of course true that engineers and pharmacologists sometimes settle on inferior designs, deliver imperfect services, or arrive at methods and procedures that could be considerably improved. Lawyers and jurists, however, are capable of making similar mistakes with the legal process itself. Without doubt, accidents outside the courtroom are socially costly. But accidents inside most assuredly can be too, in that they misallocate costs and discourage the wrong kinds of activities.

We need not resolve here whether the tort system has grown unduly fast in recent decades or whether it has just grown in step with technology and the advent of new risks. By any measures, the U.S. tort system today is a large instrument of government and social policy, certainly as expensive and far-reaching as any major government agency. Government institutions of this size and scope, whether centralized in Washington or dispersed in courthouses across the country, deserve systematic scrutiny. Even the watchdogs need to be watched; even the guardians need guarding. The difficulty of assessing the costs and benefits of the tort system cannot be sufficient excuse for simply ignoring them, or refusing to undertake any systematic inquiry at all. Certainly there *are* costs and benefits of some sort, and the entries on both sides of the ledger are potentially as large as the system itself. It is the challenge for pundits and academics to determine whether the litigation industry is delivering, all in all, a social profit or loss.

Robert M. McKenna, *The Impact of Product Liability Law on the Development of a Vaccine Against the AIDS Virus*, 55 U. CHI. L. REV. 943 (1988)*

In August 1987, the Food and Drug Administration announced that it had approved plans for the first human trials in the United States of an experimental vaccine against human immunodeficiency virus (''HIV''), the virus that causes acquired immune deficiency syndrome (''AIDS''). While federal officials cautioned that a useful vaccine would probably not be available until ''well into the 1990's,'' their announcement was nonetheless a cause for some optimism given previous projections that an effective vaccine would probably ''not become available in this century.''

Even as scientific advances bring the world closer to development of an HIV vaccine, however, the pharmaceutical industry and others argue that these advances also hasten an inevitable conflict between medical hopes and the realities of a tort law system that already has jeopardized the production of most major existing vaccines. One commentator has predicted that ''under present legal conditions, even if an HIV vaccine were available tomorrow, no one would produce it.'' Another recently stated that ''worries about product-liability lawsuits could stop any company from marketing a vaccine unless government assumes much or all of the risk.'' The California State Assembly, reacting to similar statements by companies that have invested heavily in HIV vaccine research, adopted a statute that protects the manufacturer of an FDA-approved HIV vaccine from suits brought on theories of strict liability for design or warning defects, or for breach of implied warranty.

The concerns behind these warnings stem from the liability crisis that has threatened the production and availability of vaccines against many childhood diseases. A series of product liability

*Used by permission.

cases and damage awards that began in the late 1960s has driven most manufacturers of childhood vaccines out of the market, to the point where single manufacturers supply almost all childhood disease vaccines at vastly increased prices. The premise underlying the concerns about HIV vaccine production, then, is that the legal liability associated with existing vaccines will prevent full development and production of an HIV vaccine.

The pharmaceutical industry and a number of commentators have proposed a variety of responses to this grim possibility, including (1) federal assumption of liability for injuries caused by privately manufactured vaccines, (2) statutory modification of the prevailing common law standard that makes vaccine manufacturers strictly liable for design and warning defects, and (3) judicial modification of the strict liability standard. Models for legislation in the first category are the Swine Flu Act of 1976 and the National Childhood Vaccine Injury Act of 1986, both of which established federal programs to compensate victims of vaccine-related injuries and deaths. In the second category is the California statute. The third category is exemplified by a California case, decided prior to enactment of that statute, which adopted a negligence standard for defects in a manufacturer's warnings to vaccines.

But it is incorrect to assume that the liability associated with existing vaccines will carry over to HIV vaccine; therefore, it is unnecessary to enact legislation or to modify the common law in order to guarantee that pharmaceutical companies will develop and produce the vaccine. Almost all of the pharmaceutical industry's liability for existing vaccines has arisen from the mass immunization programs through which most Americans traditionally have been inoculated.

In these programs, persons administering the vaccines make no individualized medical judgments of the risks and benefits of inoculation for each vaccinee and give few warnings of potential side effects to vaccines. As a result, vaccine manufacturers usually have not met their duty under product liability law to warn vaccinees directly of known dangers associated with their vaccines. HIV's epidemiology, however, makes mass immunization against HIV unnecessary. Compared to influenza or the major childhood diseases, HIV is not transmitted easily. Moreover, it does not spread rapidly beyond the groups whose members have been its primary victims. Public officials can therefore target immunization efforts at members of those groups. Universal inoculation is unwarranted. In addition, HIV vaccine is likely to be too scarce and too expensive to dispense indiscriminately, making universal inoculation impossible even if it were to become the preferred option of public health officials. For these reasons, the decision to vaccinate against HIV—whether it is made in an immunization clinic or in a doctor's office—will necessarily be that of a physician capable of making an individualized medical judgment.

Consequently, the learned intermediary doctrine will protect manufacturers of HIV vaccines from the liability that is associated with existing vaccines. This doctrine provides that a drug manufacturer is not liable for inadequate warnings to a drug recipient where a physician evaluates the recipient's personal circumstances and then decides to prescribe the drug. There are only two exceptions to the learned intermediary doctrine. The first involves vaccines administered in mass immunization programs. This exception to the rule does not threaten HIV manufacturers because health workers will administer the vaccine on an individualized basis. The second exception is more recent and involves oral contraceptives. HIV vaccine manufacturers might cite these cases as grounds for legislative protection, arguing that HIV vaccines share with oral contraceptives the characteristics that the courts in the oral contraceptive cases cited as the reasons for not applying the doctrine to oral contraceptives.

The HIV vaccine, however, will differ from oral contraceptives and conventional vaccines in four crucial respects. In the first place, the HIV vaccine probably will be prescribed by a physician who will have an especially active role in the vaccination decision, since the vaccine will be too expensive and scarce to administer indiscriminately. Second, communication between the physician and vaccinee will have to be substantial in order for the doctor to determine whether the vaccinee is indeed at high risk for HIV. Third, since health workers probably will not distribute the vaccine in a manner comparable to the method through which "the pill" or conventional vaccines are distributed, it is unlikely that distribution will be accompanied by massive publicity on the part of drug manufacturers aimed directly at potential vaccines. Finally, the vaccine should be very safe. Scientists are developing the vaccine by using the new technology of genetic recombination, and thus the HIV vaccine should prove much safer than conventional vaccines. The HIV vaccine will not infect a recipient with the virus from which it is made and will be so pure that it will not cause the adverse side effects associated with other vaccines. The HIV vaccine should cause few, if any, serious injuries and therefore should generate very few lawsuits. Existing standards of liability for warning defects, therefore, will adequately protect the manufacturers of HIV vaccine from the frequent lawsuits that have driven most producers of other vaccines out of the market.

Limited Vaccination

[Hepatitis B vaccine makes a useful comparison to HIV vaccine because of some points in common: its high cost (between $150 and $175 in 1987) and its association with "high-risk groups."] Because of its high cost and limited supply, hepatitis B vaccine is recommended in the United States only for high-risk groups, even though public health officials believe they could control hepatitis B completely if they administered the vaccine to all children. It is likely that the same constraints of cost and supply will force the conservation of HIV vaccine, making indiscriminate vaccination uneconomical. In order to reach poor members of high-risk groups, especially IV drug users, the government may have to purchase large quantities of the vaccine for free distribution in public health clinics. But even if the government were to do that, it would still have to limit the vaccine's administration to members of high-risk groups, out of financial necessity. The high cost of the vaccine will necessitate medical evaluation of each potential recipient, in order to determine whether he or she actually is at risk.

If a virus is capable of spreading easily and rapidly throughout the population, as are influenza and most of the major childhood diseases, then vaccination against it must be universal and rapid—that is, on a large scale and at a high rate. Thus, all states require vaccination of school-age children against the major childhood diseases. School clinics typically administer the necessary vaccines to children in an assembly-line. Similarly, health workers administered the swine flu vaccine on a massive scale to 45 million Americans. In such settings, no one makes an individualized medical judgment of the risks and benefits of inoculation for each recipient, nor does anyone directly and individually warn the recipient or the recipient's parents about potential hazards.

In contrast to the epidemiology of the childhood diseases and influenza, HIV does not spread in a manner that demands vaccination on a scale or at a rate that precludes individualized medical judgments prior to inoculation. It is true that, until recently, the Centers for Disease Control ("CDC") had estimated that HIV had infected more than 1.5 million Americans, and the CDC had projected 324,000 diagnosed cases of AIDS in the United States by the end of 1991. Many believed that HIV was spreading rapidly into the heterosexual population and that HIV was transmitted at least as readily as other sexually transmitted diseases, such as hepatitis B.

More recent estimates, however, have put the number of HIV-positive persons at between 350,000 and one million, and several studies report that the rate of increase in new AIDS cases is beginning to level off. There are other indications that HIV is not spreading rapidly among heterosexuals, except among intravenous drug users, and that the virus is actually much more difficult to transmit than was previously believed.

Thus, AIDS will continue to afflict primarily homosexual men, intravenous drug users, and the sexual partners of IV drug users. Once a vaccine is available, therefore, immunization efforts will need to reach only the members of these high-risk groups. In addition, the new HIV vaccine will be too expensive and its supply too limited to allow indiscriminate or universal distribution. Health workers will have to conserve the vaccine and administer it only to high-risk groups where it can have the greatest impact.

The HIV Vaccine Will Be Relatively Safe

HIV primarily invades white blood cells called T-lymphocytes, an essential component of the human immune system. Following infection of the lymphocyte, the virus synthesizes a DNA molecule corresponding to the code carried in its RNA. This molecule then works its way into the cell's nucleus and integrates itself among the cell's genes, where the virus remains latent until an infection stimulates the lymphocyte.

Massive suppression of the immune system is the most common effect of HIV, but HIV is also known to have a pathogenic effect on the central nervous system of some of its carriers that is independent of the immune deficiency. Furthermore, scientists have linked the virus to increased risk of at least three types of cancer.

Increasingly, scientists agree that the "only certain barrier to further spread of [AIDS] is a vaccine." The availability of new technologies such as genetic recombination have enabled relatively brisk progress in development of an HIV vaccine and are likely to result in the production of something much safer than existing conventional vaccines. Because it should be much safer, the HIV vaccine should give rise to very few lawsuits and hence, unlike its conventional counterparts, should not be a major source of legal liability for its producers.

To understand why the HIV vaccine should be safer, some background is appropriate. Vaccines work by introducing antigens which stimulate the body's production of antibodies against a particular virus prior to one's infection by the virus. The most potent forms of vaccines against viruses such as polio, rabies, and measles are those scientists prepare from the whole virus, called "whole-cell vaccines." Whole-cell vaccines come in two forms. Scientists make the first, called "live" vaccine, from a whole virus that has been attenuated but not killed completely. They make the second from the killed whole virus. Research has demonstrated that live vaccines induce longer lasting immunity than vaccines prepared from killed viruses, probably because the live vaccines are more efficient at introducing the viral antigens necessary for stimulation of antibody production. Another advantage of live vaccines is that their potency requires only one dose; they therefore involve shorter treatment. This means that they will have less of a tendency to elicit resistance in the viral population than will prolonged use of weaker doses.

Although whole-cell vaccines have the greatest potency, they pose two kinds of risks. First, they sometimes infect the vaccinee with the virus they are designed to combat. The live oral Sabin polio vaccine, for example, elicits one case of polio in every 3.2 to 8 million vaccine doses distributed. Whole-cell vaccines are capable of transmitting the target virus because they contain all of its genetic material; a virus reproduces itself by inserting its genetic material into the host cell's nucleus. The second risk posed by whole-cell vaccines is that they occasionally cause unpredictable side effects. These reactions occur because whole-cell vaccines "contain contaminating materials far exceeding, in mass, the immunogenically active ingredients."

Thus, whole-cell vaccines are somewhat risky. There are several factors, however, that would make a whole-cell HIV vaccine even riskier than existing whole-cell vaccines. First, there is the long latency period of the virus, the maximum length of which has never been established. Clinical testing of whole-cell HIV vaccine would necessarily produce uncertain results of doubtful predictive value since the virus could remain latent in the vaccinee far longer than the period of testing. In addition, anyone who would receive the vaccine would thereafter test positive for the virus because current tests identify the antibodies that the vaccine would stimulate the body to create. It therefore would be impossible to determine whether a vaccinee only had the antibodies or had been inadvertently infected with the virus itself. As a result, health workers could administer whole-cell HIV vaccine for many years before doctors discovered its infectiousness.

The possibility that a whole-cell HIV vaccine could infect a recipient with the virus has led most researchers to reject the whole-cell approach in the fight against HIV. Instead, most research focuses on the development of an "acellular" or "subunit" vaccine. A subunit vaccine cannot infect a recipient because it contains only a fragment of the target virus, a fragment lacking the genetic material necessary for the virus's reproduction. Subunit vaccines are also much less likely to produce adverse side effects, since they contain only a few essential proteins and lack the contaminating materials that inevitably accompany whole-cell preparations. The subunit vaccines already in use, such as the hepatitis B and acellular whooping cough vaccines, have demonstrated that they are much safer than whole-cell preparations. An extensive search of the case law reveals only one lawsuit in which it has been alleged that a subunit vaccine was harmful.

Conclusion

HIV is not spreading nearly as rapidly or as widely as people originally feared. Consequently, the virus does not require vaccination on such a scale and at such a rate as would preclude individualized medical evaluation of every potential vaccinee. The cost of the vaccine will in any event compel individualized medical judgments. Indiscriminate delivery of HIV vaccine will not be an option, just as it is presently not an option for the vaccine against hepatitis B, a virus that is more widespread and more easily transmitted than HIV. Because health workers will make individualized vaccination decisions in the HIV context, the learned intermediary doctrine will insulate manufacturers of HIV vaccine from the liability that has plagued manufacturers of vaccines used in mass immunization programs. In addition, while the HIV vaccine will be expensive, it should be much safer than conventional, whole-cell vaccines. It should be incapable of infecting a vaccinee with the virus, should have far fewer and much milder side effects than those vaccines, and therefore should generate few lawsuits.

Because of apprehensions over liability and claimed market uncertainty, the pharmaceutical companies argue that there are no incentives to invest in the development of new or improved vaccines. Noting that the market seems barely able to supply many existing vaccines, they contend that it could fail to develop and produce a vaccine as complex and costly as that required to immunize against HIV. Yet the reality of massive HIV vaccine research undermines this contention. Several private firms and public institutions are actively engaged in the research and development of an HIV vaccine. By August 1987, two private American firms and a health institute had sought approval for human trials of an HIV vaccine, and an FDA spokesman has confirmed that "other companies are also working on potential vaccines, as are scores if not hundreds of researchers at institutions around the world."

Thus, fear of legal liability does not appear to be inhibiting the development of an HIV vaccine. Legal liability may continue to pose a serious threat to the availability of many existing vaccines. But the HIV vaccine probably will not be like these vaccines, either in form or in the way that health workers will administer it to the public. In form, it will be most like the hepatitis B vaccine. Moreover, the inventor of an HIV vaccine will reap enormous accolades and publicity—perhaps even a Nobel prize—and, moreover, be responsible for saving hundreds of thousands of lives. Since AIDS is described as the most frightening and devastating epidemic since polio, the team or individual who solves the HIV vaccine puzzle is likely to be viewed as a latter-day Jonas Salk. The prospect of such an achievement will provide an enormous impetus to researchers worldwide.

That HIV vaccine, like hepatitis B vaccine, may cost $175 or more per vaccinee is likely to be a bigger problem for public health authorities than the threat posed to the supply of HIV vaccine by legal liability. Although manufacturers made hepatitis B vaccine available beginning in 1982, by 1985 only 20 percent of the target population had received it. Its high cost has undoubtedly deterred its administration to the groups who need it most. A steep price for HIV vaccine will deter administration to the same individuals, to the detriment of a successful immunization program.

It is imperative that scientists develop an effective HIV vaccine as soon as possible. The pharmaceutical industry and non-profit institutes are working furiously to achieve that end, and although they face considerable obstacles, legal liability is not among them. To assume that the liability burdens imposed on manufacturers by conventional, whole-cell vaccines will simply carry over to an HIV vaccine—and thereby warrant government protection for manufacturers—misconstrues the nature of the law that has imposed those burdens. This assumption also ignores the important technological characteristics that distinguish the new generation of vaccines from the conventional vaccines that they will replace.

Part VI
Perspectives on Products Liability

A. Focus on the Product

ANITA BERNSTEIN, *Product Dynamism and the Law, in* MEANING, MEASURE, AND MORALITY OF MATERIALISM (Floyd Rudmin & Marsha Richins eds., 1992)*

Almost everyone in the academy knows that objects are dynamic, capable of shaping the selves of human beings. Sociologists have described the phenomenon in their theory of symbolic interactionism. Pragmatic philosophy expresses the same insight. Works of psychology attend to the point. In literature, Nobel laureates describe the influence of objects on the self. Criminology and anthropology have their own examples. Scholars of business pursue the point through research on consumer behavior. Theology reveals the power of things in the concepts of sacred objects and Christian communion.

Law, however, lags. In legal doctrine, objects are generally regarded as simple desiderata. Who inherits the items in Uncle's house when he dies intestate? Can Lizzie Eustace sell a necklace which might be an heirloom? When lightning strikes my car in a commercial garage, must I (the bailor) suffer the loss, or may I expect the owner (the bailee) to repay me? The law does acknowledge that objects occasionally—and to my taste more interestingly—do harm. Dams break and cause floods; dynamite goes off; vicious dogs (are they objects?) bite. These problems are scattered around different areas of the law: "property," "torts," contracts," "criminal law," "decedents' estates" and elsewhere. The law perceives these events as expressions of *conduct*. And the problems are unilluminated by the simple insight, known to other disciplines, that objects act *a priori*, dynamically, as stimuli as well as responses. Here I discuss product dynamism and the law by uniting some of the areas in which the law looks at objects.

Conventional justifications for the existence of products liability have regarded products as instruments of social policy: the doctrine is usually explained by reference to "policy bases." Perhaps the most widely-known justification defends products liability as a source of social insurance or consumer protection. This justification is grounded on the absence of a comprehensive compensation scheme in the United States. Because of the absence of social insurance, injuries caused by defective products must be borne either by manufacturers or consumers. And because manufacturers

*Copyright © 1992 by the author. Used by permission.

profit from the sale of the product, they can obtain liability insurance, and they can spread the cost of all injuries among all the buyers of the product. Thus it is appropriate for manufacturers to bear the loss for all or most of the injuries caused by the product.

Another justification for the existence of products liability comes from the law-and-economics literature. Economists have suggested that a standard of strict liability for manufacturers of defective products, as opposed to the usual tort standard of negligence—which holds a defendant to the standard of a reasonable person—will give manufacturers the incentive to make their products as safe as possible. The manufacturer is said to be the "cheapest cost avoider" in many circumstances; that is, the person or entity who can anticipate a hazard and avert it without expending too much effort or money.

Products liability is also explained as a procedural device. Strict liability shifts the burden of proof from the plaintiff to the manufacturer. A plaintiff lacks the information necessary to say exactly how a product was defective: a user does not know how the product was made or whether the manufacturer acted unreasonably. Manufacturers have such knowledge. As applied, products liability serves as a rebuttable presumption of fault on the part of the manufacturer, which tends to bring out the truth. This justification implies that products liability has no meaning itself as a doctrine.

This burden-of-proof justification has escaped the scathing criticism that the first two justifications have suffered, but I find all three inadequate. As many point out, consumer protection or social insurance cannot manageably be achieved through legal liability. Compensation is not congruent with private law: the best reason for compensation is need, but private law addresses the responsibility of an actor directly, and the suffering of a victim only indirectly. If shifting wealth from powerful corporations to poor victims is the goal, why not compensate victims of illness or other nontortious misfortune by taxing product manufacturers? As for the economics argument about incentives, law-and-economics writers have turned away from strict products liability as a cureall. One view, currently in vogue, holds that strict products liability may have resulted in less safety, and more injuries. And the burden-of-proof justification, though unattacked, seems petty: a tiny, technical explanation for an enormous American phenomenon.

Hence I propose an inquiry into the nature of products themselves. Their importance, I argue, has been ignored in the law. Products describe societies. Names for the eras of human history—the Paleolithic, Neolithic, Iron, and Bronze Ages, the Industrial Revolution, the Atomic Age—reveal that the objects people could create have summed up entire eons.

Looking at objects fills a doctrinal void: A basic omission in the study of products liability is the concept of property. Products are objects, and objects are fundamental constituents of property. Because in practice products liability law seldom raises questions of ownership, it is easy to overlook property law in an attempt to explain the doctrine. The great studies of private property, however, shed light on the subjects of manufacture and use. Theorists such as Locke, who linked labor, creation, and ownership, and Hegel, who connected property with personhood, are important sources of the explanation of products liability.

Products, moreover, play an *a priori* role as stimuli to behavior. The one-way vectors of tort and contract theory—"A hit B," "A chose product X," "M manipulated C"—do not begin to describe the network binding consumers, producers, and observers who select, display, encounter, use and sell a product. In this network all things have meanings, and all products are dynamic agents. Within a subject-object dialectic, a person perceives the world around her and interprets that world to herself. Material objects make up a large share of the world perceived: members of a culture create, share, and reinterpret symbolic properties attributed to products. Because of their dynamic function, products participate in social life. They shape identities, and communicate messages to observers.

Property as a Source of Personhood

As a descriptive label, *homo faber* unites the contributions of property theory to products liability. Man is the maker and user of objects, and manufacture and use are essential elements of human existence. The concept of *homo faber* belongs as much to the domain of property law as it does to the more familiar domains of tort and contract. It is Property that notes the earlier human intentionality, that of the maker, and that grasps the unique influence of things on the formation of a person. Thus an appreciation of products liability law calls for study of the classic justifications of private property.

For centuries philosophers and legal theorists have tried to build a normative case for private ownership. Because property is so important, objects—that is, tangible and moveable property—can be understood to share in that importance. In political and legal theory the most famous defense of private property is credited to John Locke, although it had important predecessors. Locke's "labor theory" rested on the premise that persons have a property right in themselves, especially their own work. When a person mixes his work with a physical thing that is not the property of another, he has a right of ownership in that thing. This right derives from the earlier right, which Locke did not explicitly defend, of the right of property in one's person.

Convincing justifications of private property rely on concepts of personhood. Aristotle linked private property with moral development, arguing that a man needs leisure and material resources to learn civic-mindedness and friendship. Following the revival of Aristotle, the fourteenth-century Scholastics defended private property by connecting it to human nature. William of Occam argued that property is a natural human creation based on reason; Marsilius of Padua believed that private property originated in the innate sense of free will in every human being.

Denunciations of private property likewise rely on the relationship between property and personhood. To those writers who would refuse to acknowledge private ownership of things, private property corrupted the individual, usurped what was really the domain of God, betrayed a communical ideal, or oppressed those who lacked such private property. Other theorists of property such as Hobbes and Hume did not seek to abolish or defend private property but insisted that understanding property required an understanding of human desires and impulses. Tangible property is thus connected to personhood. The right to own property necessarily follows from the premise that persons own themselves.

Perhaps the most adamant insistence on the relationship between property and the individual psyche appears in the works of Hegel, especially *The Philosophy of Right*, where Hegel declares that there can be no personhood without property: "If emphasis is placed on my needs, then the possession of property appears a means to their satisfaction, but the true position is that, from the standpoint of freedom, property is the first embodiment of freedom and so is itself a substantive end." This stance is directly contrary to the conventional views of products liability. The-product-as-inert-object approach presumes that "emphasis is placed" on the needs of an individual, with products deployed to fill those needs. For Hegel this approach fails to begin at the beginning. Without a relationship to property, the individual is not a person, and cannot have the needs of a person. Human will is embedded in things, and things are embedded in human will.

Current understandings of property law have benefited from application of the Hegelian connection between objects and personhood. One important application is a distinction that Margaret Jane Radin has proposed, between property integral to personhood and property held instrumentally or for investment, with property integral to personhood warranting stronger protection in the law. In contrast, I suggest a more tentative and descriptive inference: Because property is integral to personhood, the law of injurious objects has evolved and retains conceptual appeal.

When a person combines her labor with an object, more occurs than a simple justification for ownership. According to Locke, the object changes. The person changes too: she feels different; she is entitled to feel different. For Hegel these changes are inevitable elements of human life. To presume that these changes are entirely for the good is to read into property theory a message that its authors did not write. Objects carry both benefit and detriment. The law of beneficial personalty is expressed in traditional property topics such as bailment, conversion, and decedents' estates; the law of detrimental personalty includes products liability.

The Law of Product Dynamism

Once understood as a source of personhood, the object may be seen as autonomous and dynamic. A vast literature, following Locke and Hegel, expounds this point. The early writings of Karl Marx are crucial to the understanding of the dynamic powers of products. The famous concept of alienation, for instance, expresses the transfer of vitality and freedom from the worker into the object he produces. Whereas his predecessor, the artisan, had the right and duty to control his own labor, the proletarian does work that is dictated by the nature of the product. He loses his freedom in the demands of his labor; he sells his waking hours so that he may buy other products. Out of "fetishism" he perceives powers to be vital beings in their own right.

In the twentieth-century, sociologists writing in the tradition of symbolic interactionism continued to explore the theme of object dynamism. Although not "Marxists" (in the sense of historical determinism), these writers posited a world where individuals perceived symbolic messages in the world around them. Objects are stimuli as well as responses to needs. The self, a realm of continual emergence, changes shape in response to the communication of objects.

The autonomous existence of objects recognized by Marx and the symbolic interactionists is reflected in liability doctrine. Revealing metaphors attribute vital properties to objects. Although these metaphors ultimately do not relieve human beings of responsibility—because their users acknowledge the connection between things and human choices—they help to explain the development, and persistence, of a unique legal doctrine for products.

The Object as Wrongdoer

The term *fait de la chose*, approved by the courts in France in 1897, acknowledges figuratively that there can be an "act of the thing," for which the civil liability system might blame on any of several human beings. From *fait de la chose* a variation of strict products liability has evolved in France, Belgium and Luxembourg. The idea of the act of a thing exists also in American products liability doctrine and its English antecedents.

For example, many subconcepts of products liability law isolate products as distinct from human beings and the corporations that employ them. Statutes of repose, waning in the United States because of constitutional infirmities, posit a radical separation between product and maker. After a period of years, statutes of repose disconnect products from their manufacturers by terminating the attribution of defect to the producer. This severance acknowledges that although a defective product may cause harm, the passage of years gathers all of this responsibility into the product itself (or onto another person) and away from the manufacturer. Similarly, some jurisdictions impose liability on successor corporations based on continuity via a product line, rather than continuity of individual human wrongdoers employed by a corporation. The theory behind breach of warranty avoids reference to manufacturer misconduct: it is the thing itself that must be merchantable or fit for a purpose, with little room for excuses. These doctrines are conventionally explained in terms of policy, not illustrations of the product as wrongdoer, but their focus on the object itself rather than individual or aggregate human conduct echoes *fait de la chose*.

The notion of the product as wrongdoer illuminates case law that purports to reconcile the strict liability approach used in products liability with "fault," the model of liability used in most other areas of torts. Courts have questioned whether strict products liability can accommodate other tort concepts, such as punitive damages or comparative negligence, that depend on fault. In tort doctrine, strict liability and fault stand for opposite approaches. Products liability, however, is a type of strict liability that finds a kind of fault in the harm caused by a product. If a product really were an "inert object," then it could not be a wrongdoer, and questions of damages and defenses would pose genuine conceptual trouble. Courts seem to find the issues easy, however, and have almost unanimously allowed fault-based remedies and defenses in products liability actions.

Fait de la chose suggests other lines of inquiry as well. The doctrine derives from principles of liability for harms caused by animals. The idea that nonhuman actors could be causal agents made French courts receptive to the idea that a thing too could act. English and American courts did not make this connection expressly, but modern products liability law, being "strict," traces its lineage to this older form of strict liability.

Animals and products occupy a unique place in an account of causation of harm. Semi-autonomous, they cause injury only derivatively, and what they "do" is a manifestation of a human omission or act. Their connection to human conduct must be acknowledged, for both corrective-justice reasons of attributing responsibility and for the policy of compensating a victim. But the incompleteness of that connection is expressed lexically in the term strict liability, implying that in one sense the person-defendant was not at fault.

Illustrations of this point may be found in ancient legal codes. Mosaic law provided a death penalty—stoning—for the ox that gored a man or a woman, causing the person's death. If the owner knew of the propensity of the ox to gore, and did not keep the animal restrained, the owner also faced a death penalty when the ox caused the death of a human being. Again human conduct is linked with, but also separated from, the errant activity of the nonhuman wrongdoer. As in modern strict liability the owner of the injuring animal (like the manufacturer of a product) cannot escape responsibility even when the victim does not prove fault; yet the defendant's conduct is pertinent, increasing or decreasing his culpability for the injury. The Biblical rule parallels the modern doctrine that a manufacturer is strictly liable for harms caused or occasioned by its product, and can be liable additionally (under a separate count of negligence, or for punitive damages) if the plaintiff can prove fault.

The English law of deodands, a topic that Oliver Wendell Holmes regarded as essential, attributed blame to an object that was the direct agent of a person's death. Under the law of deodands, the value of the harm-causing object was assessed, and this amount was payable to the Crown. Holmes gave the example of the wheel of a cart as a thing that could be viewed as the agent of a man's death, and forfeited. A tree that fell and killed a person was to be "executed, its corpse delivered to the person's kinsmen to chop up and put to revengeful and beneficial use at the hearth."

To some writers, notably Justice Brennan, modern forfeiture law derives from deodands: whether this association is correct as a matter of history is disputed, but forfeiture shares the theme of personification of objects. For example, the doctrine of admiralty forfeiture has historically insisted that a ship has a distinct personification. Current statutory law requires the forfeiture of boats involved in the violation of customs laws.

Like modern products liability law, deodands and its progeny have been attacked as preposterous fictions, devised with a cynical purpose in mind. Deodands is of course as obsolete as a legal notion can be; and strict products liability may follow it to oblivion. The idea of animation behind both concepts, however, continues to resonate. And as the legal historians Pollack and Maitland have suggested, it will endure as long as human beings feel impelled to curse the chairs over which they stumble.

Grieving for Lost Products

Using the metaphors of banishment, abandonment, and loss, some writers who study products liability demonstrate their belief that products are animated by a kind of life force. Manufacturers routinely and unsentimentally withdraw or decline to market products irrespective of liability considerations, yet the cessation of a line of goods because of liability concerns can provoke expressions of bereavement. The difference between products withdrawn for reasons not based on liability, and products ''driven from the market'' appears to parallel the difference between natural death and death by violence. Bad things, products liability reform proponents appear to argue, happen to good products because of liability.

Liability, according to those who grieve, eliminates products from the market in at least three ways: by obstructing innovation that would otherwise bring new technologies to the fore, by militating against the marketing of a new product, and by causing managers to decide to cease manufacture of a product.

The first category, products never made because of the decline in innovation, is dominated by contraceptives (little research into new technologies is now taking place) and, in general, any product to be used mainly by younger persons. It also features vaccines and general aviation. The second, products created but not marketed, includes miscellany such as new vaccines, a drug called Oculinum, a substitute for asbestos, and a child safety rail. The third category, products withdrawn because of liability, has received the most attention. In martyrdom are Bendectin, the morning sickness drug; CU-7, the intrauterine device that Searle withdrew; the CJ-5 and CJ-7 model Jeeps once made by American Motors; the Puritan-Bennett anesthesia gas machine. Writers have also identified imperiled products: spermicide used for barrier contraception, motorcycles, and antidepressants such as Prozac, for examples.

A complement to grieving over lost products has been agreement that some products should be banished. Even those who are habitual lamenters have agreed that certain consumer items deserved to have gone to products-liability hell. Another consensus endorses the execution of products after due process of law: the ''voluntary'' recalls of the U.S. Consumer Product Safety Commission are widely approved. This personification is crude and bipolar—products are either good or bad.

Implications

I have argued that unknown to itself, the law includes a separate doctrine for objects. Products liability is not merely accident law or the law of sellers' promises. ''Objects law'' goes beyond products liability, however. The traditional legal category of personalty may now be seen as beneficial-objects law. Detrimental objects law includes products liability, the liability rules for dangerous animals, the historical concept of deodands, and the law of forfeiture—topics generally regarded as disparate.

Two assumptions prevalent in American law must be jettisoned. The first is that some person's desire to encounter a product always precedes the encounter with the product. This assumption of conscious, rational conduct is fundamental to explanations of products liability, especially those that derive from economics. Yet as Marx, the symbolic interactionists, and others have taught, products are stimuli as well as responses. The second assumption is that products by and large are good things, except for the dangerous ones, which are bad things. Therefore the law ought to favor the continued existence of products unless they are dangerous: to paraphrase the point in jargon, products deserve protection unless their risk outweighs their utility. In earlier years American courts emphasized the badness of dangerous products; a current trend in the courts seeks protection of "innovation" and product development. This black/white view is simplistic. Products bring both detriment and benefit to the complex world in which they live.

Objects law must become another area of legal thought that advances with the help of other disciplines. Lawyers are still reluctant to surrender their notion of law as an "autonomous discipline," even though antitrust has married itself to economics; criminal law relies on psychiatry to explain its concept of *mens rea* and diminished capacity; tax law works with economics and political science; professional malpractice cases (except for those involving attorneys) cannot proceed without the expert testimony of other professionals; evidence needs epistemology and psychology; scientists must tell courts that creationism is not science—and on and on. The influences on objects law are varied. Beginning to acknowledge them would make the law more intelligible.

B. Feminism

Leslie Bender, *Feminist (Re)Torts: Thoughts on the Liability Crisis, Mass Torts, Power, and Responsibilities,* 1990 Duke L.J. 848 (1990)*

The Burden of Proof and the Presumption of Nonliability in Mass Tort Cases

In our current formulation of mass tort law, we presume the plaintiff will be "strictly liable" for her own harm unless she can prove that the defendant was "at fault," the activity was abnormally dangerous, or the product was "defective." In a tort system primarily based on fault, this presumption, in effect, results in the imposition of liability upon a "faultless" party. There is nothing natural or necessary about the presumption that the injured party should bear her own loss unless she can shift it through legal procedures. The dubious placement of the initial economic loss and the burden of proof can be attributed to two missteps in reasoning: first, the false parallels that are made between who bears the burden in criminal and civil cases, and second, the justice system's failure to consider power imbalances and inequalities in determining who should bear burdens of proof and production.

In our common law system of civil or private law justice, the state is not a party to controversies between citizens. It does however, provide a forum for the resolution of conflicts, provide the rules of law and procedure, promote an ideology about the availability of justice in that forum under those rules, decide the conflicts, and offer its power for the enforcement of its decisions. As the provider of forums for justice and as the judge, the state fails mass tort plaintiffs.

*Used by permission.

In many ways, mass tort actions are more like public law actions than the private law actions that traditionally have been used to resolve other kinds of accident disputes. Mass torts usually involve many plaintiffs, public harms that can be wide-spread or slow-developing, needs of deterrence of further similar conduct, and enormous potential burdens on the judicial system. Unlike the parties to an ordinary accident case, mass tort plaintiffs typically are less empowered than mass tort corporate defendants.

In all tort cases, but particularly in mass torts, the injured parties have multiple burdens to bear. Not only are they burdened by the pain, injustice, and disruptions caused by their injuries, but they also are tangled in a legal system which is unfamiliar, alienating and ritualized. The plaintiffs must take on the burden of rectifying the harm they suffered by identifying the harm-causers, discovering the nature and extent of the risks imposed and harms resulting, and taking corporate defendants to court to force them to take responsibility for the consequences of their actions. Since a plaintiff is required to bear the loss unless she can shift it to another, I call this presumption the "presumption of liability" or "presumption of responsibility." The presumption theoretically could be placed on any of the parties to a dispute. In mass tort cases there is a presumption of nonliability for the corporate defendant—that is, a defendant is not liable for the harms or initial out-of-pocket expenses, unless a plaintiff can prove its liability. Until they settle or win their case, the costs of the accident or injury loss falls on the plaintiff. These would not be insignificant burdens, even if imposed on healthy citizens, but in mass tort cases they rest even more heavily on physically or emotionally harmed victims. Yet there is another dynamic besides placing the burden on an already injured party that significantly disables plaintiffs in mass tort.

The crux of my argument is that parties in mass tort litigation come to the courthouse differently empowered. Because our ideology of justice includes the notion that "justice is blind"—that justice will not let differential wealth and empowerment influence her decision on the merits of the dispute—these differences are "ignored." We are encouraged to believe that our justice system and its courts are a public space where all citizens will have equal voices before the law, even if race, gender, class, sexual orientation, disability, or other factors disadvantage people elsewhere in our society. Complaints can be aired and justice sought, regardless of a party's status, wealth or power. Nevertheless, power clearly affects the judicial process. Time and again we see a judicial system in which power is confirmed, and the law privileges the privileged, in fact if not in theory. Yet the ideology of equality-before-the-law remains strong.

An equal-justice-before-the-law method for equalizing the power of the parties requires that the burden of proof (risk of nonpersuasion and nonproduction) in mass tort cases be allocated on a case-by-case basis to the more empowered party in the dispute, subject to the particularized context and parties to a lawsuit or conflict. In initial pre-complaint or pre-trial proceedings, a court should evaluate the differential power of the parties and allocate the greater burden of proof to the more empowered party. In mass torts caused by corporate conduct, this burden most often will fall on the corporate defendant. In addition, the presumption of "innocence" or "nonliability" should rest with the less empowered party to the litigation. In mass torts caused by corporate conduct, this presumption most often would attach to the injured party or parties.

I propose the following solution to the unequal power distribution in mass torts which would place the initial economic loss on a corporate defendant who created the risk of harm. When a defendant is a powerful corporation or collective organization, there should be no presumption in its favor. Instead the presumption should lie with the injured party in that case. If a plaintiff is injured or subjected to risk of injury by a mass-produced product or corporate for-profit activity, after a limited showing has been made about the corporation's creation of risk to the plaintiff, a corporate actor should be required to bear the initial economic loss (medical expenses, lost wages, or income maintenance and special out-of-pocket damages). This presumptive liability would attach to the creation of a risk of harm during activities for private profit. It would be a rebuttable presumption. The corporate actor would have the option of exculpating itself from responsibility for the harm. The goal would not be to prejudge the dispute or give an injured victim an unfair advantage, but rather to level the power of a corporate defendant's accumulated or collective resources and access to knowledge so that it is more comparable or fair with respect to a potential plaintiff's. Then parties would come before the court as relative equals.

Burden-shifting presumptions are neither foreign to courts nor to the common law of torts. Contests over burden-shifting presumptions and causation recently have preoccupied the Supreme Court in employment discrimination cases. Tort doctrines like res ipsa loquitur and alternative joint liability, some forms of enterprise or marketshare liability, and certain rules in strict products liability shift the burden of proof of either negligence, causation, or particular facts to defendants. The difference between those techniques and this proposal is that, under the current proposal, the burden of proof would be shifted for purposes of the entire litigation and for all elements of the cause of action after the plaintiff has made a limited "risk" showing that the corporate actor may have created a risk of harm to which the plaintiff was exposed. Also, the burden would be shifted, not based on the facts peculiar to the injury or product, but rather on the comparative power, resources, and access to knowledge of the parties. To that extent, it should be easier to apply and predict than the traditional burden-shifting presumptions that are often more fact-specific than party-specific.

A Feminist Exercise of Judicial and Legal Power

Professor Robin West cogently distinguishes between dominant male and female experiences of power and understandings about its use and responsibilities. West suggests that many women's experiences of having power (as opposed to the experiences of most men) arise in situations of grave inequalities of power, such as in parenting or teaching, in which women often use their power to protect and guide rather than to strong-arm or control. She explains that parental (in particular, maternal) power, derived from the power and knowledge differential between parent and child, is interpreted by its holder as a responsibility to care for the unempowered or less-empowered child, a responsibility to teach and empower. Sara Ruddick makes a similar observation about maternal power and practice. It is the very awareness of the inequality of power that prompts or produces the responsibility to protect, to enable, and to give care, rather than to overwhelm or control. The two modalities of power can be differentiated as "overpowering or controlling/protecting" (a masculinist model) and "empowering or power-balancing" (a feminist alternative).

In the masculinist model of intervention, the general power imbalance of the parties as litigants in the court is neither addressed nor altered. The court and the rules of law do not respond to a disadvantaged party's need for empowerment nor do they balance power in the courthouse so that litigants can have equal access to or opportunities for justice. Legal paternalism does not challenge the distribution of power between parties or how it impacts on the judicial process itself.

To empower a mass tort plaintiff, a court must alleviate some of the initial impediments to equal justice posed by the difficulty faced by a plaintiff in obtaining the necessary evidence to support her claim for relief. A corporate producer or actor putatively responsible for the harm has unobstructed access to the information. By shifting the burden of proof and production to the party most capable of bearing it (by virtue of wealth, power, knowledge, and access to information), a court can balance the power of the parties in their conflict and empower the disadvantaged party in her quest for justice. In addition, a court can impose the initial burden of paying for the economic loss resulting from the injury on the party better able or more empowered to bear the out-of-pocket expense.

An interesting side-effect of this change of initial responsibility for economic losses might be a greater and more immediate use of corporate political clout to lobby for socialized medical care and income maintenance for injured plaintiffs. If corporate defendants realized from the outset they would have to advance the money for medical and lost-income expenses until they could go to trial and prove that the burden should be shifted, then they might take an active role in lobbying legislatures for statutory, tax-funded compensation for these victims. At the present time, their incentive to lobby for these measures is negligible because the initial loss always falls on the injured party and his or her insurance carrier. If the law presumed that the loss initially fell on the more empowered party—in cases of mass torts and consumer products liability this party would be a corporate entity—then that party would have increased incentive to provide an alternative compensation system. Plaintiffs as a group do not have the same kind of political power to get such measures enacted because they do not have advanced knowledge that they will be plaintiffs. With a change in the burdens of proof and persuasion and the presumption of nonliability, defendant corporations immediately would face increased potential liability, and they would seek political relief or would insure accordingly.

By power-balancing or empowering a party, the court is not interfering in the merits or substance of the controversy. This feminist approach does not "decide" the case, but rather gives the parties more equal opportunities to present their claims. If we continue with only the masculinist approach taken by courts, wherein they intervene paternalistically, we ignore the role that unequal power and resources currently play in the legal conflict-resolution process itself. Even with this alteration in the burden of proof and the presumption of nonliability for the plaintiff, defendant corporations in mass tort cases would be as capable of prevailing in the litigation on the merits as they are today, but they would not be quite as advantaged in the process by their greater resources, power, or knowledge.

* * *

Thoughts About The Meaning of Responsibility in Mass Torts Caused By Corporate Defendants

Tort law has been weighted down by a language and value system that privilege economics and costs. Every time there is an injury, we determine legal responsibility by asking about the dollar and efficiency costs of paying for the harms or of avoiding them. Questions of cost have consistently been our first or second inquiry in cases of mass torts by corporate defendants.

As harms from mass tort have become more widespread, legal analysis in tort law has become desensitized to the individuals and groups of people harmed. The more people who are injured or subjected to the risk of injury, the more tort law dehumanizes people generally, views them as statistical risks, and sees their injuries as costs of economic growth and progress. If this kind of legal thinking is inconsistent with our core values, we must reject it outright as violative of human dignity and equality. Instead, we can require corporate defendants, corporate officers, and courts to be more socially and personally responsible.

Post-event responsibility ought to mean more than making reparations. A different notion of responsibility arises out of our interconnectedness as human beings, and it has to do with responding to the needs of someone through interpersonal caregiving—it means "taking care of." Although this account of responsibility seems completely absent from the law, it remains central to our life experiences. An example of a social meaning of responsibility can help to explain the need for additional understandings of post-event responsibility in law. For two reasons, I will use an example of a close, interpersonal relationship—that of parent and child. One reason was hinted at before with respect to different exercises of power and the relationship between power and responsibility. Parents are responsible for the health, safety, and well-being of their children, in part because they have far greater power within that relationship and because they have greater power with respect to the outside world to negotiate for their children's benefit. Corporate entities that mass-produce products or conduct risk-creating activities leading to mass harms also have far greater power than the individuals they harm both within the relationship and with the outside world. Perhaps if we could determine some of the meanings of responsibility associated with parental power, then we also could learn things about the meanings of responsibility associated with power in other contexts.

The second reason I am using a family relationship as an example is because it can potentially give us access to perceptions about responsibility that traditionally are absent in market-related contexts. Our understandings about responsibility, law, and power in the legal and commercial worlds were formed in an environment that excluded women. Feminist method invites us to examine systems of knowledge and power (like law) for biases and to reconstruct them with valuable aspects of excluded perspectives. To understand what women's perspectives might lend to meanings of responsibility in law or the market, we must find environments where women have exercised some responsibility and power. Even though women often have a subordinate role in families, at least they are overtly present in them. And vis-a-vis children, women often do have power. Examinations of the exercises of that power might help us rethink appropriate meanings for responsibility in the legal context. If legal thinkers are interested in learning how women's experiences and knowledges can be used to reconstruct our legal world, the family is an appropriate starting point for study.

Admittedly, there is something very different about relationships within a family or between friends and relationships between strangers or casual, business acquaintances. The affection, love, and intimacy that characterize familial and friendship relationships are absent from corporate relationships with a public that is placed at risk by corporate activities. We cannot expect the caring and caregiving behavior in families that flows from love to apply to harm-causer/mass-tort victim relationships. Nevertheless, corporate harm-causer/mass-tort victim relationships are analogous to those within the family to the extent that they involve responsibility.

Family members have an initial interpersonal responsibility of care for one another. At a minimum we understand this responsibility as an obligation to take care of or care for a family member who is unable to care for herself. Likewise, once the legal system determines that a corporation is liable or responsible for a harm, it has an obligation to remedy the harm and to take care of the people harmed. In both cases one party ends up with responsibility for another. Even though the source of the responsibility for a family member differs from the source of responsibility in a corporate-victim relationship, once responsibility attaches its source might no longer be especially relevant to its content. I would like to explore the complex nature of that responsibility. By shifting to a post-event meaning of responsibility that includes both a reparations sense and a caring sense, we can alter the way that the legal and corporate worlds function.

People responsible for the care of children understand that responsibility to and for those children involves a great deal more than money. Money might buy some of the things children need, but it cannot figure out what they need at any given time or in any given context or plan how to provide for those needs. Money doesn't listen to children, soothe their fears, show them affection, teach them values, or socialize them. People must take interpersonal responsibility for these activities—the planning, organization, and forethought, the time and emotional sharing, and attention to needs and contexts. These activities are an important part of what responsibility means in interpersonal relationships. It might include taking financial responsibility, but that aspect of responsibility is just a piece of the whole.

Because tort law was created by men (as the only participants in its writing, thinking, and practice for many years), it is not surprising that an ethic of rights, which seems to be a controlling male ethical paradigm, dominates tort analysis. Because men devised tort laws to apply to themselves, because the ethic of rights involves an implicit assumption that others are the same as oneself, and because men frequently viewed people as separate but "socially contracting" human beings, legal theorists looked for solutions to conflicts that respected separation and formalized, distanced interactions. Finally, because the men who crafted tort law were scholars, judges, and practitioners who were rarely responsible for interpersonal caregiving, they were in socially-constructed positions that defined their responsibility financially. Thus, tort law's definition of responsibility is financial. The men writing and thinking about tort law tended to universalize their experiences and concerns (failing to appreciate the existence or wisdom of other perspectives) and consequently developed a limited, incomplete definition of "legal responsibility." In its search for objective, neutral, abstract, and universal formulas for imposing responsibility, tort law became fixated on money damages.

An ethic of responsibility and care, based on perceptions of human beings as interconnected and mutually dependent, would enrich our legal post-event understanding of responsibility. This perspective understands responsibility contextually, as responsiveness to the other's or victim's particularized needs and interdependencies. This meaning of responsibility has dominated women's ethical paradigms. Since women function (or at least functioned) in family and interpersonal caregiving contexts, perhaps we can learn what responsibility involves from some of the tasks that women perform within families. From there, we can see how this interpersonal, caregiving meaning of responsibility might apply in tort law.

There is a lot of emotional work to caregiving and being responsible. The work involves physical and emotional care. Caregiving responsibility involves direct interpersonal tasks, rather than delegation, and it is time-consuming, emotionally involved, freedom-limiting (in that one must often be there in person rather than pursuing other interests), energy-draining, demanding, rewarding, and essential to human survival. This interpersonal responsibility necessitates sharing time, attention, and consciousness in a manner completely ignored by the legal system.

Currently in tort law, when we hold a defendant legally responsible for the harm caused, we make the defendant pay. This is very similar to what we do to absentee fathers when we hold them responsible. And paying is important. The money is necessary for survival and to have access to opportunities in our society. But when a tort victim is injured or incapacitated, a great deal of caregiving work is necessary no matter how much money is paid. The burden of this caregiving work traditionally falls on the family and friends of the injured, on spiritual communities, or on people hired to do some of these tasks—usually lower class women who are paid too little and given no prestige for this vital work. This responsibility is not deemed to be the responsibility of the tortfeasor.

The needs of injured victims vary according to particularized contexts, but interpersonal caregiving responsibility might include: making doctor appointments and taking the victims to that appointment, taking them to therapy, and monitoring their health care; providing transportation and medical equipment to make them mobile (e.g., wheelchairs), and altering living spaces to accommodate new physical needs; shopping, food preparation, and home repairs; managing their finances—making sure they don't lose their jobs or educational opportunities, paying bills, and helping them get benefits to which they are entitled; time-sharing and keeping company in hospitals; offering emotional support—hand-holding, tear-wiping, distracting them from pain, lifting their spirits, bearing their anger, depression, resentment, and hatred.

* * *

Conclusion

Tort law does not create injuries. It neither defines the permissible structures for corporate organizations nor sets the limits on corporate power. Tort law also does not create the social norms that value money and efficiency over health or safety. When our legal and political structures permit relatively unchecked accumulations of wealth and power in corporate for-profit enterprises and when criminal or civil sanctions are erratically imposed on corporations for their harm-causing or risk-imposing behavior, the stage is set for the problems of mass tort law.

Mass tort victims have been accused of greed and abuse of the system, but in fact it is the injured parties who have been abused by corporations' greed and abuse. Corporations undemocratically impose health and safety risks on the public in their pursuit of private profit. When a rape victim testifies about the crime perpetrated against her, our legal system questions whether she is telling the truth, whether she invited or consented to the harm, and whether what she endured is "real harm." When a mass tort victim testifies about the harm or risk imposed upon her, our legal system questions whether she is telling the truth, whether she invited the harm or consented to it, whether it is a real harm, and whether she is just after a quick buck. Rather than deal directly with male violence to eliminate rape, we turn our attention to the victim as the possible problem. Rather than deal with corporate violence and corporate organizational forms, misplaced priorities, and lack of interpersonal responsibility to end mass torts, we turn our attention to the victim and limiting access to the tort system. I ask us to examine this practice and refocus our attention on the real sources of harm.

Feminist theories and methods offer new ways to think about mass torts committed by profit-seeking corporations. Feminism teaches us that systems assumed to be neutral and necessary are in fact biased, and that systems like legal systems are based on implicit, unstated assumptions that favor those in power. It asks us to examine our social-political-legal structures for ways in which power is reinforced and groups or persons are subordinated or undervalued. Feminism also suggests alternative perspectives on human interconnection and responsibility.

If health, safety, well-being, environmental clean-up, personal relationships, and care are truly our most important values, then we cannot make them secondary to interests of efficiency or profit in tort law litigation. If health and well-being are what we would choose for ourselves in our daily lives, we also should choose them for society as a whole. We must learn that health and safety are not incompatible with or in tension with efficiency or economic progress: One need not be exchanged for the other. Ironically, the values of health, safety, and personal/community well-being have been articulated for years. In this paradigm shift we do not need to change these values, but we will need to be sincere about them this time instead of permitting them to be overridden by private pursuits of profit. Paradigm shifts are difficult, but they clearly have happened in the past and can happen now as well.

What kinds of remedies would respond better to injured persons' needs and the goals of making tortfeasors more socially and personally responsible? I do not know. Our imagination is our only limit. In the criminal law system, for example, we have developed community service obligations as social "recompense" for crime. Initially, there were grave doubts about this program's possibilities for success, but it has been implemented successfully.

We could develop interpersonal and community service obligations as legal "recompense" for tort as well. For example, corporations that cause certain kinds of harms, such as injuries to women's reproductive systems, could be required to use their own laboratories, clinics, and employees to research new reproductive technologies. Corporate officers could be required to use their skills to manage or direct these organizations for the benefit of the victims or to manage and work in hospitals, nursing homes, educational facilities, and whatever else might be appropriate. Harm-causing scientists and researchers could be required to find answers and research new technologies to benefit their victims. Corporate officers can be mandated to personally do the physical clean-up work at toxic dumps or chemical/oil spills—from cleaning off oil-soaked birds and shorelines to wearing insulated suits and scrubbing contaminated areas. These solutions are the easiest because they more closely replicate community service in criminal law and are variations on traditional monetary requirements to fund projects for the benefit of tort victims. In addition, those same defendants could be required to respond directly to the needs of one or more of their victims. That response could start with personal apologies to each victim, followed by interpersonal, caregiving work. It is hard to imagine how the tort system could make corporate defendants and corporate decisionmakers respond with direct interpersonal caregiving. But if that is our goal, and we work for it, then we can make it happen. It was probably hard to imagine strict products liability or medical monitoring damages fifty years ago.

Joan E. Steinman, *Women, Medical Care, and Mass Tort Litigation,* 68 CHI.-KENT L. REV. 409 (1992)*

[*Dow Corning whitecoat to a group of women: "We're testing breast implants on you, to see if they're safe for guinea pigs . . . ." Cartoon, © 1992 Mike Luckovich—Atlanta Constitution.*]

Everywhere I look in the popular press I see women expressing anger at their treatment in this society. One set of issues revolves around lack of equal opportunity in the workplace: unequal pay, sexual harassment on the job, exclusion from informal but important social/business networks, disadvantageous pension policies, and the like. Another set of issues revolves around women's health care. It encompasses myriad matters. A sample from recent newspapers and magazines would include:

—the low level of funding by the National Institutes of Health of scientific research involving women subjects and of health issues of special concern to women (such as research on the causes of breast cancer),

—the failure of the scientific community to aggressively pursue development of male contraceptives,

—the assault on women's health and autonomy pervading the judicial, legislative, executive and private spheres in their efforts to limit women's ability to curtail unwanted pregnancies,

—the less aggressive treatment given to women heart attack victims,

*Used by permission.

—the failure of the federal Food and Drug Administration to ensure that adequate testing has been done of the safety and efficacy of drugs and medical devices designed for women and to ensure that adequate information concerning the risks entailed by the use of such products is being made available both to doctors and to the consuming public, and

—the unacceptable risks that corporate producers of drugs and medical devices have imposed on women, while assuring us of the safety of their products.

In this essay, I would like to raise some questions about the treatment of women by the corporate businesses that provide medical products to us, the regulatory governmental structures that exist to protect consumers from hazardous drugs and medical devices, and the adjudicatory legal system that exists to redress the grievances of people injured by drugs and medical devices.

The Striking Amount of Harm Done to Women

As a teacher of "complex litigation" (which, broadly speaking, focuses on procedural and substantive law issues that arise in multi-party and multi-forum litigation), I have the impression that an awful lot of products liability personal injury litigation arises out of injuries caused by products designed for women. If one looks at the most widely used casebook, Richard Marcus' and Edward Sherman's *Complex Litigation, Cases and Materials on Advanced Civil Procedure*, one finds in it a number of judicial opinions deriving from the cases generated by the Dalkon Shield intrauterine contraceptive device, by DES, a synthetic estrogen which had been promoted by its manufacturers for use by pregnant women to prevent spontaneous abortion, and by Bendectin, an anti-nausea drug also created for pregnant women in particular, which has been alleged to cause a variety of birth defects. In addition to my exposure to these cases from teaching, I recall the harm caused by Thalidomide (arm and leg deformities due to effects on the fetus in utero), which also had been prescribed as an anti-nausea drug, and in the newspapers I read about the injuries to women that many women and their doctors believe to have been caused by silicone gel breast implants. These include scleroderma (a disorder of the skin and connective tissue), Lou Gehrig's disease (amyotrophic lateral sclerosis, a degenerative neurological condition) and auto-immune system problems such as arthritis and lupus.

To verify my impression that women seem to be disproportionately affected by harmful drugs and medical devices, I scanned the annotations of the cases described in the United States Code Annotated, in the section concerning multidistrict litigation, 28 U.S.C. § 1407. Section 1407 provides for the temporary transfer to a single federal judicial district of civil actions that share one or more common questions of fact, to facilitate coordinated or consolidated pretrial proceedings. It is likely that if many individuals believe themselves to have been injured by a product, they will sue individually, in small groups, and in some instances in proposed class actions, and that one or more of the litigants will seek to have the cases consolidated pursuant to section 1407. Consequently, the annotations to section 1407 should provide a fairly accurate portrait of the nature of product liability actions for personal injury, affecting large numbers of people, that have been filed over the last twenty-five years or so.

My examination of the annotations bore out my suspicion. I found cases about Bendectin, cases about contraceptives for women including the Dalkon Shield and other intrauterine devices such as the Lippes Loop, and cases about tampons. There were some cases that related to products for both sexes, such as intraocular lenses, aortic heart valves, swine flu vaccine, the antibiotic "Cleocin" and other drugs. There also were cases about cigarettes, which are advertised to and used by both sexes but are not prescribed as healthful, and some cases that related to products that predominantly harmed men: agent orange and asbestos, in particular. It is noteworthy, however, that the latter products were not made for men to take or use for personal purposes; they were products that men were exposed to "accidentally," as an incident of their employment in the military or in the industrial production and use of products containing asbestos. Ironically, when exposing women to hazardous substances would transfer relatively well-paying jobs to women from men, employers have been loathe to allow equal "opportunity," but when such employment effects are not obviously entailed, women's well-being seems to be of lesser concern. I do not know of a single mass tort in which men were injured by a product made for men to use or take, ostensibly to enhance their well-being. It appears that women, far more than men, take it on the chin from products made ostensibly for their good.

One has to wonder what is going on here. Are there no medical products peculiarly for men? If there are, is it mere coincidence that they have not proven to be seriously harmful? I assume that if such products had caused widespread and serious harm, the injured would have sued; evidence of the problem would appear in the case reports. But it is not there.

Although mine is not the only inference one could draw, I strongly suspect that a disparity exists between the care invested in products for men and that invested in drugs and medical devices for women. One might say that I am overstating the problem, because the troublesome products have been limited to a narrow category, to items that relate to women's reproductive and sexual functions and structures. But that is not a narrow category of products; such products are used by all of us, and millions of us use any given variety. Moreover, one has to wonder why the scientific community has placed so much emphasis on developing and marketing contraceptive drugs and devices for women, and so little emphasis on developing them for men. My own speculation is that it is because men (both the general population and the men who decide what scientific research should be conducted, in particular) don't want to mess with their own body chemistry or genitalia, or those of people like them, i.e. men. They would much prefer to let the women take the pills and the injections or have the foreign objects installed in them. After all, conception is primarily the woman's problem; fatherhood can be a five-minute proposition unless a man chooses to commit himself to it or the courts order the very limited form of responsibility that entails the payment of money, but motherhood is a long-term condition, particularly if abortion is difficult to obtain.

I cannot help wondering if the corporations which produce drugs and medical devices for women, and the people who run them, are particularly indifferent to the health and well-being of women. Perhaps the profit motive is such that these entities and individuals are nondiscriminatorily indifferent to consumers' health and well-being and, no matter what the consumer's gender, corporate decisionmakers care about causing injury and pain only when the economic consequences are sufficiently drastic that the corporation's financial condition will suffer materially adverse effects unless a change is made in a product. It would be interesting to know, through rigorous empirical study, whether there in fact has been a "disparate impact" on women from medical products ostensibly made for their benefit; whether corporate and scientific practices have unintentionally but disproportionately resulted in the marketing of products "for" women that injure women; whether there is even evidence of "disparate treatment," intentional, or more likely reckless, production and marketing of such products; whether and to what extent any disparate impacts upon or treatments of women derive from economic forces, "bean counting" that predicts that the profits to be derived from the sale of a risk-bearing product will exceed the probable liabilities; and whether and to what extent any disparate impacts upon or treatments of women derive from other factors such as attitudes toward women that denigrate the importance of the injury, impairment or pain we would suffer.

I am not in a position to do the research that would answer these queries. However, I would like, for purposes of this paper, to assume affirmative answers to all of them, to assume that there are disparate injurious impacts and treatments, and that at least some of the injuries that corporate decisionmakers inflict on women are inflicted out of a combination of economic incentives and attitudinal indifference that is greater when women are the consumer population than when men are the consumer population.

Having made this assumption, there are two broad questions I would like to consider. First, how might conditions be changed to prevent or deter these wrongs and to better redress the injuries that occur nonetheless? Second, is the legal system (including the regulatory system), which is among the forces that is intended to prevent and deter such harms and which is the primary mechanism for redressing them, significantly different than the corporate culture that permits the harms to be done? or it is similarly constrained by economic and institutional limitations and similarly infected by cultural influences that render unequal the protection that injured women are afforded by regulatory agencies and the redress that we receive when we resort to the courts?

What Can be Done?

Focusing first upon the corporate and scientific communities, the remedies for the problem (that I am assuming exists) would have to be both legal and extralegal. Some of the ''fault'' may lie in an economic system that makes profit-making the primary, if not the only, value. To the extent that money is the game, the answer would seem to lie in making it unprofitable to inflict serious injury on consumers. There is evidence that the traditional tort system does not contribute much to deterrence. In light of the uncertainty that characterizes this matter, I would err on the side of increasing the financial costs of causing injury and of causing it in a manner that disproportionately harms women. This might be accomplished in a number of ways.

Remedies could be legislated that would impose liability, punitive damages, or fines for engaging in a pattern or practice of producing and/or marketing medical products for women that prove to be injurious to them (analogous to a disparate impact claim), perhaps even if the defendant were guilty of being ''merely'' negligent in creating this pattern or practice, and for intentionally, recklessly, or perhaps even negligently producing and/or marketing such products (analogous to a disparate treatment claim). (If this proposal seems ludicrous at first blush to you, consider whether you would react the same way if you substitute ''blacks'' for ''women'' in the proposal.) In addition to imposing liability for the usual compensable injuries, under this scheme additional monetary extractions would be imposed to deter or punish societally unacceptable behavior vis-a-vis an historically abused, because undervalued and underrespected, segment of the population.

Since the corporate/scientific production of injurious medical products for women is not entirely traceable to economic forces, and since even the consequences of economic forces may not be susceptible to eradication through economic responses such as increased liability, additional responses are essential. To the extent that unduly dangerous medical products are marketed for women out of a lack of real concern for our well-being, the problem will have to be addressed through a change in basic attitudes. It would help, of course, if the obstacles to women becoming corporate and scientific decisionmakers were eliminated; having substantial numbers of women securely in positions of power, unafraid to take stands protective of women's health, would go some distance toward reducing the problem. But even women are affected by the culture's devaluation of women, so having women in influential positions would not entirely solve the problem. Again, education, a change in the society's view of the value and importance of women, seems to me critical.

How we accomplish that is a big question. It may require us to continue to increase the number and visibility of highly-achieving women, but the necessary regard is not altogether (and probably is not even primarily) a matter of respect for proven capability. To enhance the caring about women that we need, men somehow need to surrender some of their need to feel superior and their view of women as frighteningly "other." That need seems to be a very strong one, and I don't know how we moderate it.

Frances P. Kao, *Pornography as Product**

Pornography coerces women into its making; pornography injures women who are the victims of rape and battery; and pornography, through its compartmentalized and dehumanized depictions of women, is an instrument to subordinate women. Most damning, however, as pornography enjoys wide dissemination, women complaining of its harms are silenced by force or ridiculed into submission. Thus, women are deprived of the very freedom of speech pornographers enjoy via court sanction. These harms caused by pornography are too wide-ranging to be addressed by obscenity law.

In response to the courts' failures, activists Catherine MacKinnon and Andrea Dworkin drafted in 1983 a model anti-pornography ordinance ("Model Statute") that defined pornography as a violation of women's civil rights. The Model Statute stated that pornography was the depiction of women, either in words or pictures, as dehumanized sexual objects that enjoy degradation, injury, torture or other abusive contexts presented as sexual conditions.

Materials covered by the Model Statute's definition of pornography can be subject to a civil complaint under four separate sections of the statute. The first section prohibits coercion of people into taking part in the production of pornography. Liability for coercion could be imposed on the producer, seller, distributor or exhibitor of the material. A cause of action under this section can also remove the products of coercion from public view. A second section states that production, sale exhibition or distribution of pornography is discrimination against women under civil rights law. Under this provision, any woman has a cause of action against pornographers for subordination. The third section provides recourse for persons who had pornography forced upon them in the workplace, in education, in public accommodations or at home. Liability is limited to the person who forced the materials upon the plaintiff as well as to the institution where the forcible viewing occurred. Finally, the statute provides that damages may be recovered for any person who is assaulted, attacked or injured due to another person's use of pornography. The plaintiff can bring a charge against the perpetrator, the producer, distributor, seller or exhibitor of the pornography. Further, upon a finding that the pornography caused the assault, a court may enjoin further exhibition, distribution or sale of the pornography. The Model Statute was considered by the Minneapolis City Council, and passed by the Indianapolis City Council.

To be actionable, pornographic materials under the Model Statute must be sexually explicit,

*Used by permission.

and the material must subordinate women. Subordination can be effected through one of eight means:

(i) women are presented dehumanized as sexual objects, things, or commodities; or
(ii) women are presented as sexual objects who enjoy pain or humiliation; or
(iii) women are presented as sexual objects who experience sexual pleasure in rape, incest, or other sexual assault; or
(iv) women are presented as sexual objects tied up or cut up or mutilated or bruised or physically hurt;
(v) women are presented in postures or position of sexual submission or servility or display; or
(vi) women's body parts—including but not limited to vaginas, breasts and buttocks—are exhibited, such that women are reduced to those parts; or
(vii) women are presented being penetrated by objects or animals; or
(viii) women are presented in scenarios of degradation, injury, torture, shown as filthy or inferior, bleeding, bruised, or hurt in a context that makes these conditions sexual.

The Model Statute is flawed in general respects. First, it begs the question of how to define "subordination." Environment, context, and culture all play a part in its definition. A scene depicting an employee looking up at an employer (a reasonably typical recruiting poster) can be construed as a depiction of subordination. Sexually explicit photographs of a couple engaging in the missionary position can be defined as subordination. Because its definitions are so abstract, the Model Statute cannot be applied with any precision approximating equity.

Even if the definition and "context" of subordination are made more precise, many of the elements comprising "subordination" are simply too amorphous. For example, Sections (i), (ii), (v) and (vi) are vague because they deal with the "political" issues of subordination. The taboo depictions in these sections merely insinuate subordination—they do not require any graphic portrayal of such abusive actions. The difficulties inherent in prohibiting insinuations stem from the fact that insinuations are what the recipient makes of them. Given this fact, factfinders will not know by whether a given piece of work indeed conveys misogyny.

The Model Statute also lacks concern for the actual artistic merit of a piece of work. Although the fundamental tests for obscenity under *Miller v. California* are imprecise, the consideration of a work's overall artistic value ought to be maintained in order to avoid obscenity witch-hunts. Contextual analysis of pornography is important from a policy perspective. Society ought to be exposed to a variety of viewpoints, presented in a variety of mediums. Thus Robert Mapplethorpe's examination of mixed-race and sexual power relationships are presented through black and white photographs of a sexual, violent or disturbing nature. Lesbian-feminist writer Monique Wittig, in writing about male-female power struggles, chooses to do so through vivid written imagery of lesbian sexuality, decapitation and mutilation of men. Under the Model Statute, both items could reasonably be found to be pornographic and could conceivably be open to civil suits.

The various mediums used to convey ideological information are important because ideas should be made accessible to people whose ability to absorb information does not always lie in the written word. A law which allows suits based on isolated passages of a work would have a severe chilling effect on the use of art, photography or even fiction as a way of conveying ideas. It does not take a vivid imagination to envision the morally conservative faction scrutinizing texts to count the number of times epithets appear or looking for the number of times breasts or pubic areas are exposed in a collection of photography. To avoid such abuses, any law dealing with pornography must be sensitive to the context in which potentially offensive materials appear.

* * *

The Tort Approach

MacKinnon has written that a problem with First Amendment obscenity analysis is that words or pictures can be harmful only if they produce harm in a form that is considered an action—which is "linear, isolated, tortlike." If one subscribes to the civil-liability provisions of the Model Statute, it appears inevitable that tort doctrines and the notion of bipolar relationships creep into the litigation structure. For purposes of redressing the harms of pornography, this influence is a good thing; bipolarity and tort law as an answer to pornography is necessary because it is far easier for a lay jury to condemn a bad product or a heinous act than to comprehend the intellectual morass that accompanies First Amendment and civil rights analysis of pornography. But the Model Statute cannot work.

Thus building on the efforts of MacKinnon, and working within the current obscenity law as constrained by the First Amendment, I offer here an alternative: an anti-pornography law inspired by, and drawing freely on, the law of products liability. This new law would define pornography and its "ideas" as a product and it would recognize pornography's civil rights harms against women, but would incorporate some protections of the *Miller* decision. The new products liability-pornography model ("Products Model") would be structured as follows:

Section I: Statement of Policy

1. Pornography violates the civil rights of those who participate in its production as well as of those who are third party victims of its violent results.
2. Existing laws are inadequate to solve the problems presented by pornography despite the tangible physical and emotional harms which result to participants of pornography product and to third party victims of its violent results.

Section II: Definitions

1. "Pornography" shall be defined as the graphic, sexually explicit depictions of women, men and children either in pictures or graphics.
2. "Pornography" is mass produced, and disseminated as a profit-making enterprise or activity; any consideration in exchange for the pornographic material will be considered a profit to the seller and the manufacturer.
3. The allegedly pornographic material shall be considered in light of its overall artistic, literary or theoretical merit.
4. As proof of the harmful nature of the pornographic material, a person may present evidence including but not limited to a showing that the materials present:
   a) persons as sexual objects who experience sexual pleasure in being raped;
   b) persons are presented as sexual objects bound, tied up or cut up or mutilated or bruised or physically injured;
   c) persons are presented being penetrated by objects or by animals
   d) persons are presented in scenarios of injury, torture or rape in a context that makes these conditions sexual.

Section III: Causes of Action

1. Any individual harmed or injured, either mentally, emotionally or physically, as a result of the production of pornography, shall be entitled to civil suits based on the common law of torts available in the relevant state. Civil suits may be filed by a third party on behalf of an injured individual. In cases of third party suits, the complaint must be certified and the complaint must state with particularity the reasons why the injured party cannot litigate on behalf of him or herself.
2. Any individual harmed or injured, either mentally, emotionally or physically, as a result of actions imposed on that individual by another who has utilized pornography that is causally related to the pornography, shall be entitled to civil suits based on the common law of strict products liability as enumerated in Section 402A of the *Restatement (Second) of Torts*. No suits may be filed by third parties on behalf of an injured individual except in cases where the injured individual is deceased.
3. Jurisdiction is concurrent with the United States District Court and the courts of the state in which the injury arose.
4. The statute of limitations for actions is three years from the time the injury arose.

Section IV: Enforcement

1. Any person who has a cause of action under this law, or their estate, may seek nominal, compensatory, and punitive damages without limitation, including for loss, pain, suffering, and special damages as well as for reasonable costs, including attorneys' fees.
2. No damages may be sought for injuries arising before the effective date of this law.
3. No injunctions may be issued under this law against any producer, distributor, seller or exhibitor of pornography to impound, censor, or limit pornographic materials.
4. Injunctions may otherwise be issued by the court for injuries arising out of actions under this law.

The Products Model emulates MacKinnon in that it addresses pornography's real injuries to women, using traditional tort concepts. Further, the products model entitles interested third parties to sue on behalf of an individual injured during production of pornography who is afraid or unable to sue on her/his own behalf. The utility of such a law is obvious. Women injured during pornography production have a plethora of common tort complaints: battery, false imprisonment, assault, or intentional infliction of emotional distress. Tort remedies entitle the individual to a jury trial as well as punitive damages. The real test of any model anti-pornography statute is not its ability to redress direct harms but its ability to resolve harms upon third-party women. In tort-speak: bystanders. Products liability law and its societal goals are uniquely suited to the third party injuries imposed by pornography. Societal goals have largely been identified as loss spreading, loss shifting and compensation. If manufacturers whose initial intent is to serve society by producing goods can be burdened with social engineering goals, pornographers, who have been determined to serve no social function, certainly can be burdened with these social goals.

The Definitional Question

When courts try to determine whether entities are products, they often look for widespread distribution. This focal point flows logically from the social goals of imposing strict products liability: A manufacturer or seller who places items into the stream of commerce should be responsible for its injuries. This principle, in turn, is based on the notions that the manufacturer and seller is in the best position to spread the risk to all consumers, that the injured should be compensated and that the manufacturer or seller can best spread the cost of compensation across the total consumer population.

When one applies the focal point of mass production onto pornography, reasonable minds could not differ that pornography is, in fact, mass produced and marketed, primarily for a bottom-line profit. Research indicates that pornographic magazines alone account for $38,000,000 of sales monthly. Pornographic magazines, movies and books are shipped through interstate commerce and are so widely available that the distribution network for pornography is as extensive as the system for mainstream magazines such as *Time* or *Fortune*. Given such enormous financial gain, given the placement of pornography into the stream of commerce after mass production, there is no reason to insulate pornography from being labeled as a product.

First Amendment libertarians may argue that pornography is speech because it presents a viewpoint, a speech about sexual activity; thus it could not be a product. This argument is meritorious only in light of current caselaw status quo: we view pornography as speech only because we've been told that it is. Nonetheless, pornographic "speech" can be seen as more akin to maps and designs, which have been held to be products, than to protected political speech. First, pornography is not political speech because it bears no relation to speech which informs and educates people in the exercise of political rights. Second, if pornography conveys a political message, it does so in the same way that architecture or design does: in a tertiary and noncognitive way.

Maps, charts and designs, too, are expressive; yet the harms they cause are redressable. Especially in the realm of architectural and scientific designs, the "idea" or the "speech" is truly something tangible. The ideas result in the accrual of some previously unknown technology, the ideas result in the concreteness of a building, the ideas speak to new theories to be advanced. Courts are not reluctant to impose strict liability for this form of "idea" for two reasons. First, courts recognizes that, though beneficial, such designs and their attendant benefits cause injury which require redress. Second, the decisions are consistent with the traditional social rationale of products liability: society simply has a right to demand that only beneficial, non-injurious products are sold in the market. Given this context, pornography is only different in negative ways: although it is a form of idea, the idea results in no tangible benefit; it results in nothing which is concrete except its injuries to women; and it seeks to advance nothing new. If we are comfortable declaring beneficial ideas as products, then it is a judicial double-standard to not do so for analogous ideas with little or no benefit. If we are able to burden useful, real products with the social cost of compensation, it would be illogical to reverse that cost burden for non-valuable products.

Defect

Once the gap between "pornography as an idea" and "pornography as a product" is bridged, the next step is to analyze how pornographic materials can be defined as "defective." Design defect is the appropriate concept here. A defective design plea states that there is something inherently wrong with the way the product was conceived, including either lack of a safety device or inappropriate composition: this defect could well speak to the issue of pornography. In a design allegation, pornography that induces the consumer to visit violence on a third party probably is inappropriately composed, that is, different graphics depicting different, perhaps less violent sexual activity could have been substituted.

In arguing a design defect, plaintiffs are encouraged to include the presentation of an alternative, feasible design which would be commercially practicable and which does not impose unacceptable costs on the manufacturer. Thus, the plaintiff under the products model should have to suggest an alternative design. More clothes? Less violence? Representational graphics instead of actual photographs? Clearly, the alternative is commercially feasible since none of these alternatives impose any significant cost on the manufacturer. Presumably, the altered design would be acceptable to the ultimate consumer since its purpose as an ''erotic stimulant'' has not been altered substantially.

When pornography is applied to the risk-utility test it is reasonably clear that the risk of danger greatly outweighs the putative benefits to society. The Supreme Court has articulated that pornography (obscenity) is useless and people tend to agree that the very graphic, violent products targeted under the products model hold no social benefit. Given this assessment, a defect exists since the balancing comes squarely down on the side of extraordinary risk but no utility.

[Kao also contends that pornography fails the consumer expectations test.]

* * *

Causation

Cases under the Products Model would be like any products liability or tort action in that cause-in-fact can be established through expert testimony or through circumstantial evidence. Under the Products Model, the testimony of a joint tortfeasor (the assailant) can establish causation against a fellow tortfeasor (the pornographer). Expert testimony would come most frequently in the form of psychiatric research on the connection between pornography and violence. Expert testimony would also establish that the specific criminal act was a result of viewing pornography.

Expert testimony in the realm of social science data should not be controversial because there is so much evidence linking pornography to violent acts. For example, research on convicted rapists show that they find violent forms of pornography sexually arousing. Further, a rapist's level of violent and sexual behavior can be determined by his degree of sexual arousal upon viewing sexually violent images. Lest we think that only habitual criminals react to pornography, research has also shown that even so-called ''normal'' males are aroused by images of rape. Further, when questioned, these ''normal'' men said that they would commit rape if they felt they wouldn't be caught. And pornography has a very ''compulsive and obsessive'' relationship to many men's lives. The men fantasize about the images they see in pornography and they utilize the images for masturbation and for inflicting violence on victims. Given voluminous and consistent expert testimony of this nature, it is reasonable to say that some cause-in-fact element can be shown. [*Editor's note*: For a summary of the contrary evidence, see, among other sources, Marcia Pally, ''Misalliance Against Pornography,'' Sacramento Bee, Feb. 21, 1993 (available on electronic databases).]

Circumstantial evidence usually will encompass reports that the individual used pornography regularly or that the act of violence mirrored pornography used by the perpetrator. Circumstantial evidence can be presented as support for expert social science testimony. The value of circumstantial evidence is highest when the victim can testify that the violence suffered mirrored pornography that the perpetrator used.

The last type of evidence, testimony by the perpetrator, is potentially the most damaging for pornographers. In essence, the perpetrator would be ''fingering'' a certain producer's product as having induced the violent activity. In 1989, serial killer Ted Bundy stated that pornography induced him to act out his fantasies on real women. There is no dispute that violent pornography is largely the same, thus, when identification by the perpetrator is unreliable, however, there is no reason that a market share liability theory à la the DES cases can't be imposed to combat this problem.

The next causation hurdle a plaintiff must leap is proof of proximate cause. Proximate cause has been stated to be an issue of social policy: who should reasonably bear the costs of injury? Proximate cause inquiries emphasize foreseeability. This criterion assists courts in carrying out the three primary social goals of products liability—the apportionment of incentives, loss shifting and loss spreading.

Reasonable foreseeability can be proven using the numerous social science research studies conducted by psychiatrists and clinicians. Since a manufacturer is held to the standard of an expert in his field, the manufacturer is responsible for integrating outside research studies on the dangers of a particular products. Thus, pornographers will be held responsible for considering social science research and implementing that research to make their products safer.

Reasonable foreseeability also rests on whether the manufacturer had actual or constructive notice of injuries suffered as a result of marketed products. Initially, the constructive knowledge will arise from social science research. As time goes by, a manufacturer will have actual knowledge of injury from suits arise from its products. Further, manufacturers will have constructive knowledge of injury resulting from pornography due to suits filed against other, competitor manufacturers. Given the extent to which injury resulting from pornography can be foreseen, under the "reasonably foreseeable" test, proximate cause can be demonstrated.

An argument of "remoteness" can be countered by the fact that §402(A) clearly protects third parties and bystanders from product-related injuries. Violence against women is a direct result of pornography usage and can be paralleled to DES children suits against DES manufacturers. The chain of events leading to the product injury is not so attenuated and unforeseeable as to justify dismissal due to remoteness.

Conclusion

Perhaps the day has already passed when pornography can be considered a product for victim compensation purposes. It may well be that MacKinnon and Dworkin, with their insistence on the effective, political nature of the pornographic idea, have actually done more harm than good. Their theory is so widely known that courts may point out that feminists themselves believe pornography is speech and not a product.

Feminists must articulate what they want in terms of the pornography question. Do they wish to eradicate pornography or to change ingrained, powerful stereotypes about women's sexuality? If the feminist answer is to eradicate pornography, litigation can accomplish that goal. Strict liability accompanied by punitive damages has, we may presume, forced many a manufacturer out of business. These legitimate manufacturers have a benefit pornographers do not—the benefit of litigation insurance. Pornographers must bear judgment from their profits, and not many would willingly stay long in a profitless industry.

The Products Model proposed carries few of the negatives inherent in the MacKinnon-Dworkin model: the statute targets a limited pool of products; the statute does not discriminate on the basis of viewpoint; and the statute looks at the product as a whole, not mere isolated passages. Most importantly, the Products Model does not facially impound, censor, or enjoin any production or sale of pornography.

The discomfort many felt with the Model Statute stemmed from its vague wording which made practically any portion of any work open to attack. Under the Products Model, several steps must be fulfilled: the product must be mass produced and mass marketed; the product must be produced as a primary, profit-making activity; and the pornography must be graphically violent. The definition of pornography, under these terms, targets only the most objectionable material and is substantially the same as those intended to be targeted under the Model Statute. The only difference is that subjective and amorphous words such as "degrade" or "subjugate" are not implicated, thereby freeing the Products Model from embracing classic works such as those written by Joyce or

Augustine. Review of a work on its overall merit, rather than a perhaps unrepresentational portion, is another strength of the Products Model.

The Products Model also frees manufacturers to engage in any anti-female, anti-male, anti-child rhetoric or graphic necessary to the publication of the product; the Products Model only views the resulting injury and requires compensation. Because the Model compensates on the basis of injury, the statute is truly a tort law.

Use of tort principles, particularly a products liability statute, to compensate for injuries rather than to blatantly suppress pornography may eventually accomplish what a century of Supreme Court litigation could not: the eradication of violent, oppressive images that debase women.

C. Economics

Guido Calabresi and Jon T. Hirschoff, *Toward a Test for Strict Liability in Torts*, 81 Yale L.J. 1055 (1972)*

Learned Hand's test for fault defines the defendant's duty of care as a function of three variables: (1) the probability that the accident will occur, (2) the gravity of the injury which will be suffered if the accident does occur, and (3) the burden of precautions adequate to prevent such accidents. If the cost to the defendant of avoiding the accident would have been less than the cost of the accident, discounted by the probability of its occurrence, the defendant's failure to avoid the accident is termed negligence.

For the purpose of the first parts of this discussion, we will assume that the traditional test for fault, as given expression in Learned Hand's formula, was designed to do what [Richard A.] Posner says it was designed to do, namely to minimize the sum of accident costs and the costs of accident avoidance. The Learned Hand test would seem to accomplish this objective in theory, because *if it were applied perfectly,* it would put the costs of the accident on the injurer when and only when it was cheaper for him to avoid the accident costs by appropriate safety measures than to pay those costs. *Assuming injurers had the requisite foresight,* this would cause potential injurers to avoid all accidents worth avoiding, *i.e.*, those where avoidance costs less than the accident, and to have only those accidents not worth avoiding.

The application of the traditional rule of contributory negligence would make some difference, but not much. Using the rubric of the test, contributory negligence would exist when the victim, too, could have avoided the accident at a cost lower than the cost generated by the accident. Since under the traditional rule contributory negligence is a complete defense, the cost would remain on the victim despite the negligence of the injurer, *even if avoidance by the injurer would have cost less than avoidance by the victim.* Thus, even in the wonderful, let us freely admit, fantastic world of Professor Posner, in which none of the costs of an accident are borne by third parties other than the injurer and victim, and in which there is perfect foresight, the rule of contributory negligence would prevent the negligence calculus from optimizing primary accident cost reduction. The potential injurer who could avoid a $100 accident at a cost of $5, knowing that the victim

*Used by permission.

could do so at a cost of $50, might well not undertake the $5 safety measure because of his knowledge that the victim will either avoid the accident or be held contributorily negligent. Given adequate foresight, one would expect the accident to be avoided, but at a cost $45 higher than necessary.

A Learned Hand test for injurer liability with the defense of contributory negligence removed, however, would also fail to optimize accident costs, and for exactly the same reason. Under such a rule, there would be instances in which the victim who could avoid an accident more cheaply than could the injurer would fail to do so, because he would know that the injurer would nonetheless be held liable. Thus the *correct* optimizing rule, under the Learned Hand test, would be to have a doctrine of contributory negligence, but to apply it only where the cost of injurer avoidance exceeds the cost of victim avoidance.

Whatever defects the Learned Hand test may have, given the existence of an absolute defense of contributory negligence, it can at least be said that if the test worked, all the accidents worth avoiding would be avoided. If they were occasionally avoided at somewhat greater expense than necessary, that would not be a matter of great consequence. At the same time, it must be recognized that all the costs of all the accidents not worth avoiding would fall on the victim, raising distributional or justice issues. We will, however, postpone consideration of those issues to a later section of this article, and limit our discussion here to primary accident cost reduction.

If we make the assumptions under which the Learned Hand test would work adequately, the fascinating thing is that as good a result in terms of reducing primary accident costs could be achieved by a liability rule which is the exact reverse of the Learned Hand test. Under such a "reverse Learned Hand test," the costs of an accident would be borne by the *injurer* unless accident avoidance on the part of the victim would have cost less than the accident. If a reverse contributory negligence test were added, the victim would bear the accident costs only if the injurer could not also have avoided the accident at less cost than the accident entailed. A reverse Learned Hand test, in other words, which always made the injurer liable without fault unless the victim were negligent, and even then held the injurer liable if he also were negligent, would do for primary accident cost avoidance just what the actual Learned Hand test with contributory negligence is said to do. The only difference between the tests is distributional. Under the Learned Hand test, the costs of all accidents *not* worth avoiding are borne by victims, whereas under the reverse Learned Hand test they would be borne by injurers.

In focusing on the reverse Learned Hand test, we are not simply playing with mirrors. The point is that a perfect world with perfect foresight is a prerequisite to optimization of primary accident cost reduction under *either* Learned Hand type test, and that given such a world, any number of other devices would also accomplish that goal. To the extent that we are concerned with the practical minimization of accident costs, the choice among these devices will depend not on their *theoretical* ability to optimize accident costs given certain assumptions, but on the degree to which the particular assumptions required by each device actually do obtain.

Here we suggest a test that we think is much more likely than either Learned Hand type test to accomplish a satisfactory job of primary accident cost optimization. We also think that application of the proposed test requires asking questions which are closely related to those questions courts have always asked in strict liability cases. That is why we believe the proposed test is an appropriate one for defining the limits of strict liability.

The [Calabresi-Hirschoff] Strict Liability Test

When a case comes to judgment under either of the two Learned Hand type tests, a cost-benefit analysis is made by an outside governmental institution (a judge or a jury) as to the relative costs of the accident and of accident avoidance. Liability would be placed on the party initially free of responsibility only if the *decider* found the benefits of avoidance *(i.e.,* not incurring the cost of the accident) to be greater than the costs of such avoidance to that party. The strict liability test we suggest does not require that a governmental institution make such a cost-benefit analysis. It requires of such an institution only a decision as to which of the parties to the accident *is in the best position to make the cost-benefit analysis between accident costs and accident avoidance costs and to act on that decision once it is made.* The question for the court reduces to a search for the cheapest cost avoider.

So stated, the strict liability test sounds deceptively simple to apply. Instead of requiring a judgment as to whether an injurer *should* have avoided the accident costs because the costs of avoidance were less than the foreseeable accident costs as the Learned Hand test does, the strict liability test would simply require a decision as to whether the injurer or the victim was in the better position both to judge whether avoidance costs would exceed foreseeable accident costs and to act on that judgment. The issue becomes not *whether* avoidance is worth it, but which of the parties is relatively more likely to find out whether avoidance is worth it. This judgment is by no means an easy one, but we would suggest that in practice it is usually easier to make correctly than is the judgment required under either the Learned Hand test or its reverse. It also implies a lesser degree of governmental intervention than does either of the Hand type tests.

As a first step toward seeing what is implied in such a strict liability test, we propose to examine how the issues raised by courts in various areas of strict liability relate to the proposed test. We will do this first in an oversimplified context, treating accidents as though they involved only the injurer and the victim. Subsequently, we will examine what is implied for the test in considering accidents as events involving whole categories of victims, injurers and affected third parties.

In strict products liability cases, the first question asked is, "was there a defect?" A defect may be defined to mean simply that something went wrong. All that in turn means, however, is that a safer product might have been designed, and this would mean that there is a defect whenever there is an accident. If, instead, existence of a defect is defined to mean a failure of a product to meet levels deemed customary in the trade, then strict liability would be even less successful in achieving optimal reduction of primary accident costs than is the Learned Hand test and would be far narrower than fault. It is not surprising, therefore, that courts have tended to reject both of these extremes.

The courts have instead tended to determine whether a defect exists by asking a series of secondary questions relating to (a) the adequacy of warning and (b) the use to which the product was put. They have also noted that assumption of risk on the part of the victim might serve either to negate the existence of a defect or to be a defense to it. In fact, the defense of assumption of risk may be viewed as broad enough to encompass adequacy of warning and appropriateness of product use, which are in turn appropriate ways of raising some of the questions implicit in the strict liability test we have offered.

Let us look first to adequacy of warning. Suppose that a product occasionally causes the user's leg to fall off. Failure to warn the potential user that this may happen in .0001 per cent of the cases will normally result in manufacturer liability. But even such a warning is not likely to allow the user to make an intelligent cost-benefit analysis between accident and avoidance costs. Unless the user has reason to believe himself to be in the dangerous category and unless a close substitute exists which at some cost avoids the danger, the user is hardly in a position to evaluate the benefits of the product as against its costs. The producer may seem to be no better suited, but if we move from a static to a dynamic situation, this will not be the case. The producer is in a position to compare the existing accident costs with the costs of avoiding this type of accident by developing either a new product or a test which would serve to identify the risky .0001 per cent. The consumer, in practice, cannot make this comparison. Relatively, the producer is the cheapest cost avoider, the party best suited to make the cost-benefit analysis and to act upon it.

Should a patch test be developed which enables the consumer to identify himself as an especially risky user, the situation may well be changed. The existence of the patch test, sold together with the product and coupled with a warning, may be enough to make the consumer the party best able to avoid the costs of mishap. This will depend in part, but only in part, on the nature of the warning and the adequacy (including ease of use) of the patch test. Even if the warning is unmistakably clear and the patch test 100 per cent accurate, however, the manufacturer may still be in the best position to make the cost-benefit analysis. For the analysis depends not only on the adequacy of the warning and the likelihood that a risky user will be able to identify himself, but also on the availability of alternatives to the product. If the product is a cosmetic with many reasonably close substitutes, identifying and clearly warning the risky group will very likely put the user in the best position to choose. If instead the product is a medicine, the use of which is the only way of saving the user's life, identifying and warning the risky users probably would not suffice to make the users the better choosers. The manufacturer would in those circumstances be best suited to compare the cost of the occasional lost leg with the *cost of further research* designed to give rise to an adequate substitute entailing fewer risks, or equivalent risks but to another definable group.

The relevance of the use to which the product is put has seemed especially troublesome for the courts. The fact that a lawn mower was not designed to protect its driver should he care to drive it on the throughway ought not to be viewed as a design defect making the manufacturer liable either to users or to rescuers. But neither should a warning that the lawn mower ought not to be used where there are rocks preclude manufacturer's liability to passers-by hit by rocks or even to the user himself. Again, the issue is who can best make a cost benefit analysis and act on it, viewed in realistic terms. Many uses of a product, though forbidden by the producer, are actually not unexpected. Other uses, though not forbidden, are in fact so unusual as to make the user more suited to make the cost-benefit analysis than the manufacturer.

Moreover, the question whether the manufacturer could sufficiently anticipate the use as to be in a good position to make the cost-benefit analysis has little to do with whether society deems the use worth its costs. In other words, it is logically distinct from the question of whether the user was contributorily negligent. Thus a user may have an excellent reason for driving down the throughway on a lawn mower (the benefits of the use outweigh the costs), in which case the collective decider in a negligence/contributory negligence regime ought not to deem his conduct to be contributorily negligent. Yet such a user would in all probability be a better evaluator than the manufacturer of the costs and benefits involved. As a consequence, his strict liability suit against the manufacturer for injuries resulting from such driving would fail.

Conversely, the fact that a use of the product is deemed contributorily negligent does not necessarily mean that the manufacturer is not in a better position than the user to evaluate the costs and benefits. To take an example from a different area of strict liability, a worker may negligently use a piece of equipment, but his employer may nonetheless be in a better position to evaluate the relevant costs and benefits. That is, he may know the propensity to negligent use and be better able to evaluate a substitute piece of equipment which cannot readily be negligently used. This explains why contributory negligence has not been an inevitable defense to an action based on strict liability.

The greatest differences among areas of strict liability go precisely to the question of the level of generality at which a decision is made with respect to the category or party best suited to make the appropriate cost-benefit analysis. In blasting and ultrahazardous activities generally, the court-made decision that the blaster is best suited to make the cost-benefit analysis is at a high level of generality. In strict products liability, instead, the judgment, again court-made, that by and large producers are better suited than users to make the cost-benefit analysis is deemed much less generally applicable, and the manufacturer is allowed to try to show in each specific case that the user was in the best position to make the analysis. The questions asked as to the adequacy of warning and the appropriateness of use, and, in some jurisdictions, the availability of the defense of contributory negligence, suggest how far from certain courts are that the generalized premise that the producer is the cheapest cost avoider will apply to the individual case. As a result, a combination of judge and jury is allowed to find that given the availability of substitutes, the adequacy of warning and the capacity of an individual user to identify himself as being especially risky or especially safe, the general assumption as to who is better suited to compare the risks and benefits will not apply. In determining who is better suited to make a cost-benefit analysis in products liability cases, a fair degree of case by case analysis is worthwhile.

So far we have discussed the problems involved in minimizing primary accident costs as if either the injurer or the victim actually bore the losses which occurred. As has been amply discussed elsewhere, that is clearly not the case. The existence of insurance and of other ways in which a cost is removed from its initial bearer and borne ultimately by others need not be reexamined here. The effect of factors such as insurance on the choice of the party to hold liable under a strict liability test must, however, be made explicit.

It does no good to leave the accident cost on the victim in a products liability case, on the ground that he is in a better position than the injurer to make a cost-benefit analysis, if the victim will not bear the loss in any event. The issue must be whether, given the fact of this "externalization," the *actual* bearer of the loss is better suited to make the analysis than is the injurer (assuming, of course, that the injurer would bear the loss if he were held liable). The point is a simple one and need not be gone into at length. The crucial decision on who is best suited to make the appropriate cost-benefit analysis must be made among the *categories* which actually bear a loss and not among the individuals who only do so initially.

This point is, of course, equally valid for the two Learned Hand type tests. Sophisticated application of those tests would require that the collective judgment as to whether costs are worth avoiding be made at the level of categories which would end up paying, and not at the level of the single injurer and single victim. The fact that in practice this is almost impossible under existing fault rules is one of the weaknesses of the fault-insurance system as a device for reducing primary accident costs. In theory, however, it should be admitted that one could apply a Learned Hand test at a category level. Whether the language of fault with the stigma it implies would also be appropriate to such a test at a non-individual level may be quite another matter.

The Learned Hand Test Versus the Strict Liability Test

If the strict liability test is often difficult to apply correctly, and if Learned Hand type tests might, in *theory,* be just as capable of accomplishing optimal primary accident cost reduction, why have such fault-based tests fallen increasingly into disfavor? It is not likely that the answer lies simply in the existence of distributional goals which are better served by the strict liability test. That such goals are relevant we have no doubt, and we shall discuss their relevance later. But their relevance must be limited, since the two Learned Hand tests themselves accomplish diametrically different distributional results. Thus if the aim of the current trend away from the fault system were simply to favor victims as a category, this could be done as well—indeed better—by shifting from the Learned Hand test to the *reverse* Learned Hand test than by shifting to a strict liability standard. The suspicion must remain that the shift to strict liability is based in part on other grounds.

It has already been noted that the Learned Hand type tests are more "interventionistic," more collective, than is the strict liability test. Under either of the Hand tests, an organ of the state decides whether an action is worthwhile or not, and imposes the costs on the actor if it deems the action *not* worthwhile. It is not hard to see that this involves a greater degree of state involvement than that implied in the strict liability test. The latter implies state intervention only to decide which category can best determine whether an action is worthwhile, and this in turn implies less risk that traditional kinds of collective considerations will come into play. But this difference between the tests, though politically significant, hardly accounts for the decline in popularity of the fault tests. After all, we have also seen an increase in recent years in direct criminal prohibitions aimed at conduct in the accident area deemed not worthwhile. Such prohibitions surely involve greater state intervention than do even the Learned Hand tests. That political preference for laissez faire has spurred the move toward strict liability therefore seems as unlikely as the explanation that the move has been solely influenced by distributional goals. We suspect that the move to strict liability today, no less than similar moves to respondent superior, ultrahazardous activity liability and workmen's compensation in the past, are based at least in part on a desire to accomplish better primary accident cost reduction.

Earlier we noted that it seems unlikely that either Learned Hand test could effectively be applied in practice at the category level. We questioned whether at the level where it really mattered, that is at the level of who actually pays, the rubric of "fault" is likely to be congenial. And yet it is clear that if the Learned Hand tests *are* to accomplish optimal primary accident cost reduction they must be applied at that level, and not at the arbitrary level of parties to an accident who do not ultimately bear the costs and who are not therefore given any incentive to choose avoidance even where it is worthwhile. The appropriate avoidance decisions must be made at a category level, and at that level the Learned Hand tests may seem unjust. Furthermore, the categories which end up bearing the losses as a result of an application of negligence tests on a case by case basis are not likely to be those which would be selected were such tests applied at a category level, nor is this technique likely to be the most efficient way available for selecting the categories which *are* chosen. All this has been discussed at length elsewhere, and need not be gone into further, but it is important to note that the reluctance to apply the Learned Hand test to categories may be a significant underlying explanation for the current disfavor of "negligence" calculus type tests.

There is, however, another set of reasons which may explain the move away from Learned Hand tests. Hard though the strict liability test may be to apply correctly, it is nonetheless easier to apply than is the calculus of fault. We have seen that it may well be difficult to know whether the category to which a seller, user or third party belongs can best make a cost-benefit analysis of risks involved and act on that analysis. But it is more difficult still to decide correctly not only who can most cheaply act on a cost-benefit analysis, but also what the result of that cost-benefit analysis must be. Yet this is precisely what the Learned Hand-type tests require of the governmental deciders if they are to achieve optimal primary accident cost avoidance. None of the significant difficulties involved in the strict liability test are avoided, and to them is added the danger that the governmental deciders will resolve the cost-benefit analysis incorrectly.

One cannot answer, moreover, that the Learned Hand-type tests avoid some of the difficulties inherent in the strict liability test by deciding collectively whether or not avoidance is worthwhile, whereas the strict liability test leaves such judgments to the individual categories. This answer is not available because the negligence tests result in compensatory damages rather than prohibitions.

Individual categories are, therefore, allowed to decide that avoidance is *not* worthwhile despite a contrary determination by the collectivity (or vice versa). This may serve to explain the concomitant, seemingly paradoxical rise of collective prohibitions together with the less interventionistic strict liability test, at the expense of negligence type tests.

A Concluding Word About Distributional Considerations in Fashioning Liability Rules

One cannot write off distributional considerations based on ability to spread, or on wealth or caste, with a reference to Aristotle and a comment that taxation is for legislatures and not for courts. When courts chose a Learned Hand test rather than a reverse Learned Hand test, they did not simply toss a coin, given that the tests were equally efficient in theory. Distributive consequences may not have been the dominant or even a conscious motive for the decisions, but it is difficult to argue that historically these consequences were irrelevant to the choice. Similarly, too many courts have explicitly considered the ability to spread losses in torts cases as a factor in choosing one liability rule instead of another to allow us to dismiss its relevance to judicial decisions out of hand. One can, of course, question the wisdom of such decisions. One might further suggest that courts should consider such distributive effects only when they reflect reasonably explicit societal goals. Alternatively, one might maintain that courts should be free to follow their own distributional preferences so long as they do not conflict with well defined societal goals (such as, perhaps, efficiency), provided that the legislature has the power to reverse the court's judgment. Finally, one might support the position that because of the way judges are picked, they are suited to balance other goals, like efficiency, with explicitly distributional ones in choosing liability rules for a society. All these are possible approaches worth considering. What one cannot do, we would suggest, is to act as if distributional considerations did not historically play a role in judicial choice of liability rules, and must not do so today regardless of the strength and clarity of a society's commitment to specific distributional preferences.

Alan Schwartz, *The Case Against Strict Liability,* 60 FORDHAM L. REV. 819 (1992)*

In theory, society could resolve the product-defect problem by regulation; in fact, resource limitations prevent the state from regulating more than a small subset of products and product warnings. The question thus is what the "legal default" should be: in the absence of regulation, should the state delegate primary responsibility for product safety to courts or to the market? Courts now reject the market in favor of the law of strict products liability. To understand just how, realize that strict liability law has two facets. The first facet of strict liability holds that firms cannot contract out of liability for product defects. The second facet of strict liability regulates product quality. A firm is liable for both manufacturing defects and design defects. A product has a manufacturing defect when it is less well-made than the firm intended (for example, adulterated

*Used by permission.

food). A firm is liable for a manufacturing defect regardless of the degree of care the firm took. A product has a design defect when its design generates risks in excess of benefits.

Strict liability implies a rejection of the market for two related reasons. First, the market allocates risks by contract. The first facet of strict liability bans contracting about the defective product risk in favor of imposing that risk on firms. Second, and consequently, courts and juries must decide just when a product is defective. The second facet of strict liability thus regulates product quality.

* * *

The Basic Assumptions

Modern products liability law rests on six basic assumptions, some of which relate to consumer preferences and others to sources of market failure. The basic assumptions are:

A (1): Shifting accident costs from consumers to firms increases utility. This assumption actually has two aspects:

A (1.1): Utility is increased if a concentrated loss is removed from one person and spread broadly over a universe of persons. This function is performed by insurance.

A (1.2): Consumers prefer to insure with product manufacturers rather than with market insurers.

A (2): Consumers either will not or cannot read sales contracts.

A (3): Firms have monopoly power, and will use this power to degrade the "quality" of consumer contracts. This assumption also has two aspects:

A (3.1): Some firms have structural monopoly power, and monopolists are unresponsive to consumer preferences.

A (3.2): In markets with many firms, consumers will not search for contracts that contain desirable risk allocations. Sellers behave as monopolists toward consumers who do not search—that is, who will not exit a firm that offers a bad deal to try another firm.

A (4): Consumers prefer manufacturers to reduce accident risks. This assumption follows from two subassumptions:

A (4.1): Consumers prefer more safety to less.

A (4.2): Manufacturers have a comparative advantage at producing safety.

A (5): Consumers misestimate the risks that products pose. This assumption has three aspects:

A (5.1): Firms do not supply information relevant to risk; consumers cannot make correct decisions on insufficient information.

A (5.2): Consumers would ignore or misprocess information that firms could be made to supply because consumers would suffer from information overload or would make systematic cognitive errors.

A (5.3): Consumer misestimates cause consumers to purchase too many unsafe products and too little insurance coverage against product-related harms, and also induce firms to underproduce safety.

A (6): Firms use market power, when they have it, to degrade product quality (in addition to contract quality).

Which Assumptions Hold?

Assumptions A (1) – A (4) and A (6)

The first three assumptions are incorrect. A (1) can be partitioned in this way: consumers prefer to insure with product makers against (i) nonpecuniary harms such as pain and suffering and (ii) pecuniary harms such as lost earnings and medical expenses.

The first part of Assumption A (1) is incorrect because consumers prefer not to insure against nonpecuniary harm. Consumers want to equalize their marginal utility of income in all future states; hence, they will insure against events that would increase this marginal utility and bet against events that would reduce it. Consumers behave in this way because they want more income in states when their marginal utility for money is high and less in states when their marginal utility for money is low.

Injuries lower total utility but increase marginal utility insofar as the consumer's loss is "replaceable:" victims must pay doctors, make up for lost wages, and the like; a victim thus values each marginal dollar highly because it satisfies urgent needs. When the consumer's loss is not replaceable, however, marginal utility is either reduced or not affected. A wage loss is replaceable; the consumer uses an insurance payment to substitute for the lost wages. In contrast, a nonpecuniary loss, such as pain and suffering, is not replaceable; dollars cannot erase pain. An insurance payment thus would only permit the victim to purchase substitutes that would "make up for" having incurred pain, or that would take the place of activities that the victim could no longer engage in because of the accident. People apparently prefer not to buy insurance that would support spending binges to compensate for having suffered, and commonly have a lower marginal utility for replacement activities than they would have had for those activities were they uninjured. Thus, consumers would reject insurance against pain and suffering if given the opportunity to do so.

The second part of Assumption A (1) also is dubious: consumers do want insurance against events that would cause pecuniary harm (these raise the marginal utility of income), but insurance from product sellers seems a "poor buy" in contrast to market insurance. Product sellers cannot use deductibles or precise risk classifications and have little expertise evaluating claims; hence, a dollar spent buying insurance from a product seller purchases less coverage than a dollar spent with an insurance company. A (1) is incorrect because when consumers want insurance, they prefer market insurance.

Assumption A (2), that consumers do not read sales contracts, is problematic. Product-defect risks are among the most important risks that consumers face. Therefore, consumers probably are familiar with the aspects of contracts that relate to product failure. There is evidence consistent with this view. Firms often compete on warranty coverage for high-priced items. They would be unlikely to do this if consumer purchase behavior were unaffected by the defect risk allocation—if, that is, consumers do not know what the contract says. Also, the standard consumer warranty is consistent with consumer knowledge of warranty terms. This warranty imposes on firms those risks that firms could more cheaply reduce, such as the risk of harm to, or a defect in, product motors, and imposes on consumers risks that consumers could more cheaply reduce, such as the risk of harm to external trim. Such contracts maximize consumer utility by reducing purchase cost. Efficient contracts are unlikely to be exacted by persons ignorant of contract content. Finally, strict liability is too massive a response to the problem of complex contract language. The state can require firms to write simple language. Many states have done this with "plain meaning laws." Strict liability, therefore, cannot rest on the assumption that consumers do not know what their contracts contain.

Assumptions A (3) and A (6) also seem incorrect. Firms with structural market power can raise prices, degrade contract quality, or degrade product quality. The typical response is to raise prices. Some analysts show that when consumers have heterogeneous preferences for product quality, firms may discriminate against consumers who prefer low quality, by choosing contract clauses that effectively eliminate these persons from the market; that is, firms will offer higher quality products than some consumers want. When firms have market power because of insufficient consumer search, firms seldom will offer consumers worse contracts than the consumers prefer, and seem unlikely to degrade the quality of important product attributes. The common profit-maximizing response of monopolists, according to many theorists, is to exploit consumers only in the price dimension. No empirical evidence contradicts this theory. Thus, the case for strict liability cannot rest on A (3) and A (6), which state that firms exploit market power to degrade contract or product quality.

Assumption A (4) is partly correct. Consumers do prefer more safety to less, other things (such as price) being equal. Manufacturers often, but not always, have a comparative advantage at producing safety. If consumers do misestimate risks, the case for strict liability thus can rest on A (4) and A (5). Does A (5) hold?

[After analyzing empirical data and a theoretical model, Schwartz decides that the answer to this question is inconclusive. Consumers might misperceive risks in several distinct combinations. The only combinations that are stable over time are (1) consumers correctly assess the effect of both safety improvements and risk level; Schwartz calls this state "the C,C cell," with C indicating a *correct* estimate of both risk and safety improvements; and (2) "the P,P cell," where consumers are *pessimistic* about both risk and safety improvements. Pessimism about both risk and safety improvements means that firms lack sufficient incentive to improve their products, and that consumers buy too few products. Whether assumption A (5) holds depends on which of these two scenarios describes reality.]

* * *

Unregulated markets either will produce the optimal level of safety [the C,C cell] or they will not [the P,P cell]. In the latter circumstance, each product will be less safe than it should be, but fewer products will be bought than should be. Whether total accident costs are too low or too high in general is unknowable a priori. The direct evidence fails to distinguish between the relevant possibilities. If the P,P cell describes the common case, no evidence exists to show whether the improvement effect or the risk-level effect generally is the more important—that is, whether total accident costs in the United States are too high (because the improvement effect is stronger) or too low (because the risk-level effect is stronger).

Analyzing the Case For Strict Liability

A strong majority of analysts believe that strict liability is desirable. They assume that consumers make systematic errors respecting product risks and that markets respond by underproducing safety. Strict liability induces firms to make safer products. More safety is desirable for two reasons. First, safety is efficient, both because price reflects cost more accurately and because accidents create externalities. When a person has a serious injury or dies, her family and others suffer; sometimes, she or they must be rescued by the state. Producers do not take these costs into account, and therefore overproduce dangerousness. Second, and independent of efficiency, compensation can be insufficient. Perhaps no amount of money can adequately compensate a person for being horribly burned over three fourths of his body. Hence, the state should reduce the likelihood and severity of accidents. This latter reason has a neo-Kantian flavor: the state would not adequately respect persons were it to permit a state of affairs to exist—the unregulated market—that would create an excessive number of awful (and hard-to-compensate) invasions of personal integrity. Therefore, a strict liability regime is justifiable.

These arguments are problematic. First, whether consumers do systematically misperceive risks is unknown. Second, the view that consumer misperceptions (if these exist) necessarily would induce unregulated markets to produce too little safety is wrong. The aggregate effect of misperceptions actually is indeterminate because the errors that consumers are most likely to make have offsetting safety effects. As a consequence, particular markets would respond differently to consumer mistakes. For example, suppose that consumers are pessimists respecting both the risk-level and safety improvements, and that it is difficult to make a particular product safer. Medical drugs may illustrate this case. Then, that consumers would underestimate the effect of innovations that make the product safer is relatively unimportant because firms could make few such innovations. Rather, the consumer's belief that the product is more dangerous than it actually is would dominate: consumers in an unregulated market would buy too few products (and in the case of drugs there would be too much unrelieved suffering). Thus, whether there would be too few or too many accidents without strict liability (were the P,P cell to describe many cases) is context-dependent. If there would be too few, then strict liability would worsen the consumer's lot because it would further dampen demand for beneficial products.

In short, there is substantial uncertainty respecting whether consumers do misperceive risks and what the effect of likely misperceptions are. Thus, the appropriate question is what legal regime the state should adopt given uncertainty about the relevant facts. Strict liability advocates do not ask this question because they assume that they know the facts.

The case for strict liability is questionable on two other grounds. First, the neo-Kantian argument for strict liability set out above is dramatic but poorly developed. A respect for the autonomy of persons implies that invasions of physical integrity are unjustified unless there is consent. It was argued above that consumers prefer not to insure against nonpecuniary harm and would prefer to purchase insurance against pecuniary harm on the market rather than from firms. These claims imply that a consumer who purchased in an unregulated legal regime would have consented to bear the risk of the harm she later incurred; she would have the product she wanted under the contract she wanted. One may respond that such a consumer is misinformed about risk. But then the neo-Kantian case for strict liability turns on the accuracy and effect of the assumption that consumers misperceive risks.

The second ground on which to object to strict liability is that the efficiency case for it is weak even if consumers are uninformed. Initially, strict liability creates one information problem in the service of solving another. The new problem is that firms are required to compensate all consumer losses, but cannot estimate those losses, including nonpecuniary losses, with any degree of precision. As a consequence, strict liability probably does not induce the optimal provision of safety. This claim is strengthened when another implication of holding firms liable for nonpecuniary losses is pursued. Product prices in today's legal regime incorporate premiums that reflect the expected value of full ex post compensation, not the consumers' ex ante willingness to pay for safety or his willingness to insure against harm. These prices thus are "incorrect" from both safety and insurance viewpoints; they are higher than they should be. The result is excessively to dampen demand for products that could cause harm. Whatever underproduction of safety is caused in consequence of consumer risk misperceptions is partly offset (or perhaps fully overcome) by the effect of imposing liability for nonpecuniary harm on firms.

To summarize, the case for letting the market regulate product safety seems weak because consumers may be uninformed about product risks. The case for letting courts regulate product safety—the case for the first aspect of strict liability—also seems weak because consumers may be informed about product risks. Also, the effect of consumer misperceptions is hard to assess. Scholars for decades have attempted to make a "first order choice" between strict liability and the market. To make a first order choice requires the resolution of uncertainty about the true state of affairs. For example, a first order case for strict liability would establish the existence and effect of imperfect information and then show why strict liability is the appropriate public response. Debate has been inconclusive in considerable part because the true state of affairs has been very hard to discover. Below I attempt a second order approach, asking what legal regime is preferable given uncertainty about the true state of affairs.

A Second Order Case for the Market

A Methodological Introduction. Political philosophy recently has attempted to develop a "neutral liberalism." The fundamental claim that this form of liberalism makes is that society's basic institutional structure should be derived from values that all citizens would reasonably hold or would find it unreasonable to reject. The most important such values are said to be freedom, equality, and tolerance. There is an unresolved tension in neutral liberalism. The basic institutional structure could be neutral as among citizens just because every person happens to hold and rank highly the central values from which the structure is derived. This way of putting the view is troublesome because it makes the social fabric contingent on what people now believe is just; the constitution should shift with the winds of intellectual fashion. Also, few values are acceptable to everyone. A person whose religious views justify a theocracy cannot be persuaded to support religious tolerance on the ground that many people do; those people, he will think, are misguided. Liberalism could avoid these difficulties by claiming that people should hold the values of freedom, equality, and tolerance because these values are objectively correct. Kantians and utilitarians do so argue, but not everyone accepts these moral philosophies. Thus, a liberalism that claimed that its central values were correct would no longer be neutral as between every conception of the state's appropriate structure that citizens may hold.

Participants in this unresolved debate agree that the state's ordinary business can be the product of shifting consensus and compromise. They recognize the great difficulty of achieving unanimity on concrete issues of political choice because information is hard to get and because the strength with which values are held influences the assessment of inevitably inconclusive evidence. Unanimity is essential only for matters of fundamental importance, such as society's basic institutional structure. Coercion against dissenters cannot be justified respecting this matter by the need to get on with it.

There is a level of choice that is intermediate between the constitution and the concrete legal rule. This level is illustrated by the choice considered here; that is, what legal regime should regulate a broad area such as product safety? This choice should be made in as neutral a fashion as possible, which is to say that it should be derived from the values that today are most broadly held in our society. The gain from this procedure is that the legal regime so chosen would engender the least dissent, and so would be the most stable and the easiest to administer. It also is no objection to this method that the choice of legal regime could shift with shifts in intellectual fashion. In a democracy, current law is supposed to reflect current values given the basic structure that is in place.

The method of neutral choice works by asking what legal regime a representative person would prefer assuming her commitment to the central values of freedom, equality, and tolerance. To ensure neutrality, the chooser cannot have an immediate stake in the outcome. This requirement can be met in two ways: the choosing person is assumed not to know how the legal regime could affect him because he could be any (actual) one; or the choosing person should self-consciously consider the issue from all affected points of view. These differences seem more semantic than real. The policy analyst also should specify the (idealized) choosing person's attitude toward risk (the person faces uncertainty because he does not know who he will be). When choosing legal regimes within an ongoing polity rather than choosing the polity's basic institutional structure, it would be erroneous to assume that the chooser is excessively risk averse. This is because advanced societies have in place nontrivial social-safety nets.

The Argument. These methodological considerations imply that society's choice whether the market or the judicial system should govern the area of product defects should be considered from the viewpoint of a representative product purchaser. The commitment to freedom implies that consumers' choices should determine the legal regime; the commitment to equality implies that the specified chooser's view should prevail if he is relevantly like everyone else (for then his choice would not systematically disadvantage any class of persons); and the commitment to tolerance seems to provide no objection to letting the majority rule on the level of political choice now at issue. The policy question is whether such a representative consumer would prefer contracts or courts. A representative consumer knows: (a) that he will make many purchases over the course of his life, but not which ones; (b) that he may be rich, middle-class, or poor; (c) that he is ''ordinarily'' risk averse given his income level, and (d) that he is as uncertain about the existence and extent of consumer risk misperceptions as the analysis above shows he should be.

Such a person would choose the market because the market would make him substantially better off than would a regime of strict liability. A thought experiment shows why. Let the consumer be asked to choose among the legal regimes that are precisely described below. She knows that her purchase choices will not affect the total level of safety that obtains; single individuals cannot influence market outcomes. The legal regimes are:

1. Free contracting: The default rule requires firms to repair or replace defective products for a reasonable time after purchase and to compensate consumers for incidental damages, but not for consequential damages (medical expenses, lost income, pain, and suffering). Under this default contract, the consumer can insure against product accidents and purchase safety improvements as she prefers.
2. Strict liability: The consumer must buy pecuniary and nonpecuniary loss coverage from manufacturers. Consequently, the consumer's preference over legal regimes is a function only of the payoffs.

Suppose first that the P,P cell is true generally. In the first regime, products are inefficiently unsafe (they are improved less than fully informed consumers would prefer). The idealized choosing consumer knows that an actual consumer could mitigate this undesirable effect in two ways. First, when economies of scale to safety are absent—the firm can alter the safety of products as small sets of consumers desire—then the actual consumer could purchase as much safety as she prefers. For example, the consumer could purchase a car with an air bag or without, with antilock brakes or without. When economies of scale to safety exist—the product must be made safer for many consumers or for none—the consumer could buy market insurance and also purchase a warranty or a service contract. Second, the idealized consumer would be an actual pessimistic consumer, who would purchase fewer dangerous products than he would actually like.

In the strict-liability regime (again assuming the P,P cell best describes reality), when economies of scale to safety exist, strict liability can make products safer. This desirable effect is offset by undesirable effects. First, when the risk-level effect is the more important, demand is already too low. Strict liability may further dampen demand to the point where desirable products become expensive, scarce, or nonexistent. Second, strict liability requires the consumer to purchase insurance from the seller against pecuniary and nonpecuniary harm. Consumers generally prefer market insurance and only against pecuniary losses. Finally, the demand-dampening effect of strict liability is exacerbated by holding firms liable for nonpecuniary harm, because the consequent price increases can be very high.

In sum, were the P,P cell to be generally true, it is difficult to know whether a regime of free contracting would make actual consumers materially worse off relative to a strict liability regime, given the steps that actual consumers could take to protect themselves (including purchasing fewer products) and given how strict liability affects market performance.

Suppose next that the C,C cell is true generally. When the C,C cell is true, actual consumers have positive expected utility in the free-contracting regime. Products are optimally safe and the consumer can insure as she pleases. Consumers have much lower expected utility in the strict-liability regime. Strict liability forces consumers to purchase insurance they do not want and product safety they do not want, raises prices, and sometimes causes products that generate positive benefits on net not to be sold.

The ideal choosing consumer would prefer the free-contracting regime because it generates a considerably higher payoff. If the C,C cell describes reality, free contracting yields the consumer the highest possible payoff while strict liability yields the lowest; if the P,P cell describes reality, free contracting yields the consumer a payoff that exceeds the minimum while strict liability will not raise that payoff materially. Thus, free contracting will generate greater expected utility for actual consumers unless the probability that the P,P cell is true exceeds 50% by a considerable margin. Because a consumer choosing legal regimes will assign an equal probability to the C,C and P,P outcomes, she will prefer freedom of contract.

The issue, recall, is not whether the consumer would prefer an extensive or narrow warranty, or which of these would be efficient or distributionally superior. Rather, the issue is which legal regime the consumer would prefer given that the consumer is uncertain about how aggregate consumer choices influence market outcomes. For the reasons given, the representative consumer would prefer a legal regime that permits free contracting. In this regime, consumers would pay firms to make cost-justified safety improvements, and would insure against pecuniary "residual risks" (those not worth avoiding) on the market, not in the product-sales contract. Put in the language above, the best second order moral case is for a market regime of this sort rather than for a strict-liability regime.

The set of legal regimes available to society is not limited to strict liability or to an unregulated market. The state also could provide a legal regime 3, in which free contracting is permitted only if firms make particular disclosures. The idealized choosing consumer would prefer regime 3 to the free-contracting regime. The consumer would make this decision because the provision of warnings and instructions increases the probability that consumers will estimate and respond to risks correctly; that is, disclosure increases the probability that the C,C cell is true. Because the consumer prefers a legal regime that permits free contracting when she assigns a 50% probability to the C,C cell, she would value more highly a regime that increased that probability above 50%. Therefore, the representative consumer would rank regime 3 first. The "neutrality method" for choosing legal regimes according to the preferences of an ideally situated consumer thus best supports the conclusion that the state should permit free contracting supplemented by disclosure.

Summary

The state can respond to the product-defect problem primarily through its courts or through the market. It has chosen the courts on the basis of six fundamental assumptions. Four of these assumptions seem incorrect and another seems overdrawn. The truth of the last, that consumer risk misperceptions cause unregulated markets to perform poorly, is unsettled. Conventional utilitarian and autonomy-based moral notions, as instantiated in the choosing method just described, imply the repeal of strict products liability on this record. Rather, the state should rely on the market supplemented by an appropriate disclosure law.

D. Moral Philosophy

John B. Attanasio, *The Principle of Aggregate Autonomy and the Calabresian Approach to Products Liability*, 74 VA. L. REV. 677 (1988)*

In *Philosophical Explanations,* Robert Nozick connects autonomy to the essence of being human. He invokes the powerful notion of free will to describe the ideal of autonomy. Conceived in this fashion, autonomy is a social condition that is instrumentally necessary for the existence of free will. At the same time, it is also intrinsically valuable because when expressed as an individual state of being rather than a social condition, it becomes similar to the concept of free will itself. Autonomy, or free will, has intrinsic value because it endows the individual human being with dignity. Without autonomy, human beings become mere playthings of external forces. Moreover, to the extent that people are reduced to sophisticated marionettes whose behavior is determined by natural forces, they can neither actively embrace nor originate value.

I invoke the Nozickian description because it is perhaps the preeminent contemporary account of the ideal of autonomy as choice or self-determination. As will become apparent, I use it as a widely accessible and evocative starting point, yet I do not agree with all aspects of this account. Based on this Nozickian conceptualization, I develop a working definition of autonomy as that global free choice that might also be called self-determination. This vision will begin with the liberty/order tension, and culminate with the paradoxical principle of aggregate autonomy. The inspiration for these new reflections on autonomy is the Calabresian approach to strict products liability. [*Editor's note*: The "Calabresian approach" is found pervasively in many of the works of Guido Calabresi, but is especially evident in the Calabresi & Hirschoff piece reprinted above in Part IV.C.]

Typically, the Calabresian model has been criticized as narrowly utilitarian. I hope, nevertheless, to demonstrate that powerful notions of autonomy undergird Calabresian theory and that Calabresian theory sparks a new way of thinking about autonomy that I call aggregate autonomy. Essentially, the principle of aggregate autonomy introduces distributional concerns into autonomy theory. These distributive considerations starkly contrast with stringent libertarian conceptions such as Nozick's.

The Calabresian Approach to Strict Products Liability

An acceptable system of products liability, strict or otherwise, must fit the primary autonomy context of tort law. The most attractive explanations for strict liability—particularly for design and warning cases—are the theories of Guido Calabresi. The theories have been widely accepted

*Used by permission.

because they reconcile the liberty/order tension in a manner that advances both autonomy and utility.

One central tenet of Calabresi's approach dictates that society should impose accident losses on whichever party can best decide whether the potential product accident is more costly to avoid or to insure against, and subsequently act on that decision. Calabresi proffers this rule not only as a normative ideal but as a descriptive sketch of the way in which the products liability system in some degree already operates. For Calabresi, the best decider is strictly liable irrespective of the consequences of Learned Hand balancing or other fault-based systems.

The second key to the Calabresian approach is internalization: product price should reflect accident costs attributable to that product. Holding the product producer strictly liable for harms actually caused by the product will advance accurate internalization of its accident costs. Producers will consider these accident costs as part of the true costs of the product, and will increase the price accordingly. In this way, product price will incorporate the true costs of the product.

The best decider and internalization approaches obviously appeal to utility. The best decider approach nurtures utility by placing liability, and therefore incentives to avoid the accident, on whoever is best-suited to judge whether it is more efficient to avoid or absorb a potential mishap. Devolving the accident decision upon this best decider will maximize the probabilities for efficient accident avoidance: society will purchase only those safety measures that are cheaper than insurance. Similarly, by correctly reflecting the accident costs of a particular product, internalization will enable consumers to maximize their utility by making better-informed consumption choices. If one accepts the intuition that accidents are one of the most severe incursions on happiness, then reducing accidents and compensating people for them will increase the total amount of happiness in society. Described in this fashion, Calabresian theory would seem to shun autonomy, sacrificing both the individual victim and the individual tortfeasor for the good of the whole.

In a real way, however, the theory appeals to autonomy. In Calabresi's world, the law is simply attempting to strike a propitious balance between liberty and order to preserve autonomy for as many individuals in society as possible. Both the best decider and internalization theories afford primary importance to the physical integrity of the individual. Both fit the primary autonomy context of tort law. The best decider approach strives to minimize injuries by devolving safety decisions on whoever might best avert accidents. When she is not the victim, the best decider should have responsibilities other than accident avoidance. In this case, she must try to mitigate her violations of the victim's autonomy with money damages. By placing the ultimate decision about accidents in the hands of individuals, Calabresian theory overtly appeals to autonomy. This approach does not suborn individual free will with a decision by the state, or even by a state-impanelled jury as required by the Learned Hand test. The jury simply decides which party is the best decider to perform the Learned Hand calculus. That party—rather than the jury or other government institution—makes the accident decision.

Devolving such predictions on the best decider by definition entrusts them to the person who can best protect her own autonomy against infringement, as well as the autonomy of others. Central to such protection is superior knowledge regarding how to alleviate the autonomy infringement that liability exacts: among the victim, manufacturer, retailer, et cetera, the best decider has superior knowledge to elect between the options of insuring and taking safety measures. Allocating liability according to superior knowledge advances autonomy in at least four ways.

First, this superior knowledge reduces the effort necessary to make the accident decision. Extra effort reduces choice by depleting time or other resources required to participate in activities other than accident avoidance. Second, it renders the accident decision more accurate. Those held liable will be less likely to suffer severe constrictions on choice by underinsuring or by spending prohibitive amounts on safety measures. Superior knowledge will help to avoid such eventualities. Indeed, the best decider surpasses the jury itself in performing the Learned Hand ciphering.

Third, the best decider approach mitigates the grave autonomy infringements that the disarray of accidents can work on product consumers. The superior knowledge of the best decider will render more likely the introduction of prompt, cost-effective safety measures by which to reduce the severity and number of accidents.

Fourth, the best decider approach helps victims: even when insurance is cheaper than accident avoidance, the best decider will have superior knowledge about the insurance needed to redress injuries adequately. The insurance alternative attracts a rather piercing autonomy criticism, however. Arguably, the best decider approach consciously permits accidents, thereby sacrificing the individuals who will suffer them. Still, the law does not itself create accidents. Calabresi's theory simply acknowledges an unfortunate aspect of the human condition with which tort law always has grappled, albeit less openly.

Internalization theory is the other component of Calabresian analysis that sustains autonomy. According to this concept, accident costs should be incorporated into the price of a product. Like the best decider approach, internalization advances autonomy partly by increasing information. As with the best decider approach, internalization serves a variety of autonomy interests.

First, with respect to product consumers, internalization allows individuals to make more informed judgments about whether to purchase a particular product. By reflecting accident costs, internalization helps to illuminate the true cost to consumers of a particular product. Insofar as it influences consumption patterns, this cost implicitly provides some information about the extent to which a given product may, through an accident, constrict the consumer's autonomy or the autonomy of others. Both the probability and severity of the imposition will be reflected in the price of the good. Moreover, internalization gives product sellers incentives to provide additional information in the form of warnings. With price and warning information in hand, the potential user can make a more informed decision concerning consumption.

Second, internalization advances autonomy by reducing the number of autonomy infringements that consumers suffer. The internalized accident costs increase the amount of money and effort that the product exacts. Predictably, the higher price will decrease consumption of that product and therefore decrease the number of accidents caused by that product. In this way, internalization theory endeavors to satisfy the liberty/order tension: it will constrain the liberty of the consumer to purchase products to the minimum extent necessary to redress the massive liberty incursions sometimes caused by those products. The marginal increase in price attributable to accident costs will be the lesser of the amount required to render the product safe or the amount required to insure or self-insure.

Third, incorporating accident costs into product prices under internalization generates funds. This money can be used to compensate victims, purchase insurance, or otherwise redress the autonomy infringements occasioned by accidents.

Fourth, internalization can protect the autonomy of those who must ultimately shoulder liability. When the best decider is a product manufacturer or retailer, it can more easily disperse the effects of the autonomy infringements. By internalizing accident losses in each product, enterprises can spread small incremental wealth losses among all consumers of the product. Importantly, when enterprises encounter difficulty in spreading accident losses among consumers through internalization, they may still be able to spread such losses among shareholders. For product manufacturers or retailers, the ability to disperse losses, together with superior knowledge about loss spreading and avoidance, alleviates the liberty infringements that strict liability may impose on any one defendant. Moreover, if their actuarial foreseeability is blurry, manufacturers may have incentives to overinsure and to grow biased in favor of safety or physical inviolability.

Despite the strong connections to autonomy, the Calabresian approach advances this value only imperfectly. For example, with respect to internalization, firms and consumers do not always respond to higher prices and the other economic signals that the system emits. Moreover, the best decider rule would not appear to apply when the harm caused by the product is totally unforeseeable.

Some of these difficulties may be moderated through modifications in the application of the Calabresian scheme though others may not. Notwithstanding some shortcomings, the basic claim is modest. I do not contend that the Calabresian approach to products liability always or perfectly advances autonomy, but only that it is designed to advance autonomy, and does so better than a negligence system.

Why the Calabresian Approach to Products Liability is More Protective of Autonomy than Negligence

Calabresian theory frequently favors victim recovery. In the products liability context, the superior knowledge of the manufacturer will frequently render it the best decider of whether to avoid a product accident or to insure against it. Moreover, accurate internalization requires manufacturer liability whenever the harm is actually attributable to the product rather than to some assumption of risk by the consumer. The Calabresian scheme is far more protective of accident victims than negligence, which imposes many more barriers to victim compensation such as contributory negligence and the Learned Hand calculus.

Some might suppose that this victim bias unduly constrains the autonomy of manufacturers, shareholders, consumers, or others who must ultimately shoulder the additional liability imposed by the Calabresian approach. In a noncommercial context, this might be a problem. Fortunately, however, the commercial milieu in which this products liability scheme operates alleviates the autonomy infringement that liability exacts. In this context, the injurer has superior knowledge with which to minimize the loss by insurance or other measures. Moreover, the ability to spread the loss further mitigates any autonomy incursion.

In the products liability framework, Calabresian strict liability, as compared with negligence, averts more of the severe autonomy infringements on victims occasioned by product accidents. At the same time, in the commercial context, the capacity to spread the loss ensures that such strict liability generally does not infringe on defendants' self-determination much more than a negligence system. The accident costs and, consequently, product prices will be somewhat higher under Calabresian strict liability than under a negligence system. At the expense of some diminished capacity to consume products, applying the Calabresian approach will avert the profound autonomy infringements that accidents comprise for more individuals in the society as a whole. Calabresian theory thus advances autonomy and provides the starting point for the theory of aggregate autonomy, a concept I shall explain later in this paper.

Why the Calabresian Approach to Products Liability Connects More Closely to Autonomy than Utility

The best decider and internalization approaches more tightly connect with autonomy than utility. A certain indeterminance besets hedonistic act utilitarianism. Under the standard of total societal happiness, the ideal mix of order and freedom of action is virtually impossible to calculate with confidence. Even if people do regard accidents as particularly severe infringements on happiness, one would have some difficulty estimating how much of society's resources should be devoted to accident avoidance in order to maximize happiness. Calabresian theory does not pretend to advance the total happiness or material resources in society. The connection to happiness depends on some widely shared belief that the stringent protection afforded by Calabresian theory outweighs the drain in material resources it exacts. In undertaking such a utilitarian calculus, we may have to consider the distribution of the risk averse, the risk neutral, and risk preferrers. Strong risk preferrers would presumably be less enamored of the vigorous protection afforded by Calabresian theory. Then again, witnessing the restoration of accident victims might increase their total happiness, even though they do not wish similar protection for themselves. We could go on.

In contrast, the Calabresian scheme advances autonomy in far more clear and definite ways. It is concerned with minimizing and redressing the severe autonomy infringements occasioned by product accidents. Conforming with the liberty/order tension, the theory does not deter product consumption any more than necessary to redress liberty infringements caused by that product itself. It requires paying to restore victims of that consumption, or paying to produce a safer product that will not inflict the particular harm at issue.

If the utilitarian calculus could be rendered more definite, it might well reject the Calabresian scheme. Calabresian strict liability diverts even more funds than negligence systems to accident victims. As I noted earlier, utility might be increased by not wasting such large sums of money on badly mangled accident victims who sometimes suffer during the rest of their lives anyway. Spreading the major part of these damages among, for example, the poor may further augment total societal happiness. The Calabresian scheme, like the rest of tort law, focuses on the individual victim rather than on society as a whole.

* * *

Utilitarianism and Aggregate Autonomy

To support the Calabresian scheme I posit an initial formulation of the principle of *aggregate autonomy*: act to protect the individual against severe constrictions of life plans whenever such protection may be accomplished through de minimis wealth-related interference with the life plans of some members of society. The aggregation move does not conflate the theory with utilitarianism. Hedonistic-act utilitarianism focuses on whether an act advances or diminishes happiness in society as a whole. In contrast, the principle of aggregate autonomy focuses on choice and the individual. To illustrate, the principle can easily be stated in more individualistic terms than its initial formulation: Act to protect the individual from severe constrictions of life plans whenever such protection requires de minimis wealth-related interference with one's own life plans.

Unlike utilitarianism, which strives to increase happiness in the society as a whole irrespective of consequences on particular individuals, aggregate autonomy moves toward preserving a basic level of self-determination for each individual. This expanded account of autonomy that I have enlisted in Calabresi's defense dramatically differs from Nozick's approach in at least two respects. First, it does not afford so much latitude to contract escapes. The duty-premised theory of aggregate autonomy imposes certain moral obligations that parties who, for example, may have superior knowledge or bargaining power cannot simply eschew by contract. Second, the principle does not endorse the minimalist state. In my view, a vision of autonomy that incorporates notions of aggregate autonomy and extended responsibility for one's actions begins to grapple with deep problems in extreme libertarian conceptualizations of autonomy. Ironically, these narrow contract and political freedom conceptions of autonomy can engender profound autonomy infringements: protecting powerful individuals against government interference necessarily prohibits the state from protecting some meaningful level of choice for the weak. In my view, autonomy is a long-run value that a society should try to preserve over the lifetimes of as many of its members as possible. In focusing on the short-run, libertarian conceptions of autonomy shield free choice from immediate impositions, often neglecting adverse, long-term consequences.

I make a narrow claim that autonomy should incorporate some notion of responsibility for others. The context in which I make this assertion is enterprise liability. The parties at hand have interacted in the rather impersonal way that modern industry entails. They have voluntarily entered into a business relationship with each other. The enormity of modern enterprises blurs but does not undercut the existence of that relationship, a weakened yet viable expression of social cooperation (or community). The existence of these relations carefully circumscribes the scope of responsibility for others. Introducing these notions of extended responsibility and aggregation into autonomy more closely approximates the Kantian ideal. In the products liability area, these considerations require that the manufacturer and the consumer respect each other as ends rather than as mere means to a profit-seeking transaction.

Objections to an Autonomy Defense of the Calabresian Approach to Products Liability

At least three powerful objections might be raised against my aggregate autonomy defense of the Calabresian approach to products liability.

Sometimes the Calabresian Approach May Exact More Than De Minimis Wealth Infringements. One category of protests might charge that my defense is unrealistic. As formulated, the principle of aggregate autonomy only legitimates de minimis wealth incursions. Sometimes Calabresian theory may more significantly constrict choice. For example, on the demand side, strict products liability may cause a particular product to be taken off the market so that consumers may not have the option to utilize it. In the case of certain pharmaceuticals or other products, the resultant autonomy infringements may be quite harsh. On the supply side, if a manufacturer encounters difficulty in spreading damage awards, it might suffer more than small loses of wealth. Indeed, some manufacturers might be forced out of business, and certain small manufacturers might be prevented from entering a particular market altogether.

Beginning with the somewhat easier objection on the supply side, one must first assume that the wealth losses are so massive or other conditions of supply and demand are such that the producer cannot feasibly spread her loss. Even when this occurs, all that such a tortfeasor can suffer is loss of wealth. Peonage and other more intrusive infringements on debtors are no longer permitted. Moreover, other legal rules limit even the loss of wealth. At worst, the tortfeasor can declare bankruptcy. While this poses an unsavory prospect, it does construct a floor on liability; and it effectively will spread the loss among various creditors. With respect to the victim, private insurance together with government programs will have to substitute for the uncompensated part of his loss.

More importantly, a shrewd manufacturer or other potential tortfeasor can readily avail herself of other legal options to circumscribe her liability. For example, she might incorporate as a means of limiting liability. She might sell shares to others who might bear part of the loss. She might choose to sell her ideas to a larger entity that might be better able to absorb losses. Often the tortfeasor can purchase insurance that will spread the loss to a certain extent. In short, the Calabresian scheme does not close off the potential to limit losses to small amounts of wealth.

These responses do not dismiss the obligation to minimize the scope of autonomy infringements to which risk preferrers might be exposed. Concretely, the products liability system might ensure that damages are indeed allocated to the best decider and do not exceed the true costs of accidents. To reduce further the impact of wealth infringements exacted by Calabresian theory, government might also facilitate the availability of affordable insurance. While this tack impairs the accurate internalization of accident costs, the Calabresian system is not perfect; society must make hard decisions in trying to avert as many severe autonomy decisions as possible.

Turning to objections on the demand side, the Calabresian approach might cost product consumers more than small amounts of wealth. For example, Calabresian theory may exact more than de minimis wealth infringements from poor consumers. Even small product insurance premiums may be quite substantial for a poor consumer. This problem will generally be averted by market stratification stemming from unequal wealth itself. In the context of products that deprived individuals often purchase, Calabresian insurance premiums will typically be de minimis. Insofar as these often paltry internalized sums impose more than de minimis infringements, the solution to such a terrible problem is not exposing poor persons, who will almost certainly be unable to self-insure, to catastrophic accidents by doing away with the Calabresian system. A more just policy—in aggregate autonomy terms—perhaps would be to foster a more equitable distribution of wealth.

Another poignant case on the demand side is the seriously ill patient who is denied the use of a drug that accident costs render prohibitively expensive or even unmarketable. Again, the attack hits the fringe of an aggregate autonomy defense of Calabresian theory. Nevertheless, this qualification hardly rebuts the initial criticism. The hypothetical assumes a product of high necessity and expense that liability renders totally unavailable. Perhaps, in a few extreme cases similar to this one, the principle of aggregate autonomy might allow such products to be marketed without liability if appropriate warnings were given. Alternatively, society might choose to pay for the autonomy infringements caused by such products.

Aggregate Autonomy and the Compelled Overinsurance Objection to Calabresian Theory. Critics of Calabresian theory might consider my autonomy defense ironic. After all, an unencumbered private insurance option would seem to guarantee more choice. The Calabresian theory, they might argue, is an approach that compels all consumers, even risk preferrers, to purchase insurance against accidents through Calabresian internalization. Moreover, even for risk averse consumers who might desire some insurance against product accidents, the Calabresian system may force some to overinsure, as the private insurance markets generally do not even cover items like pain and suffering.

Allowing product consumers to purchase private insurance against product-related accidents would alleviate both of these problems. Still, in advancing the short-run autonomy interests of some consumers, this alternative would infringe upon the short-run and long-run autonomy interests of many more. First, it would impair the ability of consumers to make informed product choices. Second, relying on private insurance would systematically decrease product prices, thereby increasing product consumption and resultant accidents.

With respect to the first point, the private insurance alternative—and the overinsurance critique upon which it is founded—demand of the consumer far too much information and knowledge about the safety risks of each product purchase. To simplify this problem, the Calabresian scheme conveys accident information through the price of a product. While price is a crude method, price differentials will automatically convey product accident information and will modify consumption at the margin. Of course, price will only convey accident information in a uniform way that does not respect individual preferences for insurance. Still, such uniformity should, on balance, increase autonomy by fostering more informed consumption choices than could possibly be made by consumers trying to calculate the accident costs of each individual product. In addition, the Calabresian system will provide incentives for manufacturers to convey the optimal amount of accident reduction information through warnings. Manufacturers seeking to minimize the accident costs of their wares will be inclined to include the optimal amount of information that consumers can effectively digest and use to avoid accidents.

A second major difficulty with the overinsurance critique of Calabresian theory is that it impairs the deterrence goals of the tort system. Eliminating internalization of manufacturer accident costs would lessen deterrence and increase accidents for both risk preferrers and the risk averse. A system of private insurance would thus in effect allow the risk preferrer to compel the risk averse to suffer additional accidents. This result is an inevitable consequence of the interrelated nature of society. Finally, in addition to forcing people to suffer more accidents, private insurance will not adequately compensate them.

Distributive Tensions in the Principle of Aggregate Autonomy. Ceteris paribus, accident liability will probably alter the autonomy of a person of moderate wealth to a greater extent that the autonomy of one who is very poor or very rich. Accordingly, unequal wealth affects the autonomy consequences of imposing liability. For example, it limits the extent to which the Learned Hand test advances autonomy. On defendant's side, virtually no imposition on autonomy may occur when a judgment-proof poor person is held liable. Liability will also rarely affect the autonomy of a very wealthy person in a significant way. In contrast, liability can dramatically affect the autonomy of a middle-class person. Indeed, we could envision an extreme example in which the Hand test would severely constrain the autonomy of the lower-middle-class worker by making him work for years to pay for destroyed property that the wealthy owner might barely miss.

Conversely, on the plaintiff's side, negligence theory often entitles a wealthy, high-income victim to a much larger recovery than her poor, low-income counterpart. When a high-income plaintiff sues a low-income defendant, the tort system will regressively redistribute wealth. Indeed, as a general matter, the tort system will more deeply infringe on the autonomy of the relatively poor than the relatively wealthy. In the negligence system, this problem may be mitigated because the relatively wealthy can afford to pay larger damage awards than the relatively poor. Because of differences in personal wealth and insurance, the relatively poor simply will not be subjected to as large amounts of liability as the relatively wealthy. Of course, one escape for the less wealthy, who are at least able to retain counsel, may be the unhappy prospect of bankruptcy.

On plaintiff's side, the compulsory insurance imposed by Calabresian internalization, together with the exclusive recovery from the common insurance pool, incrementally exacerbates this regressive redistribution problem. Many states do require insurance to finance certain parts of the tort system; however, the Calabresian system obliges all consumers of a particular product—irrespective of their wealth—to purchase the same amount of insurance. While consumers must pay the same insurance premium for each purchase, wealthy consumers of the product will recover greater amounts than poorer ones.

Of course, the Calabresian scheme largely sheds the distribution problems that plague much of tort law on defendant's side. Because large entities will generally defend product actions, such cases will seldom result in poor defendants paying large damage awards to restore the lifestyles of wealthy plaintiffs. Still, for poor plaintiffs, strict products liability exacerbates the distributional problems of tort law because it brings into tort theory more aspects of an insurance system than does negligence.

At some level, this problem tests the distributive versus corrective justice qualities of the Calabresian system in particular, and the theory of aggregate autonomy in general. Before attacking this problem, however, let me carefully define its scope. A number of countervailing factors may limit any regressive redistribution engendered by the Calabresian system.

First, many products are themselves segregated among relatively poor or rich purchasers. A classic example is the automobile market. Such market stratification will likely mitigate the effect of relatively poor persons paying higher insurance premiums to finance the higher accident costs of comparatively wealthy accident victims. To the extent that the market is not stratified, fear of large judgments by rich persons may induce manufacturers to produce a safer product from which the poor will also benefit. Second, any critique of internalization as regressive must assume that poor persons are no more accident prone than wealthy ones. If poor persons are more accident prone—because of less education, holding onto products longer, or other factors—rich persons will be assessed the same insurance premium despite their lesser risk. Insofar as products are not stratified according to wealth, an inverse proportion between risk and wealth would mitigate or possibly reverse any regressive redistributional effects that internalization may cause in the way of greater damage awards for the wealthy.

Finally, the Calabresian system itself requires that courts consider distributional effects in determining where to place liability. In this connection, Calabresi provocatively suggests that courts might consider the ability to spread accident losses or to move toward a "given distribution of wealth, such as greater wealth equality." Taking risk spreading and wealth equality into account will help to mitigate any regressive distributional effects engendered by internalization.

My own view is that distributive difficulties have not been shown to infect Calabresian theory. Insofar as they do, corrective justice concerns embedded in the principle of aggregate autonomy should trump distributive ones. To the extent that one truly cares about distributive justice, the weak principle of aggregate autonomy might be rendered somewhat stronger and applied to other areas such as taxation and employment benefits. It might then be invoked as a justification to reduce extreme inequalities in the distribution of wealth. I do not care to examine this tantalizing suggestion at this time, as this is a paper about tort law.

* * *

Conclusion

To encapsule the argument: a libertarian version of autonomy advancing the minimalist state interposes side constraints against government involvement with the distribution of societal resources. Indeed, a Nozickian version of autonomy also appears to countenance broad-ranging contractual limitations on strict products liability. Neither of these difficulties encumbers the principle of aggregate autonomy. In defending the Calabresian approach to products liability, the principle allows small wealth infringements to avert severe constrictions of the life plans of product victims. The aggregate autonomy defense of Calabresian theory concentrates on the ready potential to incur only minimal wealth infringements. The defense also realistically reckons with the framework of societal interdependence. Finally, it advances notions of both corrective and distributive justice, but gives priority to the latter.

Calabresian theory engages the dialectic between legal example and philosophical ideal: it not only provides a theoretical basis for thinking about tort reform, but also suggests new ways of thinking about autonomy generally. Indeed, the theory's widespread appeal almost certainly derives from its intuitive connection to first principles.

Like virtually everything in an imperfect world, the Calabresian scheme has difficulties. Despite these difficulties, however, the theories remain the most sophisticated approaches to products liability puzzles yet formulated. They have retained tremendous sway precisely because they endeavor to satisfy the liberty/order tension in an elegant but practical way. In so doing the analysis engages deep ideals of utility, and particularly autonomy, that are important to all of us. Indeed, as I have endeavored to articulate, the theories provide the basis for a new way of thinking about autonomy.

This vision of autonomy takes into account the distribution of autonomy. It addresses the interdependence of modern life more realistically than narrow political freedom conceptions of autonomy. In calling the political freedom conception of autonomy narrow, I hardly mean to disparage it. The precious yet precarious nature of this narrow conception of rights has inspired many to defend it. Some may fear that expanded paradigms, enforced by governmental power, may threaten the vital core. I do not suggest that the political freedom conception of autonomy should be abandoned, but only that conceptions might be explored that include additional considerations.

At the end of the day one might ponder how the seemingly mundane and technocratic problem of products liability might broaden our vision of autonomy. The context that informs these ruminations is not products liability law but human suffering. As Calabresi and Phillip Bobbitt have so eloquently expressed: "The misery wrought by accidents thrusts upon its hapless victims a physical ordeal, and impedes human flourishing. Concurrently, it confronts the more fortunate among us who have escaped (for a time) with the moral dilemma of what to do."

David G. Owen, *The Moral Foundations of Products Liability Law: Toward First Principles,* 68 NOTRE DAME L. REV. 427 (1993)*

Products liability law lies at the center of the modern world. Whether or not humans have evolved much over the ages as moral creatures, civilization is marching into the twenty-first-century in a blaze of advancing technology. To a large extent, persons accomplish their individual and collective objectives, and relate to one another, through the products of technology—automobiles, punch presses, tractors, prescription drugs, frozen dinners, tennis rackets, perfumes, greeting cards, and airplanes (civilian and military). Matters concerning the creation and exchange of such products of technology are addressed by the law of property, contracts, and commerce. Products liability law concerns instead the consequences of modern technology gone awry—when products, or the interactions between persons and their products, fail.

But products liability law deals with matters of much greater import than merely the relationship between people and their machines. This rather sterile conception of the subject matter unhappily has dominated the thinking about products liability law since it was "invented" in modern form three decades ago. When a person is injured by a product, the principal question of interest in products liability law is whether the product was too dangerous, according to some standard of product safety. This focus of modern products liability law expressly upon the products—both the one which caused the injury, and some hypothetical one of proper safety—thus tends to direct the liability issue into a barren, technologically-based determination.

Yet the most essential question in any products liability case is not whether certain engineering,

*Used by permission. Anderson Publishing Co. bears responsibility for any errors of printing or editing.

production, or informational psychology standards were met or breached. Rather, the relationship between the maker of a product and the victim of a product accident implicates fundamental issues of moral philosophy. By choosing to expose product users and others to certain types and degrees of risk, product makers appropriate to themselves certain interests in safety—in bodily integrity—that may belong to those other persons. Similarly, by choosing to purchase products with certain inherent risks or by choosing to use such products in certain risky ways, and then by choosing to make claims against the maker for harm resulting from such risks or uses, victims of product accidents seek to appropriate to themselves economic interests that may belong to product makers and to other consumers. Both situations involve important questions of how persons should treat one another. Ethical theory, therefore, has much to say as to whether moral responsibility for product accidents lies (in part or in whole) with the maker, the user, or the victim. At bottom, product accidents are moral—not technological—events. And so the law of products liability should turn to moral theory in establishing its fundamental principles.

* * *

Freedom and Harm

The manufacture and use of products is in general good. As a form of property, products generally promote the autonomy of both their makers and their users. Makers derive profits from the manufacture and sale of products, providing opportunities, and hence more autonomy, for the persons who own the maker. The autonomy of the maker's employees is similarly promoted, as is the autonomy of the owners and employees of the maker's suppliers and distributors.

Users promote their own autonomy by purchasing goods. The very decision to purchase a product entails a choice to convert one's wealth (property) from stored (monetary) to tangible (chattel) form. The selection process involves a further exercise of choice and, hence, autonomy because the buyer must decide what other similar and dissimilar products (and services) to reject. Buyers purchase products to achieve some combination of personal objectives—a coat, for warming one's body and enhancing one's appearance; a book, for education and entertainment; a saw, for facilitating the assembly of other products to promote the user's more specific goals. Each such purchase reflects the buyer's choice to sacrifice other ends to further whatever purposes the product appears capable of helping him achieve. Thus, the very nature of product manufacture, exchange, and use is to promote the autonomy of human beings.

The problem for products liability law, however, is that products sometimes also cause accidental harm: cars sometimes crash, and toasters sometimes start fires, because they are defective or used improperly. When a person is injured accidentally by a product, his autonomy may be restricted in a variety of ways—by hospitalization, loss of bodily function, pain, loss of income, loss of property, and damage to his ability to relate to others arising from these other losses. The manufacturer often may be able to restore at least that portion of the victim's lost autonomy caused by economic deprivation. But there is no good reason in freedom theory for obligating the manufacturer in every case to compensate the victim. The resources that a manufacturer might use to relieve the victim's harm, or loss of autonomy, must come from somewhere; they must be taken from someone else. They are taken in the long run both from the maker's owners, through diminished profits, and from other consumers, through higher prices. The very difficult issue therefore becomes determining the circumstances that require one person (or group of persons) in justice to surrender his or her (or their) autonomy in order to promote the autonomy of others.

The fact that a manufacturer makes and sells products, which generally are good, is an insufficient reason for requiring a manufacturer to compensate a victim of a product accident. This activity, like any other action, always involves some harm to others. As demonstrated by the choice-harm principle discussed above, moral philosophy requires more than action, related in some manner to another's harm, for the actor to be held accountable for the harm. Moreover, the choice-harm accident paradigm involves a victim who is "passive," who is affirmatively "hurt by" an actor pursuing conflicting interests of his own. Yet, product accidents generally result from deliberative choices and actions of a product user, who has selected a particular product and reduced it to his personal dominion and control, and who is putting it (often actively) to use in the pursuit of his own chosen goals. The choice-harm paradigm of an active A hitting a passive B, therefore, simply does not fit the typical products liability case.

The products liability paradigm is more complex: A, standing at point x, makes product P; A takes P to point z where he leaves it, offering it for sale to all persons, and then returns to x where he resumes his other business; B, standing at point y, wanting a particular type of product to pursue a particular goal, leaves y and goes to various points including z to examine various products, finally deciding upon P, which he pays for and reduces to his dominion and control; B then returns to y with P, where he resumes his business, using P; in the process of using P, B is hurt. This complex paradigm of a typical product accident demonstrates that even the most attractive paradigm for compensation—A actively hits a passive B—is unable to explain the normal product accident. Even if we exclude from the paradigm the frequent fact of B's carelessness in using P, sometimes for an improper purpose, B's harm appears to be as much or more the result of his own choices and actions as of any morally relevant choice or action by A. A product user, in other words, is at least as likely the author of his own harm as the "passive victim" of the maker's conduct.

Basing liability merely on the acts of making and selling products thus would produce a general rule of strict liability that is unacceptable on moral grounds. A manufacturer's liability must rest instead on something that is wrongful in its actions. From an autonomy perspective, the maker can be held morally accountable for a harm only if it should contemplate that the product by some measure will cause unwarranted harm to the freedom of product users. Yet freedom as a naked ethic cannot provide a method for determining whether harm to product users is proper or unwarranted, or where or how the limits on a maker's or user's freedom should be drawn. For its necessary enrichment, freedom must draw from the ideals of truth, equality, and utility.

Truth and Expectations

The first key to enriching freedom, as discussed in general terms above, lies in truth. People's conceptions of the true world, their expectations as to how the future will unfold in relation to their choices and their actions, depend to a large extent on what other people say and do. Truth and expectations, rooted deeply in autonomy, therefore play a major role in determining moral accountability for product accidents. Product accidents simply would not occur at all if both the manufacturer and the user truly understood all characteristics of the product, the level of the user's knowledge and skill, and the context of the product's use.

Manufacturers and users each have certain visions of the world, which may or may not be true, that are relevant to moral accountability for product accidents. The first such visions of reality, or expectations, concern the capacity of persons (generally or in particular) to interact safely with particular products in various environments of use. The second type of expectations concerns the allocation of responsibility for safety between the maker and the user. These are a form of "background expectations" based on communal beliefs concerning moral and legal norms of behavior and personal or corporate responsibility. If, in any particular case, both forms of expectations conform to reality and hence are true, then the product can be used safely to accomplish the user's goals. If, instead, either the maker or the user misperceives the true capacities of the product or the user, an accident may result.

The first problem to consider from a truth perspective concerns express statements that affirmatively create false expectations of product safety. When the maker knowingly makes false statements about a product's safety, hoping to trick consumers into buying the product upon the belief that it is safer than it truly is, the manufacturer steals the autonomy of consumers. Thus, it should pay for any harm resulting from the theft. Even if a manufacturer's assertions of product safety are not wilful but merely negligent, they still are by definition wrongful, so that the manufacturer is morally accountable for resulting harm.

More difficult is the moral significance of a manufacturer's making an innocent but untrue statement about a product's safety. Arguably, making such a statement is merely a particular form of action, such that there should be no moral responsibility for untoward consequences because of the absence of a guilty will. Yet there are powerful reasons within the ideals of freedom and truth that support a rule of strict liability for accidental harm resulting from innocent but false assertions of product quality.

When a manufacturer makes safety "promises" in an effort to sell its products, its very purpose is to convince potential buyers that the promises concern matters that are both important and true. Safety information is important and valuable to users because it provides a "frame of reference" that permits a user to shift his limited cognitive and other resources away from self-protection, responsibility for which is thereby placed upon the manufacturer, toward the pursuit of other goals. In this manner, true safety information adds value to the product by enhancing the autonomy of the user, for which the consumer fairly pays a price. So, if the information is false, the purchaser loses both significant autonomy and the benefit of his bargain. Since an important purpose of the law is to promote autonomy and the equality of the buyer to the seller as reflected in their deal, the law should demand that the seller rectify the underlying falsity and resulting inequality in the exchange transaction if harm results—or not the seller should have realized that the price unfairly reflected value that was false. More general communal interests are also promoted by the enforcement of such promises, for the confidence of all members of the community in the trustworthiness of others is fundamental to positive interpersonal relating in general, and to commercial efficiency in particular.

Whether manufacturers are morally obligated to act affirmatively to provide consumers with information—by warning of product dangers and instructing on safe use—is a very different question that depends largely upon the availability of information to manufacturers and consumers. If the information is obvious or possessed already by consumers—that knives can cut and matches burn—there generally is no reason in moral theory for a manufacturer to warn consumers. The possibility of a duty to warn only arises, therefore, if the risk is a latent one, hidden from consumers in the product. A seller's failure to warn about such dangers, depriving consumers of the truth, was considered a form of passive fraud in Roman law and by Aquinas. At least in terms of their "background expectations," most people today probably believe that manufacturers should provide warnings about conditions that they know to be dangerous to consumers. In addition, consumers probably have a background expectation that manufacturers will seek to discover and warn about unknown but foreseeable dangers that are reasonably discoverable—discoverable, that is, at a cost justified by the product's price and proportionate to its foreseeable risks. At bottom, such expectations of reasonableness probably derive largely from equality of respect.

When a danger at the time of sale is neither known nor reasonably discoverable, the problem of moral accountability for resulting accidents becomes far more difficult. That the maker in the present context does not affirm the product's safety but is merely silent makes all the difference: the maker does not by false statements affirmatively construct a false world of value by promising potential buyers that the product is safer than in truth it is. Thus, failing to warn about an unknowable danger contrasts sharply, in terms of moral accountability, with actively (albeit innocently) misleading consumers by false statements to relinquish their normal levels of self-protection. The "silent" maker, by hypothesis, in no way wills any safety expectation or loss upon the victim; nor does the maker otherwise cause the loss, except by providing a product it reasonably thinks is good and by failing to cure a misimpression it neither made nor even knows exists.

Responsibility for harm from undiscoverable product dangers thus may be viewed most fairly as lying with the product—perhaps, in nature or in the inadequacies of science or technology—rather than with the manufacturer. That the chemistry of the world contains vast numbers of unknown dangers is a fact well known to consumers who seek the benefits of the products of modern science and technology. Especially when potent chemicals are first developed to treat serious human illnesses, consumers well understand—even if only in a subconscious, "background" kind of way—that unknowable risks may well accompany the benefits expected to result from manipulating the atoms of the universe. And notwithstanding this important background understanding or expectation, most people probably want (or "demand," from the economic perspective of product makers) manufacturers to provide them with the benefits of science and technology if and when such benefits reasonably appear to exceed the risks. If a maker does so, and an undiscoverable danger lurking in the product causes injury to a user, the maker cannot fairly be held responsible for the harm. The maker did not choose to put, nor did he unreasonably put, the danger in the product or the world, nor did the maker affirmatively mislead users into surrendering their own responsibility for self-protection. Instead, the manufacturer served in a real sense only as a conduit for consumer preferences, providing consumers with what they reasonably appeared to want. Thus, the victim of an accident from an unknowable generic product danger probably should have no claim to hold the manufacturer accountable for the loss.

Manufacturing flaw cases, however, involve entirely different types of expectations by manufacturers and consumers. The very essence of an ordinary exchange transaction involving a new product is the notion that the buyer is paying appropriate value for a certain type of "good" comprised of various utility and safety characteristics common to each unit of that type produced by the maker according to a single design. In this context, both the maker and the buyer contemplate (and hence contract for) an exchange of a standard, uniform monetary value for a standard, uniform package of utility and safety. At some level of abstract awareness, most consumers know of course that manufacturers sometimes make mistakes and that the cost of perfect production for many types of products would be exorbitant. However, while consumers may abstractly comprehend the practical necessity of allowing imperfect production, their actual expectation when purchasing a new product is that its important attributes will match those of other similar units. When a purchaser pays full value for a product that appears to be the same as every other, only to receive a product with a dangerous, hidden flaw, the product's price and appearance both generate in the buyer false expectations of safety which denies the buyer's right to truth.

Equality and Risk Control

Equality provides another important key to understanding how freedom should be defined in products liability law, as it does in accident law more generally. In making product safety decisions, a manufacturing enterprise should accord equal respect to the interests of all persons likely to be affected—its owners, potential accident victims, and the vast majority of consumers who will not be injured and who need useful products that they can afford. Thus, although a manufacturer must respect the security interests of potential accident victims, the principle of equality demands that the type and amount of that respect be limited by a "due" respect to the conflicting interests of these other groups of persons. The proper balancing of these overlapping and competing interests is fraught with difficulty and may be considered "legislative" in its nature. Manufacturers must act paternalistically to protect—with equal concern and respect—the freedom and other interests of competing constituencies: shareholders are entitled to a fair return on their investments; potential accident victims are entitled to a fair measure of product safety; and users are entitled to a fair measure of usefulness in their products, a proper but not excessive level of product safety, and the availability of products at a fair price.

Before exploring how in moral theory a manufacturer should conduct this kind of legislative balance, it should be helpful to scrutinize the common assertion that safety interests of potential victims are inherently of a higher order than the interests of actors in "mere" money and convenience. Interest ordering along these lines, whereby the bodily integrity interest is accorded a higher abstract value than property and economic interests, has a long and deep tradition in the law of torts. Yet this ethic is rooted generally in the context of truly intentional takings, of palpably identifiable property interests known to belong to specific persons targeted by the actor, where the certainty of harm to vested "property rights" is clear. This form of interest ordering fits much less comfortably in accident law, however, which generally involves only remote and contingent harm in the form of risks to speculative interests of often unknown persons. While autonomy certainly is dependent on a person's health and safety, it also depends significantly on the state of a person's wealth—holdings of money and other property. Convenience by definition is what facilitates a person's achievement of chosen goals. The choice-harm principle itself is premised on the equality of one person's interest in security, including safety, with another's freedom of action to promote chosen goals—goals which often require the use of property and may be stored in monetary form. Of course this equality is one only of interests in the abstract, so that a person's safety interests should be protected against the action interests of another when the latter's interests (in profits, convenience, or other goods) are of lesser value by some fair measure. But the converse is also true: accident victims have no inherent moral right to derogate the greater profit-seeking (hence freedom-seeking) interests of product makers.

A manufacturer, therefore, must in moral theory accord equal ("due") respect to the individual interests of potential victims, consumers generally, and its shareholders. If the maker does not do so, if it subordinates the safety interests of potential victims to shareholder and general consumer interests of lower value, then it is morally responsible for resulting harm. But if instead, the maker properly strikes the balance, according due consideration to potential victim interests in making product safety decisions, then it has fulfilled its moral obligations and may not fairly be held accountable for resulting harm. Such harm to victims of product accidents, whose safety interests have been accorded due respect, should be considered "necessary" harm within the inherent limitations of science, technology, and the social calculus. And so the principle of equality appears to demand that manufacturers improve a product's safety as much as possible without increasing its price or decreasing its utility "unreasonably."

The equality analysis may be clarified by focusing more closely on the primary determinant of whether accidents occur: risk control. Because a person's freedom depends significantly upon his power, the tremendous imbalance in the allocation of risk control or power between makers and users is of significant moral and legal interest. When persons involved together in an accident are strangers to one another, the prior allocation of power between the two, like the allocation of any resource, is generally irrelevant to the issue of responsibility for the accident. The truth of this general proposition, however, depends upon the parties being strangers before the accident, not linked together in some relationship generating rights and duties between the two. Although the maker-user relationship is not ordinarily viewed as linking the parties closely, their fortunes in fact are intertwined significantly: makers owe their very existence to user demand for their products, and the welfare of "user-constituents" depends significantly upon how makers "legislate" on product usefulness, price, and safety. This form of relationship between makers and users is a sufficient link for morals and the law to require makers to take reasonable steps to employ their resources in a manner that is likely to protect users from unreasonable risks. In the modern world, the maker-user relationship probably creates in the minds of most consumers a generalized expectation of such protection, and equality of respect appears to demand it also.

More specifically, equality of respect demands, first, that a maker provide consumers with all important information that it possesses or should possess on the dangers in its products, and of course it should promise no more safety than its products truly have. Second, manufacturers are accountable for injuries resulting from production flaws, regardless of the maker's efforts or even power to prevent such errors. The manufacturer ordinarily has virtually exclusive power to prevent errors in the manufacturing process. From this enormous imbalance of power springs the demand, from equality, that makers bear responsibility for the consequences of production defects. This is so because the maker, as a legislator, is duty-bound to treat potential victims with equal respect to consumers generally and to shareholders. A consumer injured by a production defect is subjected to a vast disparity in both risk and result from consumers generally. This inequality is unfair and should be rectified because the victim paid an equal price for what was sold as and appeared to be a product of equal quality to those supplied to other consumers. Moreover, since the price charged by the maker and paid by the victim was for a product that was "good," but was really bad, restitutionary notions behind equality compel the maker to absorb the victim's losses and to transfer them to its shareholders.

The moral questions concerning dangers in design raise very different questions of equality and risk control. If the manufacturer should foresee that some aspect of a product's design will present a danger that may be hidden from consumers, it must respect their dignity by at least warning of the risk. Yet many products, chain saws for example, contain inherent dangers in design that are obvious for all to see. With products such as these, the consumer is not tricked into thinking that the product is safer than it really is, nor does he pay for safety value that is imaginary. Instead, when persons buy and use products with obvious, inherent dangers—or dangers that have been warned about—they make personal choices to engage the risk. When consumers suffer injury from risks that they deliberately selected to accomplish their personal objectives, or willingly accepted and chose to work around, equality and risk control have much to say about moral responsibility for the accident.

Equality requires manufacturers to provide potential victims with as much respect as given others, by building into products as much safety as dictated by reasonable—optimal—care. Yet manufacturers are also bound by principles of equality to stop there and to refuse to make their products safer than the point at which a proper balance reasonably appears to be struck between product value, for consumers generally, and profits, for their shareholders. This is the point of "optimal," rather than maximum, safety, where the interests of these other groups are accorded equal respect to the interests of potential victims.

The user, like the manufacturer, is obligated in moral theory to respect the equal worth of such other persons. A user who is injured unexpectedly by an unknown product characteristic in the course of normal use is not morally accountable for the accident. But if a user chooses to take the benefits of a well-made but obviously dangerous product, or if he puts any kind of product to a uniquely adventuresome use that he should know may exceed the product's capabilities, responsibility for the product's failure and the resulting harm properly lies with him. Here the user has no fair claim to compensation from the maker, diminishing the autonomy of the maker's owners and other consumers, because the accident was caused by the victim's greed in demanding greater usefulness from the product than other consumers sought and greater usefulness than was reflected in the price he paid. The principle of equality, therefore, suggests that consumers who knowingly and voluntarily engage a product's inherent risks, and those who put products to unfair use, are morally responsible for resulting harm. Thus, equality and risk control both are central concepts in the search for moral accountability for product accidents.

Utility and Efficiency

Also important to accountability for product accidents in moral theory, and dependent to a large extent on notions of equality and risk control, are the concepts of utility and efficiency. In utilitarian theory, the manufacturer's obligation is to make its products so as to maximize the welfare, or preferences, of its shareholders and consumers. Maximizing profits is the manufacturer's classic measure of success in satisfying the welfare of its shareholders. In a sense, the welfare of consumers also has a single measure: "product value." The concept of product value is more complex than monetary value, however, and it is therefore helpful to divide it into three separate components of consumer preference: product usefulness ("utility"), price ("affordability"), and safety.

A product's utility is measured by its ability to accomplish the consumer's goals, to satisfy the consumer's other preferences. Products help humans to achieve all kinds of goals: from work, education, and nourishment in body, to recreation, rest, and nourishment in spirit. Products facilitate autonomy by permitting individuals to develop and extend themselves; products facilitate community by increasing resources and by helping individuals relate to one another.

Price, in a competitive marketplace, is closely and functionally related to a product's usefulness. Consumers prefer, of course, that manufacturers minimize product prices to make them more affordable, leaving consumers with more money to satisfy their other preferences. Manufacturers generally prefer the opposite—to maximize prices until demand begins unduly to diminish. Manufacturers of most products might charge, in freedom theory, whatever price they choose, provided that consumers could ascertain the product's true extent of utility and safety. Consumers ordinarily are free, after all, to refuse to buy the product. Yet if the product contains an unnecessary danger hidden from consumers, and the price is not discounted to reflect this fact, consumers will be paying for apparent safety value attributable to the manufacturer that is false. In such cases, in part because of the surplus price paid for the product, the manufacturer generally should bear responsibility for resulting harm.

Safety is the final component of product value. In one sense, it is a negative value, for it is defined in terms of the absence of a detriment, danger, which itself is a negative concept: perfect safety, an unattainable ideal, means zero danger. Safety is a complex value in at least two important ways. First, it frequently concerns persons other than the parties to the exchange transaction, for products typically impose some risks on third parties, usually without their consent. Second, unlike utility and price, safety often is a hidden value, and its converse, danger, is often a hidden cost. This is true especially with drugs and other toxic substances, but it is also true in important respects with durable products, such as saws and cars. As a result of both these complicating factors, the relationship between safety and price often is quite weak, although it tends to strengthen over time.

The theory of utility requires manufacturers to maximize, as best they can, profits and product value—including product usefulness, affordability, and safety to consumers and third parties. The resulting problem for the manufacturer is that the goals of increasing profits and product value often conflict, as do the individual components of product value among themselves. Improving product safety, for example, typically diminishes both profits and affordability, as well as product usefulness.

Moral theory thus forces manufacturers into a complex, decisionmaking process. This form of decisionmaking is very difficult, for it requires the manufacturer to compare—and accord equal respect to—incommensurable values of different "constituencies" or interest groups. The task is rendered even more problematic by the inherent primacy of the manufacturer's allegiance to its shareholders—the constituency that gave it birth and with which it shares an identity. Utility (and equality) theory flounders here over the difficulty of making interpersonal comparisons among incommensurable values.

This is where economic efficiency can lend assistance to utility by assigning the balancing process to the market for decisions by consumers as a group. Consumer "voters" compare the legislated packages of usefulness, price, and safety offered by competing producer candidates, and they cast their ballots for those products that appear most likely to maximize their preferences. Votes are cast in dollars, which ultimately are converted into profits (or their opposite). The market thus provides manufacturers with an incentive to maximize consumer welfare by maximizing product value. Manufacturers thereby are encouraged to legislate "correctly," or efficiently, by maximizing the sum of utility and safety at prices consumers are willing to pay.

This model of efficiency, of course, suffers from a deep and false assumption—the existence of a perfect economic world where humans act rationally to maximize their wealth and where information and transactions both are free. In the real world, of course, there is an abundance of problems with these assumptions, beginning with the supposed rationality with which persons plan and live their lives. Nor is safety information ever entirely available or completely free. As discussed above, danger is always hidden at least to some extent from all parties—manufacturers, consumers, and third parties. And bargaining transactions between the parties on types and degrees of safety exist more in the minds of theorists than in the world: bargaining on product safety is difficult, to say the least, for persons contemplating the purchase of a car; it is virtually impossible for young children, employees, patients, and bystanders confronting product hazards. The market, as a surrogate for utility, cannot handle these two problems, and so it may be said to fail.

This is where the law of accidents, and products liability law in particular, can be put to an important instrumental use to promote efficiency and hence utility by "deterring" manufacturers from selling products that contain excessive dangers. Because efficiency suffers due to an insufficient level of safety information and safety transactions, the law should seek to increase (and optimize) them both. This suggests that the purpose of the law should be to encourage all affected parties to (1) take cost-effective measures to increase the stock of safety information, (2) distribute and act upon it in a cost-effective manner, and (3) facilitate safety transactions optimally among themselves. More specifically, the law should encourage manufacturers to (1) invest in cost-effective types and levels of research to discover product dangers, (2) provide consumers with as much safety information as may cost-effectively be conveyed, and (3) reduce production and design dangers in their products to the lowest cost-effective level.

There remains the question of what to do about scientifically unavoidable risks ("undiscoverable" or "unknowable" dangers) that result when an apparently good product—one apparently containing a proper balance of risk and utility—turns out after the fact, unforeseeably, to have an excessive type or level of danger in its design. This problem sometimes manifests itself long after the product was first sold and used. The doctrinal question in such cases involving unforeseeable generic risks, as where an apparently safe drug is discovered to be a carcinogen, is whether a manufacturer should have a duty to warn of unknowable risks, as discussed above. An argument sometimes proposed in favor of such a duty is that liability for such risks may serve instrumentally as an incentive for manufacturers to increase their levels of research to discover dangers at the threshold of knowledge, which may result in a net benefit for society. If liability for failing to warn of unknowable dangers really did have this result, and if the resulting benefits to potential victims really did exceed the detriments to other consumers and to shareholders, then utility and efficiency would support a rule of liability in such cases. But manufacturers should be investing optimally in research under a negligence standard of accountability, based on knowable risks alone, and extending liability to risks that cannot reasonably be discovered probably will not cause most manufacturers to do more research than they already think is best. Moreover, there is a real risk that a rule that holds manufacturers responsible for unforeseeable harm will result in "overdeterrence," to the net detriment of society, by inducing manufacturers to delay or completely forbear marketing useful products—especially new medicines made from potent chemicals—that may contain substantial unknown risks. Utility theory, as truth and equality, thus suggests that manufacturers are not morally accountable for generic dangers that cannot reasonably be discovered.

* * *

Conclusion

This article has thus far inquired generally into moral values underlying products liability problems and has offered a preliminary ordering of the major values. The enterprise now shifts to a search for enduring principles, following from the inquiry above, that may support a moral system of products liability rules. Constructing the rules themselves or, more accurately, adjusting the current rules to fit the moral structure, must remain a major future task that far exceeds the objectives of this article. The objective here is to propose first principles, reflecting the moral considerations developed earlier, that may provide a theoretical structure for products liability law. The following set of principles appears justifiable in moral principle:

FIRST PRINCIPLES OF PRODUCTS LIABILITY LAW

PRINCIPLES OF JUSTICE

1. Manufacturers should seek and tell the truth about product dangers.
2. Manufacturers should make products as safe as reasonably possible.
3. Consumers should use products as safely as reasonably possible.

PRINCIPLES OF LIABILITY

1. Manufacturers should be responsible for foreseeable harm caused by their misrepresentations.
2. Manufacturers should be responsible for foreseeable harm caused by their production defects.
3. Manufacturers should be responsible for foreseeable harm that reasonably could have been prevented by (a) designing out unreasonable dangers, or (b) providing danger information.

4. If foreseeable harm cannot be reduced to a reasonable level by redesign or the provision of danger information, and if the harm is likely to be unexpected by consumers or excessive when balanced against the product's benefits, the manufacturer should be responsible, and the product should be banned.
5. Users should be responsible for foreseeable harm caused by product uses that they should know to be unreasonably dangerous.

E. Comparative Law

J.A. Jolowicz, *Product Liability in the EEC, in* COMPARATIVE AND PRIVATE INTERNATIONAL LAW: ESSAYS IN HONOR OF JOHN HENRY MERRYMAN ON HIS SEVENTIETH BIRTHDAY (David S. Clark ed., 1990)*

During the last twenty years or so the phrase "product liability," an import from the United States, and its approximate translation into other European languages, have come into common use in Western Europe. Books and articles are devoted to the subject: the phrase itself has been described by a British Royal Commission as "an accepted term of art;" it has developed an extensive case law or jurisprudence in many countries; the Council of Europe opened a convention on the matter for signature in 1977; and in July 1985 the Council of Ministers of the European Communities adopted a Directive "on the approximation of the laws, regulations and administrative provisions of the Member States concerning liability for defective products."

This flurry of activity has not been accompanied by agreement on what "product liability" actually means. All that can be said with confidence is that it does not include cases in which the sole cause of the damage lies in the conduct of the product's user. No one regards as within "product liability" a simple traffic accident, for example, or a case in which a product is used as a weapon. Only products that are in some sense "defective" are considered to be capable of attracting "product liability": the idea has not been taken up that even a limited right to compensation, save through the social security system, should accrue to the victim of a product-related injury where the product in question is free of defect.

A Liability for Producing or a Liability for Selling?

Product Liability as Liability for Producing. The typical channel for the distribution of marketable goods uses a chain of contracts of sale, and it is rare that the person who buys something for his own use or consumption buys it directly from its producer. This being so, and given both the flexibility of the contract of sale and the relative ease with which its incidents can be adjusted by legislation aimed, for example, at consumer protection, the traditional view almost everywhere has been that conflicts arising from the alleged defective quality of goods should be dealt with in the contractual context. It is to his seller that the dissatisfied buyer should look, and this is no less true when his complaint is that the goods caused physical damage to his person or his property than when it is that he suffered economic loss because they did not perform as well as he was entitled to expect.

*Used by permission.

It is in line with this manner of thinking that those concerned with the improvement of consumer protection tend to look to the obligations imposed by law on sellers on other contractual suppliers of goods: in England, for example, considerable effort has been devoted in recent years to legislation concerning the terms to be implied in contracts of sale and to the control of clauses purporting to exclude the seller's liability. In 1962, an English committee on consumer protection defined "consumer" as a person who purchases (or hire-purchases) goods for private use or consumption and explicitly regretted the ignorance of the general public of the fact that the law imposes obligations on the retailer rather than on the manufacturer.

Since goods sold on the retail market will have reached their ultimate buyer through a chain of contracts, any liability incurred by the retail seller to his buyer may be passed up the chain and finally reach the manufacturer, but each action in the series is independent of the others and its outcome is determined by the contract between the parties to it. The loss incurred by the immediate victim of a product-related injury may or may not be transferred to the producer of the offending product, more or less as the parties decide in each case.

This system, so to call it, provides adequate redress for the buyer of a defective product provided only that his seller is not bankrupt. It can do nothing, however, for the victim who did not himself buy the product in question from anyone—the famous "innocent bystander"—and it seems likely that development of extra-contractual liability for product-related damage derives from the need to do something for him: certainly the pursuer in the great case of *Donoghue v. Stevenson* did not herself buy the ginger beer of whose alleged defective quality she complained. Notwithstanding the frequency with which bystanders suffer damage in the conditions of modern society, notwithstanding that the retail buyer may claim against the manufacturer on grounds similar to those which may be relied on by the bystander, the extra-contractual liability of the producer tends to be seen as something exceptional which should be brought into play only where the contractual liability of the seller fails to meet the need. It is not surprising, therefore, either that the producer's extra-contractual liability should be made dependent on his fault or that it should be limited to physical damage to person or property. The person who has not bought the product from his chosen defendant, whether he bought it from someone else or not, cannot be heard to complain against that defendant that he suffered some purely economic loss such as a loss of profits simply because the product in question failed to function or because it caused damage to property not his own but on which he was economically dependent.

There can be little doubt that this way of thinking has largely informed English law up to the present time. It is true that there has been alleviation of the burden of proving the defendant producer's negligence which the law casts on the plaintiff, and it is true also that there has been a tentative move, now apparently reversed, towards allowing recovery for pure economic loss in tort, but, until compelled to do so by the Directive, the United Kingdom Parliament has consistently declined to pay serious regard to recommendations for the introduction of strict liability in tort for defective products. In contract, on the other hand, recovery for pure economic loss is a matter of routine and it has been made abundantly clear that the seller's liability is in no way dependent on his fault: in one important case the seller of a defective product which caused damage to the plaintiff's property was held liable notwithstanding that, "in the then state of knowledge, scientific and commercial, no deliberate exercise of human skill or judgment" could have avoided the defect or averted the damage.

Subject to certain specialized exceptions of which the German Law on Pharmaceutical Products of 1976 is the prime example, the approach in many Continental countries, including Germany, has been much the same even though the contractual protection may sometimes be extended beyond the actual purchaser to members of his family, his employees, and so on. It is of considerable importance for present purposes that the famous German "Fowlpest" case of 1968, generally regarded as a most important advance in product liability law, achieved its purpose through adjustment of the rules about burden of proof in tort.

The legal systems so far mentioned—most emphatically the English—thus see the liability of the producer of a defective product as falling squarely within the law of tort, and this means that they see it as a liability imposed in respect of some wrong that the producer has done—the production and marketing of defective goods. This leads to an almost instinctive sense that liability must depend on fault: why should a producer of useful goods be called upon to pay if no criticism can be legitimately levelled at his behaviour? That, of course, is not the whole story, but it does mean that those who argue that the liability of the producer of a defective product should be strict—by advancing the now familiar arguments of risk distribution, facility of insurance by the producer, proximity of producer to consumer through the advertising media, and so on—face an uphill struggle; their task is made even harder when they are met, as they are, by arguments based not just on the inherent "unfairness" of imposing tortious liability on a person who is blameless, but also on the inhibiting effect that strict liability is supposed to involve on the introduction of new products.

Product Liability as Liability for Selling. In France a different understanding of the producer's position has emerged and has led to a different conception of "product liability". That understanding, in short, takes as its starting point the fact that the producer of goods who is not also a seller of goods is *rarissima avis.* Why, then, should he not be subjected to the liabilities that are appropriate to sellers even if he did not sell the offending product directly to the victim of its defect? It is true that even the French have not been able to extend this to the case of the bystander who did not himself buy the offending product from anyone, but in French law the ultimate purchaser has a direct action in contract against the producer and the producer's liability is strict. What is more, taking the view that the distinction between the retail purchaser and the bystander in the present context cannot withstand analysis save on technical legal grounds, valiant and successful efforts have been made to give to the tortious or extra-contractual liability of the producer a content which, from a practical point of view, is virtually indistinguishable from the contractual. The manner in which French law has arrived at these results is sufficiently striking to call for brief description here.

Taken at face value, the relevant provisions of the French civil code are ill-adapted to the purposes to which they have been put. So far as contractual liability is concerned, contracts ordinarily bind only the parties to them. In the particular case of sale, the seller of goods is liable only for hidden defects under his so-called *garantie,* and then not for consequential damage unless he actually knew of the defect at the time of sale; only the seller in bad faith is obliged to do more than repay the price against return of the defective goods or reimburse the buyer for their diminished value. So far as tortious liability is concerned the principal provision imposes liability for fault alone; though there is a provision imposing liability without fault for damage done by things that one has *sous sa garde,* once a producer has sold his product into the channels of distribution it is no longer *sous sa garde,* and the provision is inapplicable.

1. *Contract.* The problem of privity was overcome long ago in a context unconnected with product liability by recognition that a direct contractual action might be brought by the person at the end of a chain of contracts against any other person in the chain, but that is barely half the battle. The essential problem was to provide the victim with a worthwhile remedy against the producer who does not actually know that his product is defective. After one false start, the way was found through the idea that a seller who, because of his own inadequacies of skill or performance, is ignorant of a defect should not on that account escape liability. This led to the introduction of a kind of rebuttable presumption of knowledge, but now, in the ease of a "professional" seller, the presumption is irrebuttable and is essentially one of law: proof by the victim of a hidden defect and of consequential damage is sufficient.

It might have been thought that this was enough, but from the victim's point of view the action based on the *garantie* against hidden defects still has some disadvantages: the defect must be "hidden" and it must be such as to render the product unfit for use; the plaintiff must prove that the defect existed, at the latest, when the product was delivered; the action must be brought within a "brief delay." To overcome these difficulties, therefore, a plaintiff is now allowed to rely on the contention that the seller's general contractual liability—his *responsabilité contractuelle de droit commun*—is engaged. Strictly speaking, once delivery has been effected, only the action on the *garantie* should be available for thereafter the buyer can demand neither the rescission of the contract nor damages for its breach. But the courts do not always adhere to this and are prepared to award damages for any carelessness or negligence on the part of the producer in the design, the manufacture, or the commercialization, including failure to give adequate warnings or instructions, of the product.

2. *Tort.* Since it is only the bystander who must (or may) rely on the extra-contractual liability of the producer, such liability plays a much less important role in the approach to product liability in France than elsewhere. In any case, as the French seem to be well aware, a producer does not become any the less a seller simply because the victim of his defective product did not himself buy it from any one. The result has been that the tortious liability of the producer is now, in its practical effect, virtually indistinguishable from the contractual.

Two techniques, one principal and one subsidiary, have been used to bring French law to this result. In the first place French courts have shown increased willingness to presume the fault on which liability normally depends, and this has gone so far that proof of defect or, rather, proof that the producer put a defective product on the market, is itself sufficient. This development was assisted by a more general movement towards the view that breach of a contractual obligation which causes damage to a third party is normally to be considered a "fault" for the purposes of extra-contractual liability.

The second device was to make use of an adaptation—admittedly a controversial one—of the rule of strict liability for damage done by a thing a person has *sous sa garde:* the French courts succeeded in dividing the concept of *garde* in such a way that the person who acquires a product acquires the *garde* only of its behaviour *(comportement); garde* of its *structure* remains with the person best able to know its internal properties and composition. It follows, for example, that in cases of explosion, of fire, or of poisoning it is sufficient for the victim to prove that his damage was caused by the "structure" of the thing—he need not even prove defect, let alone fault.

GARY T. SCHWARTZ, *Product Liability and Medical Malpractice in Comparative Context, in* THE LIABILITY MAZE: THE IMPACT OF LIABILITY LAW ON SAFETY AND INNOVATION (Peter W. Huber & Robert E. Litan eds., 1991)*

Discussions of modern American tort law often tend to assume that this law is a uniquely American phenomenon, that our own tort doctrines are vastly out of line with those accepted by

*Used by permission.

foreign legal systems. To test this assumption, I describe those tort doctrines in the fields of product liability and malpractice that prevail in England, Germany, France, and Japan. What I find, contrary to the common assumption, is that foreign tort doctrine is reasonably close to American doctrine. I also discover, however, that the rates of litigation and the costs of liability in those countries are only a small fraction of what they are here.

Since the differences in formal doctrine can account for no more than a limited part of these great differentials in tort costs, the effort to explain the latter must turn to features of the tort system other than doctrine itself. In providing this explanation, I consider, first, several ways in which American civil procedure differs from the procedures used elsewhere: here the focus is on pre-trial discovery, trial by jury, and the role played by counsel in preparing and examining witnesses. Next, I consider, in comparative context, the American system of remunerating lawyers, a system that includes both the so-called American rule and the contingent fee. I then turn to the rules and practices relied on in measuring and calculating damages. Finally, I look briefly at social welfare programs in effect in other countries, to ascertain how they might influence either the size of eventual damage awards or the more general motives for bringing suit. All these are factors that seem to be relevant to the burden of liability not only individually but in combination. What I find, in essence, is that the American tort system includes several distinctive features that interact with each other in a synergistic way. To be sure, the line that I generally draw between substantive doctrine on the one hand and procedural (and remedial) features on the other does not always hold up: at times, it is the interaction between substance and procedure that seems responsible for America's high levels of products and malpractice litigation.

[*Editor's note*: Discussions of medical malpractice law are omitted.]

While the multistate variety of American tort law makes that law somewhat difficult to summarize, the effort to understand the law of non-English-speaking countries discomforts the analyst by requiring him to rely on a limited number of secondary sources. Moreover, describing product liability doctrine in foreign legal systems turns out to be an especially daunting task. Product liability jurisprudence, though primarily tort law, tends also to include elements of contract law and sales law. The analyst can be confident that he has an insider's understanding of how this combination works within his own legal system; but as an outsider, he should be humble in making statements about what such a combination adds up to in a foreign system. Mindful of this need for humility, I set forth the following evaluations.

The practice of manufacturer "no liability" that prevailed in the United States until about 1920 survived for an additional decade or so in England. In a leading 1932 case, however, English law concluded that manufacturers can be held generally liable for their negligence; yet even after that decision English plaintiffs may have encountered difficulties in trying to prove manufacturer negligence. Before 1960, French law primarily adhered to the idea that manufacturers could be liable for fault or negligence; however, negligence could be sufficiently difficult to establish so as sometimes to provide French manufacturers with an immunity from tort liability. In Germany a practice of no liability survived until 1968. One special feature of German tort law is that it has never fully accepted the doctrine of respondeat superior (the doctrine that renders an employer automatically liable for any negligence in its employee's conduct). So, as late as the mid-1960s, even if the German consumer injured by a product defect could show that this defect was due to the negligence of the manufacturer's employee, the consumer could not recover unless there was reason to believe that the manufacturer was guilty of some negligence in either hiring or supervising the employee.

By 1980, however, all three of these legal systems had lightened the plaintiff's burden of proof in cases involving manufacturing defects. English law now allows plaintiffs who sue because of manufacturing defects to take advantage of "the doctrine of res ipsa loquitur or its practical equivalents"; as a result, under English law the manufacturer is now "virtually an insurer against manufacturing defects." As a formal caption for a legal doctrine, "res ipsa loquitur" seems unique to American and English law. Yet Germany and France, though deprived of the res ipsa caption, have reached results that are about as strong as England's. In Germany a leading 1968 case shifted the burden of proof to the manufacturer, requiring the manufacturer to explain the defect in an exonerating way in order to defeat liability; given the difficulty of discharging this burden, in manufacturing defect cases German law "greatly approximates . . . strict tort liability." In France, at least so long as the flaw in the product is "hidden," there is now a presumption of negligence running against the manufacturer that is almost conclusive; in this way French law likewise "approximate[s] strict liability." The French legal position is in part derived from a civil code section imposing liability on a person "for the injury [caused] by the act of . . . things that he has under his guard": French courts now conclude that the manufacturer has a continuing "guard" over the internal structure of the products it sells.

In defective product cases, practices in Japan provide for the possibility of two sorts of sanctions that are nearly unheard of in the United States and Europe. Social customs associated with the Japanese tort system sometimes require company officials to deliver personal apologies to victims and their families. Moreover, under Japanese law a company official who departs from the duty to avoid the sale of defective products can be subjected to criminal prosecution; apparently, however, such prosecutions are initiated only when the official's conduct seems seriously irresponsible and only if the hazardous line of products turns out to injure large numbers of consumers.

Turning now to the more conventional remedy of tort compensation, one can note that Japanese law—unlike that of America and Europe—evidently never harbored any rule or practice of no liability. Currently Japanese courts apply a negligence standard in product cases. It is, moreover, a broad version of that standard: manufacturers bear a "very high duty of care." Accordingly, a manufacturing defect in a product justifies an inference of fault on the part of the manufacturer. This inference is described as moving Japanese law "very close" to strict liability; the rule likewise renders Japanese law equivalent to the law in European countries.

How do these legal systems deal with the manufacturer's possible liability for inadequate product design? One 1982 House of Lords case makes clear that English manufacturers can incur liability for negligent design. In a 1986 case the defendant, in assembling a specialized sports car, incorporated an engine marketed by the Ford Motor Company. That engine included a design feature that entailed a small risk of a carburetor fire. Although acknowledging that the chance of a harmful incident was "quite small," an English court perceived that the harm that could ensue from such an incident would be quite serious; accordingly, the court found the design inadequate. The court also rejected the defendant's claim that it had behaved reasonably in accepting an engine marketed and recommended by an industry leader like Ford. Rather, the court reasoned, the defendant, though apparently a small-scale concern, had an obligation to conduct its own engineering review of the adequacy of the Ford design.

This case apart, English law is thin in providing helpful clarification of the meaning of the negligence concept in its application to product design issues. But there have been interesting rulings on design liability in Canada, a country whose courts take seriously the precedent of English common-law doctrine. One Canadian court has ruled that car manufacturers can be found negligent (and hence held liable) for having failed to design automobiles in an appropriate "crashworthy" way. Another Canadian court, in discussing the obligation of a manufacturer to adopt a safer alternative design when it is "available" and sufficiently "reasonable," has said that "it is not material that [this alternative design] may have been more costly"; moreover, the court made clear that the manufacturer cannot relieve itself of its obligation to adopt such a design by warning the consumer of the danger in the existing design. In light of these rulings, this case goes about as far as any American case in suggesting the breadth of manufacturers' design liability.

Claims of negligent design have clearly been permitted by German law; the plaintiff must identify a feasible alternative design that suggests that the manufacturer's chosen design poses an unreasonable risk of injury. French law likewise approves of the theory of negligent design. It is hard to figure out, however, what the criteria are for ascertaining negligence in these design cases; in particular, it is uncertain what emphasis French law places on "hidden" hazards in negligent design cases. Claims of negligent design are also viable under Japanese law. In one case involving a Mitsubishi automobile, a Japanese court ruled that since the manufacturer operates under a "high duty of care," it can be found negligent even if its design complies with both public regulation and industry practice; in this respect, Japanese law is in harmony with modern American legal norms. (French and German law also reject the defense of regulatory compliance.) In Japan the courts, in ruling that the approval of a drug by the Japanese equivalent of the Food and Drug Administration does not afford the drug manufacturer a tort defense, extend their aggressiveness by rejecting any doctrine of governmental immunity and hence holding the government liable along with the drug manufacturers on a joint-and-several basis. (To be sure, by calling for a sharing of liability between manufacturer and government, Japanese law reduces the liability the manufacturer would otherwise bear on its own.)

A manufacturer's negligent failure to warn has also produced liability under these countries' legal systems. In Japan drug manufacturers have been held responsible for side effects that they were evidently unaware of when they sold the drugs, but that they could have learned of had they done a more extensive job of premarketing testing. In France courts has been described as engaging in a "strict" and "stringent" review of the adequacy of product warnings. A 1983 case concerned an adhesive product sold in a package that contained warning labels identifying the product as "highly flammable"; despite these labels, the court found the manufacturer liable for a failure to provide explicit instructions on how to use the product safely. In Germany a 1972 case perceived that the warning obligations borne by drug manufacturers were "especially strict." In addition, German law has obliged the manufacturer to provide warnings about product hazards that relate to "the intended product use in its broadest sense"; accordingly, manufacturers, while not required to warn about clear instances of misuse, must nevertheless provide warnings that relate to a considerable range of "foreseeable misapplications." In this regard, German law has moved much of the way in the American direction. In one case a German court ruled that Honda (and its importer) had failed to warn existing owners of Honda motorcycles about the dangers of attaching to that motorcycle a windshield that another company had recently begun to market. By imposing on manufacturers (and importers) a duty to warn that continues long after the original product sale and by combining that duty with a requirement that manufacturers conduct tests on accessories produced by independent companies, this case in its own way goes further than any American failure-to-warn opinion. In England a leading failure-to-warn case is *Wright v. Dunlop Rubber Company*. *Wright* can be interestingly compared with *Borel v. Fibreboard Paper Products Corp.*, the 1973 American opinion that has provided the framework for American asbestos litigation. *Borel* holds that when a manufacturer sells a product to an employer, the manufacturer has an obligation to warn of the extent to which the workers' exposure to that product might induce instances of occupational disease. In England the year before, the *Wright* court had reached the same conclusion. To be sure, *Borel* goes further than *Wright* in specifying that the warning needs to run directly to workers; *Wright* seems to assume that a warning to the employer is sufficient. In another respect, however, *Wright* may go further than *Borel. Borel* authorizes liability whenever the manufacturer "knows or should know" of the hazard in the product it sells. Under *Wright,* however, once the manufacturer merely acquires "suspicions" of the product's hazard, the obligation to warn attaches.

In design and warning cases, English courts have thus been capable of applying the negligence standard in an aggressive way. Nevertheless, negligence rather than strict liability has been the formal standard of liability. Accordingly—and leaving aside certain very recent developments, of which more below—English courts (and European courts generally) would agree with the American view that manufacturers are not liable in design or warning cases for hazards that were not reasonably knowable at the time of original product sale. In both Germany and Japan, however, statutes have been adopted that provide remedies for patients injured by the possibly unexpected side effects of drugs. The German statute, adopted in 1976, imposes liability on the manufacturers of prescription drugs in circumstances in which

> (1) the drug has harmful effects in the course of its prescribed use which objectively exceed acceptable limits in the light of medical scientific knowledge and whose cause lies in the field of development or manufacturing or (2) the detriment has occurred as a consequence of a label, disclosure for experts or disclosure for users not in accordance with medical scientific knowledge.

Apparently, the meaning of this language has not yet been fleshed out by any major judicial opinions. German scholars tend to assume that the statute imposes strict liability. Yet the statute's emphasis on "medical scientific knowledge" raises doubt about exactly how strict its liability rule really is. Whatever the extent of this strictness, liability under the German statute is a limited liability: the drug manufacturer does not bear liability for the victim's pain and suffering, no one plaintiff can recover more that DM 500,000 (now about $325,000), and the cap on liability for any one drug is subject to a limit of DM 200 million ($134 million).

The Japanese statute, enacted in 1979, undeniably provides benefits on a no-fault basis; like the German statute, it excludes compensation for pain and suffering and places limits on the individual victim's recovery. The fund is financed partly by government contributions but primarily by levies imposed on drug manufacturers and importers according to a formula that relies largely on each manufacturer's sales proceeds; unlike the German statute, the Japanese statute does not impose actual liability on the particular manufacturer. But this manufacturer does not avoid all responsibility. For one thing, the formula for the levy takes into account the number of claims involving the manufacturer's products during the previous year. In addition, if the manufacturer is guilty of negligence in the individual case, the victim can ignore the fund and sue the manufacturer directly for full damages under a negligence theory. Or, the victim having recovered from the fund, the fund can then secure indemnification from the negligent manufacturer.

Recent Law Reform

The multinational law I have described is law that was largely in place by 1980. There are also recent law-reform efforts in Japan and Europe that need to be examined. In 1975 a number of Japanese legal scholars organized themselves and prepared a draft of a model product liability law. In many respects, this model law was designed to codify and clarify what already were

Japanese product liability practices; in other respects, the model was designed to set forth new legal standards. In particular, the model law would shift the formal standard of liability from negligence to strict liability—strict liability, that is, once the plaintiff has established some "defect" in the product itself. The draft model law goes on to define "defect" as "any flaw in a product which causes an inordinate danger to life, to the person, or to property during ordinarily foreseeable use." Also, "when determining the existence of a defect, any statements or warnings concerning the product shall be taken into account." [*Editor's note*: On June 22, 1994, the Japanese legislature enacted a revision of this model law.]

In January 1977 the Council of Europe's "Convention on Product Liability" was opened for signatures. In that year the Convention was signed by Belgium, France, Austria, and Luxembourg. However, no signatures have been obtained since 1977, largely because European countries were aware that the European Community (EC) had begun working on the draft of a directive on product liability. Moreover, even the states that signed the Convention never went on to formally ratify it; for lack of the requisite number of ratifications, the Convention has never gone into effect. Meanwhile the EC Directive, after years of discussion, was finally adopted on July 25, 1985, and then "notified" on July 30, 1985. Such directives are not generally self-enforcing; the Product Liability Directive calls on all member states to adopt implementing legislation by July 30, 1988. England complied with its obligation by adopting a Consumer Protection Act in 1987. Germany approved its implementing statute in late 1989; the statute went into effect on January 1, 1990.

What are the legal doctrines that the Directive endorses? Under article 1 of the Directive, "the producer shall be liable for damage caused by a defect in his product." Since there is no mention of negligence here, the producer's liability is implicitly strict liability. Of course, to say that a producer is strictly liable for a product "defect" is to spotlight the importance of the definition of "defect." According to article 6, "a product is defective when it does not provide the safety which a person is entitled to expect, taking all circumstances into account, indicating the presentation of the product." This is without doubt a weak definition. Indeed, it runs the risk of being viciously circular, since one is "entitled" to expect that level of safety which the law itself requires. Moreover, by requiring that "all circumstances [be taken] into account" in identifying defects, the Directive emphasizes how unstructured and open-ended its criterion of defect seems to be. The Directive's definition also makes no effort to take advantage of the American experience with the defect concept: it does not distinguish between manufacturing defects, design defects, and warning defects, nor does it establish criteria that would enable courts to identify any of those defects. The language of "the safety which a person is entitled to expect" seems to resemble the "ordinary consumer expectations" theme that once was popular in American product liability law. In America, however, that theme has declined in popularity, as judges and scholars have come to appreciate the nebulousness of the "consumer expectations" notion. American law, of course, refers to "consumer expectations," while the Directive refers to the expectations of "a person." Apparently, controversy is already raging within the Community about whether the article 6 concept of "a person" should be interpreted as including "producing persons" as well as "consumer persons."

The Directive makes clear that a product "shall not be considered defective for the *sole reason* that a better product is subsequently put into circulation" (emphasis added). This does not entail, however, the rejection of any pro-plaintiff position that an American court might adopt: the most that such a court might hold is that a later, better product is *some evidence* of the earlier product's defectiveness. The Directive also says that a manufacturer is not liable if "the defect is due to compliance . . . with mandatory regulations issued by the public authorities." This language falls short of establishing that compliance with regulations is a full defense. Rather, its point seems to be that a design that is *compelled* by public regulation cannot be regarded as defective and actionable. (Only if a design has been so compelled can it be said that the defect is "due to" the manufacturer's compliance with the regulation.) One American court has indeed ruled in favor of liability in such a case; however, that ruling seems like something of a fluke.

On one key point concerning the standard of liability, the Directive seems unintentionally ambiguous; on another key point, the Directive intentionally avoids taking a definitive position. The ambiguity relates to the Directive's attitude toward the American doctrine of "foreseeable misuse." The Directive refers to the manufacturers obligation to take precautions against "the use to which it could reasonably be expected that the product would be put." By referring to "reasonably expected" uses rather than "reasonable" uses, the language of the Directive can be read as sympathizing with the American doctrine. The preamble to the Directive disputes that doctrine, however, by indicating that the manufacturer should bear no liability in the event of consumer "misuses" of its product that are "not reasonable."

The issue on which the Directive withholds final judgment concerns the manufacturer's liability for product hazards that were not reasonably knowable at the time of original product sale. Recall that most American jurisdictions recognize a state-of-the-art limitation on liability, primarily in design and warning cases. What Americans talk about in "state-of-the-art" terms is what Europeans discuss in the language of "development risk." How to handle development risks was the most controversial issue the Community faced in preparing its Directive. In the Directive the EC Council of Ministers left this controversy unresolved. Under article 7(e) of the Directive, the producer bears no liability if the defect in the product could not have been "discovered" at the time the product was originally placed in circulation, on account of "the state of scientific and technical knowledge at the time." However, article 15.1 (b) says that member states, in passing legislation to implement the Directive, have the option of dispensing with this "unknowability" defense. Options like this obviously reduce the extent to which the Directive can achieve its stated goal of Community-wide uniformity. Acknowledging this difficulty, article 15 goes on to provide that in 1995 the Council of Ministers will reconsider the matter and make a recommendation on whether the article 7(e) defense should be repealed. Both the English and the German statutes, implementing the Directive, have incorporated the article 7(e) unknowability limitation on liability; so far, the only member state to exclude this limitation is Luxembourg. Disagreement about the limitation is apparently the prime reason that no implementing statute has yet been passed in France.

As for affirmative defenses in product liability cases, the Directive sets forth rules that do not much differ from those in effect in the United States. For example, disclaimers of liability are ineffective, and something like comparative negligence is the primary doctrinal response to issues of faulty behavior by the victim. In three other respects, however, the Directive comes across as distinctly conservative by American standards. The Directive, first of all, includes not only a conventional statute of limitations but also a statute of repose: all liabilities called for by the Directive are extinguished ten years after the date at which the product is put into circulation. Repose statutes have been adopted by American legislatures—but only in a minority of states, most of them with relatively small populations. Moreover, American repose statutes typically include important exceptions: for example, an exception for drugs that produce diseases only after long latency periods. The Directive's statute of repose is, by contrast, without exceptions; it would thus go a long way, for example, toward eliminating the liability of asbestos manufacturers and companies that make products like DES.

The Directive's damage provisions can likewise be regarded as conservative. The Directive gives countries the option of incorporating a ceiling on liability for all damages resulting from a particular product line; this ceiling "may not be less than 70 million ECU." (At the time the Directive was adopted, this sum was equivalent to $51 million; currently, it is worth more than $70 million.) No American jurisdiction currently provides any aggregate on liability of the sort the Directive authorizes. England, however, has declined the Directive's option; its 1987 implementing statute does not include any ceiling on liability. But the new German statute does incorporate a liability cap of DM 160 million (approximately $106 million). In endorsing a cap, Germany was undoubtedly drawing on the "precedent" of its earlier drug statute.

The third conservative feature in the Directive is one that needs to be carefully described. Article 9 states that the Directive, standing alone, does not provide for the award of "non-material damage"—that is, damages for pain and suffering. Article 9 then goes on to say, however, that "this Article shall be without prejudice to national provisions relating to non-material damage." In pondering the meaning of article 9, one should consider article 13, which says that the Directive "shall not affect any rights which an injured person" has under his own nation's laws "at the moment when" the Directive was notified—July 30, 1985. This article is a key part of the Directive; under its auspices, for example, plaintiffs, by relying on negligence theories endorsed by their member states in 1985, can assert claims that otherwise would be wiped out by the Directive's statute of repose or precluded by the ceiling on liability the Directive authorizes. As for article 9, it can be interpreted as deriving its meaning from article 13; under this interpretation, the plaintiff, in order to collect pain-and-suffering damages, needs to invoke article 13 and assert a claim that relies on his member state's 1985 version of negligence law.

Article 9 is, however, ambiguous. It might mean—quite independently of article 13—that the ability of the plaintiff who asserts his strict liability claim (as implemented by his member state's statute) to collect pain-and-suffering damages depends on whether those damages are recoverable in analogous circumstances under his member state's own tort law. This is the interpretation of article 9 that is supported by the EC official who has been most closely involved in the Directive's evolution. Under this interpretation, pain-and-suffering damages *can* be recovered in a strict liability action filed in England, since English tort doctrine usually allows for the recovery of pain-and-suffering damages. However, the plaintiff who files a strict liability claim under the German implementing statute would not be able to recover those damages, given the German tradition of withholding recovery for pain and suffering in the context of strict liability. But the German plaintiff, by invoking article 13, can allege negligence under 1985 German doctrine and thereby seek compensation for his pain and suffering.

Under the first interpretation of article 9, plaintiffs throughout the European Community, wanting to maximize their chances of recovering for their economic losses, will file an EC-oriented strict liability claim; however, wanting to create the possibility of recovering for pain and suffering, those same plaintiffs will also file a claim under their member states' 1985 negligence doctrines. Under article 9's second interpretation, the English plaintiff can recover all damages by suing under EC-oriented strict liability; the German plaintiff, however, will find it necessary to join an EC-oriented strict liability claim with a claim under the 1985 German version of the negligence doctrine. These patterns of claims that the Directive can be expected to produce run the risk of turning the Directive into something of a debacle. One objective commonly associated with strict liability is the simplification of litigation. Given, however, the way in which the Directive, under either interpretation, will frequently require plaintiffs to join quite different theories, one of its consequences will be to render litigation much more complex. Indeed, a major early round of litigation will be needed merely to resolve the basic ambiguity in article 9 itself; and however that ambiguity is resolved, many plaintiffs' rights to recover for pain and suffering will depend, for the indefinite future, on the fortuity of exactly what form their own member state's negligence doctrine had assumed on one magic moment in 1985. I use vivid language like this because these 1985 doctrines do seem somewhat frozen in place. It seems clear enough that they cannot be enlarged in a pro-plaintiff way by any action taken by a member state's legislature or judiciary. (Such an enlargement would lead to a greater degree of nonuniformity within the EC than is tolerated by article 13.) Moreover, given the "shall not affect any rights" language of article 13, it is at least arguable that these lawmaking bodies are not permitted to diminish plaintiffs' mid-1985 rights either.

Patterns of Litigation and Costs of Liability

United States: Then and Now. I have described above the expansion of American product liability doctrine over the last thirty years. I can now report that during that thirty-year period the number of product liability claims has increased dramatically. As it happens, claim levels seem to have remained relatively stable in the 1960s. From 1970 through the mid-1980s, however, claims rose dramatically. Indeed, between 1974 and 1986 the number of annual product liability filings in federal court increased from 1,600 to 12,500. Obviously, the expansion of doctrine in large part explains this growth in claims. But there are other explanations as well. One explanatory point is that lawyers have taken effective advantage of the opportunities afforded them by modern doctrine: they have become skillful in uncovering and proving the facts of a complicated product case. Another point—one which suggests that current claim levels might be artificially high—is that in recent years a limited number of products that have proved exceptionally hazardous (including asbestos and the Dalkon Shield) have generated a large number of claims. A third point concerns the quantum of damages. Studies undertaken by the Rand Institute for Civil Justice show that the average personal injury verdict in cases involving serious personal injury at least tripled in after-inflation dollars between the early 1960s and the early 1980s; moreover, for reasons that are not yet well understood, there now seems to be an additional "premium" in the verdicts in product liability cases (and malpractice cases as well). Undoubtedly, this surge towards much larger recoveries in product liability cases has been one factor encouraging the filing of product liability claims.

Other countries. What can be said, however, about the level of product litigation in the United States compared with the levels in other countries? A recent article by P. S. Atiyah compares liability in England and the United States. According to his calculations, the lawsuit-per-capita rate for all of tort law in the United States is about four times what it is in England; moreover, the per-capita cost of torts in this country is, in his estimate, perhaps ten times the English cost. His product liability numbers are even more one-sided: there are 70,000 product liability lawsuits in the United States annually, and only 200 in the United Kingdom. To be sure, the 350-to-1 ratio these numbers provide may be misleading. For one thing, as Atiyah makes clear, "claims" may lead to "lawsuits" more frequently in this country than they do in England; the American-English claims ratio might therefore be much less than the lawsuit ratio. Additionally, in England, as in the United States, there are large numbers of employees who have suffered disease on account of exposure to asbestos. In America tort suits resulting from these diseases are brought against manufacturers (since employers are shielded from tort liability by the exclusivity doctrine in workers' compensation). In England, however, an employee injured on the job not only has a workers' compensation-type claim (which he enforces against a government compensation fund) but also a possible tort action against his employer. Moreover, an English statute imposing on employers a near strict liability to keep job sites free of asbestos makes these tort actions against employers especially easy to win. Accordingly, asbestos victims in England usually sue their employers in tort and make no effort to bring much more complicated actions against product manufacturers. A high volume of asbestos litigation thus exists in England, but it focuses on employer defendants and so does not swell the number of product liability claims against manufacturers (as it does in the United States).

Because of factors such as these, the notion of a 350-to-1 American-English product liability relationship is not meaningful. Still, without a doubt product liability is thriving in the United States in a way that it is not in England. This point can be confirmed by two simple observations. As of 1988 no product liability verdict had ever been entered against a drug manufacturer; and until the 1986 specialty sports-car case described earlier, no auto manufacturer had ever been held liable under a theory of negligent design. Furthermore, there is reason to believe that the huge difference between the level of product liability in the United States and its level in England is matched by similar differences between the United States and other countries. John Fleming's 1982 article described the German strict liability drug statute enacted in 1976. Between 1976 and 1982 not a single claim had been filed under the statute. Five years later the liability costs that drug companies were incurring because of the statute equaled less than one-half of one percent of those companies' sales revenues. A Canadian product liability defense lawyer recently discussed one product that was widely distributed both in the United States and Canada. In the United States there were a thousand claims against the manufacturer because of that product; in Canada, only eight. One study of product liability in the Netherlands reported that in the past fifty years only five cases by injured consumers against the manufacturers of allegedly defective products resulted in published judicial opinions. The 1985 EC Directive has occasioned a spate of law review articles written (or coauthored) by European scholars. None of these articles suggest significant pre-Directive differences in the litigation patterns from one member state to another, and several articles indicate that the litigation rate in the country under study is no more than a fraction of what the rate is perceived to be in the United States.

Nor is there much indication that complying with the EC Directive will sharply increase the scope of liability within EC member states. The important limitations (and ambiguities) in the Directive have already been described. Acknowledging these limitations, one recent article concludes that the Directive ''will bring hardly any change in the pattern of products liability decisions'' in Germany, and that throughout the EC ''the Directive will not bring about much change in the failure to warn area.'' Another article perceives that ''the Directive does not markedly advance the substantive law of a country like the Netherlands.'' Insurance companies are now confirming these scholarly assessments; I am advised that when Germany's implementing statute went into effect on January 1, 1990, product liability insurers in Germany did not see fit to increase their premiums.

As described earlier, the product liability rules applied in the United States differ in certain ways from those applied in other legal systems. These differences, however, are limited rather than extreme; hence they are not capable of providing more than a portion of the explanation for the order-of-magnitude discrepancies between levels of litigation in various legal systems. It follows, then, that much of the explanation for these discrepancies must come from elements of the legal system that extend beyond product liability doctrine itself. What these elements are is a question considered in a later section.

To be sure, the discussion so far has concerned Europe rather than Japan. As far as Japan is concerned, it is often pointed out that the number of trials and lawsuits in Japan (both for personal injury and for other kinds of losses) is quite low. One explanation commonly offered for this is that the Japanese legal system is costly and inefficient in a way that discourages the presenting of claims. A second common explanation is that Japanese cultural attitudes inhibit victims from even considering bringing lawsuits. However, Mark Ramseyer, focusing on auto accidents in Japan, offers a different description. Although Ramseyer agrees that the number of Japanese auto accident cases that are finally tried in court is low, he thinks the legal system functions effectively—providing parties with such clear signals on the likely judicial results that the parties can (and do) settle claims for appropriate values without coming near the courthouse. Claims centers set up by liability insurance companies often facilitate these settlements. A small number of auto accident trials in Japan is thus compatible with a large number of claims and appropriate resolutions.

Ramseyer's account of the auto accident situation in Japan seems convincing. His evidence, however, is limited to auto cases and does not profess to relate to the situation in other areas of tort law, such as product liability and medical malpractice. As far as the former is concerned, in Japan formal litigation against manufacturers is indeed uncommon. According to one survey of 194 major Japanese manufacturers, only 24 had been sued in Japan under product liability doctrines, and only 7 of these 24 had actually been subjected to judgments requiring compensation.

Apparently, however, these Japanese litigation rates are as low as they are in part because of the availability of alternative procedures for the resolution of disputes. During a two-year period, for example, local consumer centers negotiated the outcome in more than 109 cases; personal injury damages were awarded in at least 34, with the largest award being about \$20,000. The Japanese drug statute has been described above. Between 1980 and mid-1984, 270 claims were filed against the fund that this statute creates. Of these claims, 141 resulted in payments, averaging about \$7,000. In addition, 54 products in Japan choose to carry an SG Seal. (The SG stands for Safety Goods; the 54 products are an odd assortment that includes baby carriages, swimming face-masks, mailboxes, bicycle helmets, and toilet-paper holders.) If a product marked with such a seal turns out to contain an injury-producing defect, the consumer can file a claim against the SG Association; if the claim is accepted, the largest allowable award is about \$165,000. To cover the cost of all awards, the association buys product liability insurance with the help of fees it collects from the manufacturers who elect to use its seal. This voluntary program was authorized by 1973 consumer legislation. As it happens, that legislation can be read as indicating that the association should bear liability only under Japan's ordinary negligence principles. Nevertheless, for whatever reason the association has chosen to neglect its defense of no negligence and accept liability whenever the labeled product is demonstrably defective. Between 1973 and early 1986, 132 claims—more than half of all claims filed—resulted in payments to victims by the association.

Auto manufacturers are not covered by any special program of this sort. Curious about the liability exposure of Japan's auto industry, I have been able to secure data from one of Japan's major manufacturers. This company has twice as many cars on the road in Japan as it has in the United States. Its American operations lead to about 250 product liability claims against the company each year. By contrast, in Japan the number of annual product liability filings averages about two. In a limited number of additional cases—in some years, no more than two—the company, having learned of the circumstances of a serious injury through its network of dealers, itself contacts the victim and makes what it regards as an appropriate voluntary payment.

In all, there are many ways in which Japanese manufacturers can end up encountering liability. Given this variety, one should avoid excessively confident statements about the exact level of liability in Japan. Still, the available data relating to the number of claims and the size of awards do make product liability in Japan generally appear quite modest.

* * *

Civil Procedure

A distinctive feature of American procedure is the availability of pretrial discovery. In American tort actions the plaintiff, seeking to acquire information that will support his case, can depose any potential witness and can subject the defendant to a series of written interrogatories. These are discovery techniques that are largely unavailable in European legal systems and in Japan as well. Discovery in its American form clearly makes it enormously more feasible for the plaintiff's lawyer to develop the facts of a complicated tort case. And claims in medical malpractice and product liability are usually complex. Indeed, an experienced Japanese lawyer is emphatic that the lack of discovery places the Japanese product liability plaintiff in a "very weak and difficult position."

Several writers, in comparing the American tort process to those in effect elsewhere, have focused on the availability of class actions under American law. This is, however, a feature of American civil procedure that impresses me as not being very important. For one thing, while the class action device is not available in most of Europe, "group lawsuits" *are* allowable under Japanese law, and several of the early major cases involving product liability in Japan were group actions resulting from mass torts. Furthermore, even though a country like England does not allow for class actions, when there are a large number of tort claims against particular defendants, the English legal system seems to arrange itself so as to provide a test case or "test action"—the results of which will be binding, in a somewhat de facto way, on other tort claims. In addition, even in the United States actions have been attempted in only a limited number of cases (for example, Agent Orange, and the Hyatt hotel disaster in Kansas City). And in those cases the results for plaintiffs have been sufficiently unfavorable to make it unlikely that personal injury victims (and their lawyers) will be enthusiastic about launching class actions in the future.

One distinctive feature of American procedure that clearly does make a major difference relates to the identity of the trier-of-fact. In the United States, tort cases are heard by a jury (under the supervision, to be sure, of a trial judge). But juries in tort cases are unknown in civil law countries like France and Germany; nor are juries now provided for in tort actions in Japan. In England personal injury cases were commonly heard by juries until 1883, when new rules of procedure were adopted that gave the trial judge the discretion to rule whether a jury trial is appropriate. The trial judge's discretion was reemphasized by a 1933 statute. However, judicial opinions subsequently interpreting that statute have declared that in personal injury cases jury trials should be ordered (if at all) only in exceptional circumstances. The situation in Canada offers an intermediate position between the practice in America and the practice elsewhere in the world. Under Canadian law a jury is available in a tort action in the first instance. But on the motion of either party the judge can determine that the particular case is complex in a way that makes its consideration by a jury unsatisfactory. In product and malpractice cases, defendants frequently move that the jury be dismissed—and judges frequently grant these motions and then hear the cases themselves.

What significance should be attached to the fact that in Europe and Japan malpractice and product cases are regularly considered by judges rather than juries? The widespread view among American trial lawyers is that juries tend to be sympathetic to plaintiffs: that is, they rule in favor of plaintiffs more frequently than a fair assessment of the evidence would warrant. As it happens, empirical confirmation for this widespread belief is somewhat hard to come by; but if the data do not confirm the belief, they do not refute it either. Without such a refutation, it seems appropriate to accept the view of experienced trial lawyers and to agree that trial by jury inclines American tort trials toward pro-plaintiff results. In malpractice cases English judges seem to be especially reluctant to second-guess doctors and hence rule in favor of liability. This reluctance is said to be most obvious when the plaintiff merely alleges that the doctor failed to make an appropriate diagnosis or recommend a proper treatment.

One particular mechanism by which trial by jury might affect the results of cases can be identified here. Malpractice and product cases frequently turn on the weight to be given to the testimony of expert witnesses. (Indeed, these cases frequently turn out to entail a battle of experts.) Professional judges are likely to be skilled in their ability to assess the quality of expert testimony; partisan testimony that can easily impress an American jury might if anything antagonize an English judge. Moreover, when an expert testifies in a jury case, his bedside manner may play an important role in influencing how the jury responds to his testimony. (Indeed, a top expert can exude a self-confidence that the jury might regard as off-puttingly arrogant.) Accordingly, the American practice of trial by jury may facilitate a situation in which what some call "junk science" plays an unfortunate role in determining the outcome of cases.

As for the battle of experts in product and malpractice cases, such battles are most likely in the United States and England, given the adversary system that is associated with the common law. By contrast, the civil law system that prevails in continental Europe assigns a far greater range of responsibilities to the judge. In the trial itself, it is the judge who will probably examine the expert; for that matter, the judge may well be the person who designates those experts who will testify. (For example, the Dutch judge hearing a product case involving the sleeping medication Halcion resolved to decide the case by arranging for a committee of three experts.) And even when a party is allowed to select his own expert, for that party's lawyer to interview the expert before trial might be regarded as an impropriety. For an American lawyer not to "prepare" the important witnesses in his case would be all but unthinkable; in civil law countries such preparation, far from being obligatory, is frequently just about forbidden.

What I have here claimed is that distinctive American procedures such as trial by jury and pretrial discovery probably play a significant role in explaining the difference between the size of the tort system here and its size elsewhere in the world. To be sure, these procedures have been part of American law at least since the 1940s, whereas the overall tort differential became as conspicuous as it now is only in the 1970s. For all we know, however, there might have been significant differences in earlier decades, even though they were not then frequently commented on. Moreover, at least in product cases the discrepancy in timing can be explained by referring to the interaction between the procedures themselves and the development of underlying rules of tort liability. Only in the 1970s, for example, did product liability law begin to allow plaintiffs to engage in a rather free-wheeling process of challenging the appropriateness of particular product designs. Such expansions in formal liability doctrine have thus greatly magnified the significance of the discretion the American jury possesses, and likewise have enlarged the advantage American plaintiffs can achieve by subjecting defendants to extensive discovery.

Financing Lawyers' Fees

This country's legal system differs considerably from legal systems elsewhere in how plaintiffs' lawyers and defendants' lawyers receive their compensation. As for the plaintiff's lawyer, in the United States the personal injury plaintiff routinely enters into a contingent fee arrangement with his lawyer pursuant to which the lawyer retains perhaps one-third of whatever recovery is eventually received but receives nothing if the claim is disposed of without any payment by the defendant. Contingent fee arrangements are regarded as unethical, however, by the legal systems in England and other European countries. In those legal systems, therefore, the middle-income victim who is thinking of filing a claim realizes that if his claim finally proves unsuccessful, he will be required to pay his own lawyer's fee. As for the fee of the defense counsel, the "American rule" specifies that, regardless of who finally wins the case, each side should bear its own legal costs. By contrast, the so-called English rule—which is also in effect in other European legal systems—specifies that the losing party must reimburse the prevailing party for the latter's attorney's fees. That is, the plaintiff who loses his case is required to pay not only his own lawyer's fee but also the fee of the defendant's lawyer.

Many of the scholarly articles that have considered the incentive effects of the American rule have given only limited attention to the contingent fee; moreover, articles looking at the incentive effects of the contingent fee have tended to accept the American rule as a given. In all, then, not many scholars have treated each of these practices as variables and have then assessed what their combined effects might be. Indeed, there do seem to be certain important litigation patterns for which this combination is responsible. Consider the plaintiff who is thinking of bringing a claim against the defendant and who realizes that he is an "underdog," that his chances of prevailing—while more than trivial—are still less than 50 percent. Assume, more specifically, that he has a 20 percent chance of prevailing and that his damages if he does prevail will be $100,000. Under American arrangements, so long as the plaintiff can find a lawyer who is willing to take his case, he can authorize the lawyer to proceed with the case without worrying about the expenses of litigation. His lawyer, moreover, will appreciate that the case has a settlement value of perhaps $20,000; he therefore may well agree to accept the case under a contingent fee arrangement. By contrast, in European legal systems the underdog plaintiff will need to take into account the fact that if the case goes to trial, there is a more than 50 percent possibility that he not only will receive no award but will also incur an obligation to pay both his own lawyer's bills and those of the defendant's lawyer. As compared, then, with the European alternative, the American incentive system almost certainly encourages the bringing of underdog claims.

An additional point is that the American rule may influence not only the bringing of suits but also the way in which those suits are structured. In this country a plaintiff filing suit will often find strategic value in bringing in a large number of defendants, many of whom are seemingly "peripheral"; that is, defendants whose relationship to the plaintiff's injury is questionable. By expanding his suit in this way, the plaintiff can encourage the defendants to quarrel among themselves in a manner that might eventually redound to the plaintiff's benefit. Under the English rule, however, whenever the plaintiff's claim against a peripheral defendant is dismissed, the plaintiff incurs an obligation to reimburse that defendant for its attorney's fees. That rule thus discourages plaintiffs from expanding the scope of litigation in the way that has become common in this country.

In several respects, however, the account given here of the English system needs to be rendered somewhat more complex. Under that system the solicitor's fees the loser is required to pay are those that are "reasonably incurred." Yet the full bill the defendant's solicitor runs up can easily be well in excess of what a trial judge would regard as the "reasonably incurred" figure. Accordingly, the obligation that the English rule places on the losing plaintiff is merely an obligation to pay a substantial fraction of the defendant's litigation costs. Moreover, in England there are informal practices that somewhat diminish the force of the formal rules themselves. For example, when a plaintiff of modest wealth sues in tort and loses, his solicitor is likely to "forget" the fee that he is technically owed; similarly, the defendant may well allow his right to reimbursement from such a plaintiff to go unenforced. Also, England makes available a legal aid program to low-income victims who might want to assert a tort claim. If the legal aid committee agrees to fund the victim's case, then the plaintiff is free of any compensation obligation to his solicitor; moreover, under the rules pertaining to legal aid, the acceptance of the plaintiff by the legal aid committee usually releases the plaintiff from the obligation to reimburse the defendant for its legal fees if the plaintiff fails at trial.

A legal aid committee, however, will accept a tort case only if it assesses the case as having "reasonable grounds," a "reasonable chance of success." Consider the $100,000 claim with a 20 percent chance of success. As noted, an American lawyer, operating under the contingent fee, might accept the case, perceiving that it has a settlement value of perhaps $20,000. In England, however, the legal aid committee might well conclude that the case's prospects for success were something less than "reasonable"; if so, it would decline to provide the victim with representation.

Of course, within the United States, to say that a $100,000 claim has a 20 percent chance of success may well mean that the evidence in support of the claim is objectively weak, but that it is nevertheless foreseeable that a jury, sympathizing with a badly injured plaintiff, might resolve all doubts in the plaintiff's favor. When this is the explanation for the 20 percent possibility of success, then the same lawsuit, if brought in juryless England, might have no more than a 5 percent chance of success. The American combination, then, of trial by jury and lawyers'-fee practices may *both* lower the odds against the underdog plaintiff *and* increase the likelihood that a plaintiff, facing such odds, will be able to find a lawyer who will provide him with representation.

American opponents of the contingent fee often claim that it encourages the bringing of "frivolous" cases. At one level, the arithmetic of this claim seems itself frivolous: one-third of nothing is nothing. Consider, however, the $100,000 malpractice claim that has only a 20 percent chance of success and assume as well that most of this chance is due to the possibility of unbalanced jury decisionmaking. The economist would say that this claim is far from frivolous, in the sense that it has a clear and significant expected value. It is understandable, however, that doctors, faced with the possibility of such malpractice suits, would be inclined to deride those suits as frivolous.

In acknowledging, however, the incentives for litigation afforded by American attorneys'-fee practices, one should also note that Japanese practices seem on balance even more favorable to plaintiffs. Japanese law does not prohibit, first of all, the contingent fee. What happens in Japan is that at the outset of a case the plaintiff pays his lawyer a "retainer" that corresponds to the lawyer's likely out-of-pocket expenses, along with moderate compensation for the lawyer's time. But a larger figure—called the success fee—is paid by the plaintiff to the lawyer only if the plaintiff's claim leads to a payment from the defendant. Moreover, at least in exceptional situations, Japanese lawyers apparently waive their right to the original retainer; in these cases, therefore, the plaintiff's lawyer's fee is completely contingent. Furthermore, as far as the defendant's lawyer's fees are concerned, Japanese law has developed a special practice of one-way fee shifting that applies only in personal injury cases. Under this practice a losing plaintiff is never liable to the defendant for the defendant's attorney's fees; nevertheless, if the plaintiff prevails at trial, one element of damages for which the plaintiff is entitled to compensation is a reasonable amount for his attorney's fees. In sum, Japanese plaintiffs receive the benefit of the English rule when they win and the protection of the American rule when they lose. It should be noted, by the way, that the Japanese practice of one-way fee shifting does not wipe out the significance of the Japanese practices relating to the quasi-contingent fee. For one thing, the reasonable attorney's fee for which the winning plaintiff secures compensation may well be less than the "success fee" previously agreed on by the plaintiff and his lawyer. Also, when Japanese cases are settled, it may be difficult to identify the plaintiff as an unambiguous winner; consider, for example, the $80,000 claim, with a 50 percent chance of prevailing at trial, that settles for $40,000. Since Japanese practices might not call for fee shifting in a case of this sort, the success fee might remain relevant.

Damages

The American plaintiff who prevails on the issue of liability is likely—for a combination of reasons spelled out below—to receive a much larger damage award than the plaintiff in Europe or Japan who is similarly successful. In the American tort system, personal injury awards as large as $15 million are by no means unknown. In Japan, however, even the high-income professional who is totally disabled because of a defendant's clear negligence is able to recover no more than about $1,400,000. And Japanese awards are high relative to awards in Europe. In 1989 the largest personal injury award in France was about $700,000. As of the early 1980s the largest medical malpractice award in England was $775,000. Danzon has reported that the mean payment for malpractice claims in England is currently only one-fourth of the mean payment for such claims in the United States.

Larger awards affect the burden that tort defendants bear in two obvious ways. First, even if the number of claims and verdicts is held constant, larger awards obviously result in a larger overall magnitude of liability. Second, the prospect of larger awards can be expected to increase significantly the number of suits filed in the first instance. Consider two tort claims each of which has, say, a 50 percent chance of succeeding. Claim 1, brought in the United States, will if it succeeds lead to a verdict of $100,000. Claim B, brought in Europe, will if it succeeds produce a verdict of only $40,000. As plaintiffs (and their lawyers) think about the advisability of filing suit, the American plaintiff is far more likely than his European counterpart to file, since the expected value of the American claim (50 percent times $100,000) is so much higher than that of the European claim (50 percent of $40,000).

In some respects larger damage awards in the United States are due to distinctive attributes of the American economy. For example, since real American wages remain higher than real wages elsewhere, American awards for income losses will be higher than similar awards in other parts of the world. In other respects our larger damage awards are due to distinctive features in the American law of damages. For example, American wrongful death statutes, as interpreted by American judges, provide for a measure of recovery in wrongful death actions that often greatly surpasses the damages available in such actions in countries like England. Also, English damages for income losses are measured on an after-tax basis; most American courts, by contrast, are willing to afford compensation for pretax losses. Moreover, in Germany, France, and Japan, punitive damages are understood to be simply unavailable in tort actions for personal injuries. In the United States, however, punitive damages can properly be requested in personal injury cases. They are in fact awarded in only a small proportion of product and malpractice cases. Yet this proportion has grown considerably in recent years, as courts have confirmed relatively broad interpretations of the relevant criteria for the award of punitive damages. Also, when punitive damages *are* allowed here, they are increasingly awarded in large amounts. Accordingly, by including a prayer for punitive damages in his complaint, the plaintiff may be able to increase the settlement value of his suit significantly.

One can begin, then, with the legal point that the milder European version of the collateral source rule renders the rule inapplicable to benefits provided to the victim by social welfare programs. One can then blend in the public policy observation that disability programs in Europe—though of course far less than 100 percent—are much more generous than their American counterparts, and that England, France, Germany, and Japan all operate under systems of socialized medicine (which do cover most of the costs of medical treatment). In a country like England, tort awards include almost nothing for medical costs, and the compensation they provide for income losses is reduced to acknowledge important collateral sources; moreover, as noted, the pain-and-suffering damages that those awards include are measured conservatively. In all, then, it becomes easy to understand why personal injury awards in the United States are so much larger than those in legal systems elsewhere. Sometimes it is stated that American personal injury victims are more claims conscious—more litigation-minded—than victims elsewhere in the world. ''Claims consciousness'' or ''litigiousness'' is here portrayed as an attribute in the psychology of accident victims. Though psychological notions such as claims consciousness are in my view important and intriguing, the evidence offered in support of the particular statement about American plaintiffs tends to be anecdotal or circular. The discussion above, however, may provide a somewhat more objective foundation for what may well be a claims-consciousness differential. Consider the personal injury victim who lives in a European country whose public programs provide him with the basic range of medical services and also go a considerable way toward replacing his income losses. If the American victim is more inclined than his European counterpart to consider the idea of filing a tort claim, this may well be the American's predictable and rational response to the fact that he incurs far larger pre-tort losses on account of his injury and therefore has a much greater need to turn to the tort system as a possible source of compensation.

Conclusion

To summarize, general features of the American legal system seem to be far more influential than actual differences in tort doctrine in explaining the enormous difference between the number and cost of product and malpractice claims in the United States and their number and cost in the other countries here under review. Having said this, I should make clear that my discussion of these features has for the most part tried to be nonjudgmental. To observe, for example, that a limited collateral source rule in conjunction with national health insurance functions to reduce the size of European tort awards tells us almost nothing about the analytically proper scope of the collateral source rule or about the wisdom and feasibility of American national health insurance proposals. Assuming that it is correct to say that the American system of trial by jury results in increases in both the number and the size of plaintiff verdicts, whether this result is a good thing or a bad thing depends on the assumptions that the individual analyst regards as proper. Moreover, the alternative to trial by jury is trial by judge; and in Europe and Japan this alterative may be much more attractive than the same practice would be in the United States. In countries like England and Japan, trial judges are appointed in accordance with highly meritocratic criteria. In the United States, however, these judges are designated by a political appointment process or emerge as winners in local public elections. Accordingly, among American judges there are enormous variations in outlook and ability. These variations would make trial by judge in this country a crapshoot in a way that it isn't in England or Japan.

More generally, to ascertain how extensive and demanding the torts of medical malpractice and product liability should be, one would need to understand to what extent these torts can achieve fairness as between the two parties, how effective they are in achieving socially appropriate deterrence, and what role they might play in advancing society's interests in affording compensation to accident victims. On ultimate questions of this sort, there is now an academic literature that is as voluminous as it is inconclusive.

H. Patrick Glenn, *Judicial Authority and the Liability of the Manufacturer, or* Jusqu'ou Peut-on Aller Trop Loin?, 38 AM. J. COMP. L. 555 (1990)*

What are the limits of the judiciary in providing compensation to persons injured through contact with manufactured products? Formulated in this manner, the question is not immediately suggestive of a response, since the notions of compensation, injury, contact and manufactured products direct our attention not to the process of adjudication between competing claims, but to a need for redress, brought about by circumstances which may have been entirely fortuitous. The expression "products liability" similarly occults the existence of litigation and competing claims, though we know, or are in the process of learning, that products themselves are not subject to liability, and that the existence of products in itself gives rise to no liability on the part of human defendants. Judicial limits, if they exist, must therefore be found elsewhere, in the notion of adjudication itself, or in criteria for liability which are compatible with, or even perhaps derived from, the notion of adjudication.

Why is so much current language concerning the liability of the manufacturer couched in terms which obscure the adjudicative function and the existence of competing claims? To what extent is the use of such language effective in extending the boundaries of liability and perhaps overextending the judicial function? Is it the case that the reasons for the development of such language extend beyond the province of the law of tort or obligations, such that similar results could be reached in the language of traditional concepts? In going beyond those concepts does one go too far, or, as the wonderful French phrase would have it, are there limits as to how far one can go too far? These are large questions; some attempt to answer them will be made by examining first, in a general manner, the language and results of liability said to be strict, and second, more specifically in the civil and common law context of Canada, the language and results of liability based on traditional criteria.

Liability Designated as Strict

Stricter forms of liability imply, in the modern context, a judiciary willing to examine larger slices of human activity, and a judiciary willing to do so in the field of civil liability is one which is likely to have already done so in other fields of law, where the pressure to seek general forms of solution is greater. Where the judiciary is also traditionally seen as a major source of law and where, as a natural corollary, the forms of proceeding are heavily adversarial, there is pressure which is internal to the legal order towards expansion of judicially sanctioned rules of liability. This will increase in the measure that the legal profession is a large one, and this in turn will depend greatly on whether the profession is unified or not. An expansionist legal profession is therefore one reason for the development of stricter forms of liability. This may be reflected in a broad range of procedural devices which facilitate the bringing of a large number of societal problems into the judicial range.

It is not only, however, the judicially-dominated, lawyer-heavy, adversarial, non-compensatory jurisdiction, if one should actually exist, which will look to stricter rules of manufacturers' liability. Wherever a legal tradition is said to be developed, that is to say, capable of responding in a reasonably articulate fashion to the full range of modern dilemmas, there will be a similar tendency

*Used by permission.

to burden the manufacturer with a larger compensatory role. This is not only because of the sympathy necessarily engendered by physical injury; it is also, and more importantly, because of the larger role played by the manufacturer. Manufacturing has itself been with us for millennia, but more recently that which has been made by the hand (*manufactura*) has been replaced by the product of the machine. Machine production is systemic production; systemic production requires both systemic design and systemic distribution. The notion of system implies structure and interdependence, and arguments for the internalization of social costs of production are the natural outgrowth of the process of systematization which has already taken place in the manufacturing process itself. Such costs are part of the larger universe of manufacturing; since they are part of it they must be internalized by it. Arguments for stricter forms of liability will emerge therefore in any legal tradition sufficiently developed to recognize what is occurring about it in the industrial and technological world.

* * *

Liability of the Manufacturer in Canada

The common and civil law jurisdictions of Canada are representative of much of the world in not having abandoned traditional criteria for determining the liability of a manufacturer and in not having adopted newer and stricter forms of liability. As elsewhere, there are reasons for this, and as elsewhere it is very difficult to say in what measure this affects the actual level of liability imposed on manufacturers whose products cause physical injury. There are institutional reasons which may partly explain the refusal by courts in Canada to adopt the language of stricter forms of liability. Universal compensation schemes for hospital and medical care remove one major reason for resorting to the judiciary. In Quebec, manufacturers of automobiles are also immune from suit for damage resulting from crashes of their automobiles, by virtue of the public no-fault accident compensation scheme in force in that province since 1978. Procedural considerations in all provinces discourage speculative litigation; civil juries are rare, if not prohibited outright; contingent fees are prohibited or subject to close judicial supervision; costs are born by the losing side; class actions are essentially nonexistent outside Quebec while in Quebec, where they are state-funded, they have been of no consequence in terms of the liability of the manufacturer. The Supreme Court of Canada in 1978 established a limit of $100,000 on the recovery of non-pecuniary damages in personal injury cases.

All of these circumstances limit the pressure from within the legal order itself towards more expansive forms of liability. There are also doctrinal considerations at work. Common law Canada remains very much attached to the common law of the Commonwealth, represented in large measure by English decisional law, and there is clearly an unwillingness to break rank so long as traditional criteria have not been overthrown elsewhere. It remains to be seen what effect English adherence to the European Communities Directive will have in the common law jurisdictions of the Commonwealth.

In Quebec the resistance has been largely internal, and is perhaps most rooted in a concept of fault which has thus far resisted, or largely resisted, instrumental or utilitarian analysis. Fault may be committed only by those capable of discerning right from wrong, in the language of art. 1053 of the present civil code; the leading student textbook on the law of obligations recognizes no autonomous subject of product liability; and the Supreme Court of Canada has on two recent occasions refused to venture beyond the language of fault in cases coming from Quebec and involving grievous bodily injury caused by manufactured products.

Yet manufacturers in Canada, and those from elsewhere who respond before Canadian courts, produce according to systemic methods of production and distribution, and the same arguments for internalization of costs inherent in systemic modes of activity are therefore to be found in Canadian reform proposals. In common law Canada these proposals have taken the form largely of doctrinal writing; matters have now progressed further in Quebec, where the most recent civil code revision proposals would impose liability upon the manufacturer of a product for damage caused by reason of a safety defect (defined in terms of the safety which a reasonable person is entitled to expect), while expressly preserving a state of the art defence. None of these proposals have yet however received official sanction, such that the systemic production activity of contemporary manufacturers remains subject to criteria of liability which have been traditionally applied to isolated acts of individuals. The result of this process is of some interest, however, both as an indication that courts cannot remain impervious to fundamental changes in the manner of human activity, and as an indication of the elastic character of traditional civil and common law criteria of liability, as they have been developed since the mid-twentieth-century.

The systemic, modern process of manufacture has thus been brought before Canadian courts to be judged according to traditional, non-systemic, individual criteria of liability. The pressure towards more expansive levels of liability has thus been derived from without the legal order rather than from within it, but the pressure has clearly existed. The result has been, not a broad and systemic criterion of liability, but deployment of fault criteria at strategic points in the design, production and distribution process. Since manufacturing is today more than immediate, artisanal productivity, fault can occur throughout a more extended process of activity, involving a wider array of personae exercising specialized but discrete and ascertainable functions. Doctrine here has not changed, but it is clearly being applied in circumstances which are to some extent novel, and where the consequences of liability may be substantially greater. A finding of fault in design is of greater potential consequence to a manufacturer than a finding of fault in the manufacturing process. Yet while the consequences of such a finding of fault are likely to be greater it remains a determination of fault, derived from an assessment of activity on the part of the defendant (and not his or her simple identity or status) appreciated in relation to precise damage suffered by a designated plaintiff presently before the court.

A Canadian common law judge has therefore stated that automobile manufacturers can be held accountable for negligently designed vehicles and that there is ". . . nothing new in this, it being entirely consistent with the neighbour principle enunciated in M'Alister (Donoghue) v. Stevenson . . . they must employ reasonable efforts to reduce any risk to life and limb that may be inherent in the design of their products." The tort of negligence has been extended as well to a manufacturer's failure to warn of potentially dangerous characteristics of the product, and both design fault and negligent failure to warn have been combined as separate grounds of liability on the part of a manufacturer of small garden equipment. There has as yet been no major departure from traditional requirements of proof of causation of damage by a particular manufacturer's product, but this is not to be excluded in the future. U.S developments which proportion causation amongst different defendant manufacturers in terms of their market shares have thus been described by one Canadian observer as being ones which ". . . do not undermine the conceptual centrality of causation for tort law. They carve out particular exceptions to a systemic requirement." Whether such exceptions should be created will depend once again on an assessment of the activity of the defendant, in rendering normal methods of proof impossible, as opposed to any appreciation of the defendant's identity or status.

Since the common law of negligence has proven adaptable to systemic forms of production it should follow that the civil law concept of fault, free of precedential limitations, should prove equally useful in gauging the conduct of modern manufacturers. This is borne out by the Quebec experience, which in the cadre of both contractual relations, and quasi-delictual ones, has developed the notions both of the obligation to warn of inherent dangers and that of design fault. A number of these cases have arisen with respect to foreign manufacturers, and the development of the idea of isolated faults in the production and distribution process has permitted a gradual expansion of the personal jurisdiction of Quebec courts. The precise fault of failing to warn with respect to a defective product, or failing to recall the product, is capable of being localized within the territory of Quebec and therefore providing a means of exercising jurisdiction over a foreign manufacturer on the basis of an entire cause of action arising within Quebec. The notion of "distribution fault" has been used in this regard. A similar expansion of jurisdiction has occurred in the common law provinces, though with more legislative assistance than has occurred in Quebec.

As in jurisdictions having adopted the language of strict liability it remains very difficult, however, to establish the effect of the application of these traditional criteria of liability on the manufacturing industry. There have been recent and important increases in the cost of insurance, but it appears that at least some of this increased cost results from predictions of liability arising from exports to the United States. The most evident defensive measure taken in Canada against foreign liability perceived as excessive has occurred in Quebec, where as a result of foreign asbestos litigation, the Quebec government has enacted legislation seeking to immunize Quebec asbestos producers from foreign judgments.

* * *

Conclusion

Adoption of criteria designated as strict reduces neither the need nor the complexity of litigation based on injury caused through contact with manufactured goods. Courts must continue to act as courts, and there are limits in how far they can go too far, in implementing strict criteria of liability. This is why judgments implementing criteria of so-called strict liability will generally continue to be recognized abroad, since they remain within the cadre of the judicial function, and the criteria actually used in rendering judgment may not differ markedly from those used in jurisdictions not having adopted such criteria. Adoption of such criteria appears however to increase the cost and expense of product-based litigation, making judicial recovery of damages in such cases even more radically inefficient than it normally is. Adoption of criteria of strict liability may therefore, perversely, make recovery of damages more expensive and onerous than it might otherwise be, and it has yet to be shown that the overall level of damages recovered represents a significant improvement from the perspective of the total pool of injured members of the population.

No courts can stand off from product-based litigation, however. Where traditional criteria of liability continue to be used, in an exclusive manner, they must be applied to complex and difficult questions, and the polycentric character of product-based litigation cannot be avoided. Courts refusing to adopt the language of strict liability are thus forced to decide the same type of question as courts which do adopt such language. What language should therefore be adopted by courts? Perhaps it does not matter; or perhaps it depends exclusively on local legal culture. It is also possible, and no more than this can probably be said, that courts should not promise more than they can deliver, as courts.